The Way Things Are

Basic Readings in Metaphysics

WILLIAM R. CARTER

Boston   Burr Ridge, IL   Dubuque, IA   Madison, WI
New York   San Francisco   St. Louis
Bangkok   Bogotá   Caracas   Lisbon   London   Madrid   Mexico City
Milan   New Delhi   Seoul   Singapore   Sydney   Taipei   Toronto

McGraw-Hill

*A Division of The **McGraw·Hill** Companies*

THE WAY THINGS ARE: BASIC READINGS IN METAPHYSICS

This book is printed on acid-free paper.

1 2 3 4 5 6 7 8 9 0 DOC/DOC 9 0 9 8 7

ISBN 0–07–010198–1

Editorial director: *Phillip A. Butcher*
Sponsoring editor: *Sarah Moyers*
Marketing manager: *Daniel M. Loch*
Project manager: *Christina Thornton-Villagomez*
Production supervisor: *Heather D. Burbridge*
Designer: *Michael Warrell*
Compositor: *Shepherd Incorporated*
Typeface: *10/12 Baskerville*
Printer: *R. R. Donnelley & Sons Company*

Library of Congress Cataloging-in-Publication Data
The way things are : basic readings in metaphysics / [edited by]
  William R. Carter.
      p.   cm.
    ISBN 0–07–010198–1
    1. Metaphysics.   I. Carter, William R.
  BD 111.W36   1998
  110—dc21   97–10598

http://www.mhhe.com

Contents

PART V
Causality and Free Will

Preface

Metaphysics is the systematic study of the world we inhabit and the subjects (the "we") who find ourselves in this world. There are competing theories about the structure and nature of the world, the nature of thoughtful subjects, and the relationship between the world and those subjects. This anthology is an introduction to metaphysical philosophy conceived in this broad sense. The readings focus on many of the main questions and theories developed by metaphysicians in the Western tradition.

This anthology is a companion volume to my book *The Elements of Metaphysics,* also published by McGraw-Hill. For helpful suggestions bearing on these projects I wish to thank (especially) Tom Regan, North Carolina State University; James Van Cleve, Brown University; David Sanford, Duke University; and Scott Hestevold, University of Alabama.

William R. Carter

Metaphysics—Some Questions and Arguments

We do metaphysics when we consider certain questions and reflect seriously on the answers to those questions. What sorts of questions and answers are at issue here? It is not easy to say exactly. Perhaps the best way to proceed is to consider the work of metaphysicians, to address the questions and proposed answers that philosophers who do metaphysics have set forth. The various contributions to this book reflect the nature of mainstream historical and contemporary work in the field of philosophy that is called metaphysics. As we shall see, it is a broad field of inquiry that encompasses many different, though often related, issues. As I shall attempt to explain, metaphysical questions present themselves when we consider familiar situations such as a man walking his dog. Critical reflection that focuses on commonplace things and situations gives rise to difficult and perplexing questions about personal identity, existence and nonexistence, minds and bodies, and causality and free will—topics that are addressed in the metaphysical writings collected in this volume.

Some Metaphysical Categories

Metaphysics as a discipline goes back to Aristotle, but the name "metaphysics" goes back to the Aristotelian editors of the first century BC. When Aristotle's extant works were finally ordered, fourteen associated treatises, clearly connected with the books on nature (*ta physika*), but more general and fundamental, were collected. Placed after the physical treatises, they were called "the books coming after the books on nature," *ta meta ta physika*.[1]

---

[1]Peter Simon, "Metaphysics: Definitions and Divisions," in *A Companion to Metaphysics,* ed. by Jaegwon Kim and Ernest Sosa (Oxford: Blackwell, 1995), p. 311.

Suppose we were to try to explain clearly and accurately the way things are. To start, we might say that the world contains a great many substantial things—substances—and a great many events. Events are happenings that involve substances. Consider the event that is Jack's walking his dog. The walking of the dog is something that happens— an event—but is not a substance. Jack is a constituent of this event, as is Jack's dog. Substantial things are constituents of events, but substances are not themselves events. Substances do not happen or occur, though it is true that substances exist. As Aristotle would agree, a complete inventory of substances would not be a complete inventory of what there is.

We (people) are substances, whereas our lives and histories are extended events. A normal life is a vastly complex event that in normal cases extends over a considerable temporal period. Such complex events are composed of many other, more localized events. The event that is Jack's walking of his dog is only one rather insignificant event in the extended that is Jack's life.[2] Jack himself is presumably a constituent of each event that constitutes a part of his life.

Intuitively, it seems that each of us could have—or at any rate could have had—lives different from the lives we actually have. To admit this is to have some sympathy for the idea that the world as it actually is is only one of countless *possible* but unrealized worlds. There is a possible world in which Bill Clinton never enters politics but is employed as a saxophonist in an Arkansas rock band. To reject unrealized possible worlds is to (implausibly) reject the idea that our lives could have been different from what they are. We will return to the subject of unrealized possibilities in a later section of this introduction entitled "Possible Worlds").

For the present, let's stick with the actual world. As I have said, events seem to play a prominent role in this world. Events take time. So if, as some people argue, there is no time, there really are no events. It may be hard to conceive of a world containing substances but no events, a world containing *things* in which *nothing ever happens.* Accordingly, rejections of the reality of time point toward a metaphysic that rejects both events and substantial things. It seems that our world—the actual world we inhabit—is not at all like this. Our

---

[2]For more about the distinction between events and substances, see Michael Ayers, "Substance: Prolegomena to a Realist Theory of Identity," *Journal of Philosophy,* February 1991, pp. 69–90.

world is such (many of us judge) that it is true both that a great many things happen (many events occur) and that a great many substantial things have complex careers or histories. Living substances have lives, which are extended events. Arguably, a life continues for as long, but only as long, as a certain living subject persists or endures. Since we are living subjects, our lives continue for as long (but only as long) as we persist. It is to the subject of personal persistence that I now turn.

On Identity and Persistence

> The identity question has a special urgency where living creatures are concerned, since it is connected with complicated ethical and political issues, for example the determination of death and the moral status of the foetus.[3]
>
> This then is the difficulty about describing death as change. There turns out to be nothing which can be said to change. That which was a living pheasant is not the same thing as what is now a pitiable corpse.[4]

We persist through certain temporal periods. Persistence or continued existence requires identity. Unless some individual who exists in the year 2030 is personally identical with you, *you* do not continue in 2030. Things work the same way when we turn our attention to the past. You existed 10 years ago only if the world then contained an individual who was you. The you of 10 years ago and the you of today must be identical (must be one and the same individual) if it is true that you existed 10 years ago.

Although this sounds plausible enough, the "persistence through time requires identity" thesis must be qualified. Qualification is necessary because the world contains both substantial things (including people) and events, and it is false that the persistence of an extended event requires identity.

Consider a storm that continues (persists) for a week. The stormy events that exist on the first day are constituents of the (complete) storm, as are the stormy events that exist on the last day. Nonetheless, the first-day events are not strictly identical with the last-day events. The segment of the storm that is present on the first

---

[3]Martha C. Nussbaum, "Aristotle," in *A Companion to Metaphysics,* p. 25.
[4]C. J. F. Williams, "On Dying," *Philosophy* XLIV (July 1969), p. 220.

day is numerically different from (not one and the same segment as) the segment that is present on the last day. The storm persists throughout the week even though there is no identity relation between one day's stormy events and the next day's stormy events. Thus, there can be persistence without identity.

If that is right, there is perhaps this difference between substantial things and events: The persistence of a substantial thing does, and the persistence of an event does not, require identity through time. Events are said to have temporal parts or temporal segments. The stormy events that occur on Monday are Monday's segment of the storm; the situation is similar for the stormy events that occur on Tuesday, with such events being Tuesday's segment or part of the (complete) storm. It is said that physical substances (tables and chairs, say) do not have temporal parts.[5] If that is so, nothing is both an event and a physical substance. Although physical substances are implicated in events, no physical substance *is* an event.

Since our bodies appear to be physical substances, this suggests that our bodies are not events. If it is true that we (people) are our bodies, we are not events. We do not have temporal parts if we are not events, and identity is surely what matters for our (personal) persistence if we do not have temporal parts. This points toward the following metaphysical argument (called the Identity Argument hereafter):

(1) Our bodies are physical substances.
(2) Physical substances do not have temporal parts.
(3) We are our bodies.
(4) When we are dealing with things that have no temporal parts, identity is what matters for persistence. Therefore,
(5) Our bodies do not have temporal parts. [from (1) and (2)]
(6) We do not have temporal parts. [from (3) and (5)]
(7) Identity is what matters for our (personal) persistence. [from (4) and (6)]

This does not speak against the claim that our lives persist in a way that does not involve identity. Although my life persists from yesterday to today, the segment of my life that occurs today is not identical to the segment that occurred yesterday. Our lives are extended

---

[5]Lawrence Lombard, *Events* (London: Routledge & Kegan Paul, 1986), p. 128.

events, not substantial things. The Identity Argument suggests that we (people) are substantial things, not events. That conclusion seems plausible enough, but the argument in its behalf may be challenged, as we now shall see.

Personal Beginnings and Endings

> [F]ew of the famous buried [in the Recoleta Cemetery in Buenos Aires], or elsewhere in Argentina, have found much rest in the afterlife. The corpses of many of the nation's central figures have been repeatedly exhumed, mutilated and exploited for political and financial gain.[6]

It is said that the famous people who are buried in the Recoleta Cemetery have found no rest there. That suggests that certain famous people continue to exist after they die. This sounds plausible if we assume, as the Identity Argument does, that we are our bodies. If it is true that we are (the same thing as) our bodies, we persist for precisely as long as our bodies persist. If a certain famous person is just her body and this body persists after her death as a corpse, this famous person persists—continues to exist—as a corpse. If the corpse is located in the Recoleta Cemetery, that is where the famous person is located. It is (on this conception of the matter), then, not true that our lives continue for as long as we continue. The famous person's life terminates when she dies; nonetheless, the person whose life it is continues (to exist) for some time thereafter.

When his wife Eva Peron was dying of cancer, General Juan Peron arranged to have an embalmer preserve her body. Some people judge that it is merely Eva's body and not Eva herself (the person) that continues after the embalmer does his job. If that is so, it is a mistake to judge that Eva is her body. Eva cannot *be* her body if her body continues and she herself does not continue. This reasoning opposes the third premise of the Identity Argument, suggesting that it is not true that we are our bodies.

Suppose (though this happens to be false) that the name "Robert Zimmerman" refers to my next-door neighbor and that (as is true) the name "Bob Dylan" refers to a famous musician. If I learn that these *two*

---

[6]Calvin Sims, "Eternal Rest? Not in Argentina," *New York Times*, October 13, 1996, Section 4, p. 3.

names refer to *one* individual, I know that my neighbor Zimmerman is none other than the famous Bob Dylan. Zimmerman is identical with Dylan, which means that it cannot happen that Zimmerman persists after Dylan has perished. To learn that Zimmerman and Dylan are identical is to be assured that there are not two things here, one of which can continue to exist when the other does not.

The same is true of a person and her body. The name "Eva Peron" refers to a certain famous person, while the term "Eva's body" refers to that person's body. If these terms actually refer to one thing—if, that is, the person and the body are *identical*—we do not have two things, one of which can continue to exist after the other has perished. Identity is a matter of (numerical) oneness, and it makes no sense to say that one thing does and does not perish at a certain time.

It might be proposed that Eva is identical with her living body but not with her dead body. That has to be wrong if the living body and the dead body are identical. Arguments of the following form are valid (where the equals sign "=" represents the identity relation):

$$A = B,$$
$$\text{not: } A = C, \text{ so}$$
$$\text{not: } B = C$$

If A and B are one (identical) thing and A and C are not one thing, then B and C are not one thing. The following argument (the Body Argument) is valid:

(1) Eva's dead body (Eva's corpse) = Eva's living body.
(2) not: Eva's dead body = Eva. Therefore,
(3) not: Eva's living body = Eva.

Defenders of this reasoning deny that the corpse that remains after a person dies is the person who has died. After Eva's death in 1952 her embalmed body was transported to Europe and then returned to Argentina. If the Body Argument is sound, none of this speaks for the claim that Eva herself (once an important political figure in Argentina) traveled to Europe and returned to Argentina after her death. The embalmer preserved Eva's body but not Eva herself; it is the dead body and not the person who travels to Europe and back after the person dies.

Why should we accept the Body Argument? Why deny that the dead body is Eva herself? Following the lead of the English philosopher John Locke, we might reply that the corpse has no psychology and thus has no memories of doing any of the things (only) Eva did. If such memories are a necessary condition of personal identity, as Locke maintains, it is not true that the traveling corpse is identical with the person Eva. The well-preserved corpse does not have any memories and therefore does not have memories of having once lived the life Eva lived; by Locke's reasoning, it follows that the corpse is not identical with Eva. The corpse is one thing, and Eva is (or was) another thing.

Locke's reasoning supports the second premise of the Body Argument. Since the first premise (stating that Eva's dead body is identical with her living body) looks rather plausible, Lockean assumptions point in the direction of the conclusion that we (living people) are not identical with our living bodies. That raises serious questions about the Identity Argument, which supports the claim that identity is something that matters for personal persistence; the Identity Argument rests on the premise that we are our (living) bodies, which will be challenged by Lockean theorists.

We may well ask what sorts of things we can be if indeed we are not our living bodies. I will return to this in a later section, entitled "Unsubstantial Minds." For the moment I wish only to point out that questions concerning personal persistence are closely related to the question "What sorts of things are we?" This emerges not only when we consider our endings (the times at which we perish) but also when we consider our beginnings (the times at which we first exist). It is plausible that we persist—are genuine constituents of the world—from the time we are born to the time we die. But don't we exist for a time as prenatal beings, individuals who are not yet born? This is plausible if it is true that we are our living bodies. However, the thesis that memory is necessary for personal persistence suggests that we did not exist as prenatal beings. Presumably we have no memories of prenatal existence, and so (if Locke is right) we did not once exist as prenatal beings.

Some people have deep reservations about the Lockean thesis that memory is necessary for personal identity. Arguments for the claim that we are living bodies speak against the Lockean position. If we persist as long as our bodies persist, then memory is not necessary for our continued existence (since memory is not necessary for the continued existence of our bodies). And we *do* persist for as long as our bodies persist if indeed we *are* our bodies. One argument (the Life Argument) for judging that we are our bodies goes as follows:

(1) Our bodies are currently alive.

(2) We (people) are currently alive.

(3) If (1) and (2) are true, then either we are our bodies or different lives currently coincide.

(4) It is never true that two lives coincide.[7] Therefore,

(5) Either we are our bodies or two lives currently coincide. [from (1), (2), and (3)]

(6) We are our bodies. [from (4) and (5)]

This might be challenged on the grounds that we are alive only in the sense that we (people) are closely associated with, but nonetheless distinct from, living bodies). (You are alive only in the derivative sense that you are intimately related to something that is, strictly and not derivatively, alive.) My instinct is that this is a dubious position; since I believe that the Life Argument is sound and that our (living) bodies will continue to exist for some time after we die, I maintain that we (people) will continue to exist for some time after we die. I make no claim for—and indeed reject—personal *immortality*. Our bodies are not immortal.

All this needs (what I cannot here supply) supporting arguments. In any case, it is clear that we are in deep metaphysical waters when we attempt to explain what sorts of beings we are. Since this question must be answered before we can hope to locate our temporal boundaries, we are in deep metaphysical waters when we presume to specify the time at which a person first or last exists.

Time Flies (or Does It?)

> Stop thinking about the laughter that wounded you—it no longer exists just as your years on the scaffoldings and your glory as a victim of persecution no longer exist.[8]

---

[7]This is argued by Peter van Inwagen in *Material Beings* (Ithaca, NY: Cornell University Press, 1990). Van Inwagen would not accept the conclusion of the present argument.

[8]Milan Kundera, *Slowness*, translated by Linda Asher (New York: HarperCollins, 1996).

It seems to many people that their lives pass much too quickly. One might also say that it seems to many people that time passes much too quickly. But does time really pass? We may judge that this is indisputable. It is indisputable that we change in various ways as our lives pass, and since change requires time, clearly there is such a thing as time.

The twentieth-century British metaphysician John McTaggart argues against the reality of time. McTaggart's actual argument is quite complex, and I shall make no attempt to present it here. However, the general idea is as follows (the No-Time Argument):

(1) There is no change at all unless events pass from being future to being present to being past.

(2) There is no time if there is no change.

(3) It is not true that events pass from being future to being present to being past. Therefore,

(4) There is no change at all. [from (1) and (3)]

(5) There is no time. [from (2) and (4)]

This conclusion goes very much against things most of us believe. It has been said that descriptive metaphysics is a description of the structure of our actual thoughts about the world and that real metaphysics is an accurate portrayal of how the world actually is.[9] Insofar as our conception of the world represents or corresponds to the way the world really is, descriptive metaphysics is real metaphysics. However, arguably there is no absolute guarantee that the way we *think* about the world is always the way the world really *is*. If, as some philosophers maintain, "virtually all of our common-sense beliefs are untrue,"[10] it is one thing to do descriptive metaphysics and quite another thing to do real metaphysics. Descriptive metaphysics undoubtedly will reflect the way things *appear* (to us) to be, but prominent philosophers such as McTaggart have argued that there are significant and indeed shocking divergences between appearances and reality. In theory, real metaphysics may diverge radically from descriptive metaphysics.

---

[9]John L. Tienson, "A Conception of Metaphysics," *American Philosophical Quarterly* 26 (January 1989), p. 63.

[10]Peter Unger, "I Do Not Exist," in *Material Constitution*, ed. by Michael Rea (Oxford: Rowman & Litlefield, 1997), p. 187.

That is suggested by the No-Time Argument, which indicates that our everyday conception of the world is radically misconceived. But is the argument sound? We may wonder whether premise (3) is true. In support of (3) it may be said that

> What is real, what exists, are those events that exist now, at this present moment. Past events did exist, but exist no longer, and future events, even if they will exist, do not yet exist.[11]

This has far-reaching implications. Consider the fact that some people fear death. Arguably, the events that are our deaths do not currently exist, and why fear what does not exist? A similar line can be taken for events that are in the past, not the future. You are embarrassed by your failure to do well on yesterday's math exam. This failure is in the past and so does not exist, and why be embarrassed by things that do not exist? All this points toward what I shall call the Presentist Argument:

(1) Only the present exists.

(2) Past events and future events are not in the present. Therefore,

(3) Past and future events do not exist.

A similar argument can be made for past and future times:

(1) Only the present exists.

(2*) Past times and future times are not in the present. Therefore,

(3*) Past and future times do not exist.

The Presentist Argument entails that there is no more to time than the present, but if that is so, it is hard to see how it can be true that time passes. If there are no times other than the present, presumably there are no events other than the events that currently occur. Intuitively, temporal passage seems to consist of some sort of transition from future to present to past. Events such as a person's birth or death may appear to be first in the future, later in the present, and still later in the past; time passes only if various events first approach and then recede from the present. Defenders of premise (1)— *presentists*[12]—deny that this is possible. The event that is my death

---

[11]Quenton Smith and L. Nathan Oaklander, *Time, Change and Freedom* (London: Routledge, 1995), p. 71.

[12]This term is employed by Mark Hinchliff in "The Puzzle of Change," in *Philosophical Perspectives Vol. 10,* ed. by James E. Tomberlin (Cambridge, MA: Blackwell, 1996), pp. 119–136.

cannot (it is claimed) currently be in the future. The event cannot currently *be* anywhere, since there currently *is* no such event. An event that there isn't—an event that does not exist—cannot be in the future. The same holds true for the time that is October 15, 2030. To say that this time is now in the future, presentists maintain, is to assume falsely that such a time now exists.

Science fiction writers invent stories about time travel in which a person ventures into the past or the future, but presumably we cannot travel through time if it happens that there is no time. Arguably, there is time (time exists) only if there is temporal passage, yet according to presentists, there is no such passage. Many people find it hard to believe that time does not exist. Could we be deceived in this? As we have seen, some metaphysicians distinguish between the way things appear and the way things really are, between appearance and reality. Perhaps it merely *appears* that time passes. The No-Time Argument suggests just this, indicating that past and future times do not really exist. If that is so, past and future times cannot be approaching and receding from the present. That means that there is no temporal passage, and to reject temporal passage is to reject the existence of time.

Theorists who find this intolerable may respond by rejecting the claim that only the present exists, but that rejection raises various questions. Are we to say that all times are equally real? Suppose we do say this. If all times are equally real, then presumably past and future individuals and events are no less real than are individuals and events located in the present: James Dean and John Lennon are just as real as you and I. Since Dean and Lennon are dead people, it is concluded that dead people are real people. The same is true for unborn (and not yet conceived) people. The unconceived are as real as you and I.

However, we may doubt that talk of "approaching" and "receding from" the present is intelligible on the assumption that all times are equally real. Doesn't the equalitarian conception of time (the thesis that all times are equally real) suggest that each time is present from its own perspective? And doesn't *that* conflict with the idea that there is a unique time that is "the present" from which past times recede and to which future times approach?

Time is a metaphysical troublemaker. A rejection of presentism suggests that all times are equally real and, from their own temporal perspective, equally present. If that is accepted, we cannot view presentness as a property (feature) that somehow is first instantiated by (say) October 15, 1996, and subsequently is instantiated by October 16, 1996. Just as each spatial location is *here* from its own perspective, each time is *present* from its own perspective. Once again, it does not appear that we have temporal passage, and temporal passage arguably is essential to (the reality of) time.

Change

> In fact, I cannot be said to have changed unless I am the same in the numerical sense.[13]

Critics of the egalitarian assessment of time argue that this position cannot be reconciled with the fact that things undergo changes. Suppose that presentism is false and that all times are equally real. Doesn't this mean that the Napoleon of 1796 is just as real as the Napoleon of 1806? It seems that it does. But can the Napoleon of October 15, 1796, then *be* the Napoleon of October 15, 1806? It seems not, since the former individual is (say) in France and the latter individual is not. Surely one (the same) thing cannot both be and not be in France.

The Napoleon of October 15, 1796, and the Napoleon of October 15, 1806, are discernible (different) in many ways; since identity (oneness) entails indiscernibility, it may be argued that the Napoleon of October 15, 1796, and the Napoleon of October 15, 1806, are not identical. However, as the passage cited above asserts, change *requires* identity—requires oneness or sameness "in the numerical sense." If a rejection of presentism cannot be reconciled with the claim that the Napoleon of October 15, 1796, and the Napoleon of October 15, 1806, are identical, this rejection requires that we deny that Napoleon (a certain man) undergoes a change insofar as he is located in France at the earlier time and is not located in France at the later time. Thus it seems to be a corollary of the egalitarian conception of time that change is an illusion. Although it *appears* that things change, *in reality* they do not.

We may believe that this gets things the wrong way around. If in reality things change and if such change requires a nonequalitar-

---

[13]Terence Penelhum, "Hume on Personal Identity," in *Hume*, ed. by V. C. Chappell (Garden City, NY: Doubleday, 1966), p. 227.

ian conception of time, we must accept a nonequalitarian conception of time. And doesn't that commit us to presentism (the view that only the present is real)?

Things change; things remain the same. There is nothing worrisome here if *certain* things change while *other* things remain the same, but can it happen that a *given* thing both changes and remains the same throughout a certain temporal period? We might believe that a thing that changes does not and indeed cannot also remain the same, but we should proceed cautiously. Many theorists draw a distinction between *numerical* and *qualitative* sameness. On the one hand, numerical sameness is a matter of oneness (of identity). Qualitative sameness is, on the other hand, a matter of having all and only the same intrinsic qualities (features, properties). To say that two billiard balls are qualitatively the same is to say that they are "exactly alike" with respect to their shapes, colors, weights and so on. Since *two* balls are not one (are not identical), this suggests that qualitative sameness offers no guarantee of numerical sameness. However, it is widely agreed that numerical sameness (identity) is a guarantee of qualitative sameness. Consider again the case of Robert Zimmerman and Bob Dylan. It cannot happen that Zimmerman and Dylan are qualitatively different if, as is true, Zimmerman and Dylan are identical. (How can one thing be qualitatively different from itself?)

There are, however, potential problems with this, as becomes clear when we consider the case of Morning Alice (Alice as she is in the morning) and Evening Alice (Alice as she is in the evening). Intuitively, we are speaking of one individual (one person) when we speak of Morning Alice and Evening Alice. The problem is that numerical identity entails qualitative sameness (indiscernibility). We are speaking about one individual when we refer to Morning Alice and Evening Alice only if Morning Alice and Evening Alice are qualitatively the same in all respects. (Morning Alice and Evening Alice are numerically the same individual only on the condition that Morning Alice and Evening Alice are indiscernible.) However, it may seem that Morning Alice and Evening Alice are not qualitatively the same since Morning Alice is happy and Evening Alice is not. Therefore, some people conclude that Morning Alice and Evening Alice are not identical (are not one person).

Normally we would say that Alice changes, being happy in the morning but unhappy in the evening, but is that so? Change requires identity. Since the argument we have just outlined opposes an identity assessment of Morning Alice and Evening Alice, this argument speaks against the (plausible, as most of us would judge) proposal that Alice is the subject of a change.

Presentists will be impatient with this, charging that while the world is *first* such that a certain individual (Alice) is happy, it is *later* such that the same individual is sad.[14] More generally, qualitative changes occur when a given object is first in one qualitative state or condition and later is in another such state or condition. It is denied that Morning Alice and Evening Alice are equally real. What is real is what is present, and it never happens that Morning Alice and Evening Alice are both present.

This defense of change is presumably not available to defenders of the equalitarian view of time. If all times are equally real, it seems that Morning Alice (a happy individual) and Evening Alice (one who is not happy) are equally real. Since one thing cannot be both happy and not happy, it seems that Morning Alice and Evening Alice are not one individual. Since qualitative change requires oneness (identity), defenders of the equalitarian conception of time conclude that we are mistaken in judging that Alice undergoes a qualitative change.

Presentism has its attractions, offering the prospect of judging that change is a genuine and not merely an apparent feature of the world we inhabit. Still, presentism is not without its problems. For example, some critics argue that a presentist conception of time does not allow us to accept the reality of causal relations. Suppose (as we would normally say) Jill tells a joke that causes Jack to laugh. The joke occurs first, and then the laughter occurs; accordingly, the causal relation between the joke and the laughter extends from one time to another. The problem is that according to presentists, there is no time at which both the joke and the laughter exist. When the joke exists, the laughter does not, and vice versa. At no time do we have two events one of which is the telling of the joke and the other of which is the laughter. Arguably, these two events cannot be causally related if presentism is true.[15]

---

[14]For more about this and related matters, see Trenton Merricks, "Endurance and Indiscernibility," *Journal of Philosophy* XCI (April 1994), pp. 165–184.

[15]For more about presentism and causality, see John Bigelow, "Presentism and Properties," in *Philosophical Perspectives Vol. 10*, pp. 35–52.

Events exist at certain times, as do substantial things such as people. However, talk of existence is itself a source of metaphysical controversy. It is to this topic that I now turn.

Existence and Nonexistence

> To think metaphysically is to think, without arbitrariness and dogmatism, on the most basic problems of existence.[16] Existence is that property, delicate as an eyelid, which separates the living from the dead.[17]

We can truly say of many dead people that they no longer exist, but how is it possible to speak truly of what does not exist? The statement "Joseph Stalin is dead" is true. Presumably this statement has a "truthmaker," something that *makes* the statement in question true.[18] And what is the appropriate truth-maker here? What is it that makes "Joseph Stalin is dead" true? A natural reply is that a certain man (a notorious political figure) is dead. Stalin currently has the property of being dead, a fact which accounts for the *truth* of the statement "Joseph Stalin is dead." This is not unproblematic if, as many theorists maintain, only *existing* things can have properties.[19] Without an existing thing, it seems that we lack an appropriate subject to bear (or instantiate) properties. If Stalin now has the property of being dead, it seems that Stalin currently exists. More generally, our present assumptions suggest that all dead people exist. We can truly say of *any* dead person that he or she is dead. What makes our statement true is that a certain individual—the subject about whom we speak—has the property of being dead. Since nonexisting things cannot have properties, it follows that this (dead) subject currently exists.

We may have misgivings about this conclusion, but what is wrong with the supporting argument? One proposal is that having (or, as philosophers say, instantiating) properties is not sufficient for existence. Defenders of this position may maintain that existing things are all and only things that currently have a spatial location.

---

[16]Richard Taylor, *Metaphysics* (Englewood Cliffs, NJ: Prentice-Hall, 1983), p. 1.

[17]Palle Yourgrau, "The Dead," *Journal of Philosophy,* February 1987, p. 89.

[18]See Kevin Mulligan, Peter Simons, and Barry Smith,"Truth-Makers," *Philosophy & Phenomenological Research,* March 1984, pp. 286–321.

[19]Properties are features that things have. For more about properties, see Alex Oliver, "The Metaphysics of Properties," *Mind,* January 1996, pp. 1–80.

The Eiffel Tower exists; Stalin does not. The former currently has, and the latter does not have, a spatial location. Stalin does not (at present) exist; nonetheless, Stalin currently has certain properties. Stalin currently is a dead person, which is to say that Stalin currently is an instantiator of the property of being a dead person.

If instantiation of properties is not sufficient for existence, Stalin can be dead (can have the property of being dead) and nevertheless not exist. However, if Stalin currently instantiates properties, presumably there must *be* such an individual as Stalin. Stalin does not currently have any spatial location, and so, on the assumption that all existing things have such a location, it seems that there are things that do not exist.

Some philosophers—*inflationists* as they sometimes are called[20]—distinguish between the question "What is there?" and the question "What exists?" An inflationist might hold that having a spatial location is necessary and sufficient for existence and deny that all instantiators of properties have spatial locations. There are nonexisting things. A nonexisting thing is something that has properties but lacks a spatial location. Arguably, that is Joseph Stalin's present situation. Stalin currently has various properties, and so Stalin has "reality" or "being." Nonetheless, Stalin does not currently exist. (Such existence is a matter of currently having a spatial location, and it is not true that Stalin currently has a spatial location.)

An inflationary argument might be constructed for things other than dead people. Arguably, there is such a thing as the number 7 (the Number Argument):

(1) "7 is a prime number" is a true statement.

(2) "7 is a prime number" is true only if the number 7 has the property of being prime.

(3) If the number 7 has any properties, there is such a thing as the number 7.

(4) The number 7 has at least one property. [from (1) and (2)]

(5) There is such a thing as the number 7. [from (3) and (4)]

Note that the Number Argument does not make the claim that the number 7 exists. Presumably, the number 7 has no spatial location

---

[20]This term is employed by Richard Cartwright in his contribution to this anthology. For more about inflationism, see Charles Crittenden, *Unreality: The Metaphysics of Fictional Objects* (Ithaca, NY: Cornell University Press, 1991).

and so does not exist. That is not to deny that there is such a number. Even if it is false that numbers *exist*, it may be true (as the Number Argument suggests) that there *are* numbers.[21]

A similar position is suggested when we turn to fictional objects. Consider the following:

> Mr. George Smiley was not naturally equipped for hurrying in the rain, least of all at dead of night. . . . Small, podgy, and at best middle-aged, he was by appearance one of London's meek who do not inherit the earth. His legs were short, his gait was anything but agile, his dress costly, ill-fitting, and extremely wet.[22]

Smiley is a fictional character who plays a leading role in certain spy novels. Smiley lacks a spatial location and so does not exist. Inflationists nonetheless maintain there *is* a George Smiley. Smiley is, as Stalin currently is, a nonexistent being. Unlike Stalin and other dead people, Smiley and his fellow fictional characters never existed.

In theory, we might defend an inflationary position with respect to times other than the present. As we saw earlier, to claim that time passes is to say that future events somehow are moving closer and closer to the present and that past events are moving farther and farther away from the present. How can this be if, as presentists hold, only the present exists? The inflationist's reply is that future and past times and events are nonexistent times and events. To be nonexistent is not at all the same as to not be (real). Things that have properties are in some sense real, though many such things do not exist. Consider the event that is your next birthday. This event has the property of being in the future, and so there is such an event. It is just that this event does not exist. Events exist only at the time at which they happen. Your next birthday is not currently happening, and so it does not currently exist. Nonetheless, your next birthday has various properties (among them the property of being a future event); accordingly, there *is* such an event as your next birthday.

You anticipate your next birthday. It might be said that your next birthday currently is located in your mind. Perhaps nonexistent things generally are located in (and only in) our minds. Saint Anselm argued that it is impossible that God is located only in our minds. If

---

[21]For more about numbers and abstract objects generally, see Bob Hale, *Abstract Objects* (Oxford: Blackwell, 1987).

[22]John lé Carre, *Tinker, Tailor, Soldier, Spy* (New York: Bantam Books, 1975), p. 18.

that is so and if nonexisting things are things that are located only in our minds, it is false that God is a nonexisting thing. However, on the assumption that existing things have spatial locations, we may wonder about this; we may doubt that God has a spatial location.

Arguably, there is a sense in which anything we think of is located in our minds. That is not to say that anything we think of is located *only* in our minds. We think of the Eiffel Tower, but surely the Eiffel Tower is not located only in our minds.

In some quarters it is argued that commonplace things are genuine constituents of the thoughts we have bearing on such things.[23] Our thoughts are presumably in our minds, and this suggests that constituents of our thoughts are also located in our minds. If dogs and cats (say) are constituents of our dog- and cat-directed thoughts, it turns out that dogs and cats are located in our minds (similarly for the Eiffel Tower). However, it is not plausible that dogs and cats (and the Eiffel Tower) are located in our heads. Thus, our present assumptions point toward the rather surprising (for some people) conclusion that our minds are not located in our heads.[24]

If our minds are not confined to our heads, the claim that nonexistent things are located only in our minds does not entail that nonexistent things are located only in our heads. But where could such things be located, if not in our heads?

Suppose our minds are located in (and only in) our heads. If that is so and if every object of thought is located in the mind of the person who thinks of that object, every object of thought is located in our heads. This is very implausible. I am currently thinking of the Eiffel Tower, but the Eiffel Tower is not currently (not at any time) located in my head.

Suppose Jack and Jill have simultaneous Eiffel Tower thoughts. If the Eiffel Tower is a constituent of Jack's thought and this thought is in Jack's head, it seems the Eiffel Tower is located in Jack's head. A similar argument speaks for the conclusion that the Eiffel Tower is located in Jill's head. Our present assumptions suggest that the Eiffel Tower has at least two—and indeed a great many more—locations, but isn't that absurd? Isn't it absurd to suppose that any existing thing has, at a given time, many different spatial locations?

---

[23]See Colin McGinn, *Mental Content* (Oxford: Blackwell, 1989).

[24]As McGinn says, the mind spreads itself onto the world.

Arguably, some existing things are multiply located. Consider the color red. Arguably, this color exists. Indeed, it may seem that redness (the color) is currently located in many different places. Various fire trucks, lips, roses, berries, and cherries are red. Although each red thing has one (and only one) location, it seems that *the color red* has multiple locations. A similar line may be taken for hunger or, if you will, the property of being hungry. Many individuals, located in many different places, are currently hungry. Hunger is an existing thing that has many locations.

Many, if not most, properties are multiply located; such properties are instantiated by many different things at one time. Redness is like this: There are many red things. Similarly, our world contains a great many hungry individuals. Redness exists, as does hunger. Although a substantial thing such as a person or a pebble has only one spatial location (at a given time), redness and hunger have many locations. Properties are not substantial things; nonetheless, it seems that properties exist. It is impossible for a substantial thing such as a person to exist without having properties.

It might be said that nonexistent things are things that are located in one or more minds but also are things that lack any spatial location. This won't do if it is true that our minds are located in our heads and if, moreover, every nonexistent object of thought is located in the mind of a certain thinker or thinkers. These assumptions suggest that nonexistent things have locations.

Causality and Existence

> No character . . . on stage, page, or screen has ever had the reception that God has had. God is more than a household word in the West; he is, welcome or not, a virtual member of the Western family.[25]
>
> If Pegasus existed he would indeed be in space and time, but only because the word "Pegasus" has spatio-temporal connotations and not because "exists" has spatio-temporal connotations.[26]

As the second passage above suggests, the link between existence and spatial location is problematic. Perhaps some existing things

---

[25]Jack Miles, *God: A Biography* (New York: Knopf, 1995).

[26]W. V. O. Quine, *From a Logical Point of View* (Cambridge, MA: Harvard University Press, 1961), p. 3.

have no location. A critic of the inflationary position that was out-lined above might note that George Smiley amuses and captivates many people. It seems that Smiley produces results and thus is a causally engaged individual; to be causally active is to exist. Smiley and other fictional characters are implicated in various causal rela-tions, and thus (contrary to inflationists) are existing things.

It will be objected that all existing human people have spatial lo-cations. Smiley does not have a spatial location and thus does not exist. This reasoning assumes that Smiley is a human person, but that may be denied. Arguably, Smiley is not an existing *human* but is instead an ex-isting *fictional character*.[27] Existing fictional characters such as George Smiley are abstract entities, things that exist but do not have spatial lo-cations. Spatial location is not a necessary condition of existence.

A similar line may be taken when we turn to God. We read about God, just as we read about Smiley. The biblical figure or char-acter of God captivates many people, just as the fictional character Smiley does. The (biblical) character God may cause us to lose sleep or act in certain ways. Doesn't that license the conclusion that God exists? How can something that produces results—that is causally engaged—fail to exist?

This reasoning does nothing to establish that a *supernatural being* (a creator of the world, as many people say) exists, just as the parallel reasoning concerning Smiley does not establish that there is an existing human who does the things Smiley is said to do. The pres-ent argument speaks for the existence of the biblical character God, not for the existence of a supernatural being. Biblical characters—theoretical entities of biblical scholarship—are characters who play a role in the Bible, just as fictional characters—theoretical entities of literary scholarship—are characters who appear in works of fiction. Arguably, biblical characters exist, even though, as with fictional char-acters, they lack spatial locations. On this conception of the matter, it is a mistake to equate existence with having a spatial location.

Once-existing and even currently existing people often play a role in works of fiction.[28] That means that we need to guard against equivocation. If the term "Napoleon" is employed to speak about a certain fictional character, this term does not refer to (the dead

---

[27]Peter van Inwagen, "Creatures of Fiction," *American Philosophical Quarterly*, October 1977, pp. 299–308.

[28]Van Inwagen, "Creatures of Fiction."

man) Napoleon Bonaparte. Bonaparte presumably no longer exists. Nonetheless, Napoleon, the character who appears in certain works of fiction, exists. Unlike the man, this character is an abstract entity. The man is (or was) one thing, and the fictional character is quite another. Perhaps we need two terms, "Napoleon" and "Napoleon*," one of which refers to the historical figure (the dead man) and the other of which refers to the abstract fictional character. People who believe in the existence of a supernatural being of the sort depicted in the Bible might similarly employ two expressions, "God" and "God*," to speak on the one hand of a supernatural being and on the other hand of a biblical character. It is debatable whether God created the world, but it is plainly false that God* did so. Similarly, it is false that Napoleon* lost the Battle of Waterloo but true that Napoleon lost the Battle of Waterloo. We must keep our books straight, must not confuse claims concerning fictional and biblical characters on the one hand with claims about human people and supernatural beings on the other. To establish the existence of God* is not to establish the existence of God. Of course we might construct causal arguments in support of both claims, but in the latter case it is not clear exactly how the argument would go. Skeptics will deny that we can find clear and uncontroversial cases of divine causation, maintaining that everything that happens in the natural world has a natural (and thus not a supernatural) cause. Defenders of this position may readily allow that God* causes various things to happen in the natural world.

Whatever we may think of divine causality, one thing seems certain: Commonplace things such as tables and trees are implicated in causal relations. But as we will now see, even this proposition does not go unchallenged.

Causally Inert Things (and a Word about Berkeley)

Abstract entities, by their very nature, are supposed to be causally inert.[29]

The question . . . arises, for philosophers at least, what mathematics is about. What are the truth-makers for true mathematical statements? It has often been claimed that the truth-

---

[29]Scott A. Shalkowski, "Conventions, Cognitivism and Necessity," *American Philosophy Quarterly*, October 1996, p. 376.

makers are not in space and time. If that is the true position, presumably they do not act on things in space and time.[30]

The suspicion voiced in the passages cited above is that only concrete (spatially locatable) things, not abstract (nonlocatable) objects, can be causally engaged—can cause things to happen. If existing things are things that are implicated in causal relations and abstract things are causally inert, it follows that abstract things do not exist. If God is said to be an abstract thing, our present assumptions suggest that God does not exist. The same is true of numbers and fictional objects on the assumption that such things are abstract objects.

Most people firmly believe that commonplace material things stand in various causal relations to other things. In accordance with the causal analysis of existence, which says that all and only causally active things exist, such material things exist. The eighteenth-century philosopher George Berkeley questions this reasoning. Berkeley would allow that commonplace material (as we take them to be) things exist but would deny that such things are causally active. Berkeley rejects the proposal that existence is properly understood in terms of causal activity.

Why deny that commonplace things are causally engaged? Berkeley boldly and famously argues that an ordinary "material" thing such as the Eiffel Tower is in reality nothing more than a certain collection of ideas. Berkeley does not question the existence of the Eiffel Tower; for him the Eiffel Tower is an existing collection of ideas. Berkeley argues that ideas (and collections of ideas) are causally inert. Although ideas are caused by—are products of—minds, ideas themselves are causally inactive.

Berkeley argues that only minds (spirits) are causally active. If that is correct, it is true that minds exist. Anything that is causally active exists. But is it true that *all* existing things are causally active? An affirmative answer to this question would suggest that Berkeley is committed to rejecting the existence of the material world. However, Berkeley does not agree that all existing things are causally active; he is not committed to denying the reality of the material world.

---

[30]David Armstrong, *A Combinatorial Theory of Possibility* (Cambridge: Cambridge University Press, 1989), pp. 9–10.

As we have seen, some people argue that abstract things are causally inert. If ideas (and collections of ideas) are abstract things, this vindicates Berkeley's thesis that ideas (collections of ideas) are causally inert. The problem is that commonplace things do not seem to be abstract things. The Eiffel Tower has a definite location and thus is a concrete thing, not an abstract thing. If collections of ideas are abstract things, it does not seem that the Eiffel Tower can correctly be identified with any collection of ideas.

Commonplace things have spatial locations, while abstract things do not. The Eiffel Tower is not abstract because the Eiffel Tower has a certain location. Can Berkeley grant this? We may wonder whether Berkeley can allow that there is a unique Eiffel Tower. This question arises from the conviction that

> In a strict Berkelean theory . . . a "collection" of ideas which constitutes a single object must be restricted to ideas which (1) all occur at the same time, and (2) all occur in the same mind.[31]

Berkeley seems to be facing a vexing problem. Suppose Jack and Jill travel to Paris and see "the" Eiffel Tower (ET). What we see depends on our perspective. Since Jack and Jill have somewhat different perspectives, what Jack sees is somewhat different from (though perhaps similar to) what Jill sees. Jack has one collection of ET-ideas, whereas Jill has a (somewhat) different collection of ET-ideas. If commonplace things are collections of ideas, as Berkeley apparently proposes, we seem to be left with not one but two Eiffel Towers. When the argument is extended, Berkelean assumptions seem to leave us with a great many Eiffel Towers, each of which is located in a different mind. The same conclusion emerges when we consider other commonplace things. Talk of *the world* we inhabit looks problematic if we accept Berkeley's thesis that commonplace things are collections of ideas. Jack's world contains Jack's Eiffel Tower and Jack's city of Paris, whereas Jill's world contains Jill's Eiffel Tower (a different collection of ideas) and Jill's city of Paris. Each person has her or his own world populated by his or her own commonplace objects.

This fragmentation of "the" world into many worlds is strongly counterintuitive. Berkeley's critics might argue that Berkeley's metaphysical assumptions commit us to the absurd conclusion that each person occupies his or her own (private) world. Berkeley would contest

---

[31]Jonathan Bennett, *Locke, Berkeley, Hume* (Oxford: Clarendon Press, 1989), p. 157.

this. He agrees that things that we see exist. We see the Eiffel Tower, and so the Eiffel Tower exists. If, as Berkeley maintains, we see only ideas, it follows that the Eiffel Tower is a collection of ideas. However, while it is true that the existence of ideas depends on the activity of minds (spirits), Berkeley denies that the ideas in question are dependent on *our* (human) minds. All ideas depend on minds, but the ideas that are constituents of commonplace things such as the Eiffel Tower are not dependent on our minds. Berkeley concludes that there must be an exceptional mind apart from our own finite minds that produces the collection of ideas that is the Eiffel Tower. This exceptional mind on which the commonplace world depends is none other than that of God. The commonplace world, in all its richness and diversity, exists in God's mind.

Some people find it hard to believe that Berkeley's position is defensible. Even if that is so, Berkeley offers a bold and remarkable example of how a metaphysician can argue that the way the world really is differs significantly from the way the world appears to be.

Minds

> Descartes's dualism combines substance dualism and property dualism: two disparate domains of substances and two mutually exclusive families of properties.[32]

Although most people would question Berkeley's assessment of commonplace things, they would allow that Berkeley is correct in maintaining that many minds exist. But then, what is a mind? There is much disagreement about this issue. We might say that a mind is anything that thinks, anything that has thoughts, feelings, memories, and emotions. Since we (people) have thoughts and feelings, this implies that we are minds. Somehow that seems wrong. It is one thing to say that we *have* minds and quite another to say that we *are* minds. The first claim is somehow more plausible than the second. Everyone would agree that we have hearts, but no one would say that we are our hearts. Perhaps things work the same way when we turn from hearts to minds. Our minds are, it may be said, proper parts of ourselves. If that

---

[32]Jaegwon Kim, *Philosophy of Mind* (Boulder, CO: Westview Press, 1996), p. 211.

is correct, and if, moreover, no material object is a mind,[33] it seems that we have immaterial or nonmaterial parts. This suggests that we are—a person is—a union of a certain immaterial mind and a certain material body. This position is called *substance dualism.*

Substance dualists may naturally hold that our immaterial minds have certain features or properties that are not physical features or properties. Consider the property of being angry. Conceivably a person has this property by virtue of the fact that his or her mind is angry. If minds are immaterial things and immaterial things do not have material properties, the property of being angry is not a material property. The same is true for the property of being hungry and the property of being afraid. Our present assumptions suggest that such psychological properties are not material properties. This position is called *property dualism.*

This argument for property dualism assumes the truth of substance dualism. It assumes that our minds are immaterial but also substantial things. We may find this implausible. It has been said that "the brain is where the action is, as far as our mental lives are concerned."[34] Doesn't that speak for the conclusion that our minds are (identical with) our brains? If that is so, the fact that immaterial things lack material properties does nothing to support the conclusion that psychological properties are not material properties, for although our minds have psychological properties, our minds are not (on the present view) immaterial things.

There are arguments opposing the view that our minds are our brains. Consider the sad case of Elaine Esposito, who died in 1978 after spending a remarkable 37 years and 111 days unconscious following an appendectomy at the age of six. We may judge that Esposito's mind perished at the time of her appendectomy. Her body continued to exist for the next 37 years or so, but her mind did not. Esposito's brain continued for some time after her mind had perished. But then how could her mind be her brain? Our minds cannot be identified with our brains if, as the Esposito case perhaps suggests, our brains can continue in circumstances in which our minds do not continue.

No material thing other than a brain has an apparent claim to being a mind. If our minds are not our brains, it seems that our

---

[33]As G. E. Moore maintains in *Some Main Problems of Philosophy* (New York: Collier Books, 1962), p. 147.

[34]Kim, *Philosophy of Mind,* p. 47.

minds are not material things. This reasoning speaks for the position of the substance dualist, who holds that a person is a union of a material substance (body) and an immaterial substance (a mind or a "soul," as some people say). We (normal human beings) think insofar as we have immaterial souls that think. On this conception of a mind, it is at least not obviously true that Esposito's mind ceases to exist at the time of her appendectomy. Perhaps this mind continues but no longer is united with Esposito's body. The mind–body union that is the person Esposito exists only for as long as the mind in question and the body in question interact. If there is no appropriate interaction after the appendectomy, the person Esposito no longer exists. Nonetheless, it may be true that Esposito's immaterial mind continues to exist, as does her material body. What does not continue is the mind–body union that is the person.

Critics deny that there is any reason to accept the reality of immaterial souls and so question this dualist conception of a person. Defenders of what is called the *psychophysical supervenience* thesis maintain that two physically indiscernible humans would be psychologically indiscernible, the same in all psychological respects. Such supervenience means that our psychological states are determined or fixed entirely by our physical states. If this is correct, it is hard to generate much enthusiasm for immaterial souls. Souls simply have no explanatory role to play in proper accounts of human actions, given psychophysical supervenience.

One line of attack on supervenience arises from the conviction, mentioned earlier, that commonplace things are somehow constituents of our thoughts. That suggests that there is something to be said for

> *Cognitive Externalism:* The content of our beliefs and thoughts is not determined by what is in the head of the believing or speaking subject. To determine the content of (most of) a subject's statements (thoughts) we need to take inventory of the sorts of things that are in this subject's environment.[35]

Cognitive externalists argue that the content of our thoughts is fixed by the sorts of things that populate our environment. In theory it could happen that two physically indiscernible thinkers would find themselves in radically different environments, which means (given Cogni-

---

[35]For more about this position, see McGinn, *Mental Content,* chap. 1.

tive Externalism) that those individuals would have different thoughts. Since it is possible to have physically indiscernible individuals who are nonetheless psychologically discernible, we have reason to question the thesis of psychophysical supervenience. If this is true, we should reject arguments opposing immaterial souls that appeal to supervenience.

Unsubstantial Minds

> [W]e indeed speak of the "stream" of consciousness. If the metaphor is apt, then the mind is the whole river, the totality of a systematically connected temporal stream of thoughts. None of these thoughts, and no subset of them, is identical with the mind; this does not mean, however, that they are but manifestations of an underlying substratum—a thought-stuff, soul-substance, or ghost. To have a mind is to have thoughts, and not to have something else that has them.[36]

We could consistently endorse both Cognitive Externalism and the thesis that our minds are our brains, but as we have seen, there are arguments against the identification of minds and brains. Do those arguments speak for the view that our minds are immaterial substances? Not necessarily. The move from "minds are not material substances" to "minds are immaterial substances" is not valid. Love affairs and rainstorms are not substantial things. A storm or a love affair is an extended event or process, not a substantial thing. These are exclusive categories; nothing is both an event and a substantial thing. If our minds are extended events, our minds are not substances and so are neither material substances nor immaterial substances. Theorists who deny that minds are brains thus are not committed to substance dualism (the view that our bodies are material substances while our minds are immaterial substances).

Perhaps we are unions of minds and bodies. If we are, does that make us substances or events? Conceivably the answer is neither. Suppose a person is such that the person's mind is an extended event whereas that person's body is a substantial thing. Then perhaps it is not correct to say either that a person is a substantial thing or that a person is an event.

If the event that is your mind terminates or ceases before your body perishes, the mind–body union that is you perishes before your

---

[36]Zeno Vendler, *Res Cogitans* (Ithaca, NY: Cornell University Press, 1972), p. 187.

body does. On this assessment of the matter you cannot *be* your body, since you perish before your body does. However, it does not follow *either* that you are an immaterial substance *or* that some such substance (your soul) is part of you. We can reject substance dualism and also deny that we are material substances.

An event theory of the mind is often expressed in these terms: Our minds are streams or flows of consciousness. The components of such streams are psychological events or states: occurrences of various sensations, emotions, thoughts, and memories. The stream of such events that is the mind of Elaine Esposito tragically terminates many years before her body perishes. We may judge that Esposito perishes when her mind terminates or ceases, taking the person Esposito to be a union of an event-mind and a substantial body.

One attraction of the stream of consciousness assessment of the mind lies in the fact that it enables us to reject immaterial minds. Doubts about immaterial minds arise from the conviction that human behavior can be explained satisfactorily in terms of physical causes. Indeed, some theorists accept

> *The Closure Principle:* Every physical event can be explained in physical terms. Every physical event has a physical cause.

Suppose Alice feels a draft and closes the window. The event that is Alice's closing of the window is a physical event. Accordingly, the closure principle tells us that the closing event has a physical cause. We can accept this and also allow that Alice's decision to close the window caused the closing event (the closing of the window). What we cannot allow (if we accept closure) is that this decision is a nonphysical event. However, if our minds were immaterial things, it seems that Alice's decision to close the window would be a nonphysical event. In short, closure seems to speak against the view that our minds are immaterial substances.

Defenders of an event theory of mind may agree with this and say that the various events that constitute our minds are physical events and thus are qualified for the role of causes of other physical events, such as movements of our lips (when we speak) and of our arms and legs (when we close windows). Although that sounds plausible, there is a problem. This problem emerges from the facts that (1) there is something to be said for property dualism and (2) property dualism seems to speak for event dualism, the view that psychological events are not strictly physical events. This takes some explaining. Let us start with the following:

> Most mental characteristics seem capable of being instantiated in a wide range of physical media. Can a computing machine think? One may doubt that this is so, but few nowadays would base their doubts solely on the motion that computing machines are made of the wrong "stuff." Moreover, it seems entirely within the realm of physical possibility that there are creatures elsewhere in the universe that share various mental characteristics with us but whose "biology" is vastly different from ours.[37]

We need not venture far to find cases that illustrate this, for it may well be true that the physical state of a hungry cat or dog is quite different from the physical state of a hungry human. If that is true, we cannot identify the property of hunger with the property of being in the particular physical state in which hungry humans are, since hungry dogs and cats fail to be in that physical state. All this speaks against the view that psychological properties (hunger, anger, fear, and so on) are physical properties. But plainly psychological properties are implicated in psychological events; the property of being angry is somehow a constituent of the event in which (on a certain occasion) Alice becomes angry. If psychological properties are not physical properties, then arguably psychological events are not physical events. Given the closure principle, this means that we cannot focus attention on psychological events when we try to explain why people act as they do. We would like to say that Alice closed the window because she felt a draft of cold air. The problem is that closure does not allow this sort of explanation if, as was just argued, psychological events (such as the event in which Alice feels a draft of cold air) are not physical events.

Where does this leave us? If we accept the closure principle, we will naturally maintain that psychological events are physical events (since psychological events often explain why people act in certain ways). The problem is that it seems that psychological properties such as the property of feeling cold are not physical properties. It is

---

[37]John Heil, *The Nature of True Minds* (Cambridge: Cambridge University Press, 1992), p. 64.

hard to see how psychological events can be physical events if indeed psychological properties are not physical properties.[38]

Causality and Freedom

> Suppose that a fire has broken out in a certain house. . . . Experts investigate the cause of the fire, and they conclude that it was caused by an electrical short-circuit at a certain place. What is the exact force of their statement that this short-circuit caused the fire?[39]

We often say that one event causes another when the first event is merely a conspicuous or particularly important component of a larger event that is the true (complete) cause. We say that the short circuit caused the fire, but if certain conditions had not been satisfied (e.g., the presence of oxygen in the location of the short circuit), no fire would have occurred after the short circuit happened. Specifying the true (complete) cause of the fire is a tricky business, but even if we do not succeed in this, we may naturally assume that there is (was) a cause of the fire. To believe in *universal causation* is to believe that every event has a cause, though we may not know what the cause of an event is. Causes are said to *determine* their effects. Given the occurrence of the cause-event, the effect-event is inevitable. Since the fire is not made inevitable by the short circuit, the short circuit event is not itself the complete cause of the fire. The complete cause of the fire is a complex event whose occurrence determines—makes inevitable—the event that is the fire. Determinists hold that all events are in this sense determined by previous events. All events are inevitable, given what happens previously.

If an event that occurs at time t is causally determined by a previous event that occurs at time $t-1$ and if this event is itself causally determined by a still earlier event that occurs at time $t-2$, it seems that the event that occurs at t is made inevitable—determined—by the event that occurs at $t-2$. On the assumption that every event has a cause, our present assumptions suggest that events that currently

---

[38]For more about interaction and psychological properties, see John Heil, *The Nature of True Minds* (Cambridge: Cambridge University Press, 1992).

[39]J. L. Mackie, *The Cement of the Universe* (Oxford: Oxford University Press, 1974), p. 15.

take place are causally determined by events that occurred before we were born. Human actions are events (though not all events are human actions). Thus all human actions that currently occur are (as our present assumptions suggest) determined by events that happened before the people who perform these actions (the agents) were born. If that is true, it seems that none of the agents who currently do things—fly kites, walk dogs, rob banks, and so on—could have avoided acting as they do. The question then is: How can it be true that such agents are acting freely?

The correct analysis of what it means to say that someone acts freely is a subject of considerable controversy, but suppose an agent acts freely only on the occasions when that agent has genuine alternatives. Having such alternatives means that the agent can—has the power to—not act as she or he does. One acts freely only when one has genuine alternatives, when one does not *have* to act as one does.

If the belief in universal causation is true, can we be said to act freely on any occasion? It appears not. We never act freely because in truth we never have genuine alternatives. We never have such alternatives because each of our actions is such that it is (indirectly) caused by, and thus determined by, events that occurred before we are born. We have no control over such events; since those events determine all our actions, we have no alternatives to the actions we perform. Our present assumptions concerning causality point to the disturbing conclusion that we never act freely.[40]

It may be replied that it is plainly true that people make decisions and in many cases act on the basis of those decisions. When that happens, an agent controls what she or he does and thus acts freely. However, this ignores the fact that the decisions from which your actions emerge are (by the reasoning just outlined) determined by events that occurred before you were born. It seems that no genuine alternative choices or decisions are open to you or indeed to anyone. You cannot make decisions other than the ones you make. Therefore, the making of decisions does not establish that people have control over what they do. It seems that we do not have control over our decisions.

---

[40]For a development of this reasoning, see Peter van Inwagen, *An Essay on Free Will* (Oxford: Clarendon Press, 1983).

Consider the much discussed case of Gary Gilmore, reputedly a cold-blooded murderer.[41] When Gilmore pulled the trigger in the course of killing his victim, the movement of his trigger finger presumably was caused by his decision to pull the trigger. But what caused the event that was Gilmore's decision? The thesis of universal causation may suggest that this event was determined by things that happened before Gilmore was born. If that is so, Gilmore hardly can be said to have had genuine control over either his decision to pull the trigger or the event that was the trigger pulling.

It might be said that Gilmore decided to pull the trigger because he was a mean person. In response to this, we may ask what made Gilmore the sort of person he was. Perhaps the answer lies in part with Gilmore's genetic makeup and in (large) part with the fact that Gilmore was repeatedly subjected to brutal treatment when he was a child. Causes determine their effects, and Gilmore's meanness no doubt had a cause. Therefore, it may seem that Gilmore's meanness was something over which Gilmore himself had no control, but could Gilmore then have acted freely when he pulled the trigger? It is said that to act freely an agent must be autonomous in the sense that his or her action is "up to the agent."[42] Our present assumptions concerning causality suggest that none of us is an autonomous agent. None of us, the present argument suggests, is morally responsible for what he or she does.

Possible Words

> I believe, and so do you, that things could have been different in countless ways. But what does this mean? Ordinary language permits this paraphrase: there are many ways things could have been besides the way they actually are. . . . I therefore believe in the existence of entities that might be called "ways things could have been": I prefer to call them "possible worlds."[43]

One method for reconciling free will and universal causation is to maintain that causes do not determine (or necessitate) their effects.

---

[41]For a detailed examination of Gilmore's case, see Norman Mailer, *The Executioner's Song* (New York: Warner Books, 1979).

[42]This account of autonomy is offered by Susan Wolf in *Freedom within Reason* (Oxford: Oxford University Press, 1990). Wolf denies that acting freely requires autonomy.

[43]David Lewis, *Counterfactuals* (Cambridge, MA: Harvard University Press, 1973), p. 84.

But then, what is involved when one event causes another? It is generally if not invariably true that causes precede their effects. (If event E1 causes event E2, then E1 occurs before E2.) However, there must be more to causation than this. The event that is (was) the death of Stalin occurred before the event that is (was) Bill Clinton's election as president in 1992. Stalin's death precedes but does not cause or bring about Clinton's election. Temporal priority is hardly sufficient for causality. What, then, is causality? Under what conditions can we correctly judge that one event causes another? Suppose that Alice strikes a certain match at time $t1$ and that the match ignites shortly thereafter at $t2$. To say that the striking event caused the igniting event is to say roughly that the igniting event would not have occurred at $t2$ if the striking event had not occurred at $t1$. There is no assertion here that causes determine—make inevitable—their effects. Although determinism and free will may be incompatible, perhaps we can allow universal causation—allow that every event has a cause—and also reject determinism. If so, perhaps we can have both free will and universal causation.

Counterfactual statements assert not that things *actually* happen in a certain way but that things *would have happened* in a certain way if a certain event or events had not occurred. The statement "England would have been invaded by Germany in the 1940s if Germany and the USSR had not gone to war" is counterfactual in the sense that it focuses on something that did not in fact happen (Germany and the USSR did go to war). This assumes, plausibly enough, that things might not have happened as they did happen. Germany and the Soviets did go to war in the 1940s; still, they might not have done so. If we accept this, it is hard to see why we should deny that although Gilmore did decide to pull the trigger, he might not have made that decision. If, as we may judge, Gilmore's victim would not have died (at the time at which he died) had Gilmore not decided to pull the trigger, then this decision caused the victim's death.

All this offers prospects for a world containing both universal causality and genuine alternatives. Although each person has only one actual life, each person has many possible lives. We sometimes regret that our lives have gone a certain way, as the following suggests:

> Presumably the regret that Flaubert wasn't more involved in life
> isn't just a philanthropic wish for him: if only old Gustave had

> had a wife and kiddies, he wouldn't have been so glum about
> the whole shooting-match?[44]

At the end of his life, Flaubert might have deeply regretted the fact
that he had not been a family man. Our regrets presuppose that
things *did not have to go* the way things went. Of course we cannot
change the past. Still, regret presupposes that there was a time when
we had it within our power to direct the future course of our lives in
one way rather than another. Given the way the world is and has been
at a given time, there are branching possible futures representing (or
containing) different lives we might have. Talk of possible futures (relative to a certain time) is closely related to talk of possible worlds. One
rather minimalist account of possible worlds goes like this:

> Ordinarily when we speak of things possibly having been differ-
> ent in some appropriate way from the way they in fact are and
> have been, we say that the world would have had a different his-
> tory if those imagined circumstances had obtained. . . . In-
> deed, possible worlds, as spoken of in technical discourse, are
> individuated in the same way that possible histories of the world,
> as ordinarily conceived, are individuated, so I think that the pos-
> sible *worlds* of modal logicians and philosophers really are just
> possible *histories* of the world, as ordinarily conceived.[45]

Each of Flaubert's (many) possible lives occurs in a distinct possible
world. But would the subject who lives these (different) lives really
be Flaubert? Presumably, there is a possible world in which an individual who is in many ways like Flaubert—Flaubert*, say—has a wife
and ten children. Flaubert* is decidedly good-natured, not at all
"glum about the whole shooting-match." Flaubert*'s life first diverges from Flaubert's when, at the age of thirty, Flaubert* marries
and subsequently enjoys a (largely) pleasant life as a good-humored
family man. Flaubert may well regret not living the sort of life that is
lived by Flaubert*.

   This raises a number of questions. We may wonder whether
Flaubert* is really (our) Flaubert. Flaubert*'s life differs significantly
from Flaubert's life. Isn't it a mistake to judge that we are dealing
with one person and two lives? Isn't the truth of the matter that we
are dealing with two different people who have lives of their own?

---

[44]Julian Barnes, *Flaubert's Parrot* (New York: Knopf, 1985), p. 146.

[45]Michael Slote, *Metaphysics and Essence* (Oxford: Blackwell, 1975), p. 7.

One argument in behalf of the claim that Flaubert and Flaubert* are one person focuses on the fact that Flaubert's life and Flaubert*'s life share a certain initial segment. This shared segment of life contains a precocious boy named Gustave. In the actual world there is a continuous path through space and time linking Gustave and the famous novelist and lifelong bachelor Flaubert. Similarly, in the possible Flaubert* world there is a spatiotemporal path leading from Gustave to the happy husband but literarily barren Flaubert*. Assuming that spatiotemporal paths are guarantors of identity, we then have

(1) Gustave = Flaubert

(2) Gustave = Flaubert*

Since identity is an equivalence relation, it follows that

(3) Flaubert = Flaubert*

This conclusion supports the intuition that (our) Flaubert could have been a happily married though literarily undistinguished man. As it happens, Flaubert was not such a man. Nonetheless, there is a possible but unrealized world in which Flaubert (= Flaubert*) is such a man. Judgments concerning our unrealized potentialities seem to involve (unspoken) assumptions concerning identity across possible worlds ("transworld identity"). The failed boxer who proclaims "I could have been the champ" is speaking truthfully only if there is un unrealized world in which *he* is the champ. It seems that we are not confined to the actual world; each of us occupies countless possible worlds.

All this suggests that there must be something amiss in arguments for determinism that conclude that every event is inevitable. Things could have gone quite differently for Flaubert or Gary Gilmore. An argument can be made that the recognition of unrealized possibilities is the price that must be paid for a metaphysic that allows us to act freely and bear responsibility for our actions.

Are There Many Actual Worlds?

A sorting of attributes (or properties) as essential or inessential to an object or objects is not wholly a fabrication of metaphysicians.[46]

---

[46]Ruth Barcan Marcus, *Modalities* (Oxford: Oxford University Press, 1993), p. 54.

> Metaphysical questions have answers, and among compet-
> ing answers, not all, certainly, can be true. If one man asserts a
> theory of materialism and another denies that theory, then one
> of those men is in error; and so it is with every other metaphysi-
> cal theory.[47]

An essential property (feature) of a thing is a property that that
thing has to have and thus has in every possible world in which it
exists; accidental properties of things are properties things have in
the actual world but do not have essentially. Intuitively, being a famous literary figure is an accidental property of Flaubert. There
are possible worlds in which Flaubert exists but is not a famous literary figure.

There is considerable controversy about the essential properties of things. Are we (people) essentially psychological beings? If we
answer affirmatively, we must deny that we existed as prepsychologi-
cal beings before our births. The life of a certain prenatal individual
undoubtedly merges with my life, but this prenatal individual was
not me if I am essentially a psychological being and it is not a psychological being. But how are we to determine what features are and
are not essential to a given individual? It may be argued that neither
party to an essentialist debate can win, since there is no "objective"
answer to essentialist questions. The answers to essentialist questions
"all depend on the way you view the situation." In short, we stipulate
which properties are and which are not essential to things. Essentialist questions call for *decisions,* not for *discoveries.* We can discover
what properties a thing has by carefully examining that thing, but no
examination of a thing will reveal what its essential properties are.

This has some unsettling corollaries. Earlier we considered the
charge that Berkeley's idealist assumptions should be rejected precisely because they leave us with the implausible view that there are
many worlds. A stipulative approach to essence has a similar corollary.

It may be said that the "many worlds" position is not implausible at all, for haven't we just stated that there are many possible
worlds? If there are many possible worlds, presumably there is something to the proposal that there are many worlds.

As we have seen, "possible worlds" are possible histories of the
world. We may allow that there is a plurality of possible worlds in this

---

[47]Taylor, *Metaphysics.*

sense and still doubt that there are *many actual worlds*. There is (we may judge) only one actual world, though there are countlessly many possible worlds.

Some theorists question this, maintaining that there are "multiple actual worlds."[48] This is precisely the position that is suggested by a stipulative approach to the essence–accident distinction. Suppose Jack affirms and Jill denies that people are essentially psychological beings. Suppose also that there is no "objective" answer to the question "Are people essentially psychological beings?" It then seems we are left with Jack-people (who are essentially psychological beings) and Jill-people (who are not). Things that are possible for Jill-people are not possible for Jack-people; accordingly, Jack-people cannot *be* Jill-people. We are left with two sorts of people.

If Jack's (actual) world is populated by Jack-people and Jill's (actual) world is populated by Jill-people, it seems that Jack's (actual) world is different from Jill's (actual) world. Accordingly, there is no such thing as "the actual world." There is on the one hand the actual world according to Jack and on the other hand the actual world according to Jill.

If this is accepted, the "many worlds" objection to Berkeley's idealism that was considered earlier is unsound. This objection asserted that it is absurd to judge that there are many (actual) worlds, not just one. Our present assumptions suggest that this is perfectly true.

Once it is allowed that there are many actual worlds that correspond to our favored conception of essential properties, it may be denied that any metaphysical question has a real (objective) answer. We cannot really discover the answer to a metaphysical question such as "Do we have free will?" Arguably metaphysical questions are undecidable, and undecidable questions call for stipulations (since discovery is out of the question). Since different metaphysicians can stipulate in different ways, all this points to the conclusion that there are many actual worlds corresponding to our favored stipulative "answers" to metaphysical questions. Jack's world may be a "presentist" world (in which only the present exists) whereas Jill's world is not; Jill's world may be a deterministic world whereas Jack's world is not. We are left not just with many possible worlds but with many actual worlds.

---

[48]Nelson Goodman, *Ways of Worldmaking* (Indianapolis: Hackett, 1978), p. 2.

Some people find it hard to accept this. Jack and Jill argue metaphysical issues over cups of coffee. This suggests that Jack and Jill inhabit the same world. If Jack defends and Jill opposes Berkelean idealism, it certainly is hard to believe that both parties can be right. It is true that the world as Jack takes it to be is a Berkelean world whereas the world as Jill takes it to be is not, but both parties cannot be right. Surely the world that Jack and Jill jointly inhabit cannot both be and not be a Berkelean world. It seems that one party to the Jack–Jill debate is making a mistake. And why should things turn out differently when Jack and Jill argue over the nature of time or whether we ever act freely? It is correctly said that

> there can seem to be a tension in ordinary thinking between the metaphysical autonomy of the world (its independence of us) and its epistemological accessibility (our capacity to find out about it).[49]

To maintain that metaphysics is done by stipulation is to abandon the independence assumption. The problem with the stipulative approach to metaphysics is that it leaves us with too many (actual) worlds. As even Berkeley would allow, there is a single (actual) world that is independent of our beliefs (and indeed independent of us). It is a legitimate question whether we can know what this world is like. Perhaps, as some people argue, we can never really know the answers to metaphysical questions.[50] Nonetheless, such epistemic pessimism provides no support for those who propose stipulative responses to metaphysical questions.

Of course it remains to be seen whether knowledge is possible in metaphysics. Some of us believe that we know perfectly well that time passes, that we (sometimes) act freely, and that we existed in the past. These are all metaphysical propositions. Arguably we know that (certain) metaphysical propositions are true.

---

[49]Paul Horwich, *Truth* (Oxford: Blackwell, 1990), p. 57.
[50]Taylor, *Metaphysics,* p. 5.

PART I

*I*dentity

CHAPTER 1

Of Personal Identity

David Hume

We persist throughout a certain time. You yourself exist at many times, but what sort of being are you (what is a self)? Furthermore, what conditions must be fulfilled for one person or self to exist at different times? These questions are addressed in the following selection by the eighteenth-century Scottish philosopher David Hume (1711–1776), the author of A Treatise of Human Nature *and* An Enquiry Concerning Human Understanding. *Hume raises questions about the very idea of a self but also seems to grant that people are bundles of "perceptions" or experiences. Experiences may be parts or components of the self. The question then is: Can a self continue as its parts are altered?*

There are some philosophers, who imagine we are every moment intimately conscious of what we call our SELF; that we feel its existence and its continuance in existence; and are certain, beyond the evidence of a demonstration, both of its perfect identity and simplicity. The strongest sensation, the most violent passion, say they, instead of distracting us from this view, only fix it the more intensely, and make us consider their influence on *self* either by their pain or pleasure. To attempt a farther proof of this were to weaken its evidence; since no proof can be deriv'd from any fact, of which we are so intimately conscious; nor is there any thing, of which we can be certain, if we doubt of this.

Unluckily all these positive assertions are contrary to that very experience, which is pleaded for them, nor have we any idea of *self*, after the manner it is here explain'd. For from what impression cou'd this idea be deriv'd? This question 'tis impossible to answer without a manifest contradiction and absurdity; and yet 'tis a question, which must necessarily be answer'd, if we wou'd have the idea of self pass for clear and intelligible. It must be some one impression, that gives rise to every real idea. But self or person is not any one impression, but that to which our several impressions and ideas are suppos'd to have a reference. If any impression gives rise to the idea of self, that impression must continue invariably the same, thro' the whole course of our lives; since self is suppos'd to exist after that manner. But there is no impression constant and invariable. Pain and pleasure, grief and joy, passions and sensations succeed each other, and never all exist at the same time. It cannot, therefore, be from any of these impressions, or from any other, that the idea of self is deriv'd; and consequently there is no such idea.

But farther, what must become of all our particular perceptions upon this hypothesis? All these are different, and distinguishable, and separable from each other, and may be separately consider'd, and may exist separately, and have no need of any thing to support their existence. After what manner, therefore, do they belong to self; and how are they connected with it? For my part, when I enter most intimately into what I call *myself,* I always stumble on some particular perception or other, of heat or cold, light or shade, love or hatred, pain or pleasure. I never can catch *myself* at any time without a perception, and never can observe any thing but the perception. When my perceptions are remov'd for any time, as by sound sleep; so long am I insensible of *myself,* and may truly be said not to exist. And were all my perceptions remov'd by death, and cou'd I neither think, nor feel, nor see, nor love, nor hate after the dissolution of my body, I shou'd be entirely annihilated, nor do I conceive what is farther requisite to make me a perfect non-entity. If any one upon serious and unprejudic'd reflexion, thinks he has a different notion of *himself,* I must confess I can reason no longer with him. All I can allow him is, that he may be in the right as well as I, and that we are essentially different in this particular. He may, perhaps, perceive something simple and continu'd, which he calls *himself;* tho' I am certain there is no such principle in me.

But setting aside some metaphysicians of this kind, I may venture to affirm of the rest of mankind, that they are nothing but a bundle or collection of different perceptions, which succeed each other with an inconceivable rapidity, and are in a perpetual flux and movement. Our eyes cannot turn in their sockets without varying our perceptions. Our thought is still more variable than our sight; and all our other senses and faculties contribute to this change; nor is there any single power of the soul, which remains unalterably the same, perhaps for one moment. The mind is a kind of theatre, where several perceptions successively make their appearance; pass, re-pass, glide away, and mingle in an infinite variety of postures and situations. There is properly no *simplicity* in it at one time, nor *identity* in different; whatever natural propension we may have to imagine that simplicity and identity. The comparison of the theatre must not mislead us. They are the successive perceptions only, that constitute the mind; nor have we the most distant notion of the place, where these scenes are represented, or of the materials, of which it is compos'd.

What then gives us so great a propension to ascribe an identity to these successive perceptions, and to suppose ourselves possest of an invariable and uninterrupted existence thro' the whole course of our lives? In order to answer this question, we must distinguish betwixt personal identity, as it regards our thought or imagination, and as it regards our passions or the concern we take in ourselves. The first is our present subject; and to explain it perfectly we must take the matter pretty deep, and account for that identity, which we attribute to plants and animals; there being a great analogy betwixt it, and the identity of a self or person.

We have a distinct idea of an object, that remains invariable and uninterrupted thro' a suppos'd variation of time; and this idea we call that of *identity* or *sameness*. We have also a distinct idea of several different objects existing in succession, and connected together by a close relation; and this to an accurate view affords as perfect a notion of *diversity,* as if there was no manner of relation among the objects. But tho' these two ideas of identity, and a succession of related objects be in themselves perfectly distinct, and even contrary, yet 'tis certain, that in our common way of thinking they are generally confounded with each other. That action of the imagination, by which we consider the uninterrupted and invariable object, and that by which we reflect on the succession of related objects, are almost the same to the feeling, nor is there much more effort of thought requir'd in the latter case than in the former. The relation facilitates the transition of the mind from one object to another, and renders its passage as smooth as if it contemplated one continu'd object. This resemblance is the cause of the confusion and mistake, and makes us substitute the notion of identity, instead of that of related objects. However at one instant we may consider the related succession as variable or interrupted, we are sure the next to ascribe to it a perfect identity, and regard it as invariable and uninterrupted. Our propensity to this mistake is so great from the resemblance above-mention'd, that we fall into it before we are aware; and tho' we incessantly correct ourselves by reflexion, and return to a more accurate method of thinking, yet we cannot long sustain our philosophy, or take off this biass from the imagination. Our last resource is to yield to it, and boldly assert that these different related objects are in effect the same, however interrupted and variable. In order to justify to ourselves this absurdity, we often feign some new and unintelligible principle, that connects the objects together, and prevents their interruption or variation. Thus we feign the continu'd existence of the perceptions of our senses, to remove the interruption; and run into the notion of a *soul*, and *self*, and *substance*, to disguise the variation. But we may farther observe, that where we do not give rise to such a fiction, our propension to confound identity with relation is so great, that we are apt to imagine[1] something unknown and mysterious, connecting the parts, beside their relation; and this I take to be the case with regard to the identity we ascribe to plants and vegetables. And even when this does not take place, we still feel a propensity to confound these ideas, tho' we are not able fully to satisfy ourselves in that particular, nor find any thing invariable and uninterrupted to justify our notion of identity.

Thus the controversy concerning identity is not merely a dispute of words. For when we attribute identity, in an improper sense, to variable or interrupted objects, our mistake is not confin'd to the expression, but is commonly attended with a fiction, either of something invariable and uninterrupted, or of something mysterious and inexplicable, or at least with a propensity to such fictions. What will suffice to prove this hypothesis to the satisfaction of every fair enquirer, is to shew from daily experience and observation, that the objects, which are variable or interrupted, and yet are suppos'd to continue the same, are such only as consist of a succession of parts, connected together by resemblance, contiguity, or causation. For as

---

[1]If the reader is desirous to see how a great genius may be influenc'd by these seemingly trivial principles of the imagination, as well as the mere vulgar, let him read my Lord *Shaftsbury's* reasonings concerning the uniting principle of the universe, and the identity of plants and animals. See his *Moralists:* or, *Philosophical rhapsody.*

such a succession answers evidently to our notion of diversity, it can only be by mistake we ascribe to it an identity and as the relation of parts, which leads us into this mistake, is really nothing but a quality, which produces an association of ideas, and an easy transition of the imagination from one to another, it can only be from the resemblance, which this act of the mind bears to that, by which we contemplate one continu'd object, that the error arises. Our chief business, then, must be to prove, that all objects, to which we ascribe identity, without observing their invariableness and uninterruptedness, are such as consist of a succession of related objects.

In order to this, suppose any mass of matter, of which the parts are contiguous and connected, to be plac'd before us; 'tis plain we must attribute a perfect identity to this mass, provided all the parts continue uninterruptedly and invariably the same, whatever motion or change of place we may observe either in the whole or in any of the parts. But supposing some very *small* or *inconsiderable* part to be added to the mass, or subtracted from it; tho' this absolutely destroys the identity of the whole, strictly speaking; yet as we seldom think so accurately, we scruple not to pronounce a mass of matter the same, where we find so trivial an alteration. The passage of the thought from the object before the change to the object after it, is so smooth and easy, that we scarce perceive the transition, and are apt to imagine, that 'tis nothing but a continu'd survey of the same object.

There is a very remarkable circumstance, that attends this experiment; which is, that tho' the change of any considerable part in a mass of matter destroys the identity of the whole, yet we must measure the greatness of the part, not absolutely, but by its *proportion* to the whole. The addition or diminution of a mountain wou'd not be sufficient to produce a diversity in a planet; tho' the change of a very few inches wou'd be able to destroy the identity of some bodies. 'Twill be impossible to account for this, but by reflecting that objects operate upon the mind, and break or interrupt the continuity of its actions not according to their real greatness, but according to their proportion to each other: And therefore, since this interruption makes an object cease to appear the same, it must be the uninterrupted progress of the thought, which constitutes the imperfect identity.

This may be confirm'd by another phenomenon. A change in any considerable part of a body destroys its identity; but 'tis remarkable, that where the change is produc'd *gradually* and *insensibly* we are less apt to ascribe to it the same effect. The reason can plainly be no other, than that the mind, in following the successive changes of the body, feels an easy passage from the surveying its condition in one moment to the viewing of it in another, and at no particular time perceives any interruption in its actions. From which continu'd perception, it ascribes a continu'd existence and identity to the object.

But whatever precaution we may use in introducing the changes gradually, and making them proportionable to the whole, 'tis certain, that where the changes are at last observ'd to become considerable, we make a scruple of ascribing identity to such different objects. There is, however, another artifice, by which we may induce the imagination to advance a step farther: and that is, by producing a reference of the parts to each other, and a combination to some *common end* or purpose. A ship, of which a considerable part has been chang'd by frequent reparations, is still consider'd as the same: nor does the difference of the materials hinder us from ascribing an identity to it. The common end, in which the parts conspire, is the same under all their variations, and affords an easy transition of the imagination from one situation of the body to another.

But this is still more remarkable, when we add a *sympathy* of parts to their *common end,* and suppose that they bear to each other, the reciprocal relation of cause and effect in all their actions and operations. This is the case with all animals and vegetables; where not only the several parts have a reference to some general purpose, but also a mutual dependance on, and connexion with each other. The effect of so strong a relation is, that tho' every one must allow, that in a very few years both vegetables and animals endure a *total* change, yet we still attribute identity to them, while their form, size, and substance are entirely alter'd. An oak, that grows from a small plant to a large tree, is still the same oak; tho' there be not one particle of matter, or figure of its parts the same. An infant becomes a man, and is sometimes fat, sometimes lean, without any change in his identity.

We may also consider the two following phænomena, which are remarkable in their kind. The first is, that tho' we commonly be able to distinguish pretty exactly betwixt numerical and specific identity, yet it sometimes happens, that we confound them, and in our thinking and reasoning employ the one for the other. Thus a man, who hears a noise, that is frequently interrupted and renew'd, says, it is still the same noise; tho' 'tis evident the sounds have only a specific identity or resemblance, and there is nothing numerically the same, but the cause, which produc'd them. In like manner it may be said without breach of the propriety of language, that such a church, which was formerly of brick, fell to ruin, and that the parish rebuilt the same church of free-stone, and according to modern architecture. Here neither the form nor materials are the same, nor is there any thing common to the two objects, but their relation to the inhabitants of the parish; and yet this alone is sufficient to make us denominate them the same. But we must observe, that in these cases the first object is in a manner annihilated before the second comes into existence; by which means, we are never presented in any one point of time with the idea of difference and multiplicity; and for that reason are less scrupulous in calling them the same.

Secondly, We may remark, that tho' in a succession of related objects, it be in a manner requisite, that the change of parts be not sudden nor entire, in order to preserve the identity, yet where the objects are in their nature changeable and inconstant, we admit of a more sudden transition, than wou'd otherwise be consistent with that relation. Thus as the nature of a river consists in the motion and change of parts; tho' in less than four and twenty hours these be totally alter'd: this hinders not the river from continuing the same during several ages. What is natural and essential to any thing is, in a manner, expected; and what is expected makes less impression, and appears of less moment, than what is unusual and extraordinary. A considerable change of the former kind seems really less to the imagination, than the most trivial alteration of the latter; and by breaking less the continuity of the thought, has less influence in destroying the identity.

We now proceed to explain the nature of *personal identity,* which has become so great a question in philosophy, especially of late years in *England,* where all the abstruser sciences are study'd with a peculiar ardour and application. And here 'tis evident, the same method of reasoning must be continu'd, which has so successfully explain'd the identity of plants, and animals, and ships, and houses, and of all the compounded and changeable productions either of art or nature. The identity, which we ascribe to the mind of man, is only a fictitious one, and of a like kind with that which we ascribe to vegetables and animal bodies. It cannot, therefore, have a different origin, but must proceed from a like operation of the imagination upon like objects.

But lest this argument shou'd not convince the reader; tho' in my opinion perfectly decisive: let him weigh the following reasoning, which is still closer and more immediate. 'Tis evident, that the identity, which we attribute to the human mind, however perfect we may imagine it to be, is not able to run the several different perceptions into one, and make them lose their characters of distinction and difference, which are essential to them. 'Tis still true, that every distinct perception, which enters into the composition of the mind, is a distinct existence, and is different, and distinguishable, and separable from every other perception, either contemporary or successive. But, as, notwithstanding this distinction and separability, we suppose the whole train of perceptions to be united by identity, a question naturally arises concerning this relation of identity: whether it be something that really binds our several perceptions together, or only associates their ideas in the imagination. That is, in other words, whether in pronouncing concerning the identity of a person, we observe some real bond among his perceptions, or only feel one among the ideas we form of them. This question we might easily decide, if we wou'd recollect what has been already prov'd at large, that the understanding never observes any real connexion among objects, and that even the union of cause and effect, when strictly examin'd, resolves itself into a customary association of ideas. For from thence it evidently follows, that identity is nothing really belonging to these different perceptions, and uniting them together; but is merely a quality, which we attribute to them, because of the union of their ideas in the imagination, when we reflect upon them. Now the only qualities, which can give ideas an union in the imagination, are these three relations above-mention'd. These are the uniting principles in the idea world, and without them every distinct object is separable by the mind, and may be separately consider'd, and appears not to have any more connexion with any other object, than if disjoin'd by the greatest difference and remoteness. 'Tis, therefore, on some of these three relations of resemblance, contiguity and causation, that identity depends; and as the very essence of these relations consists in their producing an easy transition of ideas; it follows, that our notions of personal identity, proceed entirely from the smooth and uninterrupted progress of the thought along a train of connected ideas, according to the principles above-explain'd.

The only question, therefore, which remains, is, by what relations this uninterrupted progress of our thought is produc'd, when we consider the successive existence of a mind or thinking person. And here 'tis evident we must confine ourselves to resemblance and causation, and must drop contiguity, which has little or no influence in the present case.

To begin with *resemblance;* suppose we cou'd see clearly into the breast of another, and observe that succession of perceptions, which constitutes his mind or thinking principle, and suppose that he always preserves the memory of a considerable part of past perceptions; 'tis evident that nothing cou'd more contribute to the bestowing a relation on this succession amidst all its variations. For what is the memory but a faculty, by which we raise up the images of past perceptions? And as an image necessarily resembles its object, must not the frequent placing of these resembling perceptions in the chain of thought, convey the imagination more easily from one link to another, and make the whole seem like the continuance of one object? In this particular, then, the memory not only discovers the identity, but also contributes to its production, by producing the relation of resemblance among the perceptions. The case is the same whether we consider ourselves or others.

As to *causation;* we may observe, that the true idea of the human mind, is to consider it as a system of different perceptions or different existences, which are link'd together by the relation of cause and effect, and mutually produce, destroy, influence, and modify each other. Our impressions give rise to their correspondent ideas; and these ideas in their turn produce other impressions. One thought chaces another, and draws after it a third, by which it is expell'd in its turn. In this respect, I cannot compare the soul more properly to any thing than to a republic or commonwealth, in which the several members are united by the reciprocal ties of government and subordination, and give rise to other persons, who propagate the same republic in the incessant changes of its parts. And as the same individual republic may not only change its members, but also its laws and constitutions; in like manner the same person may vary his character and disposition, as well as his impressions and ideas, without losing his identity. Whatever changes he endures, his several parts are still connected by the relation of causation. And in this view our identity with regard to the passions serves to corroborate that with regard to the imagination, by the making our distant perceptions influence each other, and by giving us a present concern for our past or future pains or pleasures.

As memory alone acquaints us with the continuance and extent of this succession of perceptions, 'tis to be consider'd, upon that account chiefly, as the source of personal identity. Had we no memory, we never shou'd have any notion of causation, nor consequently of that chain of causes and effects, which constitute our self or person. But having once acquir'd this notion of causation from the memory, we can extend the same chain of causes, and consequently the identity of our persons beyond our memory, and can comprehend times, and circumstances, and actions, which we have entirely forgot, but suppose in general to have existed. For how few of our past actions are there, of which we have any memory? Who can tell me, for instance, what were his thoughts and actions on the first of *January* 1715, the 11th of *March* 1719, and the 3d of *August* 1733? Or will he affirm, because he has entirely forgot the incidents of these days, that the present self is not the same person with the self of that time; and by that means overturn all the most establish'd notions of personal identity? In this view, therefore, memory does not so much *produce* as *discover* personal identity, by shewing us the relation of cause and effect among our different perceptions. 'Twill be incumbent on those, who affirm that memory produces entirely our personal identity, to give a reason why we can thus extend our identity beyond our memory.

The whole of this doctrine leads us to a conclusion, which is of great importance in the present affair, *viz.* that all the nice and subtile questions concerning personal identity can never possibly be decided, and are to be regarded rather as grammatical than as philosophical difficulties. Identity depends on the relations of ideas; and these relations produce identity, by means of that easy transition they occasion. But as the relations, and the easiness of the transition may diminish by insensible degrees, we have no just standard, by which we can decide any dispute concerning the time, when they acquire or lose a title to the name of identity. All the disputes concerning the identity of connected objects are merely verbal, except so far as the relation of parts gives rise to some fiction or imaginary principle of union, as we have already observ'd.

What I have said concerning the first origin and uncertainty of our notion of identity, as apply'd to the human mind, may be extended with little or no variation to that of *simplicity*. An object, whose different co-existent parts are bound together by a close relation, operates upon the imagination after much the same manner as one perfectly simple and indivisible, and requires not a much greater stretch of thought in order to its conception. From this similarity of operation we attribute a simplicity to it, and feign a principle of union as the support of this simplicity, and the center of all the different parts and qualities of the object.

Thus we have finish'd our examination of the several systems of philosophy, both of the intellectual and natural world; and in our miscellaneous way of reasoning have been led into several topics; which will either illustrate and confirm some preceding part of this discourse, or prepare the way for our following opinions. 'Tis now time to return to a more close examination of our subject, and to proceed in the accurate anatomy of human nature, having fully explain'd the nature of our judgment and understanding.

Suggested Further Readings

See Harold Noonan, *Personal Identity* (London: Routledge, 1991), chap. 4.

Other good discussions of Hume's views on personal identity can be found in Jonathan Bennett, *Locke, Berkeley, Hume* (Oxford: Clarendon Press, 1971), chap. XIII; David Pears, *Hume's System* (Oxford: Oxford University Press, 1990); Terence Penelhum, "Hume on Personal Identity," in *Hume*, ed. by V. C. Chappell (Garden City, NY: Doubleday, 1966); and Don Garrett, "Hume's Self-Doubts about Personal Identity," *Philosophical Review* XC (1981).

Recent work on personal identity that is said to be Humean in spirit has been done by Derek Parfit in *Reasons and Persons* (Oxford: Oxford University Press, 1984), Part Three.

There is much of interest in Barry Stroud, *Hume* (London: Routledge, 1977).

John Perry's anthology, *Personal Identity* (Berkeley: University of California Press, 1975), contains good general material on the subject of personal identity.

CHAPTER 2

Of Identity and Diversity

John Locke

The following selection is from John Locke's much-studied Essay Concerning Human Understanding *(1694). One Lockean theme is that conditions for identity over time vary, depending on the sort or kind of thing one is dealing with. Locke maintains that one analysis of identity is appropriate when we consider a human being whereas quite another is appropriate when we consider a person. If that is correct, it seems that human beings and persons are distinct entities. Locke's discussion of identity is a subject of great interest to contemporary metaphysics.*

1. *Wherein Identity Consists.* Another occasion the mind often takes of comparing, is the very being of things; when, considering anything as existing at any determined time and place, we compare it with itself existing at another time, and thereon form the ideas of identity and diversity. When we see anything to be in any place in any instant of time, we are sure (be it what it will) that it is that very thing, and not another, which at that same time exists in another place, how like and undistinguishable soever it may be in all other respects: and in this consists identity, when the ideas it is attributed to vary not at all from what they were that moment wherein we consider their former existence, and to which we compare the present. For we never finding, nor conceiving it possible, that two things of the same kind should exist in the same place at the same time, we rightly conclude, that, whatever exists anywhere at any time, excludes all of the same kind, and is there itself alone. When therefore we demand whether anything be the same or no, it refers always to something that existed

Source: John Locke, "Of Identity and Diversity," from An Essay Concerning Human Understanding, vol. 1, ed. by A. C. Fraser,(Mineola, NY: Dover Publications, Inc.) pp. 439–70, First published 1959; Reprinted by permission of Dover Publications, Inc.

such a time in such a place, which it was certain at that instant was the same with itself, and no other. From whence it follows, that one thing cannot have two beginnings of existence, nor two things one beginning; it being impossible for two things of the same kind to be or exist in the same instant, in the very same place, or one and the same thing in different places. That, therefore, that had one beginning, is the same thing; and that which had a different beginning in time and place from that, is not the same, but diverse. That which had made the difficulty about this relation has been the little care and attention used in having precise notions of the things to which it is attributed.

2. *Identity of Substances.* We have the ideas but of three sorts of substances: (1) God, (2) finite intelligences, (3) bodies. First, God is without beginning, eternal, unalterable, and everywhere; and therefore concerning his identity there can be no doubt. Secondly, finite spirits having had each its determinate time and place of beginning to exist, the relation to that time and place will always determine to each of them its identity, as long as it exists. Thirdly, the same will hold of every particle of matter, to which no addition or subtraction of matter being made, it is the same. For, though these three sorts of substances, as we term them, do not exclude one another out of the same place, yet we cannot conceive but that they must necessarily each of them exclude any of the same kind out of the same place; or else the notions and names of identity and diversity would be in vain, and there could be no such distinctions of substances, or anything else one from another. For example: could two bodies be in the same place at the same time, then those two parcels of matter must be one and the same, take them great or little; nay, all bodies must be one and the same. For, by the same reason that two particles of matter may be in one place, all bodies may be in one place; which, when it can be supposed, takes away the distinction of identity and diversity of one and more, and renders it ridiculous. But it being a contradiction that two or more should be one, identity and diversity are relations and ways of comparing well founded, and of use to the understanding.

Identity of Modes. All other things being but modes or relations ultimately terminated in substances, the identity and diversity of each particular existence of them too will be by the same way determined: only as to things whose existence is in succession, such as are the actions of finite beings, v.g., motion and thought, both which consist in a continued train of succession: concerning their diversity there can be no question; because each perishing the moment it begins, they cannot exist in different times, or in different places, as permanent beings can at different times exist in distant places; and therefore no motion or thought, considered as at different times, can be the same, each part thereof having a different beginning of existence.

3. *Principium Individuationis.* From what has been said, it is easy to discover what is so much inquired after, the *principium individuationis;* and that, it is plain, is existence itself, which determines a being of any sort to a particular time and place, incommunicable to two beings of the same kind. This, though it seems easier to conceive in simple substances or modes, yet, when reflected on, is not more difficult in compound ones, if care be taken to what it is applied: v.g., let us suppose an atom, i.e., a continued body under one immutable superfices, existing in a determined time and place; it is evident, that considered in any instant of its existence, it is in that instant the same with itself. For, being at that instant what it is, and nothing else, it is the same, and so must continue as long as its existence is continued; for so long it will be the same, and no other. In like manner, if two or more atoms be joined together into the same mass, every one of those atoms will be the same, by the foregoing rule: and whilst they exist united together, the mass, consisting of the same atoms, must be the same mass, or the same body, let the parts be ever so differently jumbled. But if one of these atoms be taken away, or one new one added, it is no longer the same mass or the same body. In the state of living creatures, their identity depends not on a mass of the same particles, but on something else. For in them the variation of great parcels of matter alters not the identity: an oak growing from a plant to a great tree, and then lopped, is still the same oak; and a colt grown up to a horse, sometimes fat, sometimes lean, is all the while the same horse: though, in both these cases, there may be a manifest change of the parts; so that truly they are not either of them the same masses of matter, though they be truly one of them the same oak, and the other the same horse. The reason whereof is, that, in these two cases, a mass of matter, and a living body, identity is not applied to the same thing.

4. *Identity of Vegetables.* We must therefore consider wherein an oak differs from a mass of matter, and that seems to me to be in this, that the one is only the cohesion of particles of matter any how united, the other such a disposition of them as constitutes the parts

of an oak; and such an organization of those parts as is fit to receive and distribute nourishment, so as to continue and frame the wood, bark, and leaves, etc., of an oak, in which consists the vegetable life. That being then one plant which has such an organization of parts in one coherent body, partaking of one common life, it continues to be the same plant as long as it partakes of the same life, though that life be communicated to new particles of matter vitally united to the living plant, in a like continued organization comformable to that sort of plants. For this organization being at any one instant in any one collection of matter, is in that particular concrete distinguished from all other, and is that individual life, which existing constantly from that moment both forwards and backwards, in the same continuity of insensibly succeeding parts united to the living body of the plant, it has that identity which makes the same plant, during all the time that they exist united in that continued organization, which is fit to convey that common life to all the parts so united.

5. *Identity of Animals*. The case is not so much different in brutes, but that any one may hence see what makes an animal and continues it the same. Something we have like this in machines, and may serve to illustrate it. For example, what is a watch? It is plain it is nothing but a fit organization or construction of parts to a certain end, which, when a sufficient force is added to it, it is capable to attain. If we would suppose this machine one continued body, all whose organized parts were repaired, increased, or diminished by a constant addition or separation of insensible parts, with one common life, we should have something very much like the body of an animal; with this difference, that, in an animal the fitness of the organization, and the motion wherein life consists, begin together, the motion coming from within; but in machines, the force coming sensibly from without, often away when the organ is in order, and well fitted to receive it.

6. *The Identity of Man*. This also shows wherein the identity of the same man consists; viz., in nothing but a participation of the same continued life, by constantly fleeing particles of matter, in succession vitally united to the same organized body. He that shall place the identity of man in anything else, but like that of other animals, in one fitly organized body, taken in any one instant, and from these continued, under one organization of life, in several successively fleeting particles of matter united to it, will find it hard to make an embryo, one of years, mad and sober, the same man, by any

supposition, that will not make it possible for Seth, Ismael, Socrates, Pilate, St. Austin, and Caesar Borgia, to be the same man. For, if the identity of soul alone makes the same man, and there be nothing in the nature of matter why the same individual spirit may not be united to different bodies, it will be possible that those men living in distant ages, and of different tempers, may have been the same man: which way of speaking must be, from a very strange use of the word man, applied to an idea, out of which body and shape are excluded. And that way of speaking would agree yet worse with the notions of those philosophers who allow of transmigration, and are of opinion that the souls of men may, for their miscarriages, be detruded into the bodies of beasts, as fit habitations, with organs suited to the satisfaction of their brutal inclinations. But yet I think nobody, could he be sure that the soul of Heliogabalus were in one of his hogs, would yet say that hog were a man or Heliogabalus.

7. *Identity Suited to the Idea.* It is not therefore unity of substance that comprehends all sorts of identity, or will determine it in every case; but to conceive and judge of it aright, we must consider what idea the word it is applied to stands for: it being one thing to be the same substance, another the same man, and a third the same person, if person, man, and substance, are three names standing for three different ideas; for such as is the idea belonging to that name, such must be the identity; which, if it had been a little more carefully attended to, would possibly have prevented a great deal of that confusion which often occurs about this matter, with no small seeming difficulties, especially concerning personal identity, which therefore we shall in the next place a little consider.

8. *Same Man.* An animal is living organized body; and consequently the same animal, as we have observed, is the same continued life communicated to different particles of matter, as they happen successively to be united to that organized living body. And whatever is talked of other definitions, ingenious observation puts it past doubt, that the idea in our minds, of which the sound man in our mouth is the sign, is nothing else but of an animal of such a certain form: since I think I may be confident, that, whoever should see a creature of his own shape or make, though it had no more reason all its life than a cat or a parrot, would call him still a man; or whoever should hear a cat or a parrot discourse, reason, and philosophize, would call or think it nothing but a cat or a parrot; and say, the one was a dull irrational man, and the other a very intelligent rational

parrot. A relation we have in an author of great note, is sufficient to countenance the supposition of a rational parrot. His words are:

> I had a mind to know, from Prince Maurice's own mouth, the account of a common, but much credited story, that I had heard so often from many others, of an old parrot he had in Brazil, during his government there, that spoke, and asked, and answered common questions, like a reasonable creature: so that those of his train there generally concluded it to be witchery or possession; and one of his chaplains, who lived long afterwards in Holland, would never from that time endure a parrot, but said they all had a devil in them. I had heard many particulars of this story, and assevered by people hard to be discredited, which made me ask Prince Maurice what there was of it. He said, with his usual plainness and dryness in talk, there was something true, but a great deal false of what had been reported. I desired to know of him what there was of the first. He told me short and coldly, that he had heard of such an old parrot when he had been at Brazil; and though he believed nothing of it, and it was a good way off, yet he had so much curiosity as to send for it: that it was a very great and a very old one; and when it came first into the room where the prince was, with a great many Dutchmen about him, it said presently, What a company of white men are here! They asked it, what it thought that man was, pointing to the prince. It answered, Some General or other. When they brought it close to him, he asked it, D'ou venez-vous? It answered, De Marinnan. The Prince, A qui estes-vous? The parrot, A un Portugais. The Prince, Que fais-tu la? Je garde les poulles. The Prince laughed, and said, Vous gardez les poulles? The parrot answered, Oui, moi, et je sçai bien faire; and made the chuck four or five times that people use to make to chickens when they call them. I set down the words of this worthy dialogue in French, just as Prince Maurice said them to me. I asked him in what language the parrot spoke, and he said in Brazilian. I asked whether he understood Brazilian; he said no: but he had taken care to have two interpreters by him, the one a Dutchman that spoke Brazilian, and the other a Brazilian that spoke Dutch; that he asked them separately and privately, and both of them agreed in telling him just the same thing that the parrot had said. I could not but tell this odd story, because it is so much out of the way, and from the first hand, and what may pass for a good one; for I dare say this prince at least believed himself in all he told me, having ever passed for a very honest and pious man: I leave it to naturalists to reason, and to

other men to believe, as they please upon it; however, it is not, perhaps, amiss to relieve or enliven a busy scene sometimes with such digressions, whether to the purpose or no.

Same Man. I have taken care that the reader should have the story at large in the author's own words, because he seems to me not to have thought it incredible; for it cannot be imagined that so able a man as he, who had sufficiency enough to warrant all the testimonies he gives of himself, should take so much pains, in a place where it had nothing to do, to pin so close not only on a man whom he mentions as his friend, but on a prince in whom he acknowledges very great honesty and piety, a story which, if he himself thought incredible, he could not but also think ridiculous. The prince, it is plain, who vouches this story, and our author, who relates it from him, both of them call this talker a parrot: and I ask any one else who thinks such a story fit to be told, whether—if this parrot, and all of its kind, had always talked, as we have a prince's word for it this one did—whether, I say, they would not have passed for a race of rational animals; but yet, whether, for all that, they would have been allowed to be men, and not parrots? For I presume it is not the idea of a thinking or rational being alone that makes the idea of a man in most people's sense, but of a body, so and so shaped, joined to it; and if that be the idea of a man, the same successive body not shifted all at once, must, as well as the same immaterial spirit, go to the making of the same man.

9. *Personal Identity.* This being premised, to find wherein personal identity consists, we must consider what person stands for; which, I think, is a thinking intelligent being, that has reason and reflection, and can consider itself as itself, the same thinking thing, in different times and places; which it does only by that consciousness which is inseparable from thinking, and, as it seems to me, essential to it: it being impossible for any one to perceive without perceiving that he does perceive. When we see, hear, smell, taste, feel, meditate, or will anything, we know that we do so. Thus it is always as to our present sensations and perceptions: and by this every one is to himself that which he calls self; it not being considered, in this case, whether the same self be continued in the same or divers substances. For, since consciousness always accompanies thinking, and it is that which makes every one to be what he calls self, and thereby distinguishes himself from all other thinking things: in this alone consists personal identity, i.e., the sameness of a rational being; and as far as

this consciousness can be extended backwards to any past action or thought, so far reaches the identity of that person; it is the same self now it was then; and it is by the same self with this present one that now reflects on it, that that action was done.

10. *Consciousness Makes Personal Identity.* But it is further inquired, whether it be the same identical substance? This, few would think they had reason to doubt of, if these perceptions, with their consciousness, always remained present in the mind, whereby the same thinking thing would be always consciously present, and, as would be thought, evidently the same to itself. But that which seems to make the difficulty is this, that this consciousness being interrupted always by forgetfulness, there being no moment of our lives wherein we have the whole train of all our past actions before our eyes in one view, but even the best memories losing the sight of one part whilst they are viewing another; and we sometimes, and that the greatest part of our lives, not reflecting on our past selves, being intent on our present thoughts, and in sound sleep having no thoughts at all, or at least none with that consciousness which remarks our waking thoughts; I say, in all these cases, our consciousness being interrupted, and we losing the sight of our past selves, doubts are raised whether we are the same thinking thing, i.e., the same substance or no. Which, however reasonable or unreasonable, concerns not personal identity at all: the question being, what makes the same person, and not whether it be the same identical substance, which always thinks in the same person; which, in this case, matters not at all: different substances, by the same consciousness (where they do partake in it) being united into one person, as well as different bodies by the same life are united into one animal, whose identity is preserved in that change of substances by the unity of one continued life. For it being the same consciousness that makes a man be himself to himself, personal identity depends on that only, whether it be annexed solely to one individual substance, or can be continued in a succession of several substances. For as far as any intelligent being can repeat the idea of any past action with the same consciousness it had of it at first, and with the same consciousness it has of any present action; so far it is the same personal self. For it is by the consciousness it has of its present thoughts and actions, that it is self to itself now, and so will be the same self, as far as the same consciousness can extend to actions past or to come; and would be by distance of time, or change of substance, no more two persons, than a man be two men

by wearing other clothes today than he did yesterday, with a long or a short sleep between: the same consciousness uniting those distant actions into the same person, whatever substances contributed to their production.

11. *Personal Identity in Change of Substances.* That this is so, we have some kind of evidence in our very bodies, all whose particles, whilst vitally united to this same thinking conscious self, so that we feel when they are touched, and are affected by, and conscious of good or harm that happens to them, are a part of ourselves; i.e., of our thinking conscious self. Thus, the limbs of his body are to every one a part of himself; he sympathizes and is concerned for them. Cut off a hand, and thereby separate it from that consciousness he had of its heat, cold, and other affections, and it is then no longer a part of that which is himself, any more than the remotest part of matter. Thus, we see the substance whereof personal self consisted at one time may be varied at another, without the change of personal identity; there being no question about the same person, though the limbs which but now were a part of it, be cut off.

12. But the question is, "Whether, if the same substance, which thinks, be changed, it can be the same person; or, remaining the same, it can be different persons."

Whether in the Change of Thinking Substances. And to this I answer: First, This can be no question at all to those who place thought in a purely material animal constitution, void of an immaterial substance. For, whether their supposition be true or no, it is plain they conceive personal identity preserved in something else than identity of substance; as animal identity is preserved in identity of life, and not of substance. And therefore those who place thinking in an immaterial substance only, before they can come to deal with these men, must show why personal identity cannot be preserved in the change of immaterial substances, or variety of particular immaterial substances, as well as animal identity is preserved in the change of material substances, or variety of particular bodies; unless they will say, it is one immaterial spirit that makes the same life in brutes, as it is one immaterial spirit that makes the same person in men; which the Cartesians at least will not admit, for fear of making brutes thinking things too.

13. But next, as to the first part of the question, "Whether, if the same thinking substance (supposing immaterial substances only to think) be changed, it can be the same person?" I answer, that cannot be resolved, but by those who know what kind of substances they

are that do think, and whether the consciousness of past actions can be transferred from one thinking substance to another. I grant, were the same consciousness the same individual action, it could not: but it being a present representation of a past action, why it may not be possible that that may be represented to the mind to have been, which really never was, will remain to be shown. And therefore how far the consciousness of past actions is annexed to any individual agent, so that another cannot possibly have it, will be hard for us to determine, till we know what kind of action it is that cannot be done without a reflex act of perception accompanying it, and how performed by thinking substances, who cannot think without being conscious of it. But that which we call the same consciousness, not being the same individual act, why one intellectual substance may not have represented to it, as done by itself, what it never did, and was perhaps done by some other agent; why, I say, such a representation may not possibly be without reality of matter of fact, as well as several representations in dreams are, which yet whilst dreaming we take for true, will be difficult to conclude from the nature of things. And that it never is so, will by us, till we have clearer views of the nature of thinking substances, be best resolved into the goodness of God, who, as far as the happiness or misery of any of his sensible creatures is concerned in it, will not, by a fatal error of theirs, transfer from one to another that consciousness which draws reward or punishment with it. How far this may be an argument against those who would place thinking in a system of fleeting animal spirits, I leave to be considered. But yet, to return to the question before us, it must be allowed, that, if the same consciousness (which, as has been shown, is quite a different thing from the same numerical figure or motion in body) can be transferred from one thinking substance to another, it will be possible that two thinking substances may make but one person. For the same consciousness being preserved, whether in the same or different substances, the personal identity is preserved.

14. As to the second part of the question, "Whether the same immaterial substance remaining, there may be two distinct persons?" which question seems to me to be built on this, whether the same immaterial being, being conscious of the action of its past duration, may be wholly stripped of all the consciousness of its past existence, and lose it beyond the power of ever retrieving it again; and so as it were beginning a new account from a new period, have a consciousness that cannot reach beyond this new state. All those who hold

pre-existence are evidently of this mind, since they allow the soul to have no remaining consciousness of what it did in that pre-existent state, either wholly separate from body, or informing any other body; and if they should not, it is plain experience would be against them. So that personal identity reaching no further than consciousness reaches, a pre-existent spirit not having continued so many ages in a state of silence, must needs make different persons. Suppose a Christian Platonist or a Pythagorean should, upon God's having ended all his works of creation the seventh day, think his soul hath existed ever since; and would imagine it has revolved in several human bodies, as I once met with one, who was persuaded his had been the soul of Socrates; (how reasonably I will not dispute; this I know, that in the post he filled, which was no inconsiderable one, he passed for a very rational man, and the press has shown that he wanted not parts or learning); would any one say, that he, being not conscious of any of Socrates' actions or thoughts, could be the same person with Socrates? Let any one reflect upon himself, and conclude that he has in himself an immaterial spirit, which is that which thinks in him, and, in the constant change of his body keeps him the same: and is that which he calls himself: let him also suppose it to be the same soul that was in Nestor or Thersites, at the siege of Troy (for souls being, as far as we know anything of them, in their nature indifferent to any parcel of matter, the supposition has no apparent absurdity in it), which it may have been, as well as it is now the soul of any other man: but he now having no consciousness of any of the actions either of Nestor or Thersites, does or can he conceive himself the same person with either of them? Can he be concerned in either of their actions? attribute them to himself, or think them his own, more than the actions of any other men that ever existed? So that this consciousness not reaching to any of the actions of either of those men, he is no more one self with either of them, than if the soul or immaterial spirit that now informs him had been created, and began to exist, when it began to inform his present body, though it were ever so true, that the same spirit that informed Nestor's or Thersites' body were numerically the same that now informs his. For this would no more make him the same person with Nestor, than if some of the particles of matter that were once a part of Nestor, were now a part of this man; the same immaterial substance, without the same consciousness, no more making the same person by being united to any body, than the same particle of matter, without consciousness united to any body, makes the same person. But let him once find himself conscious of any of the actions of Nestor, he then finds himself the same person with Nestor.

15. And thus may we be able, without any difficulty, to conceive the same person at the resurrection, though in a body not exactly in make or parts the same which he had here, the same consciousness going along with the soul that inhabits it. But yet the soul alone, in the change of bodies, would scarce to any one but to him that makes the soul the man, be enough to make the same man. "For should the soul of a prince, carrying with it the consciousness of the prince's past life, enter and inform the body of a cobbler, as soon as deserted by his own soul, every one sees he would be the same person with the prince," accountable only for the prince's actions: but who would say it was the same man? The body too goes to the making the man, and would, I guess, to everybody determine the man in this case; wherein the soul, with all its princely thoughts about it, would not make another man: but he would be the same cobbler to every one besides himself. I know that, in the ordinary way of speaking, the same person, and the same man, stand for one and the same thing. And indeed every one will always have a liberty to speak as he pleases, and to apply what articulate sounds to what ideas he thinks fit, and change them as often as he pleases. But yet, when we will inquire what makes the same spirit, man, or person, we must fix the ideas of spirit, man, or person in our minds, and having resolved with ourselves what we mean by them, it will not be hard to determine in either of them, or the like, when it is the same, and when not.

16. *Consciousness Makes the Same Person.* But though the same immaterial substance or soul does not alone, wherever it be, and in whatsoever state, make the same man; yet it is plain, consciousness, as far as ever it can be extended, should it be to ages past, unites existences and actions, very remote in time into the same person, as well as it does the existences and actions of the immediately preceding moment: so that whatever has the consciousness of present and past actions, is the same person to whom they both belong. Had I the same consciousness that I saw the ark and Noah's flood, as that I saw an overflowing of the Thames last winter, or as that I write now; I could no more doubt that I who write this now, that saw the Thames overflowed last winter, and that viewed the flood at the general deluge, was the same self, place that self in what substance you please, than that I who write this am the same myself now whilst I write (whether I consist

of all the same substance, material or immaterial, or no) that I was yesterday; for as to this point of being the same self, it matters not
whether this present self be made up of the same or other substances;
I being as much concerned, and as justly accountable for any action
that was done a thousand years since, appropriated to me now by this
self-consciousness, as I am for what I did the last moment.

17. *Self Depends on Consciousness.* Self is that conscious thinking
thing, whatever substance made up of (whether spiritual or material,
simple or compounded, it matters not), which is sensible or conscious of pleasure and pain, capable of happiness or misery, and so is
concerned for itself, as far as that consciousness extends. Thus every
one finds, that whilst comprehended under that consciousness, the
little finger is as much a part of himself as what is most so. Upon separation of this little finger, should this consciousness go along with
the little finger, and leave the rest of the body, it is evident the little
finger would be the person, the same person, and self then would
have nothing to do with the rest of the body. As in this case it is the
consciousness that goes along with the substance, when one part is
separate from another, which makes the same person, and constitutes this inseparable self; so it is in reference to substances remote
in time. That with which the consciousness of this present thinking
thing can join itself, makes the same person, and is one self with it,
and with nothing else; and so attributes to itself, and owns all the actions of that thing as its own, as far as that consciousness reaches,
and no further; as every one who reflects will perceive.

18. *Objects of Reward and Punishment.* In this personal identity is
founded all the right and justice of reward and punishment; happiness and misery being that for which every one is concerned for himself, and not mattering what becomes of any substance not joined to,
or affected with that consciousness. For as it is evident in the instance
I gave but now, if the consciousness went along with the little finger
when it was cut off, that would be the same self which was concerned
for the whole body yesterday, as making part of itself, whose actions
then it cannot but admit as its own now. Though, if the same body
should still live, and immediately from the separation of the little finger have its own peculiar consciousness, whereof the little finger knew
nothing; it would not at all be concerned for it, as a part of itself, or
could own any of its actions, or have any of them imputed to him.

19. This may show us wherein personal identity consists: not
in the identity of substance, but, as I have said, in the identity of

consciousness; wherein if Socrates and the present mayor of Queenborough agree, they are the same person: if the same Socrates waking and sleeping do not partake of the same consciousness, Socrates waking and sleeping is not the same person. And to punish Socrates waking for what sleeping Socrates thought, and waking Socrates was never conscious of, would be no more of right, than to punish one twin for what his brother-twin did, whereof he knew nothing, because their outsides were so like that they could not be distinguished; for such twins have been seen.

20. But yet possibly it will still be objected, suppose I wholly lose the memory of some parts of my life, beyond a possibility of retrieving them, so that perhaps I shall never be conscious of them again; yet am I not the same person that did those actions, had those thoughts that I once was conscious of, though I have now forgot them? To which I answer, that we must here take notice what the word I is applied to; which, in this case, is the man only. And the same man being presumed to be the same person, I is easily here supposed to stand also for the same person. But if it be possible for the same man to have distinct incommunicable consciousness at different times, it is past doubt the same man would at different times make different persons; which, we see, is the sense of mankind in the solemnest declaration of their opinions, human laws not punishing the mad man for the sober man's actions, nor the sober man for what the mad man did, thereby making them two persons: which is somewhat explained by our way of speaking in English, when we say such an one is not himself, or is beside himself; in which phrases it is insinuated, as if those who now, or at least first used them, thought that self was changed, the selfsame person was no longer in that man.

21. *Difference Between Identity of Man and Person.* But yet it is hard to conceive that Socrates, the same individual man, should be two persons. To help us a little in this, we must consider what is meant by Socrates, or the same individual man.

First, it must be either the same individual, immaterial, thinking substance; in short, the same numerical soul, and nothing else.

Secondly, or the same animal, without any regard to an immaterial soul.

Thirdly, or the same immaterial spirit united to the same animal.

Now, take which of these suppositions you please, it is impossible to make personal identity to consist in anything but consciousness, or reach any further than that does.

For, by the first of them, it must be allowed possible that a man born of different women, and in distant times, may be the same man. A way of speaking, which whoever admits, must allow it possible for the same man to be two distinct persons, as any two that have lived in different ages, without the knowledge of one another's thoughts.

By the second and third, Socrates, in this life and after it, cannot be the same man any way, but by the same consciousness; and so making human identity to consist in the same thing wherein we place personal identity, there will be no difficulty to allow the same man to be the same person. But then they who place human identity in consciousness only, and not in something else, must consider how they will make the infant Socrates the same man with Socrates after the resurrection. But whatsoever to some men makes a man, and consequently the same individual man, wherein perhaps few are agreed, personal identity can by us be placed in nothing but consciousness (which is that alone which makes what we call self), without involving us in great absurdities.

22. But is not a man drunk and sober the same person? Why else is he punished for the fact he commits when drunk, though he be never afterwards conscious of it? Just as much the same person as a man that walks, and does other things in his sleep, is the same person, and is answerable for any mischief he shall do in it. Human laws punish both, with a justice suitable to their way of knowledge; because, in these cases, they cannot distinguish certainly what is real, what counterfeit: and so the ignorance in drunkenness or sleep is not admitted as a plea. For, though punishment be annexed to personality, and personality to consciousness, and the drunkard perhaps be not conscious of what he did, yet human judicatures justly punish him, because the fact is proved against him, but want of consciousness cannot be proved for him. But in the great day, wherein the secrets of all hearts shall be laid open, it may be reasonable to think, no one shall be made to answer for what he knows nothing of; but shall receive his doom, his conscience accusing or excusing him.

23. *Consciousness Alone Makes Self.* Nothing but consciousness can unite remote existences into the same person: the identity of substance will not do it; for whatever substance there is, however framed, without consciousness there is no person: and a carcass may be a person, as well as any sort of substance be so without consciousness.

Could we suppose two distinct incommunicable consciousnesses acting the same body, the one constantly by day, the other by night; and, on the other side, the same consciousness, acting by intervals, two distinct bodies; I ask, in the first case, whether the day and the night man would not be two as distinct persons as Socrates and Plato? And whether, in the second case, there would not be one person in two distinct bodies, as much as one man is the same in two distinct clothings? Nor is it at all material to say, that this same, and this distinct consciousness, in the cases above mentioned, is owing to the same and distinct immaterial substances, bringing it with them to those bodies; which, whether true or no, alters not the case; since it is evident the personal identity would equally be determined by the consciousness, whether that consciousness were annexed to some individual immaterial substance or no. For, granting that the thinking substance in man must be necessarily supposed immaterial, it is evident that immaterial thinking thing may sometimes part with its past consciousness, and be restored to it again, as appears in the forgetfulness men often have of their past actions: and the mind many times recovers the memory of a past consciousness, which it had lost for twenty years together. Make these intervals of memory and forgetfulness to take their turns regularly by day and night, and you have two persons with the same immaterial spirit, as much as in the former instance two persons with the same body. So that self is not determined by identity or diversity of substance, which it cannot be sure of, but only by identity of consciousness.

24. Indeed it may conceive the substance whereof it is now made up to have existed formerly, united in the same conscious being; but, consciousness removed, that substance is no more itself, or makes no more a part of it, than any other substance; as is evident in the instance we have already given of a limb cut off, of whose heat, or cold, or other affections, having no longer any consciousness, it is no more of a man's self, than any other matter of the universe. In like manner it will be in reference to any immaterial substance, which is void of that consciousness whereby I am myself to myself: if there be any part of its existence which I cannot upon recollection join with that present consciousness, whereby I am now myself, it is in that part of its existence no more myself, than any other immaterial being. For whatsoever any substance has thought or done, which I cannot recollect, and by my consciousness make my own thought and action, it will no more belong to me, whether a part of me thought or did it, than if it had been thought or done by any other immaterial being anywhere existing.

25. I agree, the more probable opinion is, that this consciousness is annexed to, and the affection of, one individual immaterial substance.

But let man, according to their diverse hypotheses, resolve of that as they please; this very intelligent being, sensible of happiness or misery, must grant that there is something that is himself that he is concerned for, and would have happy; that this self has existed in a continued duration more than one instant, and therefore it is possible may exist, as it has done, months and years to come, without any certain bounds to be set to its duration; and may be the same self by the same consciousness continued on for the future. And thus, by this consciousness, he finds himself to be the same self which did such and such an action some years since, by which he comes to be happy or miserable now. In all which account of self, the same numerical substance is not considered as making the same self; but the same continued consciousness, in which several substances may have been united, and again separated from it; which, whilst they continued in a vital union with that wherein this consciousness then resided, made a part of that same self. Thus any part of our bodies vitally united to that which is conscious in us, makes a part of ourselves: but upon separation from the vital union by which that consciousness is communicated, that which a moment since was part of ourselves, is now no more so than a part of another man's self is a part of me: and it is not impossible but in a little time may become a real part of another person. And so we have the same numerical substance become a part of two different persons; and the same person preserved under the change of various substances. Could we suppose any spirit wholly stripped of all its memory or consciousness of past actions, as we find our minds always are of a great part of ours, and sometimes of them all; the union or separation of such a spiritual substance would make no variation of personal identity, and more than that of any particle of matter does. Any substance vitally united to the present thinking being, is a part of that very same self which now is; anything united to it by a consciousness of former actions, makes also a part of the same self, which is the same both then and now.

26. *Person a Forensic Term.* Person, as I take it, is the name for this self. Wherever a man finds what he calls himself there, I think, another may say is the same person. It is a forensic term, appropriating actions and their merit; and so belongs only to intelligent agents capable of a law, and happiness, and misery. This personality extends

itself beyond present existence to what is past, only by consciousness, whereby it becomes concerned and accountable, owns and imputes to itself past actions, just upon the same ground and for the same reason that it does the present. All which is founded in a concern for happiness, the unavoidable concomitant of consciousness; that which is conscious of pleasure and pain, desiring that that self that is conscious should be happy. And therefore whatever past actions it cannot reconcile or appropriate to that present self by consciousness, it can be no more concerned in, than if they had never been done; and to receive pleasure or pain, i.e., reward or punishment, on the account of any such action, is all one as to be made happy or miserable in its first being, without any demerit at all: for supposing a man punished now for what he had done in another life, whereof he could be made to have no consciousness at all, what difference is there between that punishment, and being created miserable? And therefore, conformable to this, the apostle tells us, that, at the great day, when every one shall "receive according to his doings, the secrets of all hearts shall be laid open." The sentence shall be justified by the consciousness all persons shall have, that they themselves, in what bodies soever they appear, or what substances soever that consciousness adheres to, are the same that committed those actions, and deserve that punishment for them.

27. I am apt enough to think I have, in treating of this subject, made some suppositions that will look strange to some readers, and possibly they are so in themselves. But yet, I think they are such as are pardonable, in this ignorance we are in of the nature of that thinking thing that is in us, and which we look on as ourselves. Did we know what it was, or how it was tied to a certain system of fleeting animal spirits; or whether it could or could not perform its operations of thinking and memory out of a body organized as ours is: and whether it has pleased God, that no one such spirit shall ever be united to any one but such body, upon the right constitution of whose organs its memory should depend; we might see the absurdity of some of these suppositions I have made. But, taking as we ordinarily now do, (in the dark concerning these matters), the soul of a man for an immaterial substance, independent from matter, and indifferent alike to it all, there can, from the nature of things, be no absurdity at all to suppose that the same soul may at different times be united to different bodies, and with them make up for that time one man, as well as we suppose a part of a sheep's body yesterday should

be a part of a man's body tomorrow, and in that union make a vital part of Meliboeus himself, as well as it did of his ram.

28. *The Difficulty from Ill Use of Names.* To conclude: Whatever substance begins to exist, it must, during its existence, necessarily be the same: whatever compositions of substances begin to exist, during the union of those substances the concrete must be the same; whatsoever mode begins to exist, during its existence it is the same; and so if the composition be of distinct substances and different modes, the same rule holds: whereby it will appear, that the difficulty or obscurity that has been about this matter rather rises from the names ill used, than from any obscurity in things themselves. For whatever makes the specific idea to which the name is applied, if that idea be steadily kept to the distinction of anything into the same, and divers, will easily be conceived, and there can arise no doubt about it.

29. *Continued Existence Makes Identity.* For, supposing a rational spirit be the idea of a man, it is easy to now what is the same man, viz., the same spirit, whether separate or in a body, will be the same man. Supposing a rational spirit vitally united to a body of a certain conformation of parts to make a man, whilst that rational spirit, with that vital conformation of parts, though continued in a fleeting successive body, remain, it will be the same man. But if to any one the idea of a man be but the vital union of parts in a certain shape, as long as that vital union and shape remain in a concrete no otherwise the same, but by a continued succession of fleeting particles, it will be the same man. For, whatever be the composition whereof the complex idea is made, whenever existence makes it one particular thing under any denomination, the same existence continued, preserves it the same individual under the same denomination.

Suggested Further Readings

A vast amount has been written about Locke's view on identity. A good beginning can be made with E. J. Lowe, *Locke* (London: Routledge, 1995), chap. 5; J. L. Mackie, *Problems from Locke* (Oxford: Clarendon Press, 1976), chaps. 5 and 6; Andrew Brennan, *Conditions of Identity* (Oxford: Clarendon Press, 1988), chap. 8; and James Baillie, *Problems in Personal Identity* (New York: Paragon House, 1993), chaps. 4 and 6.

See also Vere Chappell, "Locke and Relative Identity," *History of Philosophy Quarterly* 6 (1989), and Anthony Flew, "Locke and the Problem of Personal Identity," *Philosophy* Vol. XXVI (January 1951).

CHAPTER 3

Of Identity

Thomas Reid

Thomas Reid (1710–1796) was a prominent Scottish critic of Hume and Locke. In the following selection Reid addresses the role of memory in personal identity and offers a famous challenge to Locke's theory of personal identity. Reid believes that personal identity allows for various changes in a subject; in other words, we continue to exist without interruption as we change in various ways.

Of Identity

The conviction which every man has of his Identity, as far back as his memory reaches, needs no aid of philosophy to strengthen it; and no philosophy can weaken it, without first producing some degree of insanity.

The philosopher, however, may very properly consider this conviction as a phaenomenon of human nature worthy of his attention. If he can discover its cause, an addition is made to his stock of knowledge. If not, it must be held as a part of our original constitution, or an effect of that constitution produced in a manner unknown to us.

We may observe, first of all, that this conviction is indispensably necessary to all exercise of reason. The operations of reason, whether in action or in speculation, are made up of successive parts. The antecedent are the foundation of the consequent, and, without the conviction that the antecedent have been seen or done by me, I could have no reason to proceed to the consequent, in any speculation, or in any active project whatever.

Source: Thomas Reid: Excerpts from "Of Identity" from *Essays on the Intellectual Powers of Man* (1785) by Thomas Reid.

There can be no memory of what is past without the conviction that we existed at the time remembered. There may be good arguments to convince me that I existed before the earliest thing I can remember; but to suppose that my memory reaches a moment farther back than my belief and conviction of my existence, is a contradiction.

The moment a man loses this conviction, as if he had drunk the water of Lethe, past things are done away; and, in his own belief, he then begins to exist. Whatever was thought, or said, or done, or suffered before that period, may belong to some other person; but he can never impute it to himself, or take any subsequent steps that supposes it to be his doing.

From this it is evident that we must have the conviction of our own continued existence and identity, as soon as we are capable of thinking or doing anything, on account of what we have thought, or done, or suffered before; that is, as soon as we are reasonable creatures.

That we may form as distinct a notion as we are able of this phenomenon of the human mind, it is proper to consider what is meant by identity in general, what by our own personal identity, and how we are led into that invincible belief and conviction which every man has of his own personal identity, as far as his memory reaches.

Identity in general, I take to be a relation between a thing which is known to exist at one time, and a thing which is known to have existed at another time. If you ask whether they are one and the same, or two different things, every man of common sense understands the meaning of your question perfectly. Whence we may infer with certainty, that every man of common sense has a clear and distinct notion of identity.

If you ask a definition of identity, I confess I can give none; it is too simple a notion to admit of logical definition. I can say it is a relation; but I cannot find words to express the specific difference between this and other relations, though I am in no danger of confounding it with any other. I can say that diversity is a contrary relation, and that similitude and dissimilitude are another couple of contrary relations, which every man easily distinguishes in his conception from identity and diversity.

I see evidently that identity supposes an uninterrupted continuance of existence. That which hath ceased to exist, cannot be the same with that which afterwards begins to exist; for this would be to suppose a being to exist after it ceased to exist, and to have had existence before it was produced, which are manifest contradictions. Continued uninterrupted existence is therefore necessarily implied in identity.

Hence we may infer that identity cannot, in its proper sense, be applied to our pains, our pleasures, our thoughts, or any operation of our minds. The pain felt this day is not the same individual pain which I felt yesterday, though they may be similar in kind and degree, and have the same cause. The same may be said of every feeling and of every operation of mind: they are all successive in their nature, like time itself, no two moments of which can be the same moment.

It is otherwise with the parts of absolute space. They always are, and were, and will be the same. So far, I think, we proceed upon clear ground in fixing the notion of identity in general.

It is, perhaps, more difficult to ascertain with precision the meaning of Personality; but it is not necessary in the present subject: it is sufficient for our purpose to observe, that all mankind place their personality in something that cannot be divided, or consist of parts. A part of a person is a manifest absurdity.

When a man loses his estate, his health, his strength, he is still the same person, and has lost nothing of his personality. If he has a leg or an arm cut off, he is the same person he was before. The amputated member is no part of his person, otherwise it would have a right to a part of his estate, and be liable for a part of his engagements: it would be entitled to a share of his merit and demerit— which is manifestly absurd. A person is something indivisible, and is what Leibnitz calls *monad.*

My personal identity, therefore, implies the continued existence of that indivisible thing which I call myself. Whatever this self may be, it is something which thinks, and deliberates, and resolves, and acts, and suffers. I am not thought, I am not action, I am not feeling; I am something that thinks, and acts, and suffers. My thoughts, and actions, and feelings, change every moment—they have no continued, but a successive existence; but that *self* or *I,* to which they belong, is permanent, and has the same relation to all the succeeding thoughts, actions, and feelings, which I call mine.

Such are the notions that I have of my personal identity. But perhaps it may be said, this may all be fancy without reality. How do you know?—what evidence have you, that there is such a permanent self which has a claim to all the thoughts, actions, and feelings, which you call yours?

To this I answer, that the proper evidence I have of all this is remembrance. I remember that, twenty years ago, I conversed with such a person: I remember several things that passed in that conversation: my memory testifies not only that this was done, but that it was done by me who now remember it. If it was done by me, I must have existed at that time, and continued to exist from that time to the present: if the identical person whom I call myself, had not a part in that conversation, my memory is fallacious—it gives a distinct and positive testimony of what is not true. Every man in his senses believes what he distinctly remembers, and everything he remembers convinces him that he existed at the time remembered.

Although memory gives the most irresistible evidence of my being the identical person that did such a thing, at such a time, I may have other good evidence of things which befel me, and which I do not remember: I know who bare me and suckled me, but I do not remember these events.

It may here be observed, (though the observation would have been unnecessary if some great philosophers had not contradicted it,) that it is not my remembering any action of mine that makes me to be the person who did it. This remembrance makes me to know assuredly that I did it: but I might have done it though I did not remember it. That relation to me, which is expressed by saying that I did it, would be the same though I had not the least remembrance of it. To say that my remembering that I did such a thing, or, as some choose to express it, my being conscious that I did it, makes me to have done it, appears to me as great an absurdity as it would be to say, that my belief that the world was created made it to be created.

Of Mr Locke's Account of Our Personal Identity

In a long chapter upon Identity and Diversity, Mr Locke has made many ingenious and just observations, and some which I think cannot be defended. I shall only take notice of the account he gives of our own *Personal Identity*. His doctrine upon this subject has been censured by Bishop Butler, in a short essay subjoined to his "Analogy," with whose sentiments I perfectly agree.

Identity, as was observed, Chap. IV. of this Essay, supposes the continued existence of the being of which it is affirmed, and therefore can be applied only to things which have a continued existence. While any being continues to exist, it is the same being: but two beings which have a different beginning or a different ending of their existence, cannot possibly be the same. To this I think Mr Locke agrees.

He observes, very justly, that to know what is meant by the same person, we must consider what the word *person* stands for; and he defines a person to be an intelligent being, endowed with reason and with consciousness, which last he thinks inseparable from thought.

From this definition of a person, it must necessarily follow, that, while the intelligent being continues to exist and to be intelligent, it must be the same person. To say that the intelligent being is the person, and yet that the person ceases to exist, while the intelligent being continues, or that the person continues while the intelligent being ceases to exist, is to my apprehension a manifest contradiction.

One would think that the definition of a person should perfectly ascertain the nature of personal identity, or wherein it consists, though it might still be a question how we come to know and be assured of our personal identity.

Mr Locke tells us, however, "that personal identity—that is, the sameness of a rational being—consists in consciousness alone, and, as far as this consciousness can be extended backwards to any past action or thought, so far reaches the identity of that person. So that, whatever hath the consciousness of present and past actions, is the same person to whom they belong."

This doctrine hath some strange consequences, which the author was aware of, Such as, that, if the same consciousness can be transferred from one intelligent being to another, which he thinks we cannot shew to be impossible, then two or twenty intelligent beings may be the same person. And if the intelligent being may lose the consciousness of the actions done by him, which surely is possible, then he is not the person that did those actions: so that one intelligent being may be two or twenty different persons, if he shall so often lose the consciousness of his former actions.

There is another consequence of this doctrine, which follows no less necessarily, though Mr Locke probably did not see it. It is, that a man may be, and at the same time not be, the person that did a particular action.

Suppose a brave officer to have been flogged when a boy at school, for robbing an orchard, to have taken a standard from the enemy in his first campaign, and to have been made a general in advanced life: Suppose also, which must be admitted to be possible, that, when he took the standard, he was conscious of his having been flogged at school, and that when made a general he was conscious of his taking the standard, but had absolutely lost the consciousness of his flogging.

These things being supposed, it follows, from Mr Locke's doctrine, that he who was flogged at school is the same person who took the standard, and that he who took the standard is the same person who was made a general. Whence it follows, if there be any truth in logic, that the general is the same person with him who was flogged at school. But the general's consciousness does not reach so far back as his flogging—therefore, according to Mr Locke's doctrine, he is not the person who was flogged. Therefore, the general is, and at the same time is not the same person with him who was flogged at school . . .

Suggested Further Readings

Good places to begin are Keith Lehrer, *Thomas Reid* (London: Routledge, 1989), and Sydney Shoemaker, *Self-Knowledge and Self-Identity* (Ithaca, NY: Cornell University Press, 1963).

It is widely judged that Reid's argument against Locke is sound and that memory cannot be both sufficient and necessary for personal identity. For a discussion of this issue, see James Baillie, *Problems in Personal Identity* (New York: Paragon House, 1993), chap. 6.

CHAPTER 4

*R*igid Designation

Hugh S. Chandler

The study of identity is closely related to questions about the modalities of possibility and necessity, which are rich sources of metaphysical controversy. Many theorists agree that identity statements whose terms rigidly designate one individual are not only true but necessarily true. If one assumes that the proper names of commonplace things are rigid designators, an identity statement in which two names refer to the same individual is necessarily true. The following selection explains the concept of rigid designation and questions the thesis that names rigidly designate the objects to which they refer.

Hugh S. Chandler is a professor of philosophy at the University of Illinois at Urbana-Champaign. Chandler has written many papers that address problems of identity.

In *De Corpore* Hobbes asks in what sense a body can be considered sometimes the same and sometimes other than that which it was formerly. For example, is an old man the same man who was a youth, or is he, perhaps, a different man?

Hobbes notes three opinions. Some philosophers say that x at t_1 and y at t_2 are one and the same body if, and only if, x at t_1 and y at t_2 are made of the same *matter*. Others say that these things are the same if, and only if, they have the same *form*. Still others say that x and y are the same if, and only if, they are the same *aggregate of accidents*. All three theories seem to have absurd consequences.

> According to the first opinion, he that sins, and he that is punished, should not be the same man, by reason of the perpetual flux and change of man's body; nor should the city, which

Source: Hugh S. Chandler: "Rigid Designation," from *The Journal of Philosophy*, July 1995, vol. LXXII, no. 13, pp. 363–69. Reprinted by permission of The Journal of Philosophy, Inc., and the author.

makes laws in one age and abrogates them in another, be the same city; which were to confound all civil rights. According to the second opinion, two bodies existing both at once, would be one and the same numerical body. For if, for example, that ship of Theseus, concerning the difference whereof made by continual reparation in taking out the old planks and putting in new, the sophisters of Athens were wont to dispute, were, after all the planks were changed, the same numerical ship it was at the beginning; and if some man had kept the old planks as they were taken out, and by putting them afterwards together in the same order, had again made a ship of them, this, without doubt, had also been the same numerical ship with that which was at the beginning; and so there would have been two ships numerically the same, which is absurd. But, according to the third opinion, nothing would be the same it was; so that a man standing would not be the same he was sitting; nor the water, which is in the vessel, the same with that which is poured out of it.[1]

I am going to concentrate upon the story about the ship. Here is a diagram of the situation:

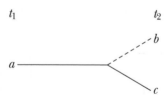

a is the original ship, b is the ship put together (following the original plans) out of planks removed from Theseus' ship. c is the ship that resulted from the gradual replacement of a's planks. a and b are made up of exactly the same planks and each plank is in its original position. Thus there is prima facie justification for the claim that a and b are the same ship. On the other hand, a and c are linked by spatiotemporal continuity. Consequently there is also prima facie justification for the claim that a and c are the same ship.

Here are five possibilities: we can hold that, at t_2, (1) a is two ships, (2) a has ceased to exist, (3) a is b, (4) a is c, or (5) a's situation is intrinsically indeterminate.

---

[1]Thomas Hobbes, *The English Works of Thomas Hobbes*, ed. by Sir William Molesworth (London: John Bohn, 1839), vol. I, *Concerning Body*, p. 136. The sentence beginning, "For if, for example, that ship of Theseus . . ." is incomplete in Hobbes's Latin.

It is, I think, entirely reasonable to decide to talk in the following way: c is the "dominant claimant" for identity with a.[2] a and c are one and the same ship because, in this sort of case, the spatiotemporal continuity relation is dominant over the same-parts-same-plan relation as justification for an identity claim.

Suppose that a's planks had been removed one by one *without being replaced*. b is then constructed just as in Hobbes's story. In this case, a and b are the same ship. What it comes to is that Theseus' ship is transported from one place to another by being disassembled and then reassembled.

The relation between a and b is *recessive*. In the absence of a dominant claimant, a and b are the same ship.

The decision to speak of dominant and recessive claimants generates a kind of *contingent identity*.[3] In what we might call the "reassembly world" (that is, the world just described) a and b are the same ship; but, if things had gone differently (that is, if they had gone as they do in Hobbes's story), a and b would *not* have been the same ship.

Now I want to advance two claims which seem to me plainly true and which are crucial to the argument of this paper: (1) a and b can be given proper names, for example, 'Anaximander' and 'Basileides'. And (2) given that real world is the reassembly world, we could, using these proper names, correctly say, "Basileides is Anaximander; but, if things had gone differently, Basileides would have been, not Anaximander, but some other ship." When I say we *could* correctly say this, I mean that it is reasonable to decide to talk in a way that makes this correct.

---

[2] The phrase is used by David Wiggins. On his view, a and c are the same ship. See *Identity and Spatio-temporal Continuity* (Oxford: Basil Blackwell, 1967), p. 37.

[3] Notice that if we had decided to say that in Hobbes's world a ceases to exist, then, in the reassembly world, the identity between a and b would again be contingent. If our decision had been that in Hobbes's world a becomes *both* b and c, it would be a contingent fact in the reassembly world that a is one individual rather than two. And if we had chosen to say that in Hobbes's world a's situation is indeterminate, then in the reassembly world the *determinacy* of the identity would be contingent.

Saul Kripke holds that no identity statement whose terms are *rigid designators* can be contingent, and that all proper names are rigid designators. What, exactly, is a "rigid designator"? Kripke[4] says that it is "a term that designates the same object in all possible worlds" (145). He also says, "when I use the notion of rigid designator, I do not imply that the object referred to necessarily exists. All I mean is that in any possible world where the object in question *does* exist, in any situation where the object *would* exist, we use the designator in question to designate that object" (146).

Of course it is a contingent fact that we use the names we do to designate particular objects. We could use the name 'Ford' to designate Agnew and 'Agnew' to designate Ford. That is to say, there is a possible world *in* which we call Agnew "Ford" and Ford "Agnew." But this is irrelevant to Kripke's sketch of rigidity. When we speak of Ford and Agnew existing in other possible worlds (wherein they have the same, or different names), the name 'Ford' designates Ford, and 'Agnew' designates Agnew. The difference between speaking *with respect to* some possible world, and speaking *in* such a world, is crucial. Presumably, a "rigid designator," when used *with respect to* various possible worlds, always designates the same object.

There is still considerable ambiguity. Kripke may be offering any of the following definitions:

> *Definition I:* Given a term that, in the real world, designates an object, the term is a "rigid designator" if, and only if, every possible world in which that object exists is one with respect to which the term designates the object.
>
> *Definition II:* Given a term that, in the real world, designates an object, the term is a "rigid designator" if, and only if, every possible world with respect to which the term designates at all is one with respect to which it designates that object.
>
> *Definition III:* Given a term that, in the real world, designates an object, the term is a "rigid designator" if, and only if, (1) every possible world in which that object exists is one with respect to which the term designates the object, and (2) every possible world with respect to which the term designates at all is one with respect to which it designates that object.

4"Identity and Necessity," in Milton K. Munitz, ed., *Identity and Individuation* (New York: NYU Press, 1971).

Do these definitions force us to hold that 'Anaximander' and 'Basileides' are rigid designators? At this point it becomes imperative that we decide how many "objects" there are in our stories about Theseus' ship. I have found only two viable theories.

The two-object theory: 'Anaximander' is just another name for Theseus' ship. But 'Basileides' is a *synonym* for some such definite description as 'the ship recently assembled out of planks P_1, P_2, P_3, . . . etc.'[5] Standing in the reassembly world, we say, "Basileides is Anaximander; but, if things had gone differently, Basileides would have been, not Anaximander, but a new and different ship," and this just means that some *description* applies to Theseus' ship (one object) which might have applied to some other ship (another object). On this theory, there is no *object* which is Theseus' ship, but which, if things had gone differently, would have been some other ship.

Here, presumably, is an analogous situation: the President of the United States is Ford; but, if things had gone differently, the President would have been someone other than Ford. Clearly we are not saying of some *object,* or *entity,* that it is Ford, but need not have been.

Given that our world is Hobbes's world, Definition I, in combination with the two-object theory, yields the conclusion that both 'Anaximander' and 'Basileides' are rigid designators. 'Anaximander' designates Theseus' ship; and every possible world in which that ship exists is one with respect to which 'Anaximander' designates just that ship. Hence 'Anaximander' is rigid. 'Basileides' designates a new and different ship, and every possible world in which *that* ship exists is one with respect to which 'Basileides' designates that ship. Hence, both terms are rigid.

I do not think that Kripke will welcome this result. In Hobbes's world, Basileides and Anaximander are only *contingently* non-identical. They are different ships; but, if things had gone differently, they would have been the same ship. As I understand it, Kripke holds that if '*a*' and '*b*' are rigid designators, *a* and *b* *cannot* be contingently non-identical.

In any case, given that our world is the *reassembly* world, Definition I and the two-object theory force one to the conclusion that 'Anaximander' is rigid and 'Basileides' *non*-rigid. 'Anaximander' still

---

[5]Kripke holds that some definite descriptions (e.g., the sum of two plus two) are rigid designators; but he would, I believe, reject the claim that the description just given is such a designator. Hence, if 'Basileides' is synonymous with that description, he should deny that 'Basileides' is rigid.

designates Theseus' ship, and designates that ship with respect to every possible world in which that ship exists. But 'Basileides' designates that ship in our world and does *not* designate it with respect to Hobbes's world. With respect to that world it designates a different ship.

Definitions II and III, plus the two-object theory, lead to the same result. Every possible world with respect to which 'Anaximander' designates at all is one with respect to which it designates Theseus' ship. On the other hand, 'Basileides' sometimes designates Theseus' ship, and sometimes designates the new ship. Hence, 'Anaximander' is rigid and 'Basileides' nonrigid.

Definitions I, II, and III, together with the two-object theory, yield the conclusion that there can be nonrigid proper names.

The three-object theory: 'Anaximander' is a name for Theseus' ship. 'Basileides' is a name of a ship (the ship recently assembled out of planks P_1, P_2, P_3, . . . etc.)—that is to say, an *object*—which is only contingently one and the same as Theseus' ship in the reassembly world. On this view, Basileides (one object) is, in fact, Theseus' ship (another object), and could have been, not Theseus' ship, but some new ship (still another object).

Those who accept this theory will say that a proper name can designate an object in two distinct ways. It can designate *directly,* or it can designate *indirectly* (*via* a contingent identity). In the reassembly world, 'Basileides' directly designates a ship only contingently one and the same as Theseus' ship, and indirectly designates Theseus' ship. On the other hand, 'Anaximander' directly designates an object contingently identical with Basileides, and only indirectly designates Basileides.

Given that our world is the reassembly world, the three-object theory, together with any of our definitions, yields the conclusion that both 'Anaximander' and 'Basileides' are nonrigid. 'Anaximander' [indirectly] designates Basileides; but Basileides exists in a possible world (namely, Hobbes's world) with respect to which 'Anaximander' designates, not Basileides, but some other ship. Similarly, 'Basileides' (indirectly) designates Anaximander; but Anaximander exists in a possible world (namely Hobbes's world) with respect to which 'Basileides' designates some other ship. Hence, both of these names designate (indirectly) in a nonrigid manner.

Since the two-object theory and the three-object theory both yield the same result, I think it is safe to conclude that some possible proper names could easily be nonrigid designators.

Suggested Further Readings

Perhaps the best place to begin is Saul A. Kripke, *Naming and Necessity* (Cambridge, MA: Harvard University Press, 1980).

See also R. Chisholm, "Identity through Possible Worlds: Some Questions," *Nous* 1 (1967), and Alvin Plantinga, "Transworld Identity or Worldbound Individuals?" in *The Possible and the Actual,* ed. by Michael J. Loux (Ithaca, NY: Cornell University Press, 1979).

A direct reply to Chandler is contained in Nathan Salmon, *Reference and Essence* (Princeton, NJ: Princeton University Press, 1981).

CHAPTER 5

*W*here Am I?

Daniel C. Dennett

Locke's famous story concerning the prince and the cobbler suggests that a person might somehow migrate from one body to another. We may question the proposition that we can be detached from our bodies, that a person can be located in a place other than where her or his body is located, but arguably there is something to be said for this idea. Conceivably our brains might be detached from our bodies. If we are our brains, then we may be detached in this manner. These possibilities are explored in the following selection. Daniel C. Dennett is director of the Center for Cognitive Studies at Tuft University. Dennett's books include Brainstorms *(1978),* Elbow Room *(1984), and* The Mind's I *(1981).*

Now that I've won my suit under the Freedom of Information Act, I am at liberty to reveal for the first time a curious episode in my life that may be of interest not only to those engaged in research in the philosophy of mind, artificial intelligence and neuroscience but also to the general public.

Several years ago I was approached by Pentagon officials who asked me to volunteer for a highly dangerous and secret mission. In collaboration with NASA and Howard Hughes, the Department of Defense was spending billions to develop a Supersonic Tunneling Underground Device, or STUD. It was supposed to tunnel through the earth's core at great speed and deliver a specially designed atomic warhead "right up the Red's missile silos," as one of the Pentagon brass put it.

The problem was that in an early test they had succeeded in lodging a warhead about a mile deep under Tulsa, Oklahoma, and they wanted me to retrieve it for them. "Why me?" I asked. Well, the mission involved some pioneering applications of current brain research, and they had heard of my interest in brains and of course my Faustian curiosity and great courage and so forth. . . . Well, how could I refuse? The difficulty that brought the Pentagon to my door was that the device I'd been asked to recover was fiercely radioactive, in a new way. According to monitoring instruments, something about the nature of the device and its complex interactions with pockets of material deep in the earth had produced radiation that could cause several abnormalities in certain tissues of the brain. No way had been found to shield the brain from these deadly rays, which were apparently harmless to other tissues and organs of the body. So it had been decided that the person sent to recover the device should *leave his brain behind*. It would be kept in a safe place where it could execute its normal control functions by elaborate radio links. Would I submit to a surgical procedure that would completely remove my brain, which would then be placed in a life-support system at the Manned Spacecraft Center in Houston? Each input and output pathway, as it was severed, would be restored by a pair of microminiaturized radio transceivers, one attached precisely to the brain, the other to the nerve stumps in the empty cranium. No information would be lost, all the connectivity would be preserved. At first I was a bit reluctant. Would it really work? The Houston brain surgeons encouraged me. "Think of it," they said, "as a mere *stretching* of the nerves. If your brain were just moved over an *inch* in your skull, that would not alter or impair your mind. We're simply going to make the nerves indefinitely elastic by splicing radio links into them."

I was shown around the life-support lab in Houston and saw the sparkling new vat in which my brain would be placed, were I to agree. I met the large and brilliant support team of neurologists, hematologists, biophysicists, and electrical engineers, and after several days of discussions and demonstrations, I agreed to give it a try. I was subjected to an enormous array of blood tests, brain scans, experiments, interviews, and the like. They took down my autobiography at great length, recorded tedious lists of my beliefs, hopes, fears, and tastes. They even listed my favorite stereo recordings and gave me a crash session of psychoanalysis.

The day for surgery arrived at last and of course I was anesthetized and remember nothing of the operation itself. When I came out of anesthesia, I opened my eyes, looked around, and asked the inevitable, the traditional, the lamentably hackneyed post-operative question: "Where am I?" The nurse smiled down at me. "You're in Houston," she said, and I reflected that this still had a good chance of being the truth one way or another. She handed me a mirror. Sure enough, there were the tiny antennae poling up through their titanium ports centered into my skull.

"I gather the operation was a success," I said, "I want to go see my brain." They led me (I was a bit dizzy and unsteady) down a long corridor and into the life-support lab. A cheer went up from the assembled support team, and I responded with what I hoped was a jaunty salute. Still feeling lightheaded, I was helped over to the life-support vat. I peered through the glass. There, floating in what looked like ginger ale, was undeniably a human brain, though it was almost covered with printed circuit chips, plastic tubules, electrodes, and other paraphernalia. "Is that mine?" I asked. "Hit the output transmitter switch there on the side of the vat and see for yourself," the project director replied. I moved the switch to OFF, and immediately slumped, groggy and nauseated, into the arms of the technicians, one of whom kindly restored the switch to its ON position. While I recovered my equilibrium and composure, I thought to myself: "Well, here I am, sitting on a folding chair, staring through a piece of plate glass at my own brain. . . . But wait," I said to myself, "shouldn't I have thought, 'Here I am, suspended in a bubbling fluid, being stared at by my own eyes'?" I tried to think this latter thought. I tried to project it into the tank, offering it hopefully to my brain, but I failed to carry off the exercise with any conviction. I tried again. "Here am *I*, Daniel Dennett, suspended in a bubbling fluid, being stared at by my own eyes." No, it just didn't work. Most puzzling and confusing. Being a philosopher of firm physicalist conviction, I believed unswervingly that the tokening of my thoughts was occurring somewhere in my brain: yet, when I thought "Here I am," where the thought occurred to me was *here*, outside the vat, where I, Dennett, was staring at my brain.

I tried and tried to think myself into the vat, but to no avail. I tried to build up to the task by doing mental exercises. I thought to myself, "The sun is shining *over there*," five times in rapid succession, each time mentally ostending a different place: in order, the sunlit corner of the lab, the visible front lawn of the hospital, Houston, Mars, and Jupiter. I found I had little difficulty in getting my "there's" to hop all over the celestial map with their proper references. I could loft a "there" in an instant through the farthest reaches of space, and then aim the next "there" with pinpoint accuracy at the upper left quadrant of a freckle on my arm. Why was I having such trouble with "here?" "Here in Houston" worked well enough, and so did "here in the lab," and even "here in this part of the lab," but "here in the vat" always seemed merely an unmeant mental mouthing. I tried closing my eyes while thinking it. This seemed to help, but still I couldn't manage to pull it off, except perhaps for a fleeting instant. I couldn't be sure. The discovery that I couldn't be sure was so unsettling. How did I know *where* I meant by "here" when I thought "here"? Could I *think* I meant one place when in fact I meant another? I didn't see how that could be admitted without untying the few bonds of intimacy between a person and his own mental life that had survived the onslaught of the brain scientists and philosophers, the physicalists and behaviorists. Perhaps I was incorrigible about where I *meant* when said "here." But in my present circumstances it seemed that either I was doomed by sheer force of mental habit to thinking systematically false indexical thoughts, or where a person is (and hence where his thoughts are tokened for purposes of semantic analysis) is not necessarily where his brain, the physical seat of his soul, resides. Nagged by confusion, I attempted to orient myself by falling back on a favorite philosopher's ploy. I began naming things.

"Yorick," I said aloud to my brain, "you are my brain. The rest of my body, seated in this chair, I dub 'Hamlet.'" So here we all are: Yorick's my brain, Hamlet's my body, and I am Dennett. *Now,* where am I? And when I think "where am I?" where's that thought tokened? Is it tokened in my brain, lounging about in the vat, or right here between my ears where it *seems* to be tokened? Or nowhere? Its *temporal* coordinates give me no trouble; must it not have spatial coordinates as well? I began making a list of the alternatives.

(1) *Where Hamlet goes, there goes Dennett.* This principle was easily refuted by appeal to the familiar brain transplant thought-experiments so enjoyed by philosophers. If Tom and Dick switch brains, Tom is the fellow with Dick's former body—just ask him; he'll claim to be Tom, and tell you the most intimate details of Tom's autobiography. It was clear enough, then, that my current body and I could part company, but not likely that I could be separated from my brain. The rule of thumb that emerged so plainly from the thought-experiments was that in a brain-transplant operation, one wanted to be the *donor,* not the recipient. Better to call such an operation a *body-transplant,* in fact. So perhaps the truth was,

(2) *Where Yorick goes, there goes Dennett.* This was not at all appealing, however. How could I be in the vat and not about to go anywhere, when I was so obviously outside the vat looking in and beginning to make guilty plans to return to my room for a substantial lunch? This begged the question, I realized, but it still seemed to be getting at something important. Casting about for some support for my intuition, I hit upon a legalistic sort of argument that might have appealed to Locke.

Suppose, I argued to myself, I were now to fly to California, rob a bank, and be apprehended. In which state would I be tried: In California, where the robbery took place, or in Texas, where the brains of the outfit were located? Would I be a California felon with an out-of-state brain, or a Texas felon remotely controlling an accomplice of sorts in California? It seemed possible that I might beat such a rap just on the undecidability of that jurisdictional question, though perhaps it would be deemed an inter-state, and hence Federal, offense. In any event, suppose I were convicted. Was it likely that California would be satisfied to throw Hamlet into the brig, knowing that Yorick was living the good life and luxuriously taking the waters in Texas? Would Texas incarcerate Yorick, leaving Hamlet free to take the next boat to Rio? This alternative appealed to me. Barring capital punishment or other cruel and unusual punishment, the state would be obliged to maintain the life-support system for Yorick though they might move him from Houston to Leavenworth, and aside from the unpleasantness of the opprobrium, I for one, would not mind at all and would consider myself a free man under those circumstances. If the state has an interest in forcibly relocating persons in institutions, it would fail to relocate me in any institution by locating Yorick there. If this were true, it suggested a third alternative.

(3) *Dennett is wherever he thinks he is.* Generalized, the claim was as follows: At any given time a person has a *point of view,* and the location of the point of view (which is determined internally by the content of the point of view) is also the location of the person.

Such a proposition is not without its perplexities, but to me it seemed a step in the right direction. The only trouble was that it seemed to place one in a heads-I-win/tails-you-lose situation of unlikely infallibility as regards location. Hadn't I myself often been wrong about where I was, and at least as often uncertain? Couldn't one get lost? Of course, but getting lost *geographically* is not the only way one might get lost. If one were lost in the woods one could attempt to reassure oneself with the consolation that at least one knew where one was: one was right *here* in the familiar surroundings of one's own body. Perhaps in this case one would not have drawn one's attention to much to be thankful for. Still, there were worse plights imaginable, and I wasn't sure I wasn't in such a plight right now.

Point of view clearly had something to do with personal location, but it was itself an unclear notion. It was obvious that the content of one's point of view was not the same as or determined by the content of one's beliefs or thoughts. For example, what should we say about the point of view of the Cinerama viewer who shrieks and twists in his seat as the roller-coaster footage overcomes his psychic distancing? Has he forgotten that he is safely seated in the theater? Here I was inclined to say that the person is experiencing an illusory shift in point of view. In other cases, my inclination to call such shifts illusory was less strong. The workers in laboratories and plants who handle dangerous materials by operating feedback-controlled mechanical arms and hands undergo a shift in point of view that is crisper and more pronounced than anything Cinerama can provoke. They can feel the heft and slipperiness of the containers they manipulate with their metal fingers. They know perfectly well where they are and are not fooled into false beliefs by the experience, yet it is as if they were inside the isolation chamber they are peering into. With mental effort, they can manage to shift their point of view back and forth, rather like making a transparent Neckar cube or an Escher drawing change orientation before one's eyes. It does seem extravagant to suppose that in performing this bit of mental gymnastics, they are transporting *themselves* back and forth.

Still their example gave me hope. If I was in fact in the vat in spite of my intuitions, I might be able to train myself to adopt that point of view even as a matter of habit. I should dwell on images of myself comfortably floating in my vat, beaming volitions to that familiar body *out there*. I reflected that the ease or difficulty of this task was presumably independent of the truth about the location of one's brain. Had I been practicing before the operation, I might now be finding it second nature. You might now yourself try such a *tromp d'oeil*. Imagine you have written an inflammatory letter which has been published in the *Times*, the result of which is that the Government has chosen to impound your brain for a probationary period of three years in its Dangerous Brain Clinic in Bethesda, Maryland. Your body of course is allowed freedom to earn a salary and thus to continue its function of laying up income to be taxed. At this moment, however, your body is seated in an auditorium listening to a peculiar account by Daniel Dennett of his own similar experience. Try it. Think yourself to Bethesda, and then hark back longingly to your body, far away, and yet *seeming* so near. It is only with long-distance restraint (yours? the Government's?) that you can control your impulse to get those hands clapping in polite applause before navigating the old body to the rest room and a well-deserved glass of evening sherry in the lounge. The task of imagination is certainly difficult, but if you achieve your goal the results might be consoling.

Anyway, there I was in Houston, lost in thought as one might say, but not for long. My speculations were soon interrupted by the Houston doctors, who wished to test out my new prosthetic nervous system before sending me off on my hazardous mission. As I mentioned before, I was a bit dizzy at first, and not surprisingly, although I soon habituated myself to my new circumstances (which were, after all, well nigh indistinguishable from my old circumstances). My accommodation was not perfect, however, and to this day I continue to be plagued by minor coordination difficulties. The speed of light is fast, but finite, and as my brain and body move farther and farther apart, the delicate interaction of my feedback systems is thrown into disarray by the time lags. Just as one is rendered close to speechless by a delayed or echoic hearing of one's speaking voice so, for instance, I am virtually unable to track a moving object with my eyes whenever my brain and my body are more than a few miles apart. In most matters my impairment is scarcely detectable, though I can no longer hit a slow curve ball with the authority of yore. There are some compensations of course. Though liquor tastes as good as ever, and warms my gullet while corroding my liver, I can drink it in any quantity I please, without becoming the slightest bit inebriated, a curiosity some of my closest friends may have noticed (though I occasionally have *feigned* inebriation, so as not to draw attention to my unusual circumstances). For similar reasons, I take aspirin orally for a sprained wrist, but if the pain persists I ask Houston to administer codeine to me *in vitro*. In times of illness the phone bill can be staggering.

But to return to my adventure. At length, both the doctors and I were satisfied that I was ready to undertake my subterranean mission. And so I left my brain in Houston and headed by helicopter for Tulsa. Well, in any case, that's the way it seemed to me. That's how I would put it, just off the top of my head as it were. On the trip I reflected

further about my earlier anxieties and decided that my first postopera-
tive speculations had been tinged with panic. The matter was not
nearly as strange or metaphysical as I had been supposing. Where was
I? In two places, clearly; both inside the vat and outside it. Just as one
can stand with one foot in Connecticut and the other in Rhode Island,
I was in two places at once. I had become one of those scattered individuals we used to hear so much about. The more I considered this
answer, the more obviously true it appeared. But, strange to say, the
more true it appeared, the less important the question to which it
could be the true answer seemed. A sad, but not unprecedented, fate
for a philosophical question to suffer. This answer did not completely
satisfy me, of course. There lingered some questions to which I should
have liked an answer, which was neither "Where are all my various and
sundry parts?" nor "What is my current point of view?" Or at least
there seemed to be such a question. For it did seem undeniable that
in some sense *I* and not merely *most of me* was descending into the
earth under Tulsa in search of an atomic warhead.

When I found the warhead, I was certainly glad I had left my
brain behind, for the pointer on the specially built Geiger counter I
had brought with me was off the dial. I called Houston on my ordinary radio and told the operation control center of my position and
my progress. In return, they gave me instructions for dismantling the
vehicle, based upon my on-site observations. I had set to work with
my cutting torch when all of a sudden a terrible thing happened. I
went stone deaf. At first I thought it was only my radio earphones
that had broken, but when I tapped on my helmet, I heard nothing.
Apparently the auditory transceivers had gone on the fritz. I could
no longer hear Houston or my own voice, but I could speak, so I
started telling them what had happened. In mid-sentence, I knew
something else had gone wrong. My vocal apparatus had become
paralyzed. Then my right hand went limp—another transceiver had
gone. I was truly in deep trouble. But worse was to follow. After a few
more minutes, I went blind. I cursed my luck, and then I cursed the
scientists who had led me into this grave peril. There I was, deaf,
dumb, and blind, in a radioactive hole more than a mile under
Tulsa. Then the last of my cerebral radio links broke, and suddenly I
was faced with a new and even more shocking problem: whereas an
instant before I had been buried alive in Oklahoma, now I was disembodied in Houston. My recognition of my new status was not immediate. It took me several very anxious minutes before it dawned

on me that my poor body lay several hundred miles away, with heart pulsing and lungs respirating, but otherwise as dead as the body of any heart transplant donor, its skull packed with useless, broken electronic gear. The shift in perspective I had earlier found well nigh impossible now seemed quite natural. Though I could think myself back into my body in the tunnel under Tulsa, it took some effort to sustain the illusion. For surely it was an illusion to suppose I was still in Oklahoma: I had lost all contact with that body.

It occurred to me then, with one of those rushes of revelation of which we should be suspicious, that I had stumbled upon an impressive demonstration of the immateriality of the soul based upon physicalist principles and premises. For as the last radio signal between Tulsa and Houston died away, had I not changed location from Tulsa to Houston at the speed of light? And had I not accomplished this without any increase in mass? What moved from A to B at such speed was surely myself; or at any rate my soul or mind—the massless center of my being and home of my consciousness. My *point of view* had lagged somewhat behind, but I had already noted the indirect bearing of point of view on personal location. I could not see how a physicalist philosopher could quarrel with this except by taking the dire and counterintuitive route of banishing all talk of persons. Yet the notion of personhood was so well entrenched in everyone's world view, or so it seemed to me, that any denial would be as curiously unconvincing, as systematically disingenuous, as the Cartesian negation, "non sum."

Suggested Further Readings

An interesting variation on Dennett's story can be found in David Hawley Sanford, "Where Was I?" in *The Mind's I,* ed. by Douglas R. Hofstadter and Daniel C. Dennett (New York: Basic Books, 1981).

Lawrence H. Davis addresses issues relating to detached brains in "Disembodied Brains," *Australasian Journal of Philosophy* 52 (1974).

For discussions of the issues raised by Dennett, see P. F. Strawson, "Self, Mind and Body," in *The Nature of Mind,* ed. by David M. Rosenthal (Oxford: Oxford University Press, 1991); Jerome Shaffer, "Persons and Bodies," *Philosophical Review* 75 (1966); and Harold Noonan, *Personal Identity* (London: Routledge, 1991), chap. 10.

PART II

Time

CHAPTER 6

The Paradoxes of Time Travel

David K. Lewis

The idea of traveling to the future or the past fascinates many people. There are many interesting stories about time travel, but we may wonder whether such a thing is possible. Might a time traveler encounter her former or future self? The following selection defends a qualified affirmative answer, maintaining that a person who engages in time travel is composed of various temporal parts or temporal stages and that "meeting oneself" at an earlier or later time occurs as a result of a certain interaction between two temporal stages of a single temporally extended individual.

David Lewis is a professor of philosophy at Princeton University. Lewis's books include Counterfactuals *(1973),* Philosophical Papers *(1983), and* On the Plurality of Worlds *(1986).*

Time travel, I maintain, is possible. The paradoxes of time travel are oddities, not impossibilities. They prove only this much, which few would have doubted: that a possible world where time travel took place would be a most strange world, different in fundamental ways from the world we think is ours.

I shall be concerned here with the sort of time travel that is recounted in science fiction. Not all science fiction writers are clear-headed, to be sure, and inconsistent time travel stories have often been written. But some writers have thought the problems through with great care, and their stories are perfectly consistent.[1]

Source: David K. Lewis: "The Paradoxes of Time Travel," from *American Philosophical Quarterly* 13 (April 1976), pp. 145–52. Reprinted by permission of *American Philosophical Quarterly* and the author.

[1] I have particularly in mind two of the time travel stories of Robert A. Heinlein: "By His Bootstraps" in R. A. Heinlein, *The Menace from Earth* (Hicksville, N.Y., 1959), and "—All You Zombies—," in R. A. Heinlein, *The Unpleasant Profession of Jonathan Hoag* (Hicksville, N.Y., 1959).

If I can defend the consistency of some science fiction stories of time travel, then I suppose parallel defenses might be given of some controversial physical hypotheses, such as the hypothesis that time is circular or the hypothesis that there are particles that travel faster than light. But I shall not explore these parallels here.

What is time travel? Inevitably, it involves a discrepancy between time and time. Any traveler departs and then arrives at his destination; the time elapsed from departure to arrival (positive, or perhaps zero) is the duration of the journey. But if he is a time traveler, the separation in time between departure and arrival does not equal the duration of his journey. He departs; he travels for an hour, let us say; then he arrives. The time he reaches is not the time one hour after his departure. It is later, if he has traveled toward the future; earlier, if he has traveled toward the past. If he has traveled far toward the past, it is earlier even than his departure. How can it be that the same two events, his departure and his arrival, are separated by two unequal amounts of time?

It is tempting to reply that there must be two independent time dimensions; that for time travel to be possible, time must be not a line but a plane.[2] Then a pair of events may have two unequal separations if they are separated more in one of the time dimensions than in the other. The lives of common people occupy straight diagonal lines across the plane of time, sloping at a rate of exactly one hour of time$_1$ per hour of time$_2$. The life of the time traveler occupies a bent path, of varying slope.

On closer inspection, however, this account seems not to give us time travel as we know it from the stories. When the traveler revisits the days of his childhood, will his playmates be there to meet him? No; he has not reached the part of the plane of time where they are. He is no longer separated from them along one of the two dimensions of time, but he is still separated from them along the other. I do not say that two-dimensional time is impossible, or that there is no way to square it with the usual conception of what time travel would be like. Nevertheless I shall say no more about two-dimensional time. Let us set it aside, and see how time travel is possible even in one-dimensional time.

---

[2]Accounts of time travel in two-dimensional time are found in Jack W. Meiland, "A Two-Dimensional Passage Model of Time for Time Travel," *Philosophical Studies,* vol. 26 (1974), pp. 153–173; and in the initial chapters of Isaac Asimov, *The End of Eternity* (Garden City, N.Y., 1955). Asimov's denouement, however, seems to require some different conception of time travel.

The world—the time traveler's world, or ours—is a four-dimensional manifold of events. Time is one dimension of the four, like the spatial dimensions except that the prevailing laws of nature discriminate between time and the others—or rather, perhaps, between various timelike dimensions and various spacelike dimensions. (Time remains one-dimensional, since no two timelike dimensions are orthogonal.) Enduring things are timelike streaks: wholes composed of temporal parts, or *stages*, located at various times and places. Change is qualitative difference between different stages—different temporal parts—of some enduring thing, just as a "change" in scenery from east to west is a qualitative difference between the eastern and western spatial parts of the landscape. If this paper should change your mind about the possibility of time travel, there will be a difference of opinion between two different temporal parts of you, the stage that started reading and the subsequent stage that finishes.

If change is qualitative difference between temporal parts of something, then what doesn't have temporal parts can't change. For instance, numbers can't change; nor can the events of any moment of time, since they cannot be subdivided into dissimilar temporal parts. (We have set aside the case of two-dimensional time, and hence the possibility that an event might be momentary along one time dimension but divisible along the other.) It is essential to distinguish change from "Cambridge change," which can befall anything. Even a number can "change" from being to not being the rate of exchange between pounds and dollars. Even a momentary event can "change" from being a year ago to being a year and a day ago, or from being forgotten to being remembered. But these are not genuine changes. Not just any old reversal in truth value of a time-sensitive sentence about something makes a change in the thing itself.

A time traveler, like anyone else, is a streak through the manifold of space-time, a whole composed of stages located at various times and places. But he is not a streak like other steaks. If he travels toward the past he is a zig-zag streak, doubling back on himself. If he travels toward the future, he is a stretched-out streak. And if he travels either way instantaneously, so that there are no intermediate stages between the stage that departs and the stage that arrives and his journey has zero duration, then he is a broken streak.

I asked how it could be that the same two events were separated by two unequal amounts of time, and I set aside the reply that time might have two independent dimensions. Instead I reply by distinguishing time itself, *external time* as I shall also call it, from the *personal time* of a particular time traveler: roughly, that which is measured by his wristwatch. His journey takes an hour of his personal time, let us say; his wristwatch reads an hour later at arrival than at departure. But the arrival is more than an hour after the departure in external time, if he travels toward the future; or the arrival is before the departure in external time (or less than an hour after), if he travels toward the past.

That is only rough. I do not wish to define personal time operationally, making wristwatches infallible by definition. That which is measured by my own wristwatch often disagrees with external time, yet I am no time traveler: what my misregulated wristwatch measures is neither time itself nor my personal time. Instead of an operational definition, we need a functional definition of personal time: it is that which occupies a certain role in the pattern of events that comprise the time traveler's life. If you take the stages of a common person, they manifest certain regularities with respect to external time. Properties change continuously as you go along, for the most part, and in familiar ways. First come infantile stages. Last come senile ones. Memories accumulate. Food digests. Hair grows. Wristwatch hands move. If you take the stages of a time traveler instead, they do not manifest the common regularities with respect to external time. But there is one way to assign coordinates to the time traveler's stages, and one way only (apart from the arbitrary choice of a zero point), so that the regularities that hold with respect to this assignment match those that commonly hold with respect to external time. With respect to the correct assignment properties change continuously as you go along, for the most part, and in familiar ways. First come infantile stages. Last come senile ones. Memories accumulate. Food digests. Hair grows. Wristwatch hands move. The assignment of coordinates that yields this match is the time traveler's personal time. It isn't really time, but it plays the role in his life that time plays in the life of a common person. It's enough like time so that we can—with due caution—transplant our temporal vocabulary to it in discussing his affairs. We can say without contradiction, as the time traveler prepares to set out, "Soon he will be in the past." We mean that a stage of him is slightly later in his personal time, but much earlier in external time, than the stage of him that is present as we say the sentence.

We may assign locations in the time traveler's personal time not only to his stages themselves but also to the events that go on around him. Soon Caesar will die, long ago; that is, a stage slightly later in the time traveler's personal time than his present stage, but long ago in external time, is simultaneous with Caesar's death. We could even extend the assignment of personal time to events that are not part of the time traveler's life, and not simultaneous with any of his stages. If his funeral in ancient Egypt is separated from his death by three days of external time and his death is separated from his birth by three score years and ten of his personal time, then we may add the two intervals and say that his funeral follows his birth by three score years and ten and three days of *extended personal time.* Likewise a bystander might truly say, three years after the last departure of another famous time traveler, that "he may even now—if I may use the phrase—be wandering on some plesiosaurus-haunted oolitic coral reef, or beside the lonely saline seas of the Triassic Age."[3] If the time traveler does wander on an oolitic coral reef three years after his departure in his personal time, then it is no mistake to say with respect to his extended personal time that the wandering is taking place "even now."

We may liken intervals of external time to distances as the crow flies, and intervals of personal time to distances along a winding path. The time traveler's life is like a mountain railway. The place two miles due east of here may also be nine miles down the line, in the westbound direction. Clearly we are not dealing here with two independent dimensions. Just as distance along the railway is not a fourth spatial dimension, so a time traveler's personal time is not a second dimension of time. How far down the line some place is depends on its location in three-dimensional space, and likewise the locations of events in personal time depend on their locations in one-dimensional external time.

Five miles down the line from here is a place where the line goes under a trestle; two miles further is a place where the line goes over a trestle; these places are one and the same. The trestle by which the line crosses over itself has two different locations along the line, five miles down from here and also seven. In the same way, an event in a time traveler's life may have more than one location in his personal time. If he doubles back toward the past, but not too far, he

---

[3]H. G. Wells, *The Time Machine, An Invention* (London, 1895), epilogue. The passage is criticized as contradictory in Donald C. Williams, "The Myth of Passage," *The Journal of Philosophy,* vol. 48 (1951), p. 463.

may be able to talk to himself. The conversation involves two of his stages, separated in his personal time but simultaneous in external time. The location of the conversation in personal time should be the location of the stage involved in it. But there are two such stages; to share the locations of both, the conversation must be assigned two different locations in personal time.

The more we extend the assignment of personal time outwards from the time traveler's stages to the surrounding events, the more will such events acquire multiple locations. It may happen also, as we have already seen, that events that are not simultaneous in external time will be assigned the same location in personal time—or rather, that at least one of the locations of one will be the same as at least one of the locations of the other. So extension must not be carried too far, lest the location of events in extended personal time loses its utility as a means of keeping track of their roles in the time traveler's history.

A time traveler who talks to himself, on the telephone perhaps, looks for all the world like two different people talking to each other. It isn't quite right to say that the whole of him is in two places at once, since neither of the two stages involved in the conversation is the whole of him, or even the whole of the part of him that is located at the (external) time of the conversation. What's true is that he, unlike the rest of us, has two different complete stages located at the same time at different places. What reason have I, then, to regard him as one person and not two? What unites his stages, including the simultaneous ones, into a single person? The problem of personal identity is especially acute if he is the sort of time traveler whose journeys are instantaneous, a broken streak consisting of several unconnected segments. Then the natural way to regard him as more than one person is to take each segment as a different person. No one of them is a time traveler, and the peculiarity of the situation comes to this: all but one of these several people vanish into thin air, all but another one appear out of thin air, and there are remarkable resemblances between one at his appearance and another at his vanishing. Why isn't that at least as good a description as the one I gave, on which the several segments are all parts of one time traveler?

I answer that what unites the stages (or segments) of a time traveler is the same sort of mental, or mostly mental, continuity and connectedness that unites anyone else. The only difference is that whereas a common person is connected and continuous with respect to external time, the time traveler is connected and continuous only with respect to his own personal time. Taking the stages in order, mental (and bodily) change is mostly gradual rather than sudden, and at no point is there sudden change in too many different respects all at once. (We can include position in external time among the respects we keep track of, if we like. It may change discontinuously with respect to personal time if not too much else changes discontinuously along with it.) Moreover, there is not too much change altogether. Plenty of traits and traces last a lifetime. Finally, the connectedness and the continuity are not accidental. They are explicable; and further, they are explained by the fact that the properties of each stage depend causally on those of the stages just before in personal time, the dependence being such as tends to keep things the same.[4]

To see the purpose of my final requirement of causal continuity, let us see how it excludes a case of counterfeit time travel. Fred was created out of thin air, as if in the midst of life; he lived a while, then died. He was created by a demon, and the demon had chosen at random what Fred was to be like at the moment of his creation. Much later someone else, Sam, came to resemble Fred as he was when first created. At the very moment when the resemblance became perfect, the demon destroyed Sam. Fred and Sam together are very much like a single person: a time traveler whose personal time starts at Sam's birth, goes on to Sam's destruction and Fred's creation, and goes on from there to Fred's death. Taken in this order, the stages of Fred-*cum*-Sam have the proper connectedness and continuity. But they lack causal continuity, so Fred-*cum*-Sam is not one person and not a time traveler. Perhaps it was pure coincidence that Fred at his creation and Sam at his destruction were exactly alike; then the connectedness and continuity of Fred-*cum*-Sam across the crucial point are accidental. Perhaps instead the demon remembered what Fred was like, guided Sam toward perfect resemblance, watched his progress, and destroyed him at the right moment. Then the connectedness and continuity of Fred-*cum*-Sam has a causal explanation, but of the wrong sort. Either way, Fred's first stages do not depend causally for their properties on Sam's last stages. So the case of Fred and Sam is rightly disqualified as a case of personal identity and as a case of time travel.

---

[4] I discuss the relation between personal identity and mental connectedness and continuity at greater length in "Survival and Identity" in *The Identity of Persons*, ed. by Amelie Rorty (forthcoming).

We might expect that when a time traveler visits the past there will be reversals of causation. You may punch his face before he leaves, causing his eye to blacken centuries ago. Indeed, travel into the past necessarily involves reversed causation. For time travel requires personal identity—he who arrives must be the same person who departed. That requires causal continuity, in which causation runs from earlier to later stages in the order of personal time. But the orders of personal and external time disagree at some point, and there we have causation that runs from later to earlier stages in the order of external time. Elsewhere I have given an analysis of causation in terms of chains of counterfactual dependence, and I took care that my analysis would not rule out causal reversal *a priori*.[5] I think I can argue (but not here) that under my analysis the direction of counterfactual dependence and causation is governed by the direction of other *de facto* asymmetries of time. If so, then reversed causation and time travel are not excluded altogether, but can occur only where there are local exceptions to these asymmetries. As I said at the outset, the time traveler's world would be a most strange one.

Stranger still, if there are local—but only local—causal reversals, then there may also be causal loops: closed causal chains in which some of the causal links are normal in direction and others are reversed. (Perhaps there must be loops if there is reversal; I am not sure.) Each event on the loop has a causal explanation, being caused by events elsewhere on the loop. That is not to say that the loop as a whole is caused or explicable. It may not be. Its inexplicability is especially remarkable if it is made up of the sort of causal processes that transmit information. Recall the time traveler who talked to himself. He talked to himself about time travel, and in the course of the conversation his older self told his younger self how to build a time machine. That information was available in no other way. His older self knew how because his younger self had been told and the information had been preserved by the causal processes that constitute recording, storage, and retrieval of memory traces. His younger self knew, after the conversation, because his older self had known and the information had been preserved by the causal processes that constitute telling. But where did the information come from in the first place? Why did the whole affair happen?

---

[5]"Causation," *The Journal of Philosophy,* vol. 70 (1973), pp. 556–567; the analysis relies on the analysis of counterfactuals given in my *Counterfactuals* (Oxford, 1973).

There is simply no answer. The parts of the loop are explicable, the whole of it is not. Strange! But not impossible, and not too different from inexplicabilities we are already inured to. Almost everyone agrees that God, or the Big Bang, or the entire infinite past of the universe, or the decay of a tritium atom, is uncaused and inexplicable. Then if these are possible, why not also the inexplicable causal loops that arise in time travel?

I have committed a circularity in order not to talk about too much at once, and this is a good place to set it right. In explaining personal time, I presupposed that we were entitled to regard certain stages as comprising a single person. Then in explaining what united the stages into a single person, I presupposed that we were given a personal time order for them. The proper way to proceed is to define personhood and personal time simultaneously, as follows. Suppose given a pair of an aggregate of person-stages, regarded as a candidate for personhood, and an assignment of coordinates to those stages, regarded as a candidate for his personal time. If the stages satisfy the conditions given in my circular explanation with respect to the assignment of coordinates, then both candidates succeed: the stages do comprise a person and the assignment is his personal time.

I have argued so far that what goes on in a time travel story may be a possible pattern of events in four-dimensional space-time with no extra time dimension; that it may be correct to regard the scattered stages of the alleged time traveler as comprising a single person; and that we may legitimately assign to those stages and their surroundings a personal time order that disagrees sometimes with their order in external time. Some might concede all this, but protest that the impossibility of time travel is revealed after all when we ask not what the time traveler *does,* but what he *could do.* Could a time traveler change the past? It seems not: the events of a past moment could no more change than numbers could. Yet it seems that he would be as able as anyone to do things that would change the past if he did them. If a time traveler visiting the past both could and couldn't do something that would change it, then there cannot possibly be such a time traveler.

Consider Tim. He detests his grandfather, whose success in the munitions trade built the family fortune that paid for Tim's time machine. Tim would like nothing so much as to kill Grandfather, but alas he is too late. Grandfather died in his bed in 1957, while Tim was a young boy. But when Tim has built his time machine and traveled to 1920, suddenly he realizes that he is not too late after all. He buys a rifle; he spends long hours in target practice; he shadows Grandfather to learn the route of his daily walk to the munitions works; he rents a room along the route; and there he lurks, one winter day in 1921, rifle loaded, hate in his heart, as Grandfather walks closer, closer. . . .

Tim can kill Grandfather. He has what it takes. Conditions are perfect in every way: the best rifle money could buy, Grandfather an easy target only twenty yards away, not a breeze, door securely locked against intruders, Tim a good shot to begin with and now at the peak of training, and so on. What's to stop him? The forces of logic will not stay his hand! No powerful chaperone stands by to defend the past from interference. (To imagine such a chaperone, as some authors do, is a boring evasion, not needed to make Tim's story consistent.) In short, Tim is as much able to kill Grandfather as anyone ever is to kill anyone. Suppose that down the street another sniper, Tom, lurks waiting for another victim, Grandfather's partner. Tom is not a time traveler, but otherwise he is just like Tim: same make of rifle, same murderous intent, same everything. We can even suppose that Tom, like Tim, believes himself to be a time traveler. Someone has gone to a lot of trouble to deceive Tom into thinking so. There's no doubt that Tom can kill his victim; and Tim has everything going for him that Tom does. By any ordinary standards of ability, Tim can kill Grandfather.

Tim cannot kill Grandfather. Grandfather lived, so to kill him would be to change the past. But the events of a past moment are not subdivisible into temporal parts and therefore cannot change. Either the events of 1921 timelessly do include Tim's killing of Grandfather, or else they timelessly don't. We may be tempted to speak of the "original" 1921 that lies in Tim's personal past, many years before his birth, in which Grandfather lived; and of the "new" 1921 in which Tim now finds himself waiting in ambush to kill Grandfather. But if we do speak so, we merely confer two names on one thing. The events of 1921 are doubly located in Tim's (extended) personal time, like the trestle on the railway, but the "original" 1921 and the "new" 1921 are one and the same. If Tim did not kill Grandfather in the "original" 1921, then if he does kill Grandfather in the "new" 1921, he must both kill and not kill Grandfather in 1921—in the one and only 1921, which is both the "new" and the "original" 1921. It is logically impossible that Tim should change the past by killing Grandfather in 1921. So Tim cannot kill Grandfather.

Not that past moments are special; no more can anyone change the present or the future. Present and future momentary events no more have temporal parts than past ones do. You cannot change a present or future event from what it was originally to what it is after you change it. What you *can* do is to change the present or the future from the unactualized way they would have been without some action of yours to the way they actually are. But that is not an actual change: not a difference between two successive actualities. And Tim can certainly do as much; he changes the past from the unactualized way it would have been without him to the one and only way it actually is. To "change" the past in this way, Tim need not do anything momentous; it is enough just to be there, however unobtrusively.

You know, of course, roughly how the story of Tim must go on if it is to be consistent: he somehow fails. Since Tim didn't kill Grandfather in the "original" 1921, consistency demands that neither does he kill Grandfather in the "new" 1921. Why not? For some commonplace reason. Perhaps some noise distracts him at the last moment, perhaps he misses despite all his target practice, perhaps his nerve fails, perhaps he even feels a pang of unaccustomed mercy. His failures by no means proves that he was not really able to kill Grandfather. We often try and fail to do what we are able to do. Success at some tasks requires not only ability but also luck, and lack of luck is not a temporary lack of ability. Suppose our other sniper, Tom, fails to kill Grandfather's partner for the same reason, whatever it is, that Tim fails to kill Grandfather. It does not follow that Tom was unable to. No more does it follow in Tim's case that he was unable to do what he did not succeed in doing.

We have this seeming contradiction: *"Tim doesn't, but can, because he has what it takes"* versus *"Tim doesn't, and can't, because it's logically impossible to change the past."* I reply that there is no contradiction. Both conclusions are true, and for the reasons given. They are compatible because "can" is equivocal.

To say that something can happen means that its happening is compossible with certain facts. *Which* facts? That is determined, but sometimes not determined well enough, by context. An ape can't speak a human language—say, Finnish—but I can. Facts about the anatomy and operation of the ape's larynx and nervous system are not compossible with his speaking Finnish. The corresponding facts about my larynx and nervous system are compossible with my speaking Finnish. But don't take me along to Helsinki as your interpreter: I can't speak Finnish. My speaking Finnish is compossible with the facts considered so far, but not with further facts about my lack of training. What I can do, relative to one set of facts, I cannot do, relative to another, more inclusive, set. Whenever the context leaves it open which facts are to count as relevant, it is possible to equivocate about whether I can speak Finnish. It is likewise possible to equivocate about whether it is possible for me to speak Finnish, or whether I am able to, or whether I have the ability or capacity or power or potentiality to. Our many words for much the same thing are little help since they do not seem to correspond to different fixed delineations of the relevant facts.

Tim's killing Grandfather that day in 1921 is compossible with a fairly rich set of facts: the facts about his rifle, his skill and training, the unobstructed line of fire, the locked door and the absence of any chaperone to defend the past, and so on. Indeed it is compossible with all the facts of the sorts we would ordinarily count as relevant in saying what someone can do. It is compossible with all the facts corresponding to those we deem relevant in Tom's case. Relative to these facts, Tim can kill Grandfather. But his killing Grandfather is not compossible with another, more inclusive set of facts. There is the simple fact that Grandfather was not killed. Also there are various other facts about Grandfather's doings after 1921 and their effects: Grandfather begat Father in 1922 and Father begat Tim in 1949. Relative to these facts, Tim cannot kill Grandfather. He can and can't, but under different delineations of the relevant facts. You can reasonably choose the narrower delineation, and say that he can; or the wider delineation, and say that he can't. But choose. What you mustn't do is waver, say in the same breath that he both can and can't, and then claim that this contradiction proves that time travel is impossible.

Exactly the same goes for Tom's parallel failure. For Tom to kill Grandfather's partner also is compossible with all facts of the sorts we ordinarily count as relevant, but not compossible with a larger set including, for instance, the fact that the intended victim lived until 1934. In Tom's case we are not puzzled. We say without hesitation that he can do it, because we see at once that the facts that are not compossible with his success are facts about the future of the time in question and therefore not the sort of facts we count as relevant in saying what Tom can do.

In Tim's case it is harder to keep track of which facts are relevant. We are accustomed to exclude facts about the future of the time in question, but to include some facts about its past. Our standards do not apply unequivocally to the crucial facts in this special case: Tim's failure, Grandfather's survival, and his subsequent doings. If we have foremost in mind that they lie in the external future of that moment in 1921 when Tim is almost ready to shoot, then we exclude them just as we exclude the parallel facts in Tom's case. But if we have foremost in mind that they precede that moment in Tim's extended personal time, then we tend to include them. To make the latter be foremost in your mind, I chose to tell Tim's story in the order of his personal time, rather than in the order of external time. The fact of Grandfather's survival until 1957 had already been told before I got to the part of the story about Tim lurking in ambush to kill him in 1921. We must decide, if we can, whether to treat these personally past and externally future facts as if they were straightforwardly past or as if they were straightforwardly future.

Fatalists—the best of them—are philosophers who take facts we count as irrelevant in saying what someone can do, disguise them somehow as facts of a different sort that we count as relevant, and thereby argue that we can do less than we think—indeed, that there is nothing at all that we don't do but can. I am not going to vote Republican next fall. The fatalist argues that, strange to say, I not only won't but can't; for my voting Republican is not compossible with the fact that it was true already in the year 1548 that I was not going to vote Republican 428 years later. My rejoinder is that this is a fact, sure enough; however, it is an irrelevant fact about the future masquerading as a relevant fact about the past, and so should be left out of account in saying what, in any ordinary sense, I can do. We are unlikely to be fooled by the fatalist's methods of disguise in this case, or other ordinary cases. But in cases of time travel, precognition, or the like, we're on less familiar ground, so it may take less of a disguise to fool us. Also, new methods of disguise are available, thanks to the device of personal time.

Here's another bit of fatalist trickery. Tim, as he lurks, already knows that he will fail. At least he has the wherewithal to know it if he thinks, he knows it implicitly. For he remembers that Grandfather was alive when he was a boy, he knows that those who are killed are thereafter not alive, he knows (let us suppose) that he is a time traveler who has reached the same 1921 that lies in his personal past, and he ought to understand—as we do—why a time traveler cannot change the past. What is known cannot be false. So his success is not only not compossible with facts that belong to the external future and his personal past, but also is not compossible with the present fact of his knowledge that he will fail. I reply that the fact of his foreknowledge, at the moment while he waits to shoot, is not a fact entirely about that moment. It may be divided into two parts. There is the fact that he then believes (perhaps only implicitly) that he will fail; and there is the further fact that his belief is correct, and correct not at all by accident, and hence qualifies as an item of knowledge. It is only the latter fact that is not compossible with his success, but it is only the former that is entirely about the moment in question. In calling Tim's state at that moment knowledge, not just belief, facts about personally earlier but externally later moments were smuggled into consideration.

I have argued that Tim's case and Tom's are alike, except that in Tim's case we are more tempted than usual—and with reason—to opt for a semi-fatalist mode of speech. But perhaps they differ in another way. In Tom's case, we can expect a perfectly consistent answer to the counterfactual question: what if Tom had killed Grandfather's partner? Tim's case is more difficult. If Tim had killed Grandfather, it seems offhand that contradictions would have been true. The killing both would and wouldn't have occurred. No Grandfather, no Father; no Father, no Tim; no Tim, no killing. And for good measure: no Grandfather, no family fortune; no fortune, no time machine; no time machine, no killing. So the supposition that Tim killed Grandfather seems impossible in more than the semi-fatalistic sense already granted.

If you suppose Tim to kill Grandfather and hold all the rest of his story fixed, of course you get a contradiction. But likewise if you suppose Tom to kill Grandfather's partner and hold the rest of his story fixed—including the part that told of his failure—you get a contradiction. If you make *any* counterfactual supposition and hold all else fixed you get a contradiction. The thing to do is rather to make the counterfactual supposition and hold all else as close to fixed as you consistently can. That procedure will yield perfectly consistent answers to the question: what if Tim had not killed Grandfather? In that case, some of the story I told would not have been true. Perhaps Tim might have been the time-traveling grandson of someone else. Perhaps he might have been the grandson of a man killed in 1921 and miraculously resurrected. Perhaps he might have been not a time traveler at all, but rather someone created out of nothing in 1920 equipped with false memories of a personal past that never was. It is hard to say what is the least revision of Tim's story to make it true that Tim kills Grandfather, but certainly the contradictory story in which the killing both does and doesn't occur is not the least revision. Hence it is false (according to the unrevised story) that if Tim had killed Grandfather then contradictions would have been true.

What difference would it make if Tim travels in branching time? Suppose that at the possible world of Tim's story the space-time manifold branches; the branches are separated not in time, and not in space, but in some other way. Tim travels not only in time but also from one branch to another. In one branch Tim is absent from the events of 1921; Grandfather lives; Tim is born, grows up, and vanishes in his time machine. The other branch diverges from the first when Tim turns up in 1920; there Tim kills Grandfather and Grandfather leaves no descendants and no fortune; the events of the two branches differ more and more from that time on. Certainly this is a consistent story; it is a story in which Grandfather both is and isn't killed in 1921 (in the different branches); and it is a story in which Tim, by killing Grandfather, succeeds in preventing his own birth (in one of the branches). But it is not a story in which Tim's killing of Grandfather both does occur and doesn't: it simply does, though it is located in one branch and not the other. And it is not a story in which Tim changes the past. 1921 and later years contain the events of both branches, coexisting somehow without interaction. It remains true at all the personal times of Tim's life, even after the killing, that Grandfather lives in one branch and dies in the other.[6]

Suggested Further Readings

A good analysis appears in Jonathan Harrison, "Doctor Who and the Philosophers or Time Travel for Beginners," *Aristotelean Society Supplement*, 1971.

For an interesting discussion of time travel and identity, see Douglas Ehring, "Personal Identity and Time Travel," *Philosophical Studies* 52 (1987).

See also Donald Williams, "The Myth of Passage," in *The Philosophy of Time*, ed. by R. M. Gale (Garden City, NY: Anchor, 1967), and Jack W. Meiland, "A Two-Dimensional Passage Model of Time Travel," *Philosophical Studies* 26 (1974).

---

[6]The present paper summarizes a series of lectures of the same title, given as the Gavin David Young Lectures in Philosophy at the University of Adelaide in July, 1971. I thank the Australian-American Educational Foundations and the American Council of Learned Societies for research support. I am grateful to many friends for comments on earlier versions of this paper; especially Philip Kitcher, William Newton-Smith, J. J. C. Smart, and Donald Williams.

CHAPTER 7

*T*ime without Change

Sydney Shoemaker

People measure time by certain changes, but could there be time without any changes? Can time pass even if nothing other than the passage of time happens? We can perhaps imagine a "frozen" world in which there is no motion—no decay, growth, or qualitative change. The question is whether a world may be frozen for a certain temporal period. Doubts about this possibility may arise from the belief that the termination of a freeze must have a cause but that no cause is available. This, and a great deal more, is addressed in the following selection.

Sydney Shoemaker is a professor of philosophy at Cornell University. He is the author of numerous articles and books, including Identity, Cause and Mind *(1984) and* Self-Knowledge and Self-Identity *(1963).*

It is a widely held view that the passage of time necessarily involves change in such a way that there cannot be an interval of time in which no changes whatever occur. Aristotle spoke of time as "a kind of affection of motion," and said that, although time cannot be simply equated with motion or with change, "neither does time exist without change."[1] Hume claimed that " 'tis impossible to conceive . . . a time when there was no succession or change in any real existence."[2] And McTaggart presented as something "universally admitted" the contention that "there could be no time if nothing changed" (from which, he claimed, it follows that everything is always changing,

---

[1]*Physics,* bk. IV, ch. II, 218b.

[2]*A Treatise of Human Nature,* ed. by L. A. Selby-Bigge (Oxford, 1888), p. 40.

at least in its relational qualities).[3] Similar claims can be found in the works of contemporary writers.[4]

The claim that time involves change must of course be distinguished from the truism that change involves time. And, as it will be understood in this essay, it must also be distinguished from a truism that Aristotle expressed by saying "if the 'now' were not different but one and the same, there would not have been time," i.e., the truism that if at time t' some time has elapsed since time t, then t' is a different time than t.[5] I do not think that this truism is what Aristotle had in mind in asserting that time involves change, but it, and certain related truisms, have seemed to some philosophers, e.g., to McTaggart, to imply that there are changes that occur with a logically necessary inevitability and relentlessness. Thus the date and time of day is constantly changing, it is constantly becoming later and later, whatever exists is constantly becoming older and older (whether or not it "shows its age"), and not a moment goes by without something that had been future becoming present and something that had been present becoming past. Such changes, if indeed they are changes, are bound to occur no matter how much things remain the same; whatever else happens or fails to happen in the next twenty-four hours, the death of Queen Anne (to use Broad's example) is bound to recede another day into the past.

I do not wish to become embroiled, in this essay, in the controversy as to whether these "McTaggartian" changes deserve to be regarded as genuine changes. My own view is that they do not. But my concern in this essay is with ordinary becoming, not "pure becoming"; my concern is with changes with respect to such properties as color, size, shape, weight, etc., i.e., properties with respect to which something *can* remain *un*changed for any length of time. And though McTaggart may be an exception, I think that philosophers who have claimed that time involves change have generally meant,

---

[3]J. M. E. McTaggart, *The Nature of Existence* (Cambridge, 1927), vol. II, p. II.

[4]See, for example, Bruce Aune's "Fatalism and Professor Taylor," *The Philosophical Review,* 71 (1962), 512–519, p. 518, and, for a somewhat more qualified statement of the view, Jonathan Bennett's *Kant's Analytic* (Cambridge, 1966), p. 175. Bennett makes the acute point that, because of multidimensionality of space and the unidimensionality of time, empty space is measurable in ways in which empty time necessarily is not.

[5]Aristotle, *Physics,* bk. IV, ch. II, 218b.

not of course that everything must always be changing with respect to every such non-McTaggartian property, but that during every interval of time, no matter how short, something or other must change with respect to some such property or other.

This view, unlike the truism that time involves McTaggartian change, has important cosmological consequences. It implies, for example, that the universe cannot have had a temporal beginning unless time itself had a beginning and that the universe cannot come to an end unless time itself can come to an end. The claim that time involves McTaggartian change is compatible with the universe having had a beginning preceded by an infinite span of empty time, for throughout such a span the beginning of the universe, and the various events in its history, would have been "moving" from the remote future toward the present, and this itself would be McTaggartian change. But the kinds of change I am here concerned with are changes of things or substances, not of events, and such a change can occur only while the subject of change exists; the occurrence of such changes involves the existence of a universe of things, and if time involves change then there can be no time during which the universe does not exist.

There is another sort of change, or ostensible change, which must be ruled out of consideration if the claim that time involves change is to assert more than a triviality. Consider Nelson Goodman's term 'grue,' and suppose that this is given the following definition (which, though not Goodman's definition, is common in the literature): "x is grue at t if and only if t is earlier than A.D. 2000 and x is green at t or t is A.D. 2000 or later and x is blue at t." Anything that is green up to A.D. 2000 and remains green for some time after A.D. 2000 necessarily changes at A.D. 2000 from being grue to being nongrue. Clearly, for any interval during which something remains unchanged with respect to any property whatever, we can invent a "grue"-like predicate which that thing either comes to exemplify or ceases to exemplify during that interval. And if we take there to be a genuine property corresponding to every grue-like predicate and count the acquisition or loss of such properties as genuine change, it follows that whenever anything remains unchanged in any respect it changes in some other respect. Now it is notoriously difficult to justify or explicate the intuition that there is a distinction between greenness and grueness which justifies regarding the former but not the latter as a genuine property, and it is correspondingly difficult to justify or explicate the intuition that something does not undergo a genuine change when at the advent of the year A.D. 2000 it ceases to be grue by continuing to be green. But I shall assume in this essay that these intuitions are well founded and shall exclude from consideration "changes" that, intuitively, consist in the acquisition or loss of "positional," i.e., grue-like, qualities. If we do not do this, the view that time involves change becomes trivially and uninterestingly true, and the considerations usually advanced in its favor become irrelevant to it.

Aristotle's statement of his grounds for thinking that time involves change is unclear but suggestive. He says that "when the state of our own minds does not change at all, or we have not noticed its changing, we do not realize that time has elapsed, any more than those who are fabled to sleep among the heroes in Sardinia do when they are awakened; for they connect the earlier 'now' with the later and make them one, cutting out the interval because of their failure to notice it" (*ibid.*). It is not clear to me why Aristotle focuses here on change of "the state of our own minds," although later on I shall venture a suggestion about this. But if we leave this aside, the argument seems to be that time involves change because the awareness, or realization, that an interval of time has elapsed necessarily involves the awareness of changes occurring during the interval. It is not a serious objection to this that sometimes, e.g., when we have been asleep, we are prepared to allow that a good deal of time has elapsed since a given event occurred even though we were not ourselves aware of any changes during the interval, for in such cases it is plausible to hold that our belief that an interval of a certain duration has elapsed is founded on the inductively grounded belief that changes did occur that we could have been aware of had we been awake and suitably situated.

What Aristotle says here seems to be supported by the obvious and often mentioned fact that it is by observing certain sorts of changes, e.g., the movements of clock hands, pendulums, and the sun and stars, that we measure time. Even if what we are measuring is the length of time during which a given object remained *un*changed, it seems necessary that something, namely whatever we are using as our clock, should have changed during that interval. This is perhaps what Aristotle meant when he said that time is directly the measure of motion and only indirectly the measure of rest. At any rate, the fact that we measure time by observing changes lends plausibility to the view that there cannot be an interval of time in which no changes occur. The contrary view can seem to lead to total skepticism about the possibility of measuring time. If it is possible for there to be changeless intervals, then it may seem compatible with my total experience that any number of such intervals, each of them lasting billions of years, should have elapsed since I ate my last meal, despite the fact that the hour hand of my watch has made only one revolution and the fact that my lunch is still being digested. For if such intervals can occur there is apparently no way in which we can be assured of their nonoccurrence; as Aristotle put it, "the non-realization of the existence of time happens to us when we do not distinguish any change" (*ibid.*). And if this is so, we can never know how much time has elapsed since the occurrence of any given past event. But, it may be held, if the supposition that changeless intervals are possible leads to this sort of skepticism, this itself is proof that the supposition is false.

Of course, it is not only by measurement, i.e., by the use of clocks and the like, that we are aware of the existence and extent of intervals of time. We are all possessed of a "sense of time," an ability to judge fairly accurately the length of intervals of time, at least of short intervals, without using any observed change as a standard; one can tell whether the second hand of a clock is slowing down without comparing its movements with those of another clock, and if one hears three sounds in succession one can often tell without the aid of a clock or metronome how the length of the interval between the first and second compares with that of the interval between the second and third. But, although the exercise of this ability to judge the length of temporal intervals need not involve *observing* any change, it is plausible to suppose that as long as one is aware of the passage of time some change must be occurring, namely, at a minimum, a change in one's own cognitive state. Suppose that throughout an interval of five minutes I observe just one object, call it 0, which remains completely unchanged throughout the interval, and that at each point during the interval I know how long I have observed 0 to remain unchanged. Then the content of my knowledge will be different at different moments during the interval. For example, at one time I will know that I have been observing 0 for two minutes, and a minute later I will know that I have been observing 0 for three minutes. And this means that there will be a constant change in my cognitive state as the interval progresses.[6] Possibly it was considerations of this sort that led Aristotle to stress change "in the state of our own minds" in his discussion of the relationship between time and change—although it does not seem to be true to say, as he does, that one must *notice* a change in the state of one's own mind in order to be aware of the passage of time.

These considerations suggest that it is logically impossible for someone to know that nothing, including the state of his own mind, is changing, i.e., for someone to be aware of the existence of a changeless interval during that interval itself. But it does not of course follow from this that it is impossible for someone to be aware of the existence of such an interval before or after its occurrence. To take an analogous case, it is logically impossible that anyone should know, at any given time, that the then current state of the universe is such as to make impossible the existence in it of life and consciousness, yet most of us believe that we have very good reasons for thinking that the universe has been in the very remote past, and will again be in the very remote future, in just such a state. In what follows I

---

[6]Suppose, however, that what I am aware of, at each moment during the interval (after the first minute of it), is only that 0 has remained unchanged—has remained in a certain state which I will call "*S*"—during the immediately preceding minute. (I have, let us suppose, an incredibly short memory span, and after the first minute of the interval my memory does not extend back to the beginning of it.) Would this continuous awareness of lack of change in 0 involve a continuous change in my own state of mind? One might argue that it does, on the grounds that at each instant I know something I did not previously know, namely that at *that* instant 0 is, and has been continuously for one minute, in state *S*. On the other hand, one could argue that my cognitive state at any instant during the interval (after the first minute) consists in a certain predicate's being true of me, namely the predicate "knows that 0 has remained in state *S* for the last minute," and that since the very *same* predicate is true of me throughout there is no change. I shall not here try to resolve the tricky issue of which of these ways of viewing the matter is correct. I shall only remark that the former, according to which awareness, even of changelessness, involves change on the part of the subject of awareness, seems to me essentially the same as C. D. Broad's view that as long as one is conscious there is a "steady movement of the quality of presentedness" along the series of one's experiences; see his *An Examination of McTaggart's Philosophy* (Cambridge, 1938), vol. II, pt. I, p. 308. My present inclination is to regard this kind of "change" as a species of McTaggartian pseudochange. The issues raised by this example are similar to those raised by a very interesting argument of Norman Kretzmann's, to the effect that God must always be changing if he always knows what time it is, and that there is therefore an incompatibility between the claim that God is omniscient and the claim that he is immutable. See Kretzmann's "Omniscience and Immutability," *The Journal of Philosophy*, 63 (1966), 409–421.

shall try to show that it is conceivable that people should have very good reasons for thinking that there are changeless intervals, that they should have well-grounded beliefs about when in the past such intervals have occurred and when in the future they will occur again, and that they should be able to say how long such intervals have lasted or will last. Of course, the fact that people might have good reasons for thinking that something happens does not prove that it is logically possible for that thing to happen; people have had good reasons for thinking that the circle has been squared. But I think that the sorts of grounds there could conceivably be for believing in the existence of changeless intervals are such that no sound argument against the possibility of such intervals can be built on a consideration of how time is measured and of how we are aware of the passage of time.

To the best of my knowledge, it follows from well-established principles of physics that our universe is a perpetually changing one. But what is in question here is not whether it is physically possible for there to be time without change but whether this is logically or conceptually possible. Accordingly, I shall allow myself in what follows to consider "possible worlds" in which the physical laws differ drastically from those which obtain in the actual world. It may be objected that scientific progress brings conceptual change and that within modern physical theory it is not possible to make any sharp distinction between those propositions about time which express logical, or conceptual, claims and those which purport to express synthetic truths of physics. But I think that it is fair to say that those philosophers who have claimed that time involves change have not generally rested their case on recent developments in physics, e.g., relativity theory, and have thought that this claim holds for our ordinary, prescientific, concept of time as well as for the more sophisticated conceptions provided by the physicists. And in dealing with such a view it seems to me legitimate to consider possible worlds in which quite different physical theories would be called for. If someone wishes to maintain that the occupants of such a world would necessarily have a different concept of time than that which the physicists tell us is applicable to our world, I have no objection to make—as long as it is granted that their concept would have enough in common with our notion of time to make it legitimate to regard it as a concept of *time*. I should concede that in allowing myself to speak of worlds that are logically but not physically possible I am making the somewhat controversial assumption that there is a tenable distinction between logically contingent and logically necessary truths. But this assumption is one that I share with the philosophers against whom I am arguing, those who say that time involves change—for I think that this claim is philosophically interesting only if we understand the 'involves' in it as meaning "necessarily involves."

Consider, then, the following world. To the best of the knowledge of the inhabitants of this world all of its matter is contained in three relatively small regions, which I shall call A, B, and C. These regions are separated by natural boundaries, but it is possible, usually, for the inhabitants of this world to pass back and forth from one region to another, and it is possible for much of what occurs in any of the regions to be seen by observers situated in the other regions. Periodically there is observed to occur in this world a phenomenon which I shall call a "local freeze." During a local freeze all processes occurring in one of the three regions come to a complete halt; there is no motion, no growth, no decay, and so on. At least this is how it appears to observers in the other regions. During a local freeze it is impossible for people from other regions to pass into the region where the freeze exists, but when inhabitants of other regions enter it immediately following the end of a freeze they find that everything is as it would have been if the period of the freeze had not occurred. Eggs laid just prior to the beginning of a freeze lasting a year are found to be perfectly fresh; a glass of beer drawn just prior to the beginning of the freeze still has its head of foam, and so forth. And this remains so even when they make the finest measurements, and the most sophisticated tests, available to them; even radioactive decay, if such exists in this world, is found to be completely arrested during the period of a local freeze. Those people who were in the region during the freeze will initially be completely unaware that the period of the freeze has elapsed, unless at the beginning of the freeze they happened to be observing one of the other regions. A man who was stopped in the middle of a sentence by the onset of the freeze will resume the sentence at the end of it, and neither he nor his hearers will be aware that there has been any interruption. However, things will seem out of the ordinary to any inhabitant of a frozen region who at the beginning of the freeze was looking into one of the other regions. To such a person it will appear as if all sorts of major changes have occurred instantaneously in the other region: people and objects will appear to have moved in a discontinuous manner or to have vanished into thin air or to have materialized out of thin air; saplings will appear to have grown instantaneously into mature trees; and so on. Although people might initially refuse to believe that events that seem to them to have only just occurred in fact occurred a year before and that they have been unconscious for a full year, it would seem that they would eventually come to believe this after hearing the reports of observers from other regions and, more important, after they themselves have observed local freezes in other regions.

The possibility of what I have described so far is compatible with the claim that there can be no time without change. That claim is that *something or other* must change during any interval of time and not that everything must change during every interval, and all that I have so far described is a case in which a fairly large percentage of the things in my imaginary world remain unchanged (or apparently unchanged) throughout an interval of time. But now the following seems possible. We can imagine, first, that the inhabitants of this world discover, by the use of clocks located in unfrozen regions, that local freezes always last the same amount of time—let us suppose that the length of freezes is always exactly one year. We can also imagine that they keep records of local freezes and find that they occur at regular intervals—let us suppose that it is found that in region A local freezes have occurred every third year, that in region B local freezes have occurred every fourth year, and that in region C local freezes have occurred every fifth year. Having noticed this they could easily calculate that, given these frequencies, there should be simultaneous local freezes in regions A and B every twelfth year, in regions A and C every fifteenth year, in regions B and C every twentieth year, and in all three regions every sixtieth year. Since these three regions exhaust their universe, to say that there will be simultaneous local freezes in all three regions every sixtieth year is to say that every sixtieth year there will be a *total* freeze lasting one year. Let us suppose that the predicted simultaneous two-region freezes are observed to occur as scheduled (the observers being, in each case, the inhabitants of whichever region remains unfrozen), that no freeze is observed to begin by anyone at the time at which local freezes are scheduled to begin simultaneously in all three regions, and that the subsequent pattern of freezes is found to be in accord with the original generalization about the frequency of freezes. If all of this happened, I submit, the inhabitants of this world would have grounds for believing that there are intervals during which no changes occur anywhere.[7]

The objections that might be made to this (and they are many) can be divided into two sorts. Objections of the first sort maintain, on various grounds, that the inhabitants of my imaginary world could not really have good reasons for believing that no changes whatever occur in a region during an ostensible local freeze in that region. For example, it might be held that, even if the hypothesis that no changes occur in such regions has survived a large number of refinements of their instruments and techniques of measurement, they could never be entitled to believe that further refinements of their instruments and techniques would not show that very slight changes occur during such intervals. Or it might be held that visual observation of an ostensibly frozen region would itself involve the occurrence of changes in that region, namely the transmission of light rays or photons. Objections of the second sort do not question the possibility of there being good reasons for believing in the occurrence of local freezes, but do question the legitimacy of extrapolating from these to the periodic occurrence of total freezes. Later on two objections of this sort will be considered in detail.

I shall not in this essay consider, except in a very general way, objections of the first sort. For though I am inclined to think that all such objections can be met, I think that such objections have limited force even if correct.[8] Even if the inhabitants of this world could not have

---

[7] It is obvious that during a local freeze objects in the frozen region will undergo changes of a kind; they will undergo changes in their relational properties in virtue of the changes that are still going on in the unfrozen regions. But during a total freeze there are no unfrozen regions, and so no changes occur even with respect to relational properties.

[8] Of the two objections of this sort I have mentioned, I think that the first can be met by supposing that the scientific investigations of these people support a "quantum" theory of change which rules out the possibility of changes so slight that they are undetectable by certain instruments. The second could be met by supposing that visual observation in this world does not involve the occurrence of processes in the vicinity of the thing perceived, does not involve the transmission at finite velocities of waves or particles. Alternatively, we can avoid the objection by supposing that while a local freeze exists in a region it is as if the region were divided from the rest of the world by an opaque (and impenetrable) curtain, and that what serves as evidence that no change occurs in regions thus insulated is the fact that when such a region again becomes observable everything appears to be just as it was immediately before the region became insulated.

good grounds for thinking there are intervals in which no changes at all occur, it seems clear that they could have good grounds for thinking there are intervals in which no changes occur that are detectable by available techniques and instruments. And this goes against the view, suggested by Aristotle's remarks, that when we have the well-grounded belief that two events are separated by an interval of time this belief is always grounded, ultimately, on evidence that changes occurred between these events, i.e., is grounded either on observations of such changes or on inductive evidence that such changes occurred. Moreover, if one thinks that the possibility of time without change can be ruled out on verificationist grounds and if it is only objections of the first sort that enable one to maintain that it is impossible to verify the existence of changeless intervals, then one seems to be committed to a view which is much stronger, and intuitively less plausible, than the view that *something or other* must change during every interval of time; one seems committed to the view that *everything* must change during every interval of time. Now there is of course a sense in which a change in any given thing involves a change in the relational properties of everything else. But it now appears that the verificationist must rest his case on the (alleged) impossibility of verifying that anything has remained wholly unchanged even with respect to its *non*relational properties and that he ought to conclude that it is logically impossible for anything to remain unchanged with respect to its nonrelational properties. But this seems no more plausible than the argument from the fact (if it is one) that it is impossible to verify that two things are exactly equal in length to the conclusion that any two things necessarily differ in length.

I turn now to objections of the second sort, and to the first objection that I shall consider in any detail. I have imagined that the inhabitants of my imaginary world come to accept the generalization that local freezes occur in region A every three years, in region B every four years, and in region C every five years, from which it follows that there is a total freeze every sixty years. But why should they accept this generalization? What they observe is equally compatible with the generalization that freezes occur with these frequencies *with the exception* that all three regions skip a freeze every fifty-nine years; or in other words (to put this in a way that makes it sound less ad hoc): one-year local freezes occur in A in cycles in which nineteen freezes occur at the rate of one every third year, with four "freeze-less" years between the last freeze of one cycle and the first freeze of the next; they occur in B in cycles in which fourteen freezes occur at the rate of one every fourth year, with six years between cycles; and they occur in C in cycles in which eleven freezes occur at the rate of one every fifth year, with eight years between cycles. This generalization does not imply that there are ever freezes in all three regions at the same time, and it may be held that for just this reason it should be preferred to the generalization that does imply this.

Now it seems to be generally agreed that if two hypotheses are compatible with the same observed data, we should prefer the simpler of the hypotheses in the absence of a good reason for preferring the other. And the first generalization stated above seems clearly simpler than the second. One reason for preferring the second is the belief that total freezes, i.e., changeless intervals, are impossible. And the most common basis for this belief is the conviction that the existence of changeless intervals is unverifiable. But, on the assumption that the simpler hypothesis is a possible one, the existence of total freezes is verifiable by standard inductive procedures; so one cannot claim that the existence of changeless intervals is unverifiable without begging the question against the possibility of the simpler hypothesis. Of course, the existence of total freezes is not "directly" verifiable, if direct verification of the occurrence of something involves knowing of its occurrence while it is actually occurring. But there are all sorts of things whose occurrence is not directly verifiable in this sense and yet is perfectly possible and knowable; it would be impossible to verify directly, in this sense, that the rotation of the earth would continue if everyone in the universe were sound asleep, yet it is clearly possible that everyone in the universe should at some time be sound asleep, and we all have excellent reasons for believing that if this ever happens the rotation of the earth will continue. I conclude that considerations of verification give no reason for preferring the second hypothesis to the first, and that the first, being simpler, should be preferred unless some other reason for preferring the second can be found.

If one does not find this wholly convincing, this is probably because the generalization that implies the existence of total freezes does not strike one as significantly simpler than its competitor, and because one views the latter not really as a "hypothesis" at all, but rather as a straightforward description of what would actually be observed over a long period of time by the inhabitants of my imaginary world. But I think that this way of viewing the matter becomes less plausible if we introduce some modifications into the example.

So far I have supposed that local freezes are always of the same length, and that whenever local freezes in different regions coincide they do so completely, i.e., begin and end at the same times. Let us now suppose instead that freezes vary in length and that sometimes freezes in two different regions overlap, so that the inhabitants of each region can observe part of the freeze in the other region, namely the part that does not coincide with a freeze in their own region. Let us further suppose that the length of local freezes is found to be correlated with other features of the world. For example, we can suppose that immediately prior to the beginning of a local freeze there is a period of "sluggishness" during which the inhabitants of the region find that it takes more than the usual amount of effort for them to move the limbs of their bodies, and we can suppose that the length of this period of sluggishness is found to be correlated with the length of the freeze. Finally, let us replace the supposition that observed freezes always last one year with the supposition that they always last longer than six months.

It now becomes possible to decide empirically between the two hypotheses stated earlier. First, it is compatible with the first and simpler hypothesis, but not with the second, that during the sixtieth year after the beginning of a cycle some periods of freeze should be observed. For now we are allowing local freezes to overlap and to last for less than a full year, and this allows freezes to be observed even in a year in which there are freezes in all three regions. Perhaps the second hypothesis could be modified in such a way as to allow there to be local freezes during the sixtieth year, as long as there is no interval during which all three regions are simultaneously frozen. This would of course involve asserting that there are exceptions to the rule that freezes always last longer than six months. Moreover, it obviously could turn out that on occasions on which the local freezes in the sixtieth year could not have lasted longer than, say, four months without there having been a period of total freeze, the periods of sluggishness preceding them were observed to be of a length that had been found in other cases to be correlated with freezes lasting, say, seven months. We can of course modify the second hypothesis still further, so that it will assert that there are exceptions to the rule that the length of the freeze is always proportional to the length of the adjacent period of sluggishness, and that these exceptions occur every fifty-nine or sixty years. But this does seem to me to make the hypothesis patently ad hoc. By positing these sorts of exceptions to observed regularities one can of course make the second hypothesis compatible with the observed facts, but it seems to me that this is no more intellectually respectable than the use of the same procedure to protect from empirical falsification the quasi-Berkelian hypothesis that objects disappear when no one is looking at them, or, to take a case closer to home, the hypothesis that it is impossible for there to be an interval of time during which everyone in the world is sound asleep.

This brings me to the last objection that I shall consider. Suppose for the moment that it is correct to describe my imaginary world as one in which there are intervals during which no changes, and hence no events or processes, occur. A question arises as to how, in such a world, processes could get started again after the end of such an interval, i.e., how a total freeze could come to an end. What could *cause* the first changes that occur after there has been a total freeze? In the case of local freezes we might initially suppose that the end of a freeze, i.e., the changes that mark its termination, are caused by immediately preceding events (changes) in regions adjoining the region in which the freeze existed. But we cannot suppose that local freezes are terminated in this way if we want to defend the legitimacy of extrapolating from the frequency of their occurrence to the periodic occurrence of total freezes. For such an extrapolation to be legitimate, we must think of a total freeze as consisting in the simultaneous occurrence of a number of local freezes, the beginnings and endings of which are caused in the same way as are those of the local freezes from which the extrapolation is made. And if a freeze is total, there is no "unfrozen" region adjoining any frozen region, and hence there is no possibility that the end of the freeze in any such region is caused by an immediately preceding event in an adjoining region. If there were evidence that the changes that terminate local freezes are always caused by immediately preceding events in adjoining regions, this would be a reason for rejecting the extrapolation to the existence of total freezes of fixed and finite durations. Nor does it seem open to a defender of the possibility of total freezes to hold that the changes that terminate freezes are uncaused events. For if that were so, it would apparently have to be sheer coincidence that observed freezes always last exactly one year (or, in the modified version of the example, that their length is proportional to that of the temporally adjoining intervals of sluggishness)—and it is illegitimate to extrapolate from an observed uniformity that one admits to be coincidental. So we are faced with the question: by what, if not by an immediately preceding event in an adjoining unfrozen region, could the end of any freeze be caused? And a special case of this is the question of how the end of a total freeze could be caused.

If we make the simplifying assumption that time is discrete, i.e., that for any instant there is a next instant and an immediately preceding instant, it is clear that the cause of the change that ends a total freeze cannot be, and cannot be part of, the state of the world in the immediately preceding instant. For the immediately preceding instant will have occurred during the freeze (will have been the last instant of the freeze), and since no change occurs during a total freeze the state of the world at that instant will be the same as its state at any other instant during the freeze, including the first one. If the state of the world at that instant were causally sufficient to produce a generically different world-state in the immediately following instant, then the freeze would not have occurred at all, for then the change that ends the freeze would have begun immediately after the first instant of the freeze—and a freeze "lasting" only an instant would be no freeze at all.

If time is dense or continuous, of course, we cannot in any case speak of a change as being caused by the state of the world at the immediately preceding instant, for in that case there is no immediately preceding instant. But I think that it is rather commonly supposed that if an event E occurs at time t and is caused, then, for any interval i, no matter how short, that begins at some time prior to t and includes all the instants between that time and t, the sequence of world states that exist during i contains a sufficient cause of E. If this is so, however, the first change that occurs after a total freeze could not have a cause. For let i be an interval with a duration of one second. If the freeze lasted more than one second, then the sequence of states that occurred during i was part of the freeze, and consequently the very same sequence of states occurred during the first second of the freeze. If the occurrence of that sequence of states had been sufficient to initiate the change that ended the freeze, the freeze could not have lasted more than one second. But since we can let i be as small an interval as we like, we can show that if the change that ends the freeze was caused, then the duration of the freeze was shorter than any assignable length, and this is to say that no freeze occurred at all.

It would seem that the only alternative to the view that the termination of a total freeze cannot be caused is the view that there can be a kind of causality that might be called "action at a temporal distance" and that the mere passage of time itself can have causal efficacy. To hold this is to deny the principle, stated above, that if an event is caused then any temporal interval immediately preceding it, no matter how short, contains a sufficient cause of its occurrence. I shall refer to this principle as "P." To suppose P false is to suppose that an event might be caused directly, and not via a mediating causal chain, by an event that occurred a year earlier, or that an event might be caused by such and such's having been the case for a period of one year, where this does not mean that it was caused by the final stage of a process lasting one year. Now I think that we are in fact unwilling to accept the existence of this sort of causality in our dealings with the actual world. If we found that a flash is always followed, after an interval of ten minutes, by a bang, we would never be willing to say that the flashes were the immediate causes of the bangs; we would look for some kind of spatiotemporally continuous causal chain connecting flashes and bangs, and would not be content until we had found one. And if we found that things always explode after having been red for an hour, we would never suppose that what causes the explosion is simply a thing's having been red for an hour; we would assume that there must be some process occurring in something that is red, e.g., the burning of a fuse or the uncoiling of a spring or the building up of an electric charge, and that the explosion occurs as the culmination of this process.

In the *Treatise* (though not in the *Inquiry*) Hume made it part of his definition of "cause" that causes are "contiguous" with their effects. And I think that there is some temptation to think that principle P, which could be thought of as expressing (among other things) the requirement that causes and their effects be temporally contiguous, is an analytic or conceptual truth. Establishing that this is so would not show directly that it is not logically possible for there to be changeless intervals, but it would undermine my strategy for arguing that this is logically possible. For, as we have seen, this would make it illegitimate for the inhabitants of my imaginary world to argue for the existence of total freezes on the basis of the observed frequency of local freezes.

But is P analytically or conceptually true? Here it is useful to distinguish two ostensible sorts of "action at a temporal distance," both of which are ruled out by P. The first might be called "delayed-action causality," and would be possible if the following were possible: X's happening at t is causally sufficient for Y's happening at a subsequent time t', and is compatible with t and t' being separated by an interval during which nothing happens that is sufficient for the occurrence of Y at t'. If in my earlier example we deny that the flash can be the "direct" cause of the bang, we are denying that this sort of causality is operating. I think that it is commonly believed that this sort of causality is logically impossible, and I am inclined to believe this myself. But in order to save the intelligibility of my freeze example we do not need to assume the possibility of this extreme sort of causality at a temporal distance. All that we need to assume is the possibility of the following: X's happening at t is a necessary but not sufficient part of an actually obtaining sufficient condition for Y's happening at t', and t and t' are separated by an interval during which nothing happens that is sufficient for Y's happening at t'. To posit this sort of causality is not necessarily to deny the principle that causes must be temporally contiguous with their effects. If we take something's exploding at t to be the result of its having been red for the preceding hour, there is a sense in which the cause (the thing's having been red for an hour) is temporally contiguous with the effect (the explosion); yet here the thing's having been red at t-minus-one-half-hour is taken to be a necessary though insufficient part of a sufficient condition of its exploding at t, and it is assumed that nothing that happens during the intervening half hour is sufficient to bring about the explosion. Likewise, if S is the state the world is in at every instant during a given total freeze and if E is the event (the change) that terminates the freeze, we can suppose that E is caused by the world's having been in state S for one year without violating the principle that causes are temporally contiguous with their effects, although not without violating principle P. Now we are, as I have already said, quite unwilling to believe that this sort of causality ever occurs in our world. But I am unable to see any conceptual reason why it could not be reasonable for the inhabitants of a world very different from ours to believe that such causality does occur in their world, and so to reject any principle, such as P, which excludes the possibility of such causality. And if this is possible, then in such a world there could, I think, be strong reasons for believing in the existence of changeless intervals.[9]

---

[9]It may be objected that allowing for this sort of causality would complicate the scientific theories of these people so much that it would always be simpler for them to avoid the need of allowing for it by adopting a hypothesis according to which total freezes never occur. But this supposes that they *can* avoid the need for allowing it by adopting such a hypothesis. It seems entirely possible to me that they might find that in order to subsume even *local* freezes under causal laws they have to accept the existence of this sort of causality (e.g., they never succeed in explaining the termination of local freezes in terms of immediately preceding events in adjacent unfrozen regions), and that they might find other phenomena in their world that they are unable to explain except on the assumption that such causality exists.

But here an important reservation must be made. Early in this essay I ruled out of consideration what I called "McTaggartian changes," and in doing so I was implicitly refusing to count certain predicates, e.g., "present" and "ten-years old," as designating genuine properties—these (which I will call "McTaggartian predicates") are predicates something comes to exemplify or ceases to exemplify simply in virtue of the passage of time. In ruling such predicates, and also grue-like predicates, out of consideration, I relied on what seem to be widely shared intuitions as to what are and what are not "genuine" changes and properties. But these intuitions become somewhat cloudy if we try to apply them to a world in which there is action (or causal efficacy) at a temporal distance. Supposing "F" to be a non-McTaggartian predicate, let us define the predicate "F'" as follows: "x is F' at t" = df "at t x is F and has been F for exactly six months." It follows from this definition that if something is F' at t it ceases to be F' immediately thereafter, simply in virtue of the "passage" of t into the past. "F'" seems clearly to be a McTaggartian predicate, like "ten-years old," and one is inclined to say that something does not undergo genuine change in coming or ceasing to be F'. But now suppose that the basic causal laws governing the world are such that the following is true: something's having been F for a period of one year is a causally sufficient condition of its becoming G at the end of that year (where "G" is another non-McTaggartian predicate), and it is not the case that something's having been F for any interval of less than a year is a causally sufficient condition of its becoming G at the end of that interval. Given this, the causal implications of something's being F' at t are different from those of its being F at t; from the fact that something is F' at t, but not from the fact that it is F at t, we can infer that if it continues to be F for another six months it will then become G. And if we introduce another predicate "F''," defining it like "F'" except that "exactly six months" is replaced by "more than six months," we see that "F'" and "F''" are incompatible predicates having different causal implications. Now we are accustomed to regarding the causal properties of things, their "powers," as intrinsic to them, and it is thus plausible to say that, when predicates differ as "F'" and "F''" do in their causal implications, then something does undergo genuine change in ceasing to exemplify one and coming to exemplify the other. But if we say this, then we will have to allow that, in remaining F for a year and not undergoing change with respect to any other non-McTaggartian property, a thing nevertheless undergoes genuine change. And this of course goes counter to the intuition that McTaggartian change is not genuine change. It remains true, I think, that the inhabitants of my imaginary world could have good reasons for thinking that there are intervals during which no non-McTaggartian changes occur— but given the sorts of causal laws they would have to accept in order for it to be reasonable for them to believe this, it is not so clear whether they would be justified, as I think we are in our world, in dismissing McTaggartian changes as not being genuine changes. The determination of whether this is so must wait on a closer examination of the considerations that underlie our intuitions as to the genuineness, or otherwise, of ostensible changes and properties.[10]

Supposing that it is possible for there to be time without change, how are we to answer the skeptical argument mentioned at the beginning of this essay—the argument that we can never be justified in believing that a given amount of time has elapsed since the occurrence of a certain event, since there is no way in which we can know that the interval between that event and the present does not contain one or more changeless intervals, perhaps lasting billions of years? I think the answer to this is that the logical possibility of such intervals, and the fact that such intervals would necessarily be unnoticed while they were occurring, do not prevent us from knowing that such intervals do not in fact occur. Given the nature of our experience of the world, the simplest theories and hypotheses that do justice to the observed facts are ones according to which changeless intervals do not occur. We do not indeed have a set of hypotheses that explain all observed phenomena, but none of the unexplained phenomena are such that there is any reason to think that positing changeless intervals would help to explain them. If our experience of the world were different in describable ways, e.g., if it were like that of the inhabitants of my imaginary world, then, so I have argued, it would be reasonable to believe in the existence of changeless intervals. But even then there would be no basis for skepticism about the measurement of time. The simplest set of hypotheses that did justice to the observed facts would then be one according to which changeless intervals occur only at specified intervals, or under

---

[10]The need for this reservation was impressed on me by Ruth Barcan Marcus, who observed in a discussion of this essay that, if the "mere" passage of time can itself have causal efficacy, it is not clear that it can be dismissed as not being genuine change.

certain specified conditions, where their existence and extent could be known (although not while they were occurring). If anything leads to skepticism it is not the claim that changeless intervals can occur but the claim that they might occur in such a way that their existence could never be detected. But it is not clear to me that even this is a *logical* impossibility, or at any rate that we must assert that it is in order to avoid skepticism. The claim that changeless intervals *do* occur in such a way that their existence cannot in any way be detected could not—and this is a logical "could not"—constitute part of the theory that provides the simplest and most coherent explanation of the observed facts, and this seems to me a sufficient reason to reject it. It is "senseless" in the sense that it could never be sensible to believe it; but it seems to me unnecessary to maintain, in order to avoid skepticism, that it is also senseless in the sense of being meaningless or self-contradictory. This is, in any case, irrelevant to what I have been arguing in this essay, for what I have suggested is that there are conceivable circumstances in which the existence of changeless intervals *could* be detected.

Suggested Further Readings

For a clear treatment of many philosophical issues concerning time, see Paul Horwich, *Asymmetries in Time* (Cambridge, MA: MIT Press, 1987).

There is also relevant material in Richard Swinburne, "The Beginning of the Universe and of Time," *Canadian Journal of Philosophy* 26 (1996); *Space and Time*, 2d ed. (London: Macmillan, 1981); and Donald C. Williams, "The Myth of Passage," *Journal of Philosophy* 48 (1951).

For an interesting discussion of change and time, see Lawrence Lombard, *Events* (London: Routledge, 1986).

CHAPTER 8

*H*ow Fast Does Time Pass?

Ned Markosian

If time does pass, we may ask how quickly it passes. This question seems ridiculous to some people, and it has been argued that the absurdity of the question gives us reason to reject the doctrine of temporal passage. The following selection critically evaluates this line of argument.

Ned Markosian is a philosopher who teaches at West Virginia University. He has written a number of papers bearing on the metaphysics of time, including "The Open Past," Philosophical Studies *vol. 79 (July 1995).*

1   Introduction

I believe that time passes. In the last one hundred years or so, many philosophers have rejected this view. Those who have done so have generally been motivated by at least one of three different arguments: (i) McTaggart's argument, (ii) an argument from the theory of relativity, and (iii) an argument concerning the alleged incoherence of talk about the rate of the passage of time. There has been a great deal of literature on McTaggart's argument (although no consensus has been reached).[1] There has been a relatively small amount of literature on the argument from the theory of relativity, but this is perhaps not surprising, since most of us philosophers

Source: Ned Markosian, "How Fast Does Time Pass?" *Philosophy & Phenomenological Research* 53 (1993):830–44.

[1]McTaggart, John M. E., "Time," in Gale, Richard M. *The Philosophy of Time* (London: Routledge & Kegan Paul, 1968), pp. 86–97. For criticism of the argument, see, for example, Prior, Arthur N., *Past, Present and Future* (Oxford: Oxford University Press, 1967), Chapter I; and Gale, *The Language of Time* (London: Routledge & Kegan Paul, 1968). For attempts to defend the argument, see, for example, Dummett, Michael, "A Defense of McTaggart's Proof of the Unreality of Time," *Philosophical Review* 69 (1960), pp. 497–504; and Mellor, D. H., *Real Time* (Cambridge, Cambridge University Press, 1981).

don't understand that theory.[2] Meanwhile, there has not been a great deal of literature on the rate of passage argument, and this *is* surprising, I think, considering that the argument is easy to understand, is quite plausible, and is suggested in one of the most famous articles in the literature on time.[3]

This paper has two main aims. The first is to say exactly what I mean by 'Time passes.' The second is to spell out the rate of passage argument, and then defend the view that time passes against that argument. In the course of trying to accomplish the first of these aims I hope to make it clear that there are really several quite distinct controversies—linguistic and metaphysical—that are relevant to the controversy over whether time passes. In the course of trying to accomplish the second of these aims I hope to show that the rate of passage argument is not a very good argument against the view that time passes.

2   What I Mean by 'Time Passes'

Let us begin by considering what is involved in saying that time passes. I think it is fair to say that anyone who asserts this is committed to the following general thesis.

> *The passage thesis:* Time is unlike the dimensions of space in at least this one respect: there are some properties possessed by time, but not possessed by any dimension of space, in virtue of which it is true to say that time passes.

In saying that time passes, then, I am baldly asserting the passage thesis. But in what specific ways do I claim that time is so strikingly different from any dimension of space that it makes sense to say that time passes while space does not? In what follows I will spell out three such ways.

To begin with, I think that there are some key linguistic differences between time and space that are relevant here. One linguistic issue that has seemed to many philosophers to be central to the debate

---

[2]For discussions of this matter, see Putnam, Hilary, "Time and Physical Geometry," in Putnam, *Mathematics, Matter and Method* (Cambridge: Cambridge University Press, 1975), pp. 198–205; and Stein, Howard, "On Einstein-Minkowski Space-Time," *Journal of Philosophy* LXV (1968), pp. 5–23.

[3]Smart, J. J. C., "The River of Time," in Flew, Antony (ed.) *Essays in Conceptual Analysis* (New York: St. Martin's Press, 1966), pp. 213–27.

over time's passage is a controversy that may be characterized by the following pair of theses.

> *The tensed view of propositions:* Propositions (or whatever entities are taken to be the bearers of truth and falsity) have truth-values *at times;* the most fundamental semantical locution is "P is v at t," where the term in place of 'P' refers to some proposition, the term in place of 'v' refers to some truth-value, and the term in place of 't' refers to some time.[4]

> *The tenseless view of propositions:* Propositions (or whatever entities are taken to be the bearers of truth and falsity) have truth-values *simpliciter;* the most fundamental semantical locution is "P is v," where the term in place of 'P' refers to some proposition and the term in place of 'v' refers to some truth-value.[5]

One who holds the tenseless view of propositions will accordingly say that a t1 token of the sentence

(1) It is snowing in Boston

expresses the proposition that it snows in Boston at t1, which is a tenseless proposition, i.e., one that simply has a truth-value (but cannot appropriately be said to have truth-values *at times*); whereas one who holds the tensed view of propositions will accordingly say that a t1 token of (1) expresses the proposition that it is snowing in Boston, which is a tensed proposition, i.e., one that has truth-values *at times.*

There is more to the controversy between the tenseless view of propositions and the tensed view of propositions than just this, however. For one who holds the tenseless view of propositions will also be naturally inclined to hold the following thesis about the correct analysis of the past and future tenses of our ordinary language.

> *The eliminability of tense:* The past and future tenses of our ordinary language are to be analyzed away.[6]

Thus, for example, one who holds the tenseless view of propositions and the eliminability of tense will say that a t1 token of the sentence

---

[4]See, for example, Prior, *Past, Present and Future* and *Papers on Time and Tense* (Oxford: Oxford University Press, 1968).

[5]See, for example, Goodman, Nelson, *The Structure of Appearance* (Cambridge: Harvard University Press, 1951), Chapter XI; Quine, Willard van Orman, *Word and Object* (Cambridge: MIT Press, 1960), pp. 170ff; and Smart, "The River of Time."

[6]See the works cited in the last footnote.

(2)   It will be snowing in Boston

is equivalent to a t1 token of some allegedly "tenseless" sentence like

(2a)   There is a time later than this token at which it snows in Boston

or

(2b)   There is a time later than t1 at which it snows in Boston.

Meanwhile, one who holds the tensed view of propositions will also be naturally inclined to hold the following thesis about the correct analysis of the past and future tenses.

> *The ineliminability of tense:* The past and future tenses of our ordinary language are, like the present tense, to be treated as primitive.[7]

Thus, for example, one who holds the tensed view of propositions and the ineliminability of tense will say that any token of (2) is in fact an irreducibly future-tensed sentence token that is not equivalent to any tenseless sentence token.

Let us call the combination of the tenseless view of propositions and the eliminability of tense "the tenseless conception of semantics," and let us call the combination of the tensed view of propositions and the ineliminability of tense "the tensed conception of semantics." Then the linguistic component of my view that time passes is the tensed conception of semantics, together with the claim that nothing analogous to the tensed conception of semantics is true with regard to any dimension of space.[8]

Next I want to discuss a controversy that combines linguistic and metaphysical issues, and that has long been thought to be central to the debate over whether time really passes. This is the issue of whether there really are such properties as the apparently monadic,

---

[7]See, for example, Prior, *Past, Present and Future* and *Papers on Time and Tense;* and Chisholm, Roderick M., *On Metaphysics* (Minneapolis: University of Minnesota Press, 1989), p. 163.

[8]For an example of one who holds spatial views analogous to the tensed conception of semantics see Sosa, Ernest, "Propositions and Indexical Attitudes," in Parret, H. (ed.), *On Believing* (Walter de Gruyter Verlag, 1983), pp. 316–32.

My reasons for rejecting the spatial analogue of the tensed conception of semantics have to do with my belief that time is strikingly different from the dimensions of space in certain metaphysical ways spelled out below. But of course a non-passage theorist will not be impressed by this argument.

temporal properties *pastness, presentness* and *futurity,* or whether, instead, talk that appears to be about such properties is really analyzable in terms of talk about such binary, temporal relations as *earlier than, simultaneous with* and *later than.*

Let us agree to refer to monadic, temporal properties such as *pastness, presentness* and *futurity*—if there are any such properties—as *A-properties.* Similarly, let us agree to refer to binary, temporal relations such as *earlier than, simultaneous with* and *later than* as *B-relations.*[9] Then the two sides to the controversy can be characterized by the following theses.

> *The A-property thesis:* There really are A-properties; talk that appears to be about the possession of A-properties by times, events or things cannot be correctly analyzed in terms of B-relations among those entities.[10]

> *The B-relation thesis:* There are no genuine A-properties: talk that appears to be about the possession of A-properties by times, events or things can be correctly analyzed in terms of B-relations among those entities.[11]

Anyone who accepts the tenseless conception of semantics should also accept the B-relation thesis. In order to see why, consider the following sentence.

(3) The 1984 World Series was nine years ago.

(3) appears to attribute to a certain event—the 1984 World Series—the property *being nine years past.* But according to the tenseless conception of semantics, (3) does no such thing. This is because, according to the tenseless conception of semantics, (3) can be correctly analyzed into something like the following.

(3a) The 1984 World Series is nine years earlier than this token.

If (3) *could* be correctly analyzed into something like (3a), then something that appears to be talk about the possession of an A-property by an event could be analyzed in terms of talk about B-relations among events. Similar remarks would, presumably, apply to the tenseless

---

[9]I am here following Gale, who in turn has followed McTaggart. See McTaggart, "Time," and Gale, *The Language of Time.*

[10]See, for example, Prior, *Past, Present and Future,* esp. pp. 4–7.

[11]See, for example, Smart, "The River of Time."

conception of semantics and its treatment of other sentences that appear to attribute A-properties to times, events or things. Thus the tenseless conception of semantics entails the *B-relation* thesis.

Meanwhile, anyone who accepts the *tensed* conception of semantics should also accept the A-property thesis. For according to the tensed conception of semantics, (3) is an irreducibly past-tensed sentence that cannot be correctly analyzed into anything like (3a). If (3) cannot be correctly analyzed into anything like (3a), this must be because (3) *expresses* something that cannot be expressed by anything like (3a). And what (3) appears to express is that the event in question possesses the property *being nine years past*, which is an A-property. Similar remarks would, presumably, apply to the tensed conception of semantics and its treatment of other sentences that appear to attribute A-properties to times, events or things. Thus the tensed conception of semantics entails the A-property thesis.

In addition, it seems to me that the A-property thesis entails the tensed conception of semantics. For suppose that there really are such monadic, temporal properties as *being nine years past*. Then presumably sentence (3) above attributes *being nine years past* to the 1984 World Series. Apparently, then, there is such a proposition as the proposition that the 1984 World Series has the property *being nine years past*. But surely this proposition is one that has been false in the past, is true now, and will be false again in the future; and if there is such a proposition then the tensed conception of semantics is correct.

The A-property thesis, together with the claim that there are no spatial properties analogous to A-properties, is the second component of my view that time passes.[12]

---

[12]Let us agree to refer to monadic, spatial properties such as *being north, being south* and *being west*—if there are any such properties—as *C-properties*. Similarly, let us agree to refer to binary, spatial relations such as *being north of, being south of* and *being west of* as *D-relations*. Then the two sides to the spatial controversy can be characterized by the following theses.

> *The C-property thesis:* There really are C-properties; talk that appears to be about the possession of C-properties by places, events or things cannot be correctly analyzed in terms of D-relations among those entities.

> *The D-relation thesis:* There are no genuine C-properties; talk that appears to be about the possession of C-properties by places, events or things can be correctly analyzed in terms of D-relations among those entities.

The C-property thesis is the spatial analogue of the A-property thesis; but although I hold the latter, I reject the former. I do not think that there are any genuine, monadic, spatial properties like *being north*.

Suppose that the A-property thesis is correct, i.e., suppose that there really are genuine, monadic, temporal properties like *being nine years past*. Then a number of questions naturally arise concerning the nature of A-properties. What exactly are A-properties? Which things may possess them? What are the conditions under which it is true that a thing possesses an A-property?

I don't know exactly how to answer all of these and related questions about the nature of A-properties. In fact, I'm not even sure that it would be appropriate to try to answer all of these questions. In particular, I think that it would be a mistake to try to analyze talk about A-properties in terms of some other, allegedly better understood, concepts (even if those other concepts were not B-relations). I think that this would be a mistake for two main reasons. First, I can't imagine what such an analysis would look like. What might be the other concepts in terms of which we could analyze talk about A-properties? And second, given that it is impossible to analyze everything, so that it is necessary to take some concepts as primitive, it seems to me that A-properties are excellent candidates for the kind of property that we ought to take as primitive. After all, everyone already has a fairly intuitive sense of what it means to say that a certain time or event is *past*. So there is no particularly pressing need to come up with a scheme for analyzing away such talk.

Still, it may be helpful to say some things about the nature of A-properties. For starters we can safely say that times and events are among the things that may possess A-properties. Thus, for example, we can say that the year 2000 currently possesses the property *being future*, and that the 1984 World Series currently possesses the property *being past*.

Another point that seems to me an important component of the A-property thesis is that talk about A-properties does not merely describe some linguistic or mind-dependent phenomenon. That is, it seems to me that it is a genuine and objective fact about the world that 3:38 P.M., Thursday, March 19 is currently present, that various other times are currently past or future, and that, moreover, these things would be true even if there were no conscious beings and no language users in the world.

Another crucial point to be made about A-properties is that there is a certain inexorability about the process by which times and events successively possess different A-properties. January 1st, 2000 is currently future, but it is becoming less and less remotely future all the time, and there is nothing that anyone can do to halt or even to slow this process.

A final point that it seems to me important to make about A-properties is that there is no spatial analogue to any phenomenon involving A-properties. There are no genuine, monadic, spatial properties analogous to pastness, presentness and futurity; there are certainly no such properties as *being north, being south* or *being west,* although there are such binary, spatial relations as *being north of, being south of* and *being west of.* Since there are no spatial analogues of the A-properties, it of course follows that there is no spatial analogue to the process by which times and events successively possess different A-properties. Moreover, there is not any sense in which either locations in space or events successively stand in different binary, spatial relations—like *being north of*—to one another in some *inexorable* way.

In what follows, I will refer to the process by which times and events successively possess different A-properties as *the pure passage of time,* and I will refer to the thesis that there is such a process as *the pure passage of time thesis*. It should be obvious, given these definitions, that anyone who holds the A-property thesis should also hold the pure passage of time thesis.[13] The pure passage of time thesis, then, together with the claim that there is no spatial analogue to the pure passage of time, is the third component of my view that time passes.[14]

At the beginning of this section I characterized the passage thesis as saying that there are certain properties possessed by time, but not possessed by any dimension of space, in virtue of which it is true to say that time passes. So far I have said that I hold several different

---

[13]I suppose it would be consistent to hold that there really are A-properties, but deny that times and events successively possess different A-properties. That is, there would be no outright contradiction in holding the A-property thesis and at the same time rejecting the pure passage of time thesis. For one could hold, in effect, that time is stuck; i.e., that 3:38 P.M. on March 19th, 1992, for example, is, always has been and always will be present, while certain other times always have been and always will be past, while still others always have been and always will be future. But I can't imagine why anyone would hold such a thing.

[14]I'm not sure what the spatial analogue of the pure passage of time thesis would amount to, actually, but I'm sure that I would want to deny it if I understood it. For I don't think that locations in space or events undergo any kind of change that could be considered the spatial analogue of the pure passage of time.

views about time: the tensed conception of semantics, the A-property thesis, and the pure passage of time thesis. I've also said that I reject the spatial analogues of these theses. Now, I think it is pretty clear that my subscription to a package consisting of the relevant theses that I hold about time, together with the rejections of their spatial analogues, gives me ample justification for saying that time passes.

Here are just two reasons for this claim. (i) In virtue of my subscription to the tensed conception of semantics, and my rejection of its spatial analogue, I can justifiably say that many propositions (or whatever are the bearers of the truth-values) pass, over time, from being true to being false and *vice versa*, whereas no proposition does any such thing over any dimension of space. (ii) In virtue of my subscription to the A-property thesis and the pure passage of time thesis, together with the denial of their spatial analogues, I can justifiably say that times and events pass inexorably, over time, from being future to being present and then on to being more and more remotely past, whereas places and events do no analogous thing over any dimension of space. Note that while (i) involves a semantical claim, (ii) involves a purely metaphysical claim. As I see it, the A-property thesis and the pure passage of time thesis together constitute the essential, metaphysical core of the view that time passes, while the tensed conception of semantics is simply the semantical view that naturally accompanies that metaphysical core.

3   The Rate of Passage Arguments

In this section I will discuss two distinct but closely related arguments that have been brought against the view that time passes. As far as I can tell, these arguments, or arguments very much like them, were first suggested in the literature by C. D. Broad.[15] But J. J. C. Smart has probably been the most earnest proponent of The Rate of Passage Arguments, and it is to him that I will look for a statement of the arguments.

---

[15]Broad, C. D., "Ostensible Temporality," in Gale, *The Philosophy of Time*, p. 124. See also Smart, "The River of Time," pp. 214–16; Smart, *Philosophy and Scientific Realism*, p. 136; Prior, "Changes in Events and Changes in Things"; Schlesinger, "How Time Flies," *Mind* XCI (1982), pp. 501–23, esp. 507ff; and Zwart, *About Time* (Amsterdam: North Holland Publishing Co., 1976), chapter V.

In his famous article, "The River of Time," Smart argues against the idea that time can properly be thought of as something that flows like a river.

> If time is a flowing river we must think of events taking time to float down this stream, and if we say 'time has flowed faster to-day than yesterday' we are saying that the stream flowed a greater distance to-day than it did in the same time yesterday. That is, we are postulating a second time-scale with respect to which the flow of events along the first time-dimension is measured. 'To-day', 'to-morrow', 'yesterday', become systematically ambiguous. They may represent positions in the first time-dimension, as in 'to-day I played cricket and to-morrow I shall do so again', or they may represent positions in the second time-dimension, as in 'to-day time flowed faster than it did yesterday'. Nor will it help matters to say that time always flows at the *same* rate. Furthermore, just as we thought of the first time-dimension as a stream, so will we want to think of the second time-dimension as a stream also; now the speed of flow of the second stream is a rate of change with respect to a third time-dimension, and so we can go on indefinitely postulating fresh streams without being any better satisfied.[16]

As I see it, the argument that Smart is suggesting here begins with the claim that we can understand the idea of time's *flowing* or *passing* only if we posit some second time-dimension in terms of which we can explicate the flowing or passing of normal time. This claim would presumably be justified by an appeal to some principle about the meaning of the words 'flow' and 'pass' when applied to time. The principle might be formulated as follows.

> *P1:*   For any time-dimension, T, if T *flows* or *passes,* then there is some time-dimension, T′, such that T′ is distinct from T, and the flow or passage of events in T is to be measured with respect to T′.

The argument also involves the claim that if time flows or passes, then in order for *any* time-dimension to be a legitimate

---

[16]Smart, "The River of Time," pp. 214–15.

time-dimension, it must flow or pass. This claim would presumably be defended by appeal to a principle that could be formulated as follows.

> *P2:* If flowing or passing is a characteristic of time, then flowing or passing must be an essential characteristic of any time-dimension.

More is needed, however, in order to ensure that, as Smart says, "we can go on indefinitely." It must also be claimed that the passage of any time-dimension is to be measured only with respect to some previously unmentioned time-dimension. This principle might be formulated as follows.

> *P3:* For any series of time-dimensions, T1, . . ., Tn, such that the passage of each of the first n-1 members of the series is to be measured with respect to the next member of the series, the passage of Tn must be measured with respect to some time-dimension, Tm, such that Tm is distinct from each member of the series T1–Tn.

Now the argument can be formulated as follows.

The First Rate of Passage Argument

(1) If time flows or passes, then there is some second time-dimension with respect to which the passage of normal time is to be measured.

(2) If there is some second time-dimension with respect to which the passage of normal time is to be measured, then the second time-dimension must flow or pass.

(3) If the second time-dimension flows or passes, then there must be some third time-dimension with respect to which the passage of the second time-dimension is to be measured, and, hence, some fourth time-dimension with respect to which the passage of the third time-dimension is to be measured, and so on *ad infinitum.*

(4) It's not the case that there is some third time-dimension with respect to which the passage of the second time-dimension is to be measured, and, hence, some fourth time-dimension with respect to which the passage of the third time-dimension is to be measured, and so on *ad infinitum.*

---

(5) It's not the case that time flows or passes.

Whatever plausibility this argument has is due to premises (2)–(4). If acceptance of the view that time passes commits one to some kind of infinite series of time-dimensions, then that view would surely be untenable to any but the most wildly free-spending of ontologists. But I can see no reason why I should accept premise (1) of this argument, or P1, the principle on which that premise is based. For although the linguistic and metaphysical components of my view give me ample reason for asserting the passage thesis. Smart has said nothing yet to demonstrate that I am in any way committed to a second time-dimension with respect to which the passage of normal time is to be measured. So I reject premise (1) of The First Rate of Passage Argument. (I will have more to say below about the details of my rejection of premise (1) of The First Rate of Passage Argument.)

Immediately after the passage quoted above from "The River of Time," Smart goes on to say some things that are, I think, intended to provide justification for the claim that if time flows or passes, then there must be some second time-dimension with respect to which the passage of normal time is to be measured.

> A connected point is this: with respect to motion in space it is always possible to ask 'how fast is it?' An express train, for example, may be moving at 88 feet per second. The question, 'How fast is it moving?' is a sensible question with a definite answer: '88 feet per second.' We may not in fact know the answer, but we do at any rate know what sort of answer is required. Contrast the pseudo-question 'How fast am I advancing through time?' or 'How fast did time flow yesterday?' We do not know how we ought to set about answering it. What sort of measurements ought we to make? We do not even know the sort of units in which our answer should be expressed. 'I am advancing through time at how many seconds per___?' we might begin, and then we should have to stop. What could possibly fill in the blank? Not 'seconds' surely. In that case the most we could hope for would be the not very illuminating remark that there is just one second in every second.[17]

The argument suggested here, it seems to me, is based on the claim that to say that time passes is to raise a question that cannot be coherently answered. The question is 'How fast does time pass?'

---

[17]Smart, "The River of Time," p. 215.

That this question arises from the claim that time passes would presumably be defended by an appeal to something like the following principle.

P4: For any thing, x, if x changes, then x changes at some rate.

That the question 'How fast does time pass?' cannot be coherently answered would presumably be defended in part by an appeal to a definition like the following.

R is a *rate* = df there is some parameter, P, and number, n, such that R = n units of P per unit of time.

To this definition would be added two further claims: (i) the claim that the first parameter involved in the rate of the passage of time would have to be time, so that the rate of the passage of time would be something of the form "n units of time per unit of time"; and (ii) a claim to the effect that something of the form "n units of time per unit of time" does not express a coherent rate. The definition of 'rate,' then, together with these two claims, would justify the premise that the question 'How fast does time pass?' cannot be coherently answered.

Finally, the argument also depends on some principle like the following.

P5: For any thing, x, if x flows or passes, then it is possible to state coherently the rate at which x flows or passes.

This second rate of passage argument can now be formulated as follows.

The Second Rate of Passage Argument

(1) If it makes sense to say that time passes, then it makes sense to ask 'How fast does time pass?'

(2) If it makes sense to ask 'How fast does time pass?', then it's possible for there to be a coherent answer to this question.

(3) It's not possible for there to be a coherent answer to this question.

(4) It doesn't make sense to say that time passes.

This, it seems to me, is a very interesting argument, and one that raises several important issues about the ways in which we talk about the passage of time, in particular, and rates of change, in general. But

I also think that once these issues are spelled out, it can be shown that the argument fails.

In order to explain this it will first be necessary to say some things about rates. In order to discuss a paradigm case involving the rate of some process, let us suppose that it is 1964 and we are watching Abebe Bikila run in the Olympic marathon in Tokyo. For the sake of simplicity we will suppose that Bikila's rate is constant throughout the race. What exactly is the procedure that we would go through in order to find out how fast Bikila is running? Well, it might be something like this: we first check Bikila's position on the course by noting that he is passing a certain mile-marker, and, at roughly the same time, we check the time; then we note when Bikila passes the next mile-marker, and again check the time; if we find that five minutes have passed while Bikila has run one mile then we will know that he is running at the rate of one mile per five minutes, or twelve miles per hour.

But of course we check the time at the appropriate moments during this procedure by consulting a clock. Thus, our investigation reveals that while Bikila's position on the course changes by one mile, the position of the hands on the clock change by the amount that marks off five minutes. Since we can assume that the rate of Bikila's change in position is constant, and also that the rate of the change in position of the hands on the clock is constant, we are in effect comparing the rates of these two changes to one another. But, of course, we really have no special interest in the rate of the change in position of the hands on that particular clock; our interest in the clock is only due to the fact that we take it to be so calibrated that it changes at a constant rate; a rate, that is, that by convention we use to measure periods of time. This conventional rate is not just any old rate; it is supposed to be the rate at which the sun changes its position in the sky. Really, then, the clock is a stand-in for the sun; and what we have really done in carrying out our procedure is to compare the rate of Bikila's change of position to the rate of the sun's change of position. Our investigation has revealed that while Bikila's position on the course changes by one mile, the sun's position in the sky changes by roughly one and one-quarter degrees.

Such are the mechanics of our talk about the rates of such physical processes as Bikila's motion. It may seem, however, that there is something deeper going on when we make the appropriate investigations and find out that Bikila is traveling at the rate of twelve miles per hour. While we have in practice merely compared the rate of one physical change to the rate of another, it may seem that we have at least *attempted* to do something quite different. For just as we are not really interested in the rate of the change of position of the hands on our clock, so we are not, it seems, really interested in the rate of the change of position of the sun: the latter change is also meant to be a stand-in for a more important change, namely, the pure passage of time. Indeed, it seems that our assumption that the sun's position changes at a constant rate amounts to the assumption that the sun's position changes at the rate of *fifteen degrees per hour,* i.e., that every time the sun moves fifteen degrees across the sky, one hour of pure time passes. So it at least appears that what we are after in trying to determine the rates of various physical processes, such as Bikila's running of the marathon, are the rates at which those processes occur in comparison to the rate of the pure passage of time.

Of course, such comparisons are not possible if the pure passage of time thesis is false. For suppose that the pure passage of time thesis is false. Then the sentence 'Bikila is running at the rate of twelve miles per hour' cannot mean that Bikila runs twelve miles in each hour of pure time; rather, it must mean something like this: Bikila runs twelve miles each time the sun's position changes by fifteen degrees. This latter change would then be simply a standard, chosen by convention, for comparing rates and lengths of various changes. But the standard wouldn't stand for anything else—it would not serve as a marker for approximating the pure passage of time. And if it should turn out one day that the motion of the sun in the sky appears to speed up drastically relative to other changes, then we should say, not that the motion of the sun has sped up drastically relative to the pure passage of time, while every other change has maintained its rate, but, rather simply that the sun's motion has sped up relative to the other normal changes. We may then want to choose another standard for comparing the rates and lengths of changes, especially if the speed of the sun seems to have become erratic.

So if the pure passage of time thesis is false, then all of our talk about the rates of different changes must be understood as talk that is meant to compare the rate of one ordinary change to the rate of another; a question such as 'How fast does x change?' must be a question about the speed of the change in x relative to the speed of some other change(s). It just so happens that in answering such questions we generally select the change in the position of the sun as the second change, to which the first one is compared.

On the other hand, if the pure passage of time thesis is true, as I think it is, then talk about rates can be understood in either of several ways. We could say that such talk simply consists of comparisons between the rates of different changes, sometimes including the pure passage of time; or we could say that talk about rates essentially involves comparisons between the rates of different changes and the rate of the pure passage of time. If we say the latter, then we must say that whenever we select some observable change (such as the change in the position of the sun, or the change in the position of the hands on a clock) for the purpose of measuring a particular change whose rate we are interested in, that observable change is merely a stand-in for the pure passage of time.

Two main questions arise, then, concerning our talk about rates: Is there really such a thing as the pure passage of time? And even if there is such a thing, what is essential about rate talk—the comparison of any two changes, or the comparison of one change to the pure passage of time?

All of this is relevant to The Second Rate of Passage Argument, since, as one who says that time passes, I am compelled to answer these two questions. I have already made it clear that I give an affirmative answer to the first question. Since I say that there is such a thing as the pure passage of time, it at least appears that I should admit that 'Time passes' is literally true, so that I cannot easily reject premise (1) of The Second Rate of Passage Argument. But I have a choice to make about how to answer the second question about rate talk.

Suppose I claim that talk about any rate essentially involves a comparison between two different changes, but that it need not be the case that one of the changes compared is the pure passage of time. (I might support this position by pointing out that in at least some instances we speak of a certain rate without appearing to make any reference to time. For example, one can sensibly say that during the 1989 NFL season, Joe Montana's passing totals increased at the rate of 21 completions per game.) Then I will think that any time one gives the rate of some change in terms of some second change, one has likewise given the rate of the second change. (If, for example, I tell you that Montana's passing totals increased at the rate of 21 completions per game, then I have also told you that the games progressed at the rate of one game per 21 completions by Montana). Hence, whenever one gives the rate of some normal change in what is admittedly the standard way, i.e., in terms of the pure passage of time, then one has likewise given the rate of the pure passage of time in terms of the first change. If I tell you that Bikila is running at the rate of twelve miles per hour of the pure passage of time, for example, then I have also told you that the pure passage of time is flowing at the rate of one hour for every twelve miles run by Bikila.

If I take this line then I should reject premise (3) of The Second Rate of Passage Argument, while still insisting that it is literally true that time passes. For I will in this case think that it is possible to state coherently the rate at which time passes, and that this information is in fact given each time the rate of some normal change is described in terms of the pure passage of time. Moreover, if I take this line then I will be rejecting premise (1) of The First Rate of Passage Argument on the grounds that the passage line is a change whose rate may be measured with respect to the rate of any normal change, so that there is no need for me to posit any second time-dimension with respect to which the passage of normal time is to be measured.

Suppose I claim that all talk about rates is essentially talk comparing some change to the pure passage of time; there is still, it seems to me, an important choice for me to make with regard to how we are to understand rate talk. For I might believe that there are no restrictions on what kinds of change can be sensibly compared to the pure passage of time; in particular, it may be sensible to compare the pure passage of time to itself. According to this view, the question 'How fast does time pass?' is a sensible question with a sensible answer: time passes at the rate of one hour per hour. Thus, if I take this line, then I should reject premise (3) of The Second Rate of Passage Argument, but I will still be able to maintain that it is literally true that time passes.[18] Moreover, if I take this line, then I will be rejecting premise (1) of The First Rate of Passage Argument on the grounds that the passage of time is a change whose rate may be measured with respect to itself, so that there is no need for me to posit any second time-dimension with respect to which the passage of normal time is to be measured.

Finally, I may choose to say that what is essential about rate talk is that it involves a comparison between some normal change and the pure passage of time. According to this view, it does not make sense to ask about the rate of the passage of time, for to do so is to make a category mistake: the answer would have to involve a comparison between

---

[18]Prior suggests something like this as a possible response in "Changes in Events and Changes in Things," pp. 2–3.

the pure passage of time and the pure passage of time, but such an answer would not make sense because the pure passage of time has a unique status among changes—it is the one to which other, normal changes are to be compared. It is the paradigm, and, as such, it alone among changes cannot be measured.[19] If I take this line then I should accept premise (3) of The Second Rate of Passage Argument, but then I will be compelled to reject premise (1) of that argument, and I will still be able to maintain that time literally passes. Moreover, if I take this line then I will be rejecting premise (1) of The First Rate of Passage Argument on the grounds that the passage of time is a change whose rate simply cannot be measured, so that there is no need to posit any second time-dimension with respect to which the passage of normal time is supposed to be measured.

4 Conclusion

I have spelled out what I mean by 'Time passes.' Then I have considered two related arguments, suggested by Smart, against my view. The first of these involves a premise that says that if time passes then there is some second time-dimension with respect to which the passage of normal time is to be measured. I claimed that there was no reason for me to accept this premise, and so I rejected the first of Smart's arguments.

Consideration of The Second Rate of Passage Argument proved to be more complicated. But I have argued that that argument raises certain questions about how we should understand our talk about rates. Then I have tried to show that, whichever one I choose from among the coherent ways of answering those questions, there is some premise of Smart's argument that is, according to the way I have answered the relevant questions, clearly false.

---

[19]Wittgenstein makes analogous remarks about the standard meter: "There is *one* thing of which one can say neither that it is one metre long, nor that it is not one metre long, and that is the standard metre in Paris.—But this is, of course, not to ascribe any extraordinary property to it, but only to mark its peculiar role in the language-game of measuring with a metre-rule." (Wittgenstein, Ludwig, *Philosophical Investigations,* translated by G. E. M. Anscombe, third edition (New York: Macmillan Publishing Co., 1968), 50.)

I conclude that, while the rate of passage arguments raise some interesting questions about the pure passage of time and how we ought to understand our talk about the rates of various changes, these arguments pose no real threat to my version of the view that time passes.[20]

Suggested Further Readings

See George Schlesinger, "How Time Flies," *Mind* XCI (1982), and J. J. C. Smart, "The River of Time," in *Essays in Conceptual Analysis,* ed. by Antony Flew (New York: St. Martin's Press, 1966).

See also Clifford Williams, "The Metaphysics of A- and B-Time," *Philosophical Quarterly* (1996).

---

[20]I am grateful to Mark Aronszajn, Fred Feldman, Edmund Gettier, Gareth B. Matthews, Theodore R. Sider and Timm Triplett for helpful comments on earlier versions of this paper. I am also grateful to the members of the philosophy departments at the University of New Hampshire and West Virginia University, where earlier versions of this paper were discussed in departmental colloquia. Finally, I am indebted to several journal referees for helpful comments on earlier versions of this paper.

PART III

*E*xistence

CHAPTER 9

Space, Time, and Universals

Nicholas Wolterstorff

Some metaphysicians draw a distinction between particular things (particulars) and universal things (universals). This issue is addressed in the following selection. Is the particular–universal distinction a distinction between things that are not repeatable and things that are repeatable? We need an analysis of repeatability. The cat that I currently see has a definite location. The cat is not repeatable in the sense of having many different locations at a given time, but some things may be repeatable in this sense. This proposal is explored here by Nicholas Wolterstorff.

Nicholas Wolterstorff, professor of philosophy at Yale University, is the author of many philosophy papers and of On Universals *(1970).*

1.   Thus far in our discussion we have been dealing with what I have called *predicables*. We have distinguished predicables from nonpredicables, or *substances;* and we have drawn this distinction by using the concept of (nonlinguistic) predication. A predicable is what can be predicated, a substance is what cannot be predicated.

It turns out, on these definitions, that the class of substances is a very mixed bag of things. Not only exemplifications, but also cases of predicables are substances; for example, not only Napoleon, but also Napoleon's brashness. And among those substances which are exemplifications of predicables are to be found not only events and physical objects and persons, but also such entities as poems, symphonies, species, classes, groups, organizations, stuffs, and propositions. For though, to give but one example, one can of course predicate *being*

Bartok's Fifth Quartet of something, one cannot predicate Bartok's Fifth Quartet itself.

Among predicables, further, we drew a distinction between those which can fittingly be called *universals* and those which cannot be. The distinction was that between those which can be truly predicated of more than one thing, and those which can not be truly predicated of more than one thing. *Being identical with Napoleon* is a predicable nonuniversal, as is *being a round square;* whereas *being identical with someone named "Napoleon"* is a predicable universal, for it is possible that it should be truly predicated of more than one thing.

Just as there can be exemplifications of a single predicable universal, so, analogously, there can be many copies, and many recitations, of a single literary work (for example, "Sailing to Byzantium"). There can be many performances of a single musical work (Bartok's Fifth Quartet). There can be many copies, and many showings, of a single film ("Blowup"). There can be many inscriptions, and many utterances, of a single word or sequence of words. There can be many impressions of a single art-print (Rembrandt's "Hundred Guilder Print"). There can be many performances of a single dance (The Zuni Rain Dance). There can be many castings of a single sculpture (Rodin's "The Thinker"). There can be many productions of a single car-model (the '32 Ford Victoria), of a single house-model (the Tech-Bilt House), of a single chair-model (the Barcelona Chair), of a single flag (the American Flag). There can be many playings of a single game (baseball). There can be many copies, and many productions, and many performances, of a single drama. There can be many issues of a single newspaper (*The Grand Rapids Press*), many numbers of a single journal, many editions of a single book. There can be many executions of a single play or move in a game (the Draw-Play). There can be many doings of a single exercise (the push-up). There can be many uses of a single argument. There can be many printings of a single stamp. There can be many mintings of a single coin (the Buffalo-Head Nickel). There can be many examples of a single genus or species (the Lion). There can be many cases of a single disease.

In all these cases one feels, I think, a strong analogy between the fact cited, and the fact that there can be many exemplifications of a predicable. Now in every such case there is present, of course, a one–many contrast. But the feeling of analogy must have deeper roots than this. For everything whatsoever is such that it bears *some*

relation to many things. A painting, for example, can have many re-
productions; a father, many children; a house, many doors; but we
do not feel any strong analogy between these facts and the fact that a
predicable can have many exemplifications. Nor, I think, do we feel
any strong analogy between this fact and the facts that a class can
have many members, that a group or organization can have many
members, and that a stuff can have many quantities of it.

It is well known that more sorts of things than predicables have
been called universals. The whole medieval and ancient tradition regarded natural kinds—species and genera—as universals; and contemporary philosophers have frequently cited such things as literary
works and musical works as examples of universals. In this and the
following chapter I wish to see what, if anything, can be made of this
concept of universal, a concept such that both predicables and nonpredicables fall under it. Is there any significant analogy between the
relation of a predicable to its exemplifications, on the one hand,
and, on the other, the relation of a kind to its many examples, a literary work to its many copies, a musical work to its many performances? Or is our feeling, that there is a significant analogy here, illusory, having no solid basis in fact? Is there any rationale for
speaking of substance-universals as well as of predicable-universals?

2.   It is common practice, among philosophers of modern and
contemporary times, to draw a distinction between those entities
which are capable of recurrence, or repetition in space-time, and
those which are not. Whitehead, for example, makes the distinction
very deliberately. Calling properties and qualities "objects" he says,
"We are comparing objects in events whenever we can say, 'There it
is again.' Objects are the elements in nature which can be again."[1] In
another place he says, "A colour is eternal. It haunts time like a
spirit. It comes and it goes. But where it comes, it is the same color."[2]
In yet another place he says, "The same object can be found in different parts of space and time, and this cannot hold for events."[3]
"Objects have the possibility of recurrence in experience."[4] The very
same sort of distinction appears, this time almost offhandedly, in

---

[1] A. N. Whitehead, *Concept of Nature* (Cambridge, 1920), p. 144.

[2] A. N. Whitehead, *Science and the Modern World* (New York, 1931), p. 126.

[3] A. N. Whitehead, *Principles of Natural Knowledge* (Cambridge, 1919), p. 66.

[4] Ibid., p. 64.

Miss Anscombe's book on the *Tractatus*. Criticizing F. P. Ramsey's contention that, since red and something which is red can both enter into several facts, there is no fundamental distinction between them, she says, critically, "It takes a little mental habituation to think that existence in several facts is the only feature that counts, so that since both A and red can exist in several facts, we should not be impressed by A's at least existing in only one place at a time, while red can exist in so many."[5]

Usually the distinction between entities capable of recurrence in space-time and those not capable of such recurrence, has been denominated as the distinction between *universals* and *particulars*. Thus far in our discussion we have ignored this universal–particular distinction. We have concentrated solely on the predicable-substance distinction. Let us now pick up this thus-far neglected distinction and see whether it sheds light on the problem at hand. Is it the case that those predicables which can be truly predicated of many are spatio-temporally repeatable? Is it the case that those which cannot be truly predicated of many are not spatio-temporally repeatable? And is it the case that those things which we feel to be radically different from predicables—events, physical objects, persons—are not spatio-temporally repeatable? And where do such things as musical works, literary works, and natural kinds fall? Are they too repeatable? Is it the case that they, along with those predicables which are truly predicable of many, fit into the framework of space and time in a fundamentally different way from the way of events and physical objects and persons? Is it the case that a single predicable, a single species, a single musical work, a single literary work, a single game, a single word, a single dance, can each be in many different places and/or times; and do they differ in this way from events, physical objects, and persons? If so, this would no doubt ground our feeling of a close analogy between the things in the list given earlier, and justify us in calling them all *universals*.

Whitehead spoke of a thing as being again, whereas Anscombe spoke of one thing as being in different places at the same time. Which of these is to be used to draw the distinction we are concerned with? Or should we put them together, and say that a thing is repeatable just in case it can be again, or can be in different places at the

---

[5]G. Anscombe, *Introduction to Wittgenstein's Tractatus* (London, 1959), p. 109.

same time? But then, is being again to be regarded as happening whenever a thing exists at two different times? And is a desk, which has a size of five feet by three feet by two and one-half feet, thereby in many different places at once? Evidently to answer these questions, and so to arrive at a suitable definition of "repeatability," we shall have to look into some of the ways in which things can be in space and time.

3.   Let us notice, first, that something may be or take place somewhere, without being or taking place anywhere in space. Suppose, for example, that with my eyes shut there is presented to me a red patch with a black dot superimposed. Then it might be that the black dot is in the middle of the red patch which I am now seeing. Still, I think it is clear that the black dot is not anywhere in space; one thing can bear a spatial relation to another thing, without either of the things being in space. There are, though, other states of consciousness which, so it seems, can be somewhere in space, for example, bodily pains. When I have a pain in my finger, that pain is somewhere in space; and amputees testify that they sometimes have pains in places not occupied by any part of their bodies. There is another class of states of consciousness which seem, in the respects mentioned, a good deal like pains, but which are not, I think, anywhere in space; these are those afterimages which we see somewhere—when we look, for example, from a sheet on which there is a red area surrounded by green, to a white sheet. In such cases, though one sees the gray afterimage *on* the white sheet, and thus sees it somewhere, perhaps even sees it somewhere in space, it would certainly be misleading to say that that is where it is. Thus one can see something somewhere in space, without that thing's *being* anywhere in space.

For the sake of convenience, then, let us henceforth use the phrase "location in space" as follows. A location of a thing in space at a certain time is any place where it is or takes place in space at that time. It is what, if anything, can be given as a true answer to the question, asked of the thing in question, "Where is it, or where does it take place, in space?"

The reason for not saying merely "is in space," but adding "or takes place in space" is this: There are some entities such that though they take place somewhere, still they *are* not anywhere. For example, there is no correct answer to the question, asked of some collision or some performance of a symphony, "Where is it?" though there is a correct answer to the question, "Where did it take place?"

And if it is in space that something takes place, as it often is, then we shall say that it has a location in space—its location being, of course, *where* it takes place.

Let us notice, next, that though collisions and symphonic performances do have location in space, they yet do not have a north half and a southern half, a left half and a right half, a top half and a bottom half. On the other hand, my desk, which likewise has location in space, does have a north and south, left and right, top and bottom, half. Thus some of the things which have location in space have spatial parts and some do not. It may be noted that some of the things which lack location in space yet have spatial parts, for example, afterimages.

We are now in a position to distinguish between what I shall call *multiple location in space* and *divided location in space*. A thing which is located in space will be said to have *multiple* location in space at a given time if it has more than one location in space at that time. A thing which is located in space will be said to have *divided* location in space at a given time if at that time it has at least two spatial parts having different spatial locations. The crucial difference, be it noted, is the difference between one thing being at different places in space at a given time, and one thing having spatial parts which are at different places at a given time.

It is evident that physical objects have divided, but not multiple, location. They themselves cannot be in different places at the same time, but they do have parts which are in different locations at the same time. It would seem to be the view of Whitehead and Anscombe that predicables, on the other hand, are capable of multiple location. Whether this view is correct will be considered shortly.

To say that an entity can have multiple location in space at a given time is to say that one of its locations can be to the north of, or above, or to the left of, another of its locations. Now this is different from saying that the *thing* is to the north of, or above, or to the left of, itself. One can hold that things are capable of multiple location in space, without holding that spatial-ordering relations are reflexive.

Our definition of multiple location allows for both the case in which there is spatial discontinuity among the locations of a thing at a time, and the case in which there is no discontinuity. Predicables are, by reputation, not only capable of multiple location, but capable of spatial discontinuity in their locations at a given time. Perhaps the French Revolution is another example of the same phenomenon. In principle there could, however, also be entities which, though capable of multiple location, are not capable of *discontinuous* multiple locations. Such entities, though they could be in different places at the same time, could only be in adjoining places.

Also our definition of divided location allows for both the case in which there is spatial discontinuity among the locations of a thing's spatial parts, and the case in which there is no such discontinuity. An obvious case of such discontinuity would be the case of a suite of furniture which, as a whole, has a spatial location in a certain room. The part constituting one of the pieces of furniture is spatially disconnected from the part constituting one of the other pieces; there is no place between them which is in turn the location of some spatial part of the thing.

Now before we put these distinctions to use in trying to formulate a satisfactory definition of repeatability, let us make a series of comparable distinctions for the relation of things to time.

We saw, earlier, that a thing could be somewhere, without being somewhere in space. Something similar is to be found in the case of time. In a dream, for example, there are before and after relations among the dreamed events. But these events do not themselves take place in time (though the *dreaming* of them does). So let us define "position in time." A position in time of some thing is whenever it is (was, will be) or takes (took, will take) place in time. It is any time at which or during which it is (was, will be) or takes (took, will take) place. It would seem that everything whatsoever that is (was, will be) or takes (took, will take) place in time has some position in time.

Such a thing as a race, be it noted, can be half over at a certain point. Within the stretch of time from the beginning of the race to that point, the race itself does not take place, only half of the race does. That stretch of time does not constitute the temporal position of the race; rather, it constitutes the temporal position of the first half of the race. But now suppose that my desk endures throughout today—today then being one of its positions in time. It also exists at each component stretch of time—the *desk* does, not half of it, or a quarter of it. And if my green ashtray gradually, over the years of its existence, becomes blackened, it is not the case that part of the ashtray was green, part black, and part somewhere in between. Physical objects, in short, do not have temporal parts, whereas such things as races do. Of course, corresponding to a physical object is what we might call the *life* or *history* of the object. And *that* has temporal parts. During a certain stretch of time not the whole history of my ashtray but only half of it, is to be found. And, for each of us, our life is half over at a certain point, though we ourselves are not; in the stretch of time from our birth to that point is to be found half of our life, but not half of ourself. We are not our histories; we are not our lives.

Corresponding to the distinction between multiple and divided location in space, let us distinguish between *multiple* and *divided* position in time. A thing which is positioned within time will be said to have *multiple position in time* if it is positioned at or during more than one time. And a thing which is positioned in time will be said to have *divided position in time* if it has at least two temporal parts which have different temporal locations. What is to be noted here is just the distinction between the case in which one thing has more than one position in time, and the case in which one temporal part of a thing has one position in time and another temporal part another position in time.

Since physical objects do not have temporal parts, they do not have divided position in time. Obviously, however, they do have multiple position in time; my desk exists now—*it* does, and not some temporal part of it; it also existed a minute ago—*it* did, and not some temporal part of it. Predicables, likewise, have multiple but not divided position in time, and it was this similarity between physical objects and predicables which led Whitehead to assimilate them to each other and call both "objects." A musical performance is a good example of something which has divided position in time, but is incapable of multiple position; for there can be one, and only one, time during which it takes place.

We must distinguish, as we did in the case of space, between the temporal relations of things, and the temporal relations of the temporal positions of things. One of the temporal positions of a thing may be before another; indeed, this will be the case if a thing has more than one temporal position. But it does not follow from this that, in such a case, the thing is before itself. One can allow that some things have multiple positions in time, without allowing that all temporal-ordering relations are reflexive.

Our definition of multiple position in time allows for both the case in which there is temporal discontinuity among the positions of a thing in time, and the case in which there is no such discontinuity— that is, for the case in which a thing is or takes place at or during one time, and another time, and no intervening time; and the case in which, if a thing is or takes place at or during one time, and another time, it also is or takes place at every intervening time. Similarly, our definition of divided position in time allows for both the case in which there is temporal discontinuity among the positions in time of a thing's temporal parts, and the case in which there is no such discontinuity. A symphonic performance, in which there is a pause between the movements, would be an example of the former. At a certain time during the time of the entire performance, no part of the performance is taking place.

4.   In one sense, of course, no entity is repeatable; there can be only one of each thing. But quite clearly, when philosophers have spoken of certain entities as repeatable, or capable of recurring, they had in mind the relation of such entities to space and/or time. And no doubt what they were pointing to was the phenomenon of *multiple,* as distinguished from *divided,* location or position. Whether it was the phenomenon of multiple location in space that they had in mind, or multiple position in time, or both, is less clear. To mention just the two cases we have cited, Whitehead seems to have had chiefly multiple position in time in mind, whereas Anscombe seems to have had multiple location in space in mind. Let us then consider the various possibilities.

Suppose we say that a thing is repeatable just in case it can have multiple position in space at a given time. Can we then single out universals as being those entities which are repeatable? That is to say, do multiply-predicable predicables, and entities which we feel to bear a significant analogy to them, turn out to be distinguished from other entities as being repeatable?

A question to be raised at once is whether predicables, musical works, literary works, natural kinds, and others have spatial locations at all, let alone multiple locations. Are there correct answers to such questions as these:

Where is the property of being six feet tall?
Where is the lion?
Where is Bartok's Fifth Quartet?
Where is Yeats' "Sailing to Byzantium"?

If a copy of "Sailing to Byzantium" is on the mantel, then I think that a perfectly appropriate and true answer to the question

"Where is Yeats' 'Sailing to Byzantium'?" is this: "On the mantel." It might be argued that if we regard this as a true answer, then we are really interpreting the question as one which would more strictly be asked with these words: "Where is a *copy* of Yeats' 'Sailing to Byzantium'?" For, the argument would go, a *copy* of Yeats' poem can well be on the mantel, but the poem itself cannot be. And the fact that we can appropriately and correctly answer "On the mantel" to the question "Where is Yeats' 'Sailing to Byzantium'?" just indicates that this is an ambiguous form of words, failing to distinguish between a poem and a copy of a poem.

I see no reason to suppose that this objection is correct. Why should not "On the mantel" be a correct answer to "Where is Yeats' poem 'Sailing to Byzantium'?" as well as to, "Where is a *copy* of Yeats' poem 'Sailing to Byzantium'?" Why should not a poem be wherever some copy of it is? Perhaps, even, we should not regard the question "Where is Yeats' poem 'Sailing to Byzantium'?" and the question "Where is a copy of Yeats' poem 'Sailing to Byzantium'?" as two different questions having the very same answer, but rather as one question asked with two different word-sequences, the same question being also askable with these words: "Where is Yeats' 'Sailing to Byzantium'?"

I think it is much less clear, however, that there is an appropriate and true answer to the question "Where is the property of being six feet tall?" Indeed, it seems to me quite clear that there is no appropriate and true answer to this question. But if not, then, by our definitions, *the property of being six feet tall* turns out to be *non*repeatable. For, being then susceptible of no location in space, it is of course not susceptible of multiple location.

Now quite clearly the basic assumption of those who have tried to distinguish between universals and particulars by reference to the concept of repeatability in space, is that a poem is where its copies are, a musical work where its performances are, a kind where its examples are, a predicable where its exemplifications are. We have seen reason to doubt that this assumption holds for *all* such cases. But suppose it be granted. By granting it, do we achieve the result that universals are those entities which are repeatable in space?

Not at all. Not even all *predicable* universals are repeatable in space. For not all predicables are such that their *exemplifications* have spatial location. *The property of being a thought* is one such, *the property of having no spatial location* is another such. And so the concept of repeatability in space is obviously inadequate for the work we want done. The matter is not improved if we start with the concept of *non*-repeatability, define "a particular" as any object which has location in space but is not capable of having multiple location, and define "a universal" simply as a nonparticular. On this definition, *the property of being a thought* and *the property of having no spatial location* would indeed turn out to be universals. But so would God, and angels, and numbers, all of them entities which lack the analogy to predicable universals that we are requiring of universals generally.

What, then, about repeatability in time? Suppose we say that an entity is repeatable just in case it can have multiple position in time. Can we then single out universals as being those entities which are repeatable *in time?*

No. This too is unsatisfactory. For on this definition it turns out that such things as physical objects and persons are universals, since physical objects and persons, as we saw, have multiple position in time. A minute ago was a time at which my desk existed, and half a minute ago was another time at which my desk existed.

At this point it might be suggested that, though predicables and physical objects are alike in that they are both capable of multiple location in time, what differentiates them is that predicables can *be again,* whereas physical objects can only *be yet*—that is, that predicables, unlike physical objects, are capable of *discontinuous* multiple position in time.

Suppose, then, that "a universal" were defined as what is capable of discontinuous multiple position in time. Would *this* be satisfactory for our purposes?

One question to raise, obviously, is whether it is in fact impossible for persons and physical objects to have discontinuous multiple position in time. Is it impossible, *logically* impossible, that a certain sofa should exist for a while, then go out of existence for a time, and then come back into existence? And is it logically impossible that a person should exist for a time, then die and go out of existence, and then be resurrected?

These are difficult questions, involving subtle issues of identity. They must, of course, be answered if the definition at hand proves satisfactory in all other respects. But I think that that is just what it does *not* do.

We saw earlier that the words "there is," when used in connection with predicables, are ambiguous. For example, in assertively uttering, with normal meaning, the words "There is such a thing as the property of being green," I may be asserting a proposition equivalent to the claim that something is green, or one equivalent to the claim that possibly something is green. Now if the condition for there being such a property as being green is understood to be that possibly something is green, then the property of being green cannot go out of and come back into being. But if the condition for there being such a property as being green is understood to be that something is green, then the property of being green can go out of and come back into being. It is, in short, capable of discontinuous multiple position in time. And so far, then, the definition of "universal" as what is capable of discontinuous multiple position in time is satisfactory.

But there are many predicables which are necessarily exemplified at all times; and so, no matter how we understand "being" when used in connection with predicables, these are not capable of discontinuous multiple position in time. One example of such a predicable is this: *Being an animal if a cat.* And another is this: *Being a predicable.*

So neither the concept of repeatability in time, nor the concept of discontinuous repeatability in time, is satisfactory for distinguishing universals from nonuniversals in the manner we desire. And nothing is gained if we use *both* the concept of repeatability in space and the concept of repeatability in time. For if we say that something is a universal just in case it is capable of *both* multiple location in space and multiple position in time, then the predicable *being a thought* turns out not to be a universal, for it cannot have location in space at all. And if we say that something is a universal just in case it is capable of *either* multiple location in space *or* multiple position in time, then physical objects and persons turn out to be universals, for they have multiple position in time.

We have not rung quite all the changes on the concept of repeatability, but enough has been said to show this: Our feeling that there is a fundamental similarity between predicables on the one hand, and such entities as natural kinds, literary works, musical works, and the like, on the other, is not based on the fact that all such entities, as distinguished from those which seem clearly different, are *repeatable*. Even more generally, the various properties of space and time can of course be used to draw various distinctions between sorts of entities. But they will not serve to distinguish universals from nonuniversals in the fashion that we are requiring.

Suggested Further Readings

A good beginning can be found in Peter Strawson, "Universals," and Richard Grandy, "Universals or Family Resemblances?" *Midwest Studies in Philosophy* IV (1979).

See also D. M. Armstrong, "Universals," in *A Companion to Metaphysics*, ed. by Jaegwon Kim and Ernest Sosa (Oxford: Blackwell, 1995); Ian Hacking, "A Language without Particulars," Mind LXXVII (1968); and M. J. Loux, *Substance and Attribute* (Dordrecht: D. Reidel, 1978), Part One.

CHAPTER 10

*N*egative Existentials

Richard Cartwright

Common sense says that ghosts and unicorns do not exist. These are denials of existence, or what are often called negative existential statements. The following selection explains why negative existentials are troublemakers and sets forth two classic responses to the problems posed by such statements.

Richard Cartwright is a professor of philosophy at MIT. He is the author of Philosophical Essays *and many important papers bearing on philosophical logic and metaphysics.*

Sentences of the forms 'There is no such thing (person, place, etc.) as . . .' and 'There are no such things (persons, places, etc.) as . . . (s)' are characteristically used to make statements which I shall call *negative existentials.* A negative existential which can be formulated in a sentence of the first form is *singular;* one which takes a sentence of the second form is *general.* Sentences of other forms can also be used to formulate negative existentials, singular or general. Instead of 'There is no such person as Santa Claus' we may have 'Santa Claus does not exist' or 'No such person as Santa Claus really exists'; and instead of 'There are no such things as unicorns' we may have 'There are no unicorns' or 'No such animal as a unicorn exists'. I will not attempt a review of the subtle differences among the various ways in which negative existentials may be formulated. For some purposes this might be desirable or even necessary; but for my purposes here it is not.

Since ancient times negative existentials have been a source of puzzlement. Although it is plain that among them some are true and some false, it has sometimes appeared on reflection that none can possibly be true. Several lines of argument have seemed to lead to this conclusion, and prominent among them is the following. To deny the existence of something—of unicorns, for example—we must indicate *what* it is the existence of which is denied; and this requires that unicorns be *referred to,* or *mentioned:* the negative existential must be *about* them. But things which do not exist cannot be referred to or mentioned; no statement can be about them. So, given that we have denied their existence, unicorns must after all exist. The apparently true negative existential is thus either false or not really a statement at all; and since the argument applies as well in any other case, we seem forced to conclude that there are no true negative existentials.

Presumably the argument tempts no one to renounce his cherished denials of existence. Nevertheless, as do other such puzzles, it focuses attention on a question of fundamental importance to logical theory. To formulate this question precisely, it is convenient first to state the argument (or rather, a slightly altered version of it) in a standard logical form. Let S be any negative existential, and let a (or K's, where S is general) be what in S is said not to exist. The argument is then as follows:

    (i) S is about a (or, K's);
    (ii) If S is about a (or, K's), there is such a thing as a (or, there are such things as K's);
    (iii) If there is such a thing as a (or, there are such things as K's), S is false;

therefore,

    (iv) S is false.

Clearly, the argument is formally valid; but its conclusion is obviously false. Hence, there must be some defect in the premises—either plain falsity or the sort which gives rise to an informal fallacy. The question is, What is this defect?

Two proposed answers are by now classic. I shall begin by expounding these; then, through commenting on them, I shall make some suggestions of my own.

Proponents of the first answer, whom I shall call Inflationists, regard the argument as involving a fallacy of equivocation. According to them, the words 'there is,' and consequently the term 'negative existential,' are ambiguous; and it is by surreptitiously trading on this ambiguity that the argument simultaneously enjoys both an appearance of soundness and an air of paradox. Inflationists contend that so-called existential statements, whether positive or negative, are of two quite different kinds. Some are affirmations or denials of *being*, others are affirmations or denials of *existence*. Taken as denials of being, "negative existentials" *are* one and all false. Thus, in a famous passage, Russell wrote:

> *Being* is that which belongs to every conceivable term, to every possible object of thought. . . . Being belongs to whatever can be counted. If *A* be any term that can be counted as one, it is plain that *A* is something, and therefore that *A* is. "*A* is not" must always be either false or meaningless. For if *A* were nothing, it could not be said not to be; "*A* is not" implies that there is a term *A* whose being is denied, and hence that *A* is. Thus unless "*A* is not" be an empty sound, it must be false—whatever *A* may be, it certainly is. . . . Thus being is a general attribute of everything, and to mention anything is to show that it is.

But, taken as denials of existence, not all "negative existentials" are false; for, as Russell remarked "*existence* is the prerogative of some only amongst beings." As to *how* existence is to be distinguished from being, there is apparently not much to be said; but it seems that only such things as are in some sense "concrete," or occupy some portion of space or time, enjoy existence as well as being.

As applied to the argument under discussion, the Inflationist distinction between being and existence is said to have this effect. If "negative existentials" are understood as denials of being, and if the words 'there is' are correspondingly interpreted, then each of (i) through (iv) is true. But this need not be viewed as paradoxical. For "negative existentials" are more naturally taken as denials of existence; and when (i) through (iv) are interpreted accordingly, (ii)— as well as (iv)—is false. In order to be mentionable, a thing need only *be;* it need not exist.

To treat the Inflationist fairly—especially to mitigate the distressingly ad hoc character which otherwise attaches to the distinction between being and existence, it is necessary to remark that what I have presented as a solution to a problem more often appears as an independent argument for the necessity of that distinction. The argument is a familiar one: given that some denials of existence are true, that which, in any of them, is truly said not to exist must nevertheless be; for a denial of existence is about what it says not to exist—which is possible only if what it claims not to *exist* nevertheless *is*. From this argument I have extracted, in an obvious way, the Inflationist solution to the problem before us.

Although classic, the Inflationist solution is not popular. Indeed, it has become a favorite whipping boy of metaphysical economists. They, in turn, propose an alternative which I shall call the Deflationist solution. Expositions of it vary in detail from one author to another, but the central point in each is the contention that (i) is simply false. Negative existentials are *not* about those things the existence of which they deny. They may *seem* to be; but this, Deflationists say, is mere semantic appearance, resulting from the misleading verbal form in which they are cast.

Again, this contention typically appears as the conclusion of an argument, not as an ad hoc device for avoiding a paradox. Deflationists argue that no negative existential is about that which it denies to exist; for, if true, there is no such thing for it to be about. Thus Ryle wrote:

> Suppose I assert of (apparently) the general subject 'carnivorous cows' that they 'do not exist', and my assertion is true. I cannot really be talking about carnivorous cows, for there are none. So it follows that the expression 'carnivorous cows' is not really being used, though the grammatical appearances are to the contrary, to denote the thing or things of which the predicate is being asserted.

Contrary to what the quotation might suggest. Ryle does not intend to limit the conclusion to true negative existentials. It is easily extended to false ones as well by adding the premise that a false statement is about only what it would be about if true.

Deflationists characteristically proceed to tell us what negative existentials are *really* about; and here the main variations occur. Russell, once he disavowed Inflationism, regarded them as being about *propositional functions.* To say there are no unicorns is, on this view, to say of the function *x is a unicorn* that it is "always false"; and to deny the existence of the present king of France is to say of *x is a present king of France* that it is not uniquely satisfied. Others have said that a negative existential asserts of an *attribute (characteristic, property, concept)* either that it is not exemplified at all or (where the negative existential is singular) that it is not uniquely exemplified. But the variations are less important than the theme; for they would not have been fashioned were it not for the conviction that negative existentials are not about what they seem to be.

The classic answers invite obvious objections. It is a commonplace to point out that the Inflationist peoples the world not only with fictitious, mythical, and imaginary beings but also with such thoroughgoing nonexistents as carnivorous cows and such contradictions as round squares. If, in defense, it is said that he grants these "being" but not "existence," it may well be replied that he thereby parries the charge of overpopulation only by invoking an unexplained concept of being. The result is to dispel a paradox by substituting for it a mystery. The Deflationist, on the other hand, avoids mystery—but only at the cost of creating a new paradox. For if it is paradoxical to say that all negative existentials are false, it is at least disturbing to be told that when we finally tell our children that Santa Claus does not exist, we say nothing about Santa Claus. Presumably they *expect* to hear something about him—the truth about him, one way or the other; and it is scarcely believable that the hard facts of semantics force us to disappoint them. Nor is it much consolation (to us or to them) to be told that we say nothing about him *in the same sense* as that in which we say something about Caesar when we say he crossed the Rubicon; for it is not clear that 'about' has an appropriately different sense. Perhaps a Deflationist can simply *give* it one; but then it is left open whether he says anything relevant to our problem.

Perhaps these objections are too easy to be decisive. Still, they suggest a need for reexamination of the classical theories.

Suggested Further Readings

There is much of interest in James Cargile *Paradoxes* (Cambridge, MA: Cambridge University Press, 1979), chap. 5.

See also Charles Crittenden, *Unreality* (Ithaca, NY: Cornell University Press, 1991); A. Meinong, "The Theory of Objects," in *Realism and the Background of Phenomenology,* ed. by R. Chisholm (Glencoe, IL: Free Press, 1960); George Edward Moore, "Is Existence a Predicate?" in *Philosophical Papers* (London: George Allen & Unwin Ltd, 1959); Terence Parsons, *Nonexistent Objects* (New Haven, CT: Yale University Press, 1980); Bertrand Russell: "On Denoting," *Mind* 14 (1905); and Peter van Inwagen, "Creatures of Fiction," *American Philosophical Quarterly* 14 (1977).

CHAPTER 11

The Ontological Argument

William L. Rowe

Anselm of Canterbury (1033–1109) formulated a famous "ontological" argument in support of the proposition that God exists. That argument is set forth in the following selection. Anselm's reasoning depends on a distinction between things that exist only in the understanding (mind) and things that exist in reality. To say that there are no unicorns is to say that unicorns are in the former category and not the latter category, but could that be the way things work with God? Anselm thinks not and provides an interesting argument in support of this position. (Professor Rowe's critical assessment of Anselm's argument is not included here.)

William L. Rowe is a professor of philosophy at Purdue University.

Arguments for the existence of God are commonly divided into a posteriori and a priori arguments. An a posteriori argument depends on a principle or premise that can be known only by means of our experience of the world. And a priori argument, on the other hand, purports to rest on principles which can be known independently of our experience of the world, just by reflecting on and understanding them. Of the three major arguments for the existence of God—the Cosmological, Teleological, and Ontological—only the last is entirely a priori. In the Cosmological argument one starts from some simple fact about the world, such as the fact that it contains things which are caused to exist by other things. In the Teleological argument a somewhat more complicated fact about the world serves as a starting point: the fact that the world exhibits order and

Source: William L. Rowe: Excerpts from "The Ontological Argument," in *Reason and Responsibility*, 9th ed., edited by Joel Feinberg. Copyright 1974; pp. 8–11, 21–30. Reprinted by permission of Wadsworth Publishing Co. and the author.

design. In the Ontological argument, however, one begins simply with a concept of God.

It is perhaps best to think of the Ontological argument as a family of arguments, each member of which begins with a concept of God, and by appealing only to a priori principles, endeavors to establish that God actually exists. Within this family of arguments the most important historically is the argument set forth by Anselm in the second chapter of his *Proslogium* (A Discourse). Indeed, the Ontological argument begins with chapter II of Anselm's *Proslogium*. In an earlier work, *Monologium* (A Soliloquy), Anselm had endeavored to establish the existence and nature of God by weaving together several versions of the Cosmological argument. In the Preface to *Proslogium* Anselm remarks that after the publication of *Monologium* he began to search for a single argument which alone would establish the existence and nature of God. After much strenuous but unsuccessful effort, he reports that he sought to put the project out of his mind in order to turn to more fruitful tasks. The idea, however, continued to haunt him until one day the proof he had so strenuously sought became clear to his mind. Anselm sets forth this proof in the second chapter of *Proslogium*.

Before discussing Anselm's argument in step-by-step fashion, there are certain concepts that will help us understand some of the central ideas of the argument. Suppose we draw a vertical line in our imagination and agree that on the left side of our line are all the things which exist, while on the right side of the line are all the things which don't exist. We might then begin to make a list of some of the things on both sides of our imaginary line, as follows:

THINGS WHICH EXIST	THINGS WHICH DON'T EXIST
The Empire State Building	The Fountain of Youth
Dogs	Unicorns
The planet Mars	The Abominable Snowman

Now each of the things (or sorts of things) listed thus far has (have) the following feature: it (they) logically might have been on the other side of the line. The Fountain of Youth, for example, is on the right side of the line, but *logically* there is no absurdity in the idea that it might have been on the left side of the line. Similarly, although dogs do exist, we surely can imagine without logical absurdity that they might not have existed, that they might have been on the right side of the line. Let us then record this feature of the things thus far listed by introducing the idea of a *contingent thing* as a thing that logically might have been on the other side of the line from the side it actually is on. The planet Mars and the Abominable Snowman are contingent things, even though the former happens to exist and the latter does not.

Suppose we add to our list the phrase "the object which is completely round and completely square at the same time" on the right side of our line. The round square, however, unlike the other things thus far listed on the right side of our line, is something that *logically could not* have been on the left side of the line. Noting this, let us introduce the idea of an *impossible thing* as a thing that is on the right side of the line and logically could not have been on the left side of the line.

Looking again at our list, we wonder if there is anything on the left side of our imaginary line which, unlike the things thus far listed on the left side, *logically could not* have been on the right side of the line. At this point we don't have to answer this question, but it is useful to have a concept to apply to any such things, should there be any. Accordingly, let us say that a *necessary thing* is a thing on the left side of our imaginary line and logically could not have been on the right side of the line.

Finally, a *possible thing* is any thing that is either on the left side of our imaginary line or logically might have been on the left side of the line. Possible things, then, will be all those things that are not impossible things—that is, all those things that are either contingent or necessary. If there are no necessary things, then all possible things will be contingent and all contingent things will be possible. If there is a necessary thing, however, then there will be a possible thing which is not contingent.

Armed with these concepts, we can clarify certain important distinctions and ideas in Anselm's thought. The first of these is his distinction between *existence in the understanding* and *existence in reality*. Anselm's notion of existence in reality is the same as our notion of existence; that is, being on the left side of our imaginary line. Since the Fountain of Youth is on the right side of the line, it does not exist in reality. The things which exist are, to use Anselm's phrase, the things which exist in reality. Anselm's notion of existence in the understanding, however, is not the same as any idea we normally employ. When we think of a certain thing, say the Fountain of Youth, then that thing, on Anselm's view, exists in the understanding. Also, when we think of an existing thing like the Empire State Building, it, too, exists in the understanding. So some of the things on both sides of our imaginary line exist in the understanding, but only those on the left side of our line exist in reality. Are there any things that don't exist in the understanding? Undoubtedly there are, for there are things, both existing and non-existing, of which we have not really thought. Now suppose I assert that the Fountain of Youth does not exist. Since to meaningfully deny the existence of something I have to have that thing in mind. I have to think of it, it follows on Anselm's view that whenever someone asserts that some thing does not exist, that thing *does* exist in the understanding. So in asserting that the Fountain of Youth does not exist, I imply that the Fountain of Youth does exist in the understanding. And in asserting that it does not exit I have asserted (on Anselm's view) that it does not exist in reality. This means that my simple assertion amounts to the somewhat more complex claim that the Fountain of Youth exists in the understanding but does not exist in reality—in short, that the Fountain of Youth exists *only* in the understanding.

We can now understand why Anselm insists that anyone who hears of God, thinks about God, or even denies the existence of God is, nevertheless, committed to the view that God exists in the understanding. Also, we can understand why Anselm treats what he calls "the fool's claim" that God does not exist as the claim that God exists *only* in the understanding—that is, that God exists in the understanding but does not exist in reality.

In *Monologium* Anselm sought to prove that among those beings which do exist there is one which is the greatest, highest, and the best. But in *Proslogium* he undertakes to prove that among those beings which exist there is one which is not just the greatest among existing beings, but is such that no conceivable being is greater. We need to distinguish these two ideas: (1) a being than which *no existing being* is greater, and (2) a being than which *no conceivable being* is greater. If the only things in existence were a stone, a frog, and a man, the last of these would satisfy our first idea but not our second—for we can conceive of a being (an angel or God) greater than a man. Anselm's idea of God, as he expresses it in *Proslogium* II, is the same as (2) above; it is the idea of "a being than which nothing greater can be conceived." It will facilitate our understanding of Anselm's argument if we make two slight changes in the way he has expressed his idea of God. For his phrase I shall substitute the following: '*the* being than which none greater *is possible.*' This idea says that if a certain being is God then no *possible being* can be greater than it, or conversely, if a certain being is such that it is even *possible* for there to be a being greater than it, then that being is not God. What Anselm proposes to prove, then, is that the being than which none greater is possible exists in reality. If he proves this he will have proved that God, as he conceives of Him, exists in reality.

But what does Anselm mean by "greatness"? Is a building, for example, greater than a man? In *Monologium,* chapter II. Anselm remarks: "But I do not mean physically great, as a material object is great, but that which, the greater it is, is the better or the more worthy— wisdom, for instance." Contrast wisdom with size. Anselm is saying that wisdom is something that contributes to the greatness of a thing. If a thing comes to have more wisdom than it did before then (given that its other characteristics remain the same), that thing has become a greater, better, more worthy thing than it was. Wisdom, Anselm is saying, is a great-making quality. However, the mere fact that something increases in size (physical greatness) does not make that thing a better thing than it was before, so size is not a great-making quality. By "greater than" Anselm means "better than," "superior to," or "more worthy than," and he believes that some characteristics, like wisdom and moral goodness, are great-making characteristics in that anything which has them is a *better thing* than it would be (other characteristics of it remaining the same) were it to lack them.

We come now to what we may call the *key idea* in Anselm's Ontological argument. Anselm believes that *existence in reality is a great-making quality*. Does Anselm mean that anything that exists is a greater thing than anything that doesn't? Although he does not ask or answer the question, it is perhaps reasonable to believe that Anselm did not mean this. When he discusses wisdom as a great-making quality he is careful not to say that any wise thing is better than any unwise thing—for he recognizes that a just but unwise man might be a better being than a wise but unjust man. I suggest that what Anselm means is that anything that doesn't exist but might have existed (is on the right side of our line but might have been on the left) would have been a greater thing if it had existed (if it had been on the left side of our line). He is not comparing two different things (one existing and one not existing) and saying that the first is therefore greater than the second. Rather, he is talking about *one* thing and pointing out that if it does not exist but might have existed, then *it* would have been a greater thing if it had existed. Using Anselm's distinction between existence in the understanding and existence in reality, we may express the key idea in Anselm's reasoning as follows: If something exists only in the understanding but might have existed in reality, then it might have been greater than it is. Since the Fountain of Youth, for example, exists only in the understanding but (unlike the round square) might have existed in reality, it follows by Anselm's principle that the Fountain of Youth might have been a greater thing than it is.

We can now consider the step-by-step development of Anselm's Ontological argument. I shall use the term "God" in place of the longer phrase "the being than which none greater is possible"— wherever the term "God" appears we are to think of it as simply an abbreviation of the longer phrase.

(1) God exists in the understanding.

As we have noted, anyone who hears of the being than which none greater is possible is, on Anselm's view, committed to premise (1).

(2) God might have existed in reality (God is a possible being).

Anselm, I think, assumes the truth of (2) without making it explicit in his reasoning. By asserting (2) I do not mean to imply that God does not exist in reality, but that, unlike the round square, God is a possible being.

(3) If something exists only in the understanding and might have existed in reality, then it might have been greater than it is.

As we noted, this is the key idea in Anselm's Ontological argument. It is intended as a general principle, true of anything whatever.

Steps (1)–(3) constitute the basic premises of Anselm's Ontological argument. From these three items, Anselm believes, it follows that God exists in reality. But how does Anselm propose to convince us that if we accept (1)–(3) we are committed by the rules of logic to accept his conclusion that God exists in reality? Anselm's procedure is to offer what is called a *reductio ad absurdum* proof of his conclusion. Instead of showing directly that the existence of God follows from steps (1)–(3), Anselm invites us to *suppose* that God does not exist (i.e., that the conclusion he wants to establish is false) and then shows how this supposition, when conjoined with steps (1)–(3), leads to an absurd result, a result that couldn't possibly be true because it is contradictory. Since the supposition that God does not exist leads to an absurdity, that supposition must be rejected in favor of the conclusion that God does exist.

Does Anselm succeed in reducing the "fool's belief" that God does not exist to an absurdity? The best way to answer this question is to follow the steps of his argument.

(4) Suppose God exists only in the understanding.

This supposition, as we saw earlier, is Anselm's way of expressing the belief that God does not exist.

(5) God might have been greater than He is. (2, 4, and 3)

Step (5) follows from steps (2), (4), and (3). Since (3), if true, is true of anything whatever, it will be true of God. Therefore, (3) implies that if God exists only in the understanding and might have existed in reality, then God might have been greater than He is. If so, then given (2) and (4), (5) must be true. For what (3) says when applied to God is that given (2) and (4), it follows that (5).

(6) God is a being than which a greater is possible. (5)

Surely if God is such that He logically might have been greater, then He is such than which a greater is possible.

We can now appreciate Anselm's *reductio* argument. He has shown that if we accept steps (1)–(4), we must accept step (6). But (6) is unacceptable; it is the absurdity Anselm was after. By replacing "God" in (6) with the longer phrase it abbreviates, we see that (6) amounts to the absurd assertion:

(7) The being than which none greater is possible is a being than which a greater is possible.

Now since step (1)–(4) have led us to an obviously false conclusion, and if we accept Anselm's basic premises (1)–(3) as true, then (4), the supposition that God exists only in the understanding, must be rejected as false. Thus we have shown that:

(8) It is false that God exists only in the understanding.

But since premise (1) tells us that God does exist in the understanding and (8) tells us that God does not exist only there, we may infer that

(9) God exists in reality as well as in the understanding. (1, 8)

Suggested Further Readings

The best place to begin is with *St. Anselm's Proslogium with a Reply on Behalf of the Fool by Gaunilo and the Author's Reply to Gaunilo* (Oxford: Clarendon Press, 1965).

See also Peter van Inwagen, *God, Knowledge and Mystery* (Ithaca, NY: Cornell University Press, 1995), Part I.1; Alvin Plantinga, *The Nature of Necessity* (Oxford: Oxford University Press, 1974), chap. X; and Norman Malcolm, "Anselm's Ontological Arguments," in *Knowledge and Certainty* (Englewood Cliffs, NJ: Prentice-Hall, 1963).

*T*he First Dialogue

George Berkeley

The famous Irish philosopher George Berkeley (1685–1753) defends a meta-physical position that many people regard as being sharply in opposition to common sense. Although Berkeley does not deny the reality of familiar things such as hawks and handsaws, he argues that those things are mind-dependent—are in fact located only in people's minds. Berkeley questions the assumption that, as an Anselmean might put it, commonplace things exist both in the mind and out of the mind. Minds themselves have a special place in Berkeley's meta-physic. With the exception of minds, Berkeley holds that to exist is to be perceived and that what is perceived is located in the mind. The character Hylas speaks for the position (arguably the commonsense position) that commonplace things are independent of minds. This is challenged by the character Philonous, who speaks for Berkeley.

Philonous.   Good morrow, Hylas: I did not expect to find you abroad so early.

Hylas.   It is indeed something unusual: but my thoughts were so taken up with a subject I was discoursing of last night, that finding I could not sleep, I resolved to rise and take a turn in the garden.

Phil.   It happened well, to let you see what innocent and agreeable pleasures you lose every morning. Can there be a pleasanter time of the day, or a more delightful season of the year? That purple sky, those wild but sweet notes of birds, the fragrant bloom upon the trees and flowers, the gentle influence of the rising sun, these and a thousand nameless beauties of nature inspire the soul with secret

---

Source: George Berkeley: Excerpt reprinted by permission of Open Court Trade & Academic Books, a division of Carus Publishing Company, Peru, IL, from *Three Dialogues between Hylas and Philonous* by George Berkeley. Copyright 1901: pp. 149–92.

transports; its faculties too being at this time fresh and lively, are fit
for these meditations, which the solitude of a garden and tranquillity
of the morning naturally dispose us to. But I am afraid I interrupt
your thoughts; for you seemed very intent on something.

Hyl. It is true, I was, and shall be obliged to you if you will
permit me to go on in the same vein: not that I would by any means
deprive myself of your company, for my thoughts always flow more
easily in conversation with a friend, than when I am alone: but my re-
quest is, that you would suffer me to impart my reflections to you.

Phil. With all my heart, it is what I should have requested myself, if you had not prevented me.

Hyl. I was considering the odd fate of those men who have in
all ages, through an affectation of being distinguished from the vulgar, or some unaccountable turn of thought, pretended either to believe nothing at all, or believe the most extravagant things in the
world. This however might be borne, if their paradoxes and scepticism did not draw after them some consequences of general disad-
vantage to mankind. But the mischief lieth here; that when men of
less leisure see them who are supposed to have spent their whole
time in the pursuits of knowledge, professing an entire ignorance of
all things, or advancing such notions as are repugnant to plain and
commonly received principles, they will be tempted to entertain sus-
picions concerning the most important truths, which they had hitherto held sacred and unquestionable.

Phil. I entirely agree with you, as to the ill tendency of the affected doubts of some philosophers, and fantastical conceits of others. I am even so far gone of late in this way of thinking, that I have
quitted several of the sublime notions I had got in their schools for
vulgar opinions. And I give it you on my word, since this revolt from
metaphysical notions to the plain dictates of nature and common
sense, I find my understanding strangely enlightened, so that I can
now easily comprehend a great many things which before were all
mystery and riddle.

Hyl. I am glad to find there was nothing in the accounts I
heard of you.

Phil. Pray, what were those?

Hyl. You were represented in last night's conversation, as one
who maintained the most extravagant opinion that ever entered into
the mind of man, to wit, that there is no such thing as *material substance* in the world.

Phil.   That there is no such thing as what philosophers call *material substance,* I am seriously persuaded: but if I were made to see any thing absurd or sceptical in this, I should then have the same reason to renounce this, that I imagine I have now to reject the contrary opinion.

Hyl.   What! can any thing be more fantastical, more repugnant to common sense, or a more manifest piece of scepticism, than to believe there is no such thing as *matter?*

Phil.   Softly, good Hylas. What if it should prove, that you who hold there is, are by virtue of that opinion a greater sceptic, and maintain more paradoxes and repugnancies to common sense, than I who believe no such thing?

Hyl.   You may as soon persuade me, the part is greater than the whole, as that, in order to avoid absurdity and scepticism, I should ever be obliged to give up my opinion in this point.

Phil.   Well then, are you content to admit that opinion for true, which upon examination shall appear most agreeable to common sense, and remote from scepticism?

Hyl.   With all my heart. Since you are for raising disputes about the plainest things in nature, I am content for once to hear what you have to say.

Phil.   Pray, Hylas, what do you mean by a *sceptic?*

Hyl.   I mean what all men mean, one that doubts of every thing.

Phil.   He then who entertains no doubt concerning some particular point, with regard to that point cannot be thought a *sceptic.*

Hyl.   I agree with you.

Phil.   Whether doth doubting consist in embracing the affirmative or negative side of a question?

Hyl.   In neither; for whoever understands English, cannot but know that *doubting* signifies a suspense between both.

Phil.   He then that denieth any point, can no more be said to doubt of it than he who affirmeth it with the same degree of assurance.

Hyl.   True.

Phil.   And consequently, for such his denial is no more to be esteemed a *sceptic* than the other.

Hyl.   I acknowledge it.

Phil.   How cometh it to pass then, Hylas, that you pronounce me a *sceptic,* because I deny what you affirm, to wit, the existence of matter? Since, for aught you can tell, I am as peremptory in my denial, as you in your affirmation.

Hyl. Hold, Philonous, I have seen a little out in my definition; but every false step a man makes in discourse is not to be insisted on. I said, indeed, that a *sceptic* was one who doubted of every thing; but I should have added, or who denies the reality and truth of things.

Phil. What things? Do you mean the principles and theorems of sciences? but these you know are universal intellectual notions, and consequently independent of matter; the denial therefore of this doth not imply the denying them.

Hyl. I grant it. But are there no other things? What think you of distrusting the senses, of denying the real existence of sensible things, or pretending to know nothing of them? Is not this sufficient to denominate a man a *sceptic*?

Phil. Shall we therefore examine which of us it is that denies the reality of sensible things, or professes the greatest ignorance of them; since, if I take you rightly, he is to be esteemed the greatest *sceptic*?

Hyl. That is what I desire.

Phil. What mean you by sensible things?

Hyl. Those things which are perceived by the senses. Can you imagine that I mean any thing else?

Phil. Pardon me, Hylas, if I am desirous clearly to apprehend your notions, since this may much shorten our inquiry. Suffer me then to ask you this further question. Are those things only perceived by the senses which are perceived immediately? or may those things properly be said to be *sensible*, which are perceived mediately, or not without the intervention of others?

Hyl. I do not sufficiently understand you.

Phil. In reading a book, what I immediately perceive are the letters, but mediately, or by means of these, are suggested to my mind the notions of God, virtue, truth, &c. Now that the letters are truly sensible things, or perceived by sense, there is no doubt: but I would know whether you take the things suggested by them to be so too.

Hyl. No. certainly, it were absurd to think *God* or *virtue* sensible things, though they may be signified and suggested to the mind by sensible marks, with which they have an arbitrary connexion.

Phil. It seems then, that by *sensible things* you mean those only which can be perceived immediately by sense.

Hyl. Right.

Phil. Doth it not follow from this, that though I see one part of the sky red, and another blue, and that my reason doth thence evidently conclude there must be some cause of that diversity of colours, yet that cause cannot be said to be a sensible thing, or perceived by the sense of seeing?

Hyl. It doth.

Phil. In like manner, though I hear variety of sounds, yet I cannot be said to hear the causes of those sounds.

Hyl. You cannot.

Phil. And when by my touch I perceive a thing to be hot and heavy, I cannot say with any truth or propriety, that I feel the cause of its heat or weight.

Hyl. To prevent any more questions of this kind, I tell you once for all, that by *sensible things* I mean those only which are perceived by sense, and that in truth the senses perceive nothing which they do not perceive immediately: for they make no inferences. The deducing therefore of causes or occasions from effects and appearances, which alone are perceived by sense, entirely relates to reason.

Phil. This point then is agreed between us, that *sensible things are those only which are immediately perceived by sense.* You will further inform me, whether we immediately perceive by sight any thing beside light, and colours, and figures: or by hearing any thing but sounds: by the palate, any thing besides tastes: by the smell, besides odours: or by the touch, more than tangible qualities.

Hyl. We do not.

Phil. It seems therefore, that if you take away all sensible qualities, there remains nothing sensible.

Hyl. I grant it.

Phil. Sensible things therefore are nothing else but so many sensible qualities, or combinations of sensible qualities.

Hyl. Nothing else.

Phil. Heat then is a sensible thing.

Hyl. Certainly.

Phil. Doth the reality of sensible things consist in being perceived? or is it something distinct from their being perceived, and that bears no relation to the mind?

Hyl. To *exist* is one thing, and to be *perceived* is another.

Phil. I speak with regard to sensible things only; and of these I ask, whether by their real existence you mean a subsistence exterior to the mind, and distinct from their being perceived?

Hyl. I mean a real absolute being, distinct from, and without any relation to their being perceived.

Phil.   Heat, therefore, if it be allowed a real being, must exist without the mind.

Hyl.   It must.

Phil.   Tell me, Hylas, is this real existence equally compatible to all degrees of heat, which we perceive: or is there any reason why we should attribute it to some, and deny it others? and if there be, pray let me know that reason.

Hyl.   Whatever degree of heat we perceive by sense, we may be sure the same exists in the object that occasions it.

Phil.   What, the greatest as well as the least?

Hyl.   I tell you, the reason is plainly the same in respect of both: they are both perceived by sense; nay, the greater degree of heat is more sensibly perceived; and consequently, if there is any difference, we are more certain of its real existence than we can be of the reality of a lesser degree.

Phil.   But is not the most vehement and intense degree of heat a very great pain?

Hyl.   No one can deny it.

Phil.   And is any unperceiving thing capable of pain or pleasure?

Hyl.   No, certainly.

Phil.   Is your material substance a senseless being, or a being endowed with sense and perception?

Hyl.   It is senseless without doubt.

Phil.   It cannot therefore by the subject of pain.

Hyl.   By no means.

Phil.   Nor consequently of the greatest heat perceived by sense, since you acknowledge this to be no small pain.

Hyl.   I grant it.

Phil.   What shall we say then of your external object; is it a material substance, or no?

Hyl.   It is a material substance with the sensible qualities inhering in it.

Phil.   How then can a great heat exist in it, since you own it cannot in a material substance? I desire you would clear this point.

Hyl.   Hold, Philonous; I fear I was out in yielding intense heat to be a pain. It should seem rather, that pain is something distinct from heat, and the consequence or effect of it.

Phil.   Upon putting your hand near the fire, do you perceive one simple uniform sensation, or two distinct sensations?

Hyl.   But one simple sensation.
Phil.   Is not the heat immediately perceived?
Hyl.   It is.
Phil.   And the pain?
Hyl.   True.
Phil.   Seeing therefore they are both immediately perceived at
the same time, and the fire affects you only with one simple, or un-
compounded idea, it follows that this same simple idea is both the
intense heat immediately perceived, and the pain; and consequently,
that the intense heat immediately perceived, is nothing distinct from
a particular sort of pain.
Hyl.   It seems so.
Phil.   Again, try in your thoughts, Hylas, if you can conceive a
vehement sensation to be without pain, or pleasure.
Hyl.   I cannot.
Phil.   Or can you frame to yourself an idea of sensible pain or
pleasure in general, abstracted from every particular idea of heat,
cold, tastes, smells, &c.?
Hyl.   I do not find that I can.
Phil.   Doth it not therefore follow, that sensible pain is noth-
ing distinct from those sensations or ideas, in an intense degree?
Hyl.   It is undeniable; and to speak the truth, I begin to sus-
pect a very great heat cannot exist but in a mind perceiving it.
Phil.   What! are you then in that *sceptical* state of suspense, be-
tween affirming and denying?
Hyl.   I think I may be positive in the point. A very violent and
painful heat cannot exist without the mind.
Phil.   It hath not therefore, according to you, any real being.
Hyl.   I own it.
Phil.   Is it therefore certain, that there is no body in nature
really hot?
Hyl.   I have not denied there is any real heat in bodies. I only
say, there is no such thing as an intense real heat.
Phil.   But did you not say before, that all degrees of heat were
equally real: or if there was any difference, that the greater were
more undoubtedly real than the lesser?
Hyl.   True: but it was, because I did not then consider the
ground there is for distinguishing between them, which I now plainly
see. And it is this: because intense heat is nothing else but a particular
kind of painful sensation; and pain cannot exist but in a perceiving

being; it follows that no intense heat can really exist in an unperceiving corporeal substance. But this is no reason why we should deny heat in an inferior degree to exist in such a substance.

Phil. But how shall we be able to discern those degrees of heat which exist only in the mind, from those which exist without it?

Hyl. That is no difficult matter. You know, the least pain cannot exist unperceived; whatever therefore degree of heat is a pain, exists only in the mind. But as for all other degrees of heat, nothing obliges us to think the same of them.

Phil. I think you granted before, that no unperceiving being was capable of pleasure, any more than of pain.

Hyl. I did.

Phil. And is not warmth, or a more gentle degree of heat than what causes uneasiness, a pleasure?

Hyl. What then?

Phil. Consequently it cannot exist without the mind in any unperceiving substance, or body.

Hyl. So it seems.

Phil. Since therefore, as well those degrees of heat that are not painful, as those that are, can exist only in a thinking substance; may we not conclude that external bodies are absolutely incapable of any degree of heat whatsoever?

Hyl. On second thoughts, I do not think it so evident that warmth is a pleasure, as that a great degree of heat is a pain.

Phil. I do not pretend that warmth is as great a pleasure as heat is a pain. But if you grant it to be even a small pleasure, it serves to make good my conclusion.

Hyl. I could rather call it an *indolence*. It seems to be nothing more than a privation of both pain and pleasure. And that such a quality or state as this may agree to an unthinking substance, I hope you will not deny.

Phil. If you are resolved to maintain that warmth, or a gentle degree of heat, is no pleasure, I know not how to convince you otherwise, than by appealing to your own sense. But what think you of cold?

Hyl. The same that I do of heat. An intense degree of cold is a pain; for to feel a very great cold, is to perceive a great uneasiness: it cannot therefore exist without the mind; but a lesser degree of cold may, as well as a lesser degree of heat.

Phil. Those bodies therefore, upon whose application to our own we perceive a moderate degree of heat, must be concluded to have a moderate degree of heat or warmth in them; and those, upon whose application we feel a like degree of cold, must be thought to have cold in them.

Hyl.   They must.

Phil.   Can any doctrine be true that necessarily leads a man into an absurdity?

Hyl.   Without doubt it cannot.

Phil.   Is it not an absurdity to think that the same thing should be at the same time both cold and warm?

Hyl.   It is.

Phil.   Suppose now one of your hands hot, and the other cold, and that they are both at once put into the same vessel of water, in an intermediate state; will not the water seem cold to one hand, and warm to the other?

Hyl.   It will.

Phil.   Ought we not therefore by your principles to conclude, it is really both cold and warm at the same time, that is, according to your own concession, to believe an absurdity?

Hyl.   I confess it seems so.

Phil.   Consequently, the principles themselves are false, since you have granted that no true principle leads to an absurdity.

Hyl.   But after all, can any thing be more absurd than to say, *there is no heat in the fire?*

Phil.   To make the point still clearer; tell me, whether in two cases exactly alike, we ought not to make the same judgment?

Hyl.   We ought.

Phil.   When a pin pricks your finger, doth it not rend and divide the fibres of your flesh?

Hyl.   It doth.

Phil.   And when a coal burns your finger, doth it any more?

Hyl.   It doth not.

Phil.   Since therefore you neither judge the sensation itself occasioned by the pin, nor any thing like it to be in the pin; you should not, conformably to what you have now granted, judge the sensation occasioned by the fire, or any thing like it, to be in the fire.

Hyl.   Well, since it must be so, I am content to yield this point, and acknowledge, that heat and cold are only sensations existing in our minds: but there still remain qualities enough to secure the reality of external things.

Phil.   But what will you say, Hylas, if it shall appear that the case is the same with regard to all other sensible qualities, and that they can no more be supposed to exist without the mind, than heat and cold?

Hyl.   Then indeed you will have done something to the purpose; but that is what I despair of seeing proved.

Phil.   Let us examine them in order. What think you of tastes, do they exist without the mind, or no?

Hyl.   Can any man in his senses doubt whether sugar is sweet, or wormwood bitter?

Phil.   Inform me, Hylas. Is a sweet taste a particular kind of pleasure or pleasant sensation, or is it not?

Hyl.   It is.

Phil.   And is not bitterness some kind of uneasiness or pain?

Hyl.   I grant it.

Phil.   If therefore sugar and wormwood are unthinking corporeal substances existing without the mind, how can sweetness and bitterness, that is, pleasure and pain, agree to them?

Hyl.   Hold, Philonous; I now see what it was deluded me all this time. You asked whether heat and cold, sweetness and bitterness, were not particular sorts of pleasure and pain; to which I answered simply, that they were. Whereas I should have thus distinguished: those qualities, as perceived by us, are pleasures or pains, but not as existing in the external objects. We must not therefore conclude absolutely, that there is no heat in the fire, or sweetness in the sugar, but only that heat or sweetness, as perceived by us, are not in the fire or sugar. What say you to this?

Phil. I say it is nothing to the purpose. Our discourse proceeded altogether concerning sensible things, which you defined to be the things we *immediately perceive by our senses.* Whatever other qualities therefore you speak of, as distinct from these, I know nothing of them, neither do they at all belong to the point in dispute. You may indeed pretend to have discovered certain qualities which you do not perceive, and assert those insensible qualities exist in fire and sugar. But what use can be made of this to your present purpose, I am at a loss to conceive. Tell me then once more, do you acknowledge that heat and cold, sweetness and bitterness (meaning those qualities which are perceived by the senses), do not exist without the mind?

Hyl. I see it is to no purpose to hold out, so I give up the cause as to those mentioned qualities. Though I profess it sounds oddly, to say that sugar is not sweet.

Phil. But for your further satisfaction, take this along with you: that which at other times seems sweet, shall to a distempered palate appear bitter. And nothing can be plainer, than that divers persons perceive different tastes in the same food, since that which one man delights in, another abhors. And how could this be, if the taste was something really inherent in the food?

Hyl. I acknowledge I know not how.

Phil. In the next place, odours are to be considered. And with regard to these, I would fain know, whether what hath been said of tastes doth not exactly agree to them? Are they not so many pleasing or displeasing sensations?

Hyl. They are.

Phil. Can you then conceive it possible that they should exist in an unperceiving thing?

Hyl. I cannot.

Phil. Or can you imagine, that filth and ordure affect those brute animals that feed on them out of choice, with the same smells which we perceive in them?

Hyl. By no means.

Phil. May we not therefore conclude of smells, as of the other forementioned qualities, that they cannot exist in any but a perceiving substance or mind?

Hyl. I think so.

Phil. Then as to sounds, what must we think of them: are they accidents really inherent in external bodies, or not?

Hyl. That they inhere not in the sonorous bodies, is plain from hence; because a bell struck in the exhausted receiver of an air-pump, sends forth no sound. The air therefore must be thought the subject of sound.

Phil. What reason is there for that, Hylas?

Hyl. Because when any motion is raised in the air, we perceive a sound greater or lesser, in proportion to the air's motion; but without some motion in the air, we never hear any sound at all.

Phil. And granting that we never hear a sound but when some motion is produced in the air, yet I do not see how you can infer from thence, that the sound itself is in the air.

Hyl.   It is this very motion in the external air, that produces in the mind the sensation of *sound*. For striking on the drum of the ear, it causeth a vibration, which by the auditory nerves being communicated to the brain, the soul is thereupon affected with the sensation called *sound.*

Phil.   What! is sound then a sensation?

Hyl.   I tell you, as perceived by us, it is a particular sensation in the mind.

Phil.   And can any sensation exist without the mind?

Hyl.   No, certainly.

Phil.   How then can sound, being a sensation, exist in the air, if by the *air* you mean a senseless substance existing without the mind.

Hyl.   You must distinguish, Philonous, between sound, as it is perceived by us, and as it is in itself; or, (which is the same thing) between the sound we immediately perceive, and that which exists without us. The former indeed is a particular kind of sensation, but the latter is merely a vibrative or undulatory motion in the air.

Phil.   I thought I had already obviated that distinction by the answer I gave when you were applying it in a like case before. But to say no more of that: are you sure then that sound is really nothing but motion?

Hyl.   I am.

Phil.   Whatever therefore agrees to real sound, may with truth be attributed to motion.

Hyl.   It may.

Phil.   It is then good sense to speak of *motion,* as of a thing that is *loud, sweet, acute,* or *grave.*

Hyl.   I see you are resolved not to understand me. Is it not evident, those accidents or modes belong only to sensible sound, or *sound* in the common acceptation of the word, but not to *sound* in the real and philosophic sense, which, as I just now told you, is nothing but a certain motion of the air?

Phil.   It seems then there are two sorts of sound, the one vulgar, or that which is heard, the other philosophical and real.

Hyl.   Even so.

Phil.   And the latter consists in motion.

Hyl.   I told you so before.

Phil.   Tell me, Hylas, to which of the senses, think you, the idea of motion belongs: to the hearing?

Hyl.   No, certainly, but to the sight and touch.

Phil.   It should follow then, that according to you, real sounds may possibly be *seen* or *felt,* but never *heard.*

Hyl.   Look you, Philonous, you may if you please make a jest of my opinion, but that will not alter the truth of things. I own, indeed, the inferences you draw me into sound something oddly: but common language, you know, is framed by, and for the use of the vulgar: we must not therefore wonder, if expressions adapted to exact philosophic notions, seem uncouth and out of the way.

Phil.   Is it come to that? I assure you, I imagine myself to have gained no small point, since you make so light of departing from common phrases and opinions; it being a main part of our inquiry, to examine whose notions are widest of the common road, and most repugnant to the general sense of the world. But can you think it no more than a philosophical paradox, to say that *real sounds are never hard,* and that the idea of them is obtained by some other sense. And is there nothing in this contrary to nature and the truth of things?

Hyl.   To deal ingenuously, I do not like it. And after the concessions already made, I had as well grant that sounds too have no real being without the mind.

Phil.   And I hope you will make no difficulty to acknowledge the same of colours.

Hyl.   Pardon me; the case of colours is very different. Can any thing be plainer, than that we see them on the objects?

Phil.   The objects you speak of are, I suppose, corporeal substances existing without the mind.

Hyl.   They are.

Phil.   And have true and real colours inhering in them?

Hyl.   Each visible object hath that colour which we see in it.

Phil.   How! is there any thing visible but what we perceive by sight?

Hyl.   There is not.

Phil.   And do we perceive any thing by sense, which we do not perceive immediately?

Hyl.   How often must I be obliged to repeat the same thing? I tell you, we do not.

Phil.   Have patience, good Hylas; and tell me once more whether there is any thing immediately perceived by the senses, except sensible qualities. I know you asserted there was not: but I would not be informed, whether you still persist in the same opinion.

Hyl. I do.

Phil. Pray, is your corporeal substance either a sensible quality or made up of sensible qualities?

Hyl. What a question that is! who ever thought it was?

Phil. My reason for asking was, because in saying, *each visible object hath that colour which we see in it,* you make visible objects to be corporeal substances; which implies either that corporeal substances are sensible qualities, or else that there is something beside sensible qualities perceived by sight: but as this point was formerly agreed between us, and is still maintained by you, it is a clear consequence, that your corporeal substance is nothing distinct from sensible qualities.

Hyl. You may draw as many absurd consequences as you please, and endeavour to perplex the plainest things; but you shall never persuade me out of my senses. I clearly understand my own meaning.

Phil. I wish you would make me understand it too. But since you are unwilling to have your notion of corporeal substance examined, I shall urge that point no further. Only be pleased to let me know, whether the same colours which we see, exist in external bodies, or some other.

Hyl. The very same.

Phil. What! are then the beautiful red and purple we see on yonder clouds, really in them? Or do you imagine they have in themselves any other form than that of a dark mist or vapour?

Hyl. I must own, Philonous, those colours are not really in the clouds as they seem to be at this distance. They are only apparent colours.

Phil. *Apparent* call you them? how shall we distinguish these apparent colours from real?

Hyl. Very easily. Those are to be thought apparent, which, appearing only at a distance, vanish upon a nearer approach.

Phil. And those I suppose are to be thought real, which are discovered by the most near and exact survey.

Hyl. Right.

Phil. Is the nearest and exactest survey made by the help of a microscope, or by the naked eye?

Hyl. By a microscope, doubtless.

Phil. But a microscope often discovers colours in an object different from those perceived by the unassisted sight. And in case we had microscopes magnifying to any assigned degree; it is certain, that no object whatsoever viewed through them, would appear in the same colour which it exhibits to the naked eye.

Hyl. And what will you conclude from all this? You cannot argue that there are really and naturally no colours on objects; because by artificial managements they may be altered, or made to vanish.

Phil. I think it may evidently be concluded from your own concessions, that all the colours we see with our naked eyes, are only apparent as those on the clouds, since they vanish upon a more close and accurate inspection, which is afforded us by a microscope. Then as to what you say by way of prevention; I ask you, whether the real and natural state of an object is better discovered by a very sharp and piercing sight, or by one which is less sharp.

Hyl. By the former without doubt.

Phil. Is it not plain from *dioptrics,* that microscopes make the sight more penetrating, and represent objects as they would appear to the eye, in case it were naturally endowed with a most exquisite sharpness?

Hyl. It is.

Phil. Consequently the microscopical representation is to be thought that which best sets forth the real nature of the thing, or what it is in itself. The colours therefore by it perceived, are more genuine and real, than those perceived otherwise.

Hyl. I confess there is something in what you say.

Phil. Besides, it is not only possible but manifest, that there actually are animals, whose eyes are by nature framed to perceive those things, which by reason of their minuteness escape our sight. What think you of those inconceivably small animals perceived by glasses? Must we suppose they are all stark blind? Or, in case they see, can it be imagined their sight hath not the same use in preserving their bodies from injuries, which appears in that of all other animals? And if it hath, is it not evident they must see particles less than their own bodies, which will present them with a far different view in each object, from that which strikes our senses? Even our own eyes do not always represent objects to us after the same manner. In the *jaundice,* every one knows that all things seem yellow. Is it not therefore highly probable, those animals in whose eyes we discern a very different texture from that of ours, and whose bodies abound with different humours, do not see the same colours in every object that we do? From all of which, should it not seem to follow that all colours are equally apparent, and that none of those which we perceive are really inherent in any outward object?

Hyl.   It should.

Phil.   The point will be past all doubt, if you consider, that in case colours were real properties or affections inherent in external bodies, they could admit of no alteration, without some change wrought in the very bodies themselves; but is it not evident from what hath been said, that upon the use of microscopes, upon a change happening in the humours of the eye, or a variation of distance, without any manner of real alteration in the thing itself, the colours of any object are either changed, or totally disappear? Nay, all other circumstances remaining the same, change but the situation of some objects, and they shall present different colours to the eye. The same thing happens upon viewing an object in various degrees of light. And what is more known, than that the same bodies appear differently coloured by candle-light from what they do in the open day? Add to these the experiments of a prism, which, separating the heterogeneous rays of light, alters the colour of any object; and will cause the whitest to appear of a deep blue or red to the naked eye. And now tell me, whether you are still of opinion, that every body hath its true, real colour inhering in it; and if you think it hath, I would fain know further from you, what certain distance and position of the object, what peculiar texture and formation of the eye, what degree or kind of light is necessary for ascertaining that true colour, and distinguishing it from apparent ones.

Hyl.   I own myself entirely satisfied, that they are all equally apparent; and that there is no such thing as colour really inhering in external bodies, but that it is altogether in the light. And what confirms me in this opinion, is, that in proportion to the light, colours are still more or less vivid; and if there be no light, then are there no colours perceived. Besides, allowing there are colours on external objects, yet how is it possible for us to perceive them? For no external body affects the mind, unless it act first on our organs of sense. But the only action of bodies is motion; and motion cannot be communicated otherwise than by impulse. A distant object therefore cannot act on the eye, nor consequently make itself or its properties perceivable to the soul. Whence it plainly follows, that it is immediately some contiguous substance, which operating on the eye occasions a perception of colours: and such is light.

Phil.   How! is light then a substance?

Hyl.   I tell you, Philonous, external light is nothing but a thin fluid substance, whose minute particles being agitated with a brisk motion, and in various manners reflected from the different surfaces of outward objects to the eyes, communicate different motions to the optic nerves; which being propagated to the brain, cause therein various impressions: and these are attended with the sensations of red, blue, yellow, &c.

Phil.   It seems, then, the light doth no more than shake the optic nerves.

Hyl.   Nothing else.

Phil.   And consequent to each particular motion of the nerves the mind is affected with a sensation, which is some particular colour.

Hyl.   Right.

Phil.   And these sensations have no existence without the mind.

Hyl.   They have not.

Phil.   How then do you affirm that colours are in the light, since by *light* you understand a corporeal substance external to the mind?

Hyl.   Light and colours, as immediately perceived by us, I grant cannot exist without the mind. But in themselves they are only the motions and configurations of certain insensible particles of matter.

Phil.   Colours then, in the vulgar sense, or taken for the immediate objects of sight, cannot agree to any but a perceiving substance.

Hyl.   That is what I say.

Phil.   Well then, since you give up the point as to those sensible qualities, which are alone thought colours by all mankind beside, you may hold what you please with regard to those invisible ones of the philosophers. It is not my business to dispute about them; only I would advise you to bethink yourself, whether, considering the inquiry we are upon, it be prudent for you to affirm *the red and blue which we see are not real colours, but certain unknown motions and figures which no man ever did or can see, are truly so.* Are not these shocking notions, and are not they subject to as many ridiculous inferences, as those you were obliged to renounce before in the case of sounds?

Hyl.   I frankly own, Philonous, that it is in vain to stand out any longer. Colours, sounds, tastes, in a word, all those termed *secondary qualities*, have certainly no existence without the mind. But by this acknowledgment I must not be supposed to derogate any thing from the reality of matter or external objects, seeing it is no more than several philosophers maintain, who nevertheless are the furthest imaginable from denying matter. For the clearer understanding of this, you must know sensible qualities are by philosophers divided into *primary* and *secondary*. The former are extension, figure, solidity, gravity, motion, and rest. And these they hold exist really in bodies. The latter are those above enumerated; or briefly, all sensible qualities beside the primary, which they assert are only so many sensations or ideas existing no where but in the mind. But all this, I doubt not, you are already apprised of. For my part, I have been a long time sensible there was such an opinion current among philosophers, but was never thoroughly convinced of its truth till now.

Phil.   You are still then of opinion, that extension and figures are inherent in external unthinking substances.

Hyl.   I am.

Phil.   But what if the same arguments which are brought against secondary qualities, will hold proof against these also?

Hyl.   Why then I shall be obliged to think, they too exist only in the mind.

Phil.   Is it your opinion, the very figure and extension which you perceive by sense, exist in the outward object or material substance?

Hyl.   It is.

Phil.   Have all other animals as good grounds to think the same of the figure and extension which they see and feel?

Hyl.   Without doubt, if they have any thought at all.

Phil.   Answer me, Hylas. Think you the senses were bestowed upon all animals for their preservation and well-being in life? or were they given to men alone for this end?

Hyl.   I make no question but they have the same use in all other animals.

Phil.   If so, is it not necessary they should be enabled by them to perceive their own limbs, and those bodies which are capable of harming them?

Hyl.   Certainly.

Phil.   A mite therefore must be supposed to see his own foot, and things equal or even less than it, as bodies of some considerable dimension; though at the same time they appear to you scarce discernible, or at best as so many visible points.

Hyl.   I cannot deny it.

Phil.   And to creatures less than the mite they will seem yet larger.

Hyl.   They will.

Phil.   Insomuch that what you can hardly discern, will to another extremely minute animal appear as some huge mountain.

Hyl.   All this I grant.

Phil.   Can one and the same thing be at the same time in itself of different dimensions?

Hyl.   That were absurd to imagine.

Phil.   But from what you have laid down it follows, that both the extension by you perceived, and that perceived by the mite itself, as likewise all those perceived by lesser animals, are each of them the true extension of the mite's foot, that is to say, by your own principles you are led into an absurdity.

Hyl.   There seems to be some difficulty in the point.

Phil.   Again, have you not acknowledged that no real inherent property of any object can be changed, without some change in the thing itself?

Hyl.   I have.

Phil.   But as we approach to or recede from an object, the visible extension varies, being at one distance ten or a hundred times greater than at another. Doth it not therefore follow from hence likewise, that it is not really inherent in the object?

Hyl.   I own I am at a loss what to think.

Phil.   Your judgment will soon be determined, if you will venture to think as freely concerning this quality, as you have done concerning the rest. Was it not admitted as a good argument, that neither heat nor cold was in the water, because it seemed warm to one hand, and cold to the other?

Hyl.   It was.

Phil.   Is it not the very same reasoning to conclude, there is no extension or figure in an object, because to one eye it shall seem little, smooth, and round, when at the same time it appears to the other, great, uneven, and angular?

Hyl.   The very same. But doth this latter fact ever happen?

Phil.   You may at any time make the experiment, by looking with one eye bare, and with the other through a microscope.

Hyl. I know not how to maintain it, and yet I am loath to give up *extension,* I see so many odd consequences following upon such a concession.

Phil. Odd, say you? After the concessions already made, I hope you will stick at nothing for its oddness. But on the other hand should it not seem very odd, if the general reasoning which includes all other sensible qualities did not also include extension? If it be allowed that no idea nor any thing like an idea can exist in an unperceiving substance, then surely it follows, that no figure or mode of extension, which we can either perceive or imagine, or have any idea of, can be really inherent in matter; not to mention the peculiar difficulty there must be, in conceiving a material substance, prior to and distinct from extension, to be the *substratum* of extension. Be the sensible quality what it will, figure, or sound, or colour; it seems alike impossible it should subsist in that which doth not perceive it.

Hyl. I give up the point for the present, reserving still a right to retract my opinion, in case I shall hereafter discover any false step in my progress to it.

Phil. That is a right you cannot be denied. Figures and extension being despatched, we proceed next to *motion.* Can a real motion in any external body be at the same time both very swift and very slow?

Hyl. It cannot.

Phil. Is not the motion of a body swift in a reciprocal proportion to the time it takes up in describing any given space? Thus a body that describes a mile in an hour, moves three times faster than it would in case it described only a mile in three hours.

Hyl. I agree with you.

Phil. And is not time measured by the succession of ideas in our minds?

Hyl. It is.

Phil. And is it not possible ideas should succeed one another twice as fast in your mind, as they do in mine, or in that of some spirit of another kind?

Hyl. I own it.

Phil. Consequently the same body may to another seem to perform its motion over any space in half the time that it doth to you. And the same reasoning will hold as to any other proportion: that is to say, according to your principles (since the motions perceived are both really in the object) it is possible one and the same body shall be really moved the same way at once, both very swift and very slow. How is this consistent either with common sense, or with what you just now granted?

Hyl.   I have nothing to say to it.

Phil.   Then as for *solidity:* either you do not mean any sensible quality by that word, and so it is beside our inquiry: or if you do, it must be either hardness or resistance. But both the one and the other are plainly relative to our senses: it being evident, that what seems hard to one animal, may appear soft to another, who hath greater force and firmness of limbs. Nor is it less plain, that the resistance I feel is not in the body.

Hyl.   I own the very sensation of resistance, which is all you immediately perceive, is not in the *body,* but the cause of that sensation is.

Phil.   But the causes of our sensations are not things immediately perceived, and therefore not sensible. This point I thought had been already determined.

Hyl.   I own it was; but you will pardon me if I seem a little embarrassed: I know not how to quit my old notions.

Phil.   To help you out, do but consider, that if extension be once acknowledged to have no existence without the mind, the same must necessarily be granted of motion, solidity, and gravity, since they all evidently suppose extension. It is therefore superfluous to inquire particularly concerning each of them. In denying extension, you have denied them all to have any real existence.

Hyl.   I wonder, Philonous, if what you say be true, why those philosophers who deny the secondary qualities any real existence, should yet attribute it to the primary. If there is no difference between them, how can this be accounted for?

Phil.   It is not my business to account for every opinion of the philosophers. But among other reasons which may be assigned for this, it seems probable, that pleasure and pain being rather annexed to the former than the latter, may be one. Heat and cold, tastes and smells, have something more vividly pleasing or disagreeable than the ideas of extension, figure, and motion, affect us with. And it being too visibly absurd to hold, that pain or pleasure can be in an unperceiving substance, men are more easily weaned from believing the external existence of the secondary, than the primary qualities. You will be satisfied there is something in this, if you recollect the difference you made between an intense and more moderate degree of heat, allowing the one a real existence, while you denied it to the other. But after all, there is no rational ground for that distinction; for surely an indifferent sensation is as truly *a sensation,* as one more pleasing or painful; and consequently should not any more than they be supposed to exist in an unthinking object.

Hyl.   It is just come into my head, Philonous, that I have some-where heard of a distinction between absolute and sensible extension. Now though it be acknowledged that *great* and *small,* consisting merely in the relation which other extended beings have to the parts of our own bodies, do not really inhere in the substances themselves; yet noth-ing obliges us to hold the same with regard to *absolute extension,* which is something abstracted from *great* and *small,* from this or that particular magnitude or figure. So likewise as to motion, *swift* and *slow* are alto-gether relative to the succession of ideas in our own minds. But it doth not follow, because those modifications of motion exist not without the mind, that therefore absolute motion abstracted from them doth not.

Phil.   Pray what is it that distinguishes one motion, or one part of extension from another? Is it not something sensible, as some de-gree of swiftness or slowness, some certain magnitude or figure pecu-liar to each?

Hyl.   I think so.

Phil.   These qualities therefore, stripped of all sensible proper-ties, are without all specific and numerical differences, as the schools call them.

Hyl.   They are.

Phil.   That is to say, they are extension in general, and motion in general.

Hyl.   Let it be so.

Phil.   But it is a universally received maxim, that *every thing which exists is particular.* How then can motion in general, or exten-sion in general, exist in any corporeal substance?

Hyl.   I will take time to solve your difficulty.

Phil.   But I think the point may be speedily decided. Without doubt you can tell, whether you are able to frame this or that idea. Now I am content to put our dispute on this issue. If you can frame in your thoughts a distinct abstract idea of motion or extension, di-vested of all those sensible modes, as swift and slow, great and small, round and square, and the like, which are acknowledged to exist only in the mind, I will then yield the point you contend for. But if you cannot, it will be unreasonable on your side to insist any longer upon what you have no notion of.

Hyl.   To confess ingenuously, I cannot.

Phil.   Can you even separate the ideas of extension and motion, from the ideas of all those qualities which they who make the distinction term *secondary*?

Hyl.   What! is it not an easy matter, to consider extension and motion by themselves, abstracted from all other sensible qualities? Pray how do the mathematicians treat of them?

Phil.   I acknowledge, Hylas, it is not difficult to form general propositions and reasonings about those qualities, without mentioning any other; and in this sense to consider or treat of them abstractedly. But how doth it follow that because I can pronounce the word *motion* by itself, I can form the idea of it in my mind exclusive of body? Or because theorems may be made of extension and figures, without any mention of *great* or *small*, or any other sensible mode or quality; that therefore it is possible such an abstract idea of extension, without any particular size or figure, or sensible quality, should be distinctly formed, and apprehended by the mind? Mathematicians treat of quantity, without regarding what other sensible qualities it is attended with, as being altogether indifferent to their demonstrations. But when laying aside the words, they contemplate the bare ideas, I believe you will find, they are not the pure abstracted ideas of extension.

Hyl.   But what say you to *pure intellect*? May not abstracted ideas be framed by that faculty?

Phil.   Since I cannot frame abstract ideas at all, it is plain, I cannot frame them by the help of *pure intellect*, whatsoever faculty you understand by those words. Besides—not to inquire into the nature of pure intellect and its spiritual objects, as *virtue, reason, God,* or the like—thus much seems manifest, that sensible things are only to be perceived by sense, or represented by the imagination. Figures therefore and extension, being originally perceived by sense, do not belong to pure intellect. But for your further satisfaction, try if you can frame the idea of any figure, abstracted from all particularities of size, or even from other sensible qualities.

Hyl.   Let me think a little—I do not find that I can.

Phil.   And can you think it possible, that should really exist in nature, which implies a repugnancy in its conception?

Hyl.   By no means.

Phil.   Since therefore it is impossible even for the mind to disunite the ideas of extension and motion from all other sensible qualities, doth it not follow, that where the one exist, there necessarily the other exist likewise?

Hyl. It should seem so.

Phil. Consequently the very same arguments which you admitted, as conclusive against the secondary qualities, are without any further application of force against the primary too. Besides, if you will trust your senses, is it not plain all sensible qualities co-exist, or to them appear as being in the same place? Do they ever represent a motion, or figure, as being divested of all other visible and tangible qualities?

Hyl. You need say no more on this head. I am free to own, if there be no secret error or oversight in our proceedings hitherto, that all sensible qualities are alike to be denied existence without the mind. But my fear is, that I have been too liberal in my former concessions, or overlooked some fallacy or other. In short, I did not take time to think.

Phil. For that matter, Hylas, you may take what time you please in reviewing the progress of our inquiry. You are at liberty to recover any slips you might have made, or offer whatever you have omitted, which makes for your first opinion.

Hyl. One great oversight I take to be this: that I did not sufficiently distinguish the *object* from the *sensation*. Now though this latter may not exist without the mind, yet it will not thence follow that the former cannot.

Phil. What object do you mean? The object of the senses?

Hyl. The same.

Phil. It is then immediately perceived?

Hyl. Right.

Phil. Make me to understand the difference between what is immediately perceived, and a sensation.

Hyl. The sensation I take to be an act of the mind perceiving; beside which, there is something perceived; and this I call the *object*. For example, there is red and yellow on that tulip. But then the act of perceiving those colours is in me only, and not in the tulip.

Phil. What tulip do you speak of? it is that which you see?

Hyl. The same.

Phil. And what do you see beside colour, figure, and extension?

Hyl. Nothing.

Phil. What you would say then is, that the red and yellow are co-existent with the extension; is it not?

Hyl.   That is not all: I would say, they have a real existence without the mind, in some unthinking substance.

Phil.   That the colours are really in the tulip which I see, is manifest. Neither can it be denied, that this tulip may exist independent of your mind or mine; but that any immediate object of the senses, that is, any idea, or combination of ideas, should exist in an unthinking substance, or exterior to all minds, is in itself an evident contradiction. Nor can I imagine how this follows from what you said just now, to wit that the red and yellow were on the tulip *you saw,* since you do not pretend to *see* that unthinking substance.

Hyl.   You have an artful way, Philonous, of diverting our inquiry from the subject.

Phil.   I see you have no mind to be pressed that way. To return then to your distinction between *sensation* and *object;* if I take you right, you distinguish in every perception two things, the one an action of the mind, the other not.

Hyl.   True.

Phil.   And this action cannot exist in, or belong to any unthinking thing; but whatever beside is implied in a perception, may.

Hyl.   That is my meaning.

Phil.   So that if there was a perception without any act of the mind, it were impossible such a perception should exist in an unthinking substance.

Hyl.   I grant it. But it is impossible there should be such a perception.

Phil.   When is the mind said to be active?

Hyl.   When it produces, puts and end to, or changes any thing.

Phil.   Can the mind produce, discontinue, or change any thing but by an act of the will?

Hyl.   It cannot.

Phil.   The mind therefore is to be accounted active in its perceptions, so far forth as volition is included in them.

Hyl.   It is.

Phil.   In plucking this flower, I am active, because I do it by the motion of my hand, which was consequent upon my volition; so likewise in applying it to my nose. But is either of these smelling?

Hyl.   No.

Phil.   I act too in drawing the air through my nose; because my breathing so rather than otherwise, is the effect of my volition.

But neither can this be called *smelling:* for if it were, I should smell every time I breathed in that manner.

Hyl.   True.

Phil.   Smelling then is somewhat consequent to all this.

Hyl.   It is.

Phil.   But I do not find my will concerned any further. Whatever more there is, as that I perceive such a particular smell or any smell at all, this is independent of my will, and therein I am altogether passive. Do you find it otherwise with you, Hylas?

Hyl.   No, the very same.

Phil.   Then as to seeing, is it not in your power to open your eyes, or keep them shut; to turn them this or that way?

Hyl.   Without doubt.

Phil.   But doth it in like manner depend on your will, that in looking on this flower, you perceive *white* rather than any other colour? Or directing your open eyes towards yonder part of the heaven, can you avoid seeing the sun? Or is light or darkness the effect of your volition?

Hyl.   No, certainly.

Phil.   You are then in these respects altogether passive.

Hyl.   I am.

Phil.   Tell me now, whether *seeing* consists in perceiving light and colours, or in opening and turning the eyes?

Hyl.   Without doubt, in the former.

Phil.   Since, therefore you are in the very perception of light and colours altogether passive, what is become of that action you were speaking of, as an ingredient in every sensation? And doth it not follow from your own concessions, that the perception of light and colours, including no action in it, may exist in an unperceiving substance? And is not this a plain contradiction?

Hyl.   I know not what to think of it.

Phil.   Besides, since you distinguish the *active* and *passive* in every perception, you must do it in that of pain. But how is it possible that pain, be it as little active as you please, should exist in an unperceiving substance? In short, do but consider the point, and then confess ingenuously, whether light and colours, tastes, sounds, &c., are not equally passions or sensations in the soul. You may indeed call them *external objects,* and give them in words what subsistence you please. But examine your own thoughts, and then tell me whether it be not as I say?

Hyl.   I acknowledge, Philonous, that upon a fair observation of what passes in my mind. I can discover nothing else, but that I am a thinking being, affected with variety of sensations; neither is it possible to conceive how a sensation should exist in an unperceiving substance. But then on the other hand, when I look on sensible things in a different view, considering them as so many modes and qualities. I find it necessary to suppose a material *substratum*, without which they cannot be conceived to exist.

Phil.   *Material substratum* call you it? Pray, by which of your senses came you acquainted with that being?

Hyl.   It is not itself sensible; its modes and qualities only being perceived by the senses.

Phil.   I presume then, it was by reflection and reason you obtained the idea of it.

Hyl.   I do not pretend to any proper positive idea of it. However I conclude it exists, because qualities cannot be conceived to exist without a support.

Phil.   It seems then you have only a relative notion of it, or that you conceive it not otherwise than by conceiving the relation it bears to sensible qualities.

Hyl.   Right.

Phil.   Be pleased therefore to let me know wherein that relation consists.

Hyl.   Is it not sufficiently expressed in the term *substratum*, or *substance*?

Phil.   If so, the word *substratum* should import, that it is spread under the sensible qualities or accidents.

Hyl.   True.

Phil.   And consequently under extension.

Hyl.   I own it.

Phil.   It is therefore somewhat in its own nature entirely distinct from extension.

Hyl.   I tell you, extension is only a mode, and matter is something that supports modes. And is it not evident the thing supported is different from the thing supporting?

Phil.   So that something distinct from, and exclusive of extension, is supposed to be the *substratum* of extension?

Hyl.   Just so.

Phil.   Answer me, Hylas. Can a thing be spread without extension? or is not the idea of extension necessarily included in *spreading*?

Hyl. It is.

Phil. Whatsoever therefore you suppose spread under any thing, must have in itself an extension distinct from the extension of that thing under which it is spread.

Hyl. It must.

Phil. Consequently every corporeal substance being the *substratum* of extension must have in itself another extension by which it is qualified to be a *substratum;* and so on to infinity. And I ask whether this be not absurd in itself, and repugnant to what you granted just now, to wit, that the *substratum* was something distinct from, and exclusive of extension.

Hyl. Aye but Philonous, you take me wrong. I do not mean that matter is *spread* in a gross literal sense under extension. The word *substratum* is used only to express in general the same thing with *substance.*

Phil. Well then, let us examine the relation implied in the term *substance.* Is it not that it stands under accidents?

Hyl. The very same.

Phil. But that one thing may stand under or support another, must it not be extended?

Hyl. It must.

Phil. Is not therefore this supposition liable to the same absurdity with the former?

Hyl. You still take things in a strict literal sense: that is not fair, Philonous.

Phil. I am not for imposing any sense on your words: you are at liberty to explain them as you please. Only I beseech you, make me understand something by them. You tell me, matter supports or stands under accidents. How! is it as your legs support your body?

Hyl. No; that is the literal sense.

Phil. Pray let me know any sense, literal or not literal, that you understand it in.—How long must I wait for an answer, Hylas?

Hyl. I declare I know not what to say. I once thought I understood well enough what was meant by matter's supporting accidents. But now the more I think on it, the less can I comprehend it; in short, I find that I know nothing of it.

Phil. It seems then you have no idea at all, neither relative nor positive, of matter; you know neither what it is in itself, nor what relation it bears to accidents.

Hyl. I acknowledge it.

Phil.   And yet you asserted, that you could not conceive how qualities or accidents should really exist, without conceiving at the same time a material support of them.

Hyl.   I did.

Phil.   That is to say, when you conceive the real existence of qualities, you do withal conceive something which you cannot conceive.

Hyl.   It was wrong, I own. But still I fear there is some fallacy or other. Pray what think you of this? It is just come into my head, that the ground of all our mistake lies in your treating of each quality by itself. Now, I grant that each quality cannot singly subsist without the mind. Colour cannot without extension, neither can figure without some other sensible quality. But as the several qualities united or blended together form entire sensible things, nothing hinders why such things may not be supposed to exist without the mind.

Phil.   Either, Hylas, you are jesting, or have a very bad memory. Though indeed we went through all the qualities by name one after another; yet my arguments, or rather your concessions no where tended to prove, that the secondary qualities did not subsist each alone by itself: but that they were not *at all* without the mind. Indeed in treating of figure and motion, we concluded they could not exist without the mind, because it was impossible even in thought to separate them from all secondary qualities, so as to conceive them existing by themselves. But then this was not the only argument made use of upon that occasion. But (to pass by all that hath been hitherto said, and reckon it for nothing, if you will have it so) I am content to put the whole upon this issue. If you can conceive it possible for any mixture or combination of qualities, or any sensible object whatever, to exist without the mind, then I will grant it actually to be so.

Hyl.   If it comes to that, the point will soon be decided. What more easy than to conceive a tree or house existing by itself, independent of, and unperceived by any mind whatsoever? I do at this present time conceive them existing after that manner.

Phil.   How say you, Hylas, can you see a thing which is at the same time unseen?

Hyl.   No, that were a contradiction.

Phil.   Is it not as great a contradiction to talk of *conceiving* a thing which is *unconceived*?

Hyl. It is.

Phil. The tree or house therefore which you think of, is conceived by you.

Hyl. How should it be otherwise?

Phil. And what is conceived is surely in the mind.

Hyl. Without question, that which is conceived is in the mind.

Phil. How then came you to say, you conceived a house or tree existing independent and out of all minds whatsoever?

Hyl. That was, I own, an oversight; but stay, let me consider what led me into it.—It is a pleasant mistake enough. As I was thinking of a tree in a solitary place, where no one was present to see it, methought that was to conceive a tree as existing unperceived or unthought of, not considering that I myself conceived it all the while. But now I plainly see, that all I can do is to frame ideas in my own mind. I may indeed conceive in my own thoughts the idea of a tree, or a house, or a mountain, but that is all. And this is far from proving, that I can conceive them *existing out of the minds of all spirits.*

Phil. You acknowledge then that you cannot possibly conceive how any one corporeal sensible thing should exist otherwise than in a mind.

Hyl. I do.

Phil. And yet you will earnestly contend for the truth of that which you cannot so much as conceive.

Hyl. I profess I know not what to think, but still there are some scruples remain with me. Is it not certain I see things at a distance? Do we not perceive the stars and moon, for example, to be a great way off? Is not this, I say, manifest to the senses?

Phil. Do you not in a dream too perceive those or the like objects?

Hyl. I do.

Phil. And have they not then the same appearance of being distant?

Hyl. They have.

Phil. But you do not thence conclude the apparitions in a dream to be without the mind?

Hyl. By no means.

Phil. You ought not therefore to conclude that sensible objects are without the mind, from their appearance or manner wherein they are perceived.

Hyl.   I acknowledge it. But doth not my sense deceive me in those cases?

Phil.   By no means. The idea or thing which you immediately perceive, neither sense nor reason inform you that it actually exists without the mind. By sense you only know that you are affected with such certain sensations of light and colours, &c. And these you will not say are without the mind.

Hyl.   True: but beside all that, do you not think the sight suggests something of *outness* or *distance?*

Phil.   Upon approaching a distant object, do the visible size and figure change perpetually, or do they appear the same at all distances?

Hyl.   They are in a continual change.

Phil.   Sight therefore doth not suggest or in any way inform you, that the visible object you immediately perceive, exists at a distance, or will be perceived when you advance further onward, there being a continued series of visible objects succeeding each other, during the whole time of your approach.

Hyl.   It doth not; but still I know, upon seeing an object, what object I shall perceive after having passed over a certain distance: no matter whether it be exactly the same or no: there is still something of distance suggested in the case.

Phil.   Good Hylas, do but reflect a little on the point, and then tell me whether there be any more in it than this. From the ideas you actually perceive by sight, you have by experience learned to collect what other ideas you will (according to the standing order of nature) be affected with after such a certain succession of time and motion.

Hyl.   Upon the whole, I take it to be nothing else.

Phil.   Now is it not plain, that if we suppose a man born blind was on a sudden made to see, he could at first have no experience of what may be suggested by sight?

Hyl.   It is.

Phil.   He would not then, according to you, have any notion of distance annexed to the things he saw; but would take them for a new set of sensations existing only in his mind.

Hyl.   It is undeniable.

Phil.   But to make it still more plain: is not *distance* a line turned endwise to the eye?

Hyl.   It is.

Phil.   And can a line so situated be perceived by sight?

Hyl. It cannot.

Phil. Doth it not therefore follow that distance is not properly and immediately perceived by sight?

Hyl. It should seem so.

Phil. Again, is it your opinion that colours are at a distance?

Hyl. It must be acknowledged, they are only in the mind.

Phil. But do not colours appear to the eye as co-existing in the same place with extension and figures?

Hyl. They do.

Phil. How can you then conclude from sight, that figures exist without, when you acknowledge colours do not; the sensible appearance being the very same with regard to both?

Hyl. I know not what to answer.

Phil. But allowing that distance was truly and immediately perceived by the mind, yet it would not thence follow it existed out of the mind. For whatever is immediately perceived is an idea: and can any *idea* exist out of the mind?

Hyl. To suppose that were absurd: but inform me, Philonous, can we perceive or know nothing beside our ideas?

Phil. As for the rational deducing of causes from effects, that is beside our inquiry. And by the senses you can best tell, whether you perceive any thing which is not immediately perceived. And I ask you, whether the things immediately perceived, are other than your own sensations or ideas? You have indeed more than once, in the course of this conversation, declared yourself on those points; but you seem, by this last question, to have departed from what you then thought.

Hyl. To speak the truth, Philonous, I think there are two kinds of objects, the one perceived immediately, which are likewise called *ideas;* the other are real things or external objects perceived by the mediation of ideas, which are their images and representations. Now I own, ideas do not exist without the mind; but the latter sort of objects do. I am sorry I did not think of this distinction sooner; it would probably have cut short your discourse.

Phil. Are those external objects perceived by sense, or by some other faculty?

Hyl. They are perceived by sense.

Phil. How! is there any thing perceived by sense, which is not immediately perceived?

Hyl.   Yes, Philonous, in some sort there is. For example, when I look on a picture or statue of Julius Caesar, I may be said, after a manner, to perceive him (though not immediately) by my senses.

Phil.   It seems, then, you will have our ideas, which alone are immediately perceived, to be pictures of external things: and that these also are perceived by sense, inasmuch as they have a conformity or resemblance to our ideas.

Hyl.   That is my meaning.

Phil.   And in the same way that Julius Caesar, in himself invisible, is nevertheless perceived by sight: real things, in themselves imperceptible, are perceived by sense.

Hyl.   In the very same.

Phil.   Tell me, Hylas, when you behold the picture of Julius Caesar, do you see with your eyes any more than some colours and figures, with a certain symmetry and composition of the whole?

Hyl.   Nothing else.

Phil.   And would not a man, who had never known any thing of Julius Caesar, see as much?

Hyl.   He would.

Phil.   Consequently he hath his sight, and the use of it, in as perfect a degree as you.

Hyl.   I agree with you.

Phil.   Whence comes it then that your thoughts are directed to the Roman emperor and his are not? This cannot proceed from the sensations or ideas of sense by you then perceived; since you acknowledge you have no advantage over him in that respect. It should seem therefore to proceed from reason and memory: should it not?

Hyl.   It should.

Phil.   Consequently it will not follow from that instance, that any thing is perceived by sense which is not immediately perceived. Though I grant we may in one acceptation be said to perceive sensible things mediately by sense: that is, when from a frequently perceived connexion, the immediate perception of ideas by one sense suggests to the mind others perhaps belonging to another sense, which are wont to be connected with them. For instance, when I hear a coach drive along the streets, immediately I perceive only the sound; but from the experience I have had that such a sound is connected with a coach, I am said to hear the coach. It is nevertheless evident, that in truth and strictness, nothing can be *heard* but *sound:*

and the coach is not then properly perceived by sense, but suggested from experience. So likewise when we are said to see a red-hot bar of iron; the solidity and heat of the iron are not the objects of sight, but suggested to the imagination by the colour and figure, which are properly perceived by that sense. In short, those things alone are actually and strictly perceived by any sense, which would have been perceived, in case that same sense had then been first conferred on us. As for other things, it is plain they are only suggested to the mind by experience grounded on former perceptions. But to return to your comparison of Caesar's picture, it is plain, if you keep to that, you must hold the real things or archetypes of our ideas are not perceived by sense, but by some internal faculty of the soul, as reason or memory. I would therefore fain know, what arguments you can draw from reason for the existence of what you call *real things* or *material objects;* or whether you remember to have seen them formerly as they are in themselves; or if you have heard or read of any one that did.

Hyl. I see, Philonous, you are disposed to raillery; but that will never convince me.

Phil. My aim is only to learn from you the way to come at the knowledge of *material beings.* Whatever we perceive, is perceived either immediately or mediately: by sense, or by reason and reflection. But as you have excluded sense, pray show me what reason you have to believe their existence; or what *medium* you can possibly make use of to prove it, either to mine or your own understanding.

Hyl. To deal ingenuously, Philonous, now I consider the point, I do not find I can give you any good reason for it. But thus much seems pretty plain, that it is at least possible such things may really exist; and as long as there is no absurdity in supposing them, I am resolved to believe as I did, till you bring good reasons to the contrary.

Phil. What! is it come to this, that you only believe the existence of material objects, and that your belief is founded barely on the possibility of its being true? Then you will have me bring reasons against it: though another would think it reasonable, the proofs should lie on him who holds the affirmative. And after all, this very point which you are now resolved to maintain without any reason, is, in effect, what you have more than once, during this discourse, seen good reason to give up. But to pass over all this; if I understand you rightly, you say our ideas do not exist without the mind; but that they are copies, images, or representations of certain originals that do.

Hyl.   You take me right.

Phil.   They are then like external things.

Hyl.   They are.

Phil.   Have those things a stable and permanent nature independent of our senses; or are they in a perpetual change, upon our producing any motions in our bodies, suspending, exerting, or altering our faculties or organs of sense?

Hyl.   Real things, it is plain, have a fixed and real nature, which remains the same, notwithstanding any change in our senses, or in the posture and motion of our bodies; which, indeed, may affect the ideas in our minds, but it were absurd to think they had the same effect on things existing without the mind.

Phil.   How then is it possible, that things perpetually fleeting and variable as our ideas, should be copies or images of any thing fixed and constant? or in other words, since all sensible qualities, as size, figure, colour, &c., that is, our ideas, are continually changing upon every alteration in the distance, medium, or instruments of sensation; how can any determinate material objects be properly represented or painted forth by several distinct things, each of which is so different from and unlike the rest? Or if you say it resembles some one only of our ideas, how shall we be able to distinguish the true copy from all the false ones?

Hyl.   I profess, Philonous, I am at a loss. I know not what to say to this.

Phil.   But neither is this all. Which are material objects in themselves, perceptible or imperceptible?

Hyl.   Properly and immediately nothing can be perceived but ideas. All material things therefore are in themselves insensible, and to be perceived only by their ideas.

Phil.   Ideas then are sensible, and their archetypes or originals insensible.

Hyl.   Right.

Phil.   But how can that which is sensible be like that which is insensible? Can a real thing in itself *invisible* be like a *colour;* or a real thing which is not *audible,* be like a *sound?* In a word, can any thing be like a sensation or idea, but another sensation or idea?

Hyl.   I must own, I think not.

Phil.   Is it possible there should be any doubt in the point? Do you not perfectly know your own ideas?

Hyl. I know them perfectly; since what I do not perceive or know, can be no part of my idea.

Phil. Consider therefore, and examine them, and then tell me if there be any thing in them which can exist without the mind: or if you can conceive any thing like them existing without the mind.

Hyl. Upon inquiry, I find it is impossible for me to conceive or understand how any thing but an idea can be like an idea. And it is most evident, that *no idea can exist without the mind.*

Phil. You are therefore by your principles forced to deny the reality of sensible things, since you made it to consist in an absolute existence exterior to the mind. That is to say, you are a downright sceptic. So I have gained my point, which was to show your principles led to scepticism.

Hyl. For the present I am, if not entirely convinced, at least silenced.

Phil. I would fain know what more you would require in order to a perfect conviction. Have you not had the liberty of explaining yourself all manner of ways? Were any little slips in discourse laid hold and insisted on? Or were you not allowed to retract or reinforce any thing you had offered, as best served your purpose? Hath not every thing you could say been heard and examined with all the fairness imaginable? In a word, have you not in every point been convinced out of your own mouth? And if you can at present discover any flaw in any of your former concessions or think of any remaining subterfuge, any new distinction, colour, or comment whatsoever, why do you not produce it?

Hyl. A little patience, Philonous. I am at present so amazed to see myself ensnared, and as it were imprisoned in the labyrinths you have drawn me into, that on the sudden it cannot be expected I should find my way out. You must give me time to look about me, and recollect myself.

Phil. Hark; is not this the college-bell?

Hyl. It rings for prayers.

Phil. We will go in then if you please, and meet here again to-morrow morning. In the mean time you may employ your thoughts on this morning's discourse, and try if you can find any fallacy in it, or invent any new means to extricate yourself.

Hyl. Agreed.

Suggested Further Readings

A good discussion of Berkeley's metaphysical position can be found in George S. Pappas, "Berkeley on Common-Sense Realism, *History of Philosophy Quarterly* 8 (1991).

A number of other good papers appear in *Locke and Berkeley: A Collection of Critical Essays,* ed. by C. B. Martin and D. M. Armstrong (New York: 1968), and *Berkeley's Principles of Human Knowledge: Critical Studies,* ed. by Gale W. Engle and Gabriele Taylor (Belmont, CA: 1968).

See also Jonathan Bennett, *Locke, Berkeley, Hume: Central Themes* (Oxford: Clarendon Press, 1971); G. J. Warnock, *Berkeley* (Harmondsworth, England: Penguin, 1969); C. D. Broad, "Berkeley's Denial of Material Substance," *Philosophical Review* 77 (1954); G. E. Moore, "The Refutation of Idealism," in *Philosophical Studies* (London: Routledge, 1922); and K. P. Winkler, *Berkeley: An Interpretation* (Oxford: Clarendon Press, 1989).

PART IV

Mind and Body

CHAPTER 13

On the Nature of the Human Mind

René Descartes

The work of René Descartes (1596–1650) is widely regarded as a beginning point in modern philosophy. In the following selection Descartes constructs a famous argument that attempts to show that our minds are not material entities. Descartes maintains that thought or, more broadly, psychological activity is essential to and sufficient for the continued existence of a person. Thought is quite clearly not essential to the continued existence of the object that is Descartes's body, and so it appears that the person Descartes cannot be the object that is Descartes's body.

The Meditation of yesterday filled my mind with so many doubts that it is no longer in my power to forget them. And yet I do not see in what manner I can resolve them; and, just as if I had all of a sudden fallen into very deep water, I am so disconcerted that I can neither make certain of setting my feet on the bottom, nor can I swim and so support myself on the surface. I shall nevertheless make an effort and follow anew the same path as that on which I yesterday entered, i.e. I shall proceed by setting aside all that in which the least doubt could be supposed to exist, just as if I had discovered that it was absolutely false; and I shall ever follow in this road until I have met with something which is certain, or at least, if I can do nothing else, until I have learned for certain that there is nothing in the world that is certain. Archimedes, in order that he might draw the terrestrial globe out of its place, and transport it elsewhere, demanded

Source: René Descartes: "Of the Nature of the Human Mind," from *The Philosophical Works of Descartes,* vol. 1. edited by Elizabeth Haldane and G. R. T. Ross (translation). Copyright 1931; pp. 149–157. Reprinted with the permission of Cambridge University Press.

only that one point should be fixed and immoveable; in the same way I shall have the right to conceive high hopes if I am happy enough to discover one thing only which is certain and indubitable.

I suppose, then, that all the things that I see are false; I persuade myself that nothing has ever existed of all that my fallacious memory represents to me. I consider that I possess no senses; I imagine that body, figure, extension, movement and place are but the fictions of my mind. What, then, can be esteemed as true? Perhaps nothing at all, unless that there is nothing in the world that is certain.

But how can I know there is not something different from those things that I have just considered, of which one cannot have the slightest doubt? Is there not some God, or some other being by whatever name we call it, who puts these reflections into my mind? That is not necessary, for is it not possible that I am capable of producing them myself? I myself, am I not at least something? But I have already denied that I had senses and body. Yet I hesitate, for what follows from that? Am I so dependent on body and senses that I cannot exist without these? But I was persuaded that there was nothing in all the world, that there was no heaven, no earth, that there were no minds, nor any bodies: was I not then likewise persuaded that I did not exist? Not at all; of a surety I myself did exist since I persuaded myself of something [or merely because I thought of something]. But there is some deceiver or other, very powerful and very cunning, who ever employs his ingenuity in deceiving me. Then without doubt I exist also if he deceives me, and let him deceive me as much as he will, he can never cause me to be nothing so long as I think that I am something. So that after having reflected well and carefully examined all things, we must come to the definite conclusion that this proposition: I am, I exist, is necessarily true each time that I pronounce it, or that I mentally conceive it.

But I do not yet know clearly enough what I am, I who am certain that I am; and hence I must be careful to see that I do not imprudently take some other object in place of myself, and thus that I do not go astray in respect of this knowledge that I hold to be the most certain and most evident of all that I have formerly learned. That is why I shall now consider anew what I believed myself to be before I embarked upon these last reflections; and of my former opinions I shall withdraw all that might even in a small degree be invalidated by the reasons which I have just brought forward, in order that there may be nothing at all left beyond what is absolutely certain and indubitable.

What then did I formerly believe myself to be? Undoubtedly I believed myself to be a man. But what is a man? Shall I say a reasonable animal? Certainly not; for then I should have to inquire what an animal is, and what is reasonable; and thus from a single question I should insensibly fall into an infinitude of others more difficult; and I should not wish to waste the little time and leisure remaining to me in trying to unravel subtleties like these. But I shall rather stop here to consider the thoughts which of themselves spring up in my mind, and which were not inspired by anything beyond my own nature alone when I applied myself to the consideration of my being. In the first place, then, I considered myself as having a face, hands, arms, and all that system of members composed of bones and flesh as seen in a corpse which I designated by the name of body. In addition to this I considered that I was nourished, that I walked, that I felt, and that I thought, and I referred all these actions to the soul: but I did not stop to consider what the soul was, or if I did stop, I imagined that it was something extremely rare and subtle like a wind, a flame, or an ether, which was spread throughout my grosser parts. As to body I had no manner of doubt about its nature, but thought I had a very clear knowledge of it; and if I had desired to explain it according to the notions that I had then formed of it, I should have described it thus: By the body I understand all that which can be defined by a certain figure: something which can be confined in a certain place, and which can fill a given space in such a way that every other body will be excluded from it; which can be perceived either by touch, or by sight, or by hearing, or by taste, or by smell: which can be moved in many ways not, in truth, by itself, but by something which is foreign to it, by which it is touched [and from which it receives impressions]: for to have the power of self-movement, as also of feeling or of thinking, I did not consider to appertain to the nature of body: on the contrary, I was rather astonished to find that faculties similar to them existed in some bodies.

But what am I, now that I suppose that there is a certain genius which is extremely powerful, and, if I may say so, malicious, who employs all his powers in deceiving me? Can I affirm that I possess the least of all those things which I have just said pertain to the nature of body? I pause to consider. I revolve all these things in my mind, and I find none of which I can say that it pertains to me. It would be tedious to stop to enumerate them. Let us pass to the attributes of soul and see if there is any one which is in me? What of nutrition or walking [the first mentioned]? But if it is so that I have no body it is also true that I can neither walk nor take nourishment. Another attribute is sensation. But one cannot feel without body, and besides I have thought I perceived many things during sleep that I recognised in my waking moments as not having been experienced at all. What of thinking? I find here that thought is an attribute that belongs to me; it alone cannot be separated from me. I am, I exist, that is certain. But how often? Just when I think; for it might possibly be the case if I ceased entirely to think, that I should likewise cease altogether to exist. I do not now admit anything which is not necessarily true: to speak accurately I am not more than a thing which thinks, that is to say a mind or a soul, or an understanding, or a reason, which are terms whose significance was formerly unknown to me. I am, however, a real thing and really exist; but what thing? I have answered: a thing which thinks.

And what more? I shall exercise my imagination [in order to see if I am not something more]. I am not a collection of members which we call the human body: I am not a subtle air distributed through these members, I am not a wind, a fire, a vapour, a breath, nor anything at all which I can imagine or conceive; because I have assumed that all these were nothing. Without changing that supposition I find that I only leave myself certain of the fact that I am somewhat. But perhaps it is true that these same things which I supposed were non-existent because they are unknown to me, are really not different from the self which I know. I am not sure about this, I shall not dispute about it now; I can only give judgment on things that are known to me. I know that I exist, and I inquire what I am, I whom I know to exist. But it is very certain that the knowledge of my existence taken in its precise significance does not depend on things whose existence is not yet known to me; consequently it does not depend on those which I can feign in imagination. And indeed the very term *feign* in imagination[1] proves to me my error, for I really do this if I image myself a something, since to imagine is nothing else than to contemplate the figure or image of a corporeal thing. But I already know for certain that I am, and that it may be that all these images, and, speaking generally, all things that relate to the nature of body are nothing but dreams [and chimeras]. For this reason I see clearly that I have as little reason to say, 'I shall stimulate my imagination in order to know more

---

[1]Or 'form an image' (effingo).

distinctly what I am,' than if I were to say, 'I am now awake, and I perceive somewhat that is real and true: but because I do not yet perceive it distinctly enough, I shall go to sleep of express purpose, so that my dreams may represent the perception with greatest truth and evidence.' And, thus, I know for certain that nothing of all that I can understand by means of my imagination belongs to this knowledge which I have of myself, and that it is necessary to recall the mind from this mode of thought with the utmost diligence in order that it may be able to know its own nature with perfect distinctness.

But what then am I? A thing which thinks. What is a thing which thinks? It is a thing which doubts, understands, [conceives], affirms, denies, wills, refuses, which also imagines and feels.

Certainly it is no small matter if all these things pertain to my nature. But why should they not so pertain? Am I not that being who now doubts nearly everything, who nevertheless understands certain things, who affirms that one only is true, who denies all the others, who desires to know more, is averse from being deceived, who imagines many things, sometimes indeed despite his will, and who perceives many likewise, as by the intervention of the bodily organs? Is there nothing in all this which is as true as it is certain that I exist, even though I should always sleep and though he who has given me being employed all his ingenuity in deceiving me? Is there likewise any one of these attributes which can be distinguished from my thought, or which might be said to be separated from myself? For it is so evident of itself that it is I who doubts, who understands, and who desires, that there is no reason here to add anything to explain it. And I have certainly the power of imagining likewise; for although it may happen (as I formerly supposed) that none of the things which I imagine are true, nevertheless this power of imagining does not cease to be really in use, and it forms part of my thought. Finally, I am the same who feels, that is to say, who perceives certain things, as by the organs of sense, since in truth I see light, I hear noise, I feel heat. But it will be said that these phenomena are false and that I am dreaming. Let it be so; still it is at least quite certain that it seems to me that I see light, that I hear noise and that I feel heat. That cannot be false; properly speaking it is what is in me called feeling[2]; and used in this precise sense that is no other thing than thinking.

---

[2]Sentire.

From this time I begin to know what I am with a little more clearness and distinction than before; but nevertheless it still seems to me, and I cannot prevent myself from thinking, that corporeal things, whose images are framed by thought, which are tested by the senses, are much more distinctly known than that obscure part of me which does not come under the imagination. Although really it is very strange to say that I know and understand more distinctly these things whose existence seems to me dubious, which are unknown to me, and which do not belong to me, than others of the truth of which I am convinced, which are known to be and which pertain to my real nature, in a word, than myself. But I see clearly how the case stands: my mind loves to wander, and cannot yet suffer itself to be retained within the just limits of truth. Very good, let us once more give it the freest rein, so that, when afterwards we seize the proper occasion for pulling up, it may the more easily be regulated and controlled.

Let us begin by considering the commonest matters, those which we believe to be the most distinctly comprehended, to wit, the bodies which we touch and see; not indeed bodies in general, for these general ideas are usually a little more confused, but let us consider one body in particular. Let us take, for example, this piece of wax: it has been taken quite freshly from the hive, and it has not yet lost the sweetness of the honey which it contains; it still retains somewhat of the odour of the flowers from which it has been culled; its colour, its figure, its size are apparent; it is hard, cold, easily handled, and if you strike it with the finger, it will emit a sound. Finally all the things which are requisite to cause us distinctly to recognise a body, are met within it. But notice that while I speak and approach the fire what remained of the taste is exhaled, the smell evaporates, the colour alters, the figure is destroyed, the size increases, it becomes liquid, it heats, scarcely can one handle it, and when one strikes it, no sound is emitted. Does the same wax remain after this change? We must confess that it remains; none would judge otherwise. What then did I know so distinctly in this piece of wax? It could certainly be nothing of all that the senses brought to my notice, since all these things which fall under taste, smell, sight, touch, and hearing, are found to be changed, and yet the same wax remains.

Perhaps it was what I now think, viz. that this wax is not that sweetness of honey, nor that agreeable scent of flowers, nor that particular whiteness, nor that figure, nor that sound, but simply a body which a little while before appeared to me as perceptible under these forms, and which is not perceptible under others. But what, precisely, is it that I imagine when I form such conceptions? Let us attentively consider this, and, abstracting from all that does not belong to the wax, let us see what remains. Certainly nothing remains excepting a certain extended thing which is flexible and movable. But what is the meaning of flexible and movable? Is it not that I imagine that this piece of wax being round is capable of becoming square and of passing from a square to a triangular figure? No, certainly it is not that, since I imagine it admits of an infinitude of similar changes, and I nevertheless do not know how to compass the infinitude by my imagination, and consequently this conception which I have of the wax is not brought about by the faculty of imagination. What now is this extension? Is it not also unknown? For it becomes greater when the wax is melted, greater when it is boiled, and greater still when the heat increases; and I should not conceive [clearly] according to truth what wax is, if I did not think that even this piece that we are considering is capable of receiving more variations in extension than I have ever imagined. We must then grant that I could not even understand through the imagination what this piece of wax is, and that it is my mind[3] alone which perceives it. I say this piece of wax in particular for as to wax in general it is yet clearer. But what is this piece of wax which cannot be understood excepting by the [understanding or] mind? It is certainly the same that I see, touch, imagine, and finally it is the same which I have always believed it to be from the beginning. But what must particularly be observed is that its perception is neither an act of vision, nor of touch, nor of imagination, and has never been such although it may have appeared formerly to be so, but only an intuition[4] of the mind, which may be imperfect and confused as it was formerly, or clear and distinct as it is at present, according as my attention is more or less directed to the elements which are found in it, and of which it is composed.

Yet in the meantime I am greatly astonished when I consider [the great feebleness of mind] and its proneness to fall [insensibly] into error; for although without giving expression to my thoughts I consider all this in my own mind, words often impede me and I am almost deceived by the terms of ordinary language. For we say that we

---

[3]entendement F., mens L.

[4]inspectio.

see the same wax, if it is present, and not that we simply judge that it is the same from its having the same colour and figure. From this I should conclude that I knew the wax by means of vision and not simply by the intuition of the mind; unless by chance I remember that, when looking from a window and saying I see men who pass in the street, I really do not see them, but infer that what I see is men, just as I say that I see wax. And yet what do I see from the window but hats and coats which may cover automatic machines? Yet I judge these to be men. And similarly solely by the faculty of judgment which rests in my mind, I comprehend that which I believed I saw with my eyes.

A man who makes it his aim to raise his knowledge above the common should be ashamed to derive the occasion for doubting from the forms of speech invented by the vulgar; I prefer to pass on and consider whether I had a more evident and perfect conception of what the wax was when I first perceived it, and when I believed I knew it by means of the external senses or at least by the common sense[5] as it is called, that is to say by the imaginative faculty, or whether my present conception is clearer now that I have most carefully examined what it is, and in what way it can be known. It would certainly be absurd to doubt as to this. For what was there in this first perception which was distinct? What was there which might not as well have been perceived by any of the animals? But when I distinguish the wax from its external forms, and when, just as if I had taken from it its vestments, I consider it quite naked, it is certain that although some error may still be found in my judgment, I can nevertheless not perceive it thus without a human mind.

But finally what shall I say of this mind, that is, of myself, for up to this point I do not admit in myself anything but mind? What then, I who seem to perceive this piece of wax so distinctly, do I not know myself, not only with much more truth and certainty, but also with much more distinctness and clearness? For if I judge that the wax is or exists from the fact that I see it, it certainly follows much more clearly that I am or that I exist myself from the fact that I see it. For it may be that what I see is not really wax, it may also be that I do not possess eyes with which to see anything; but it cannot be that when I see, or (for I no longer take account of the distinction) when I think I see, that I myself who think am nought. So if I judge that the wax

---

[5]sensus communis.

exists from the fact that I touch it, the same thing will follow, to wit, that I am; and if I judge that my imagination, or some other cause, whatever it is, persuades me that the wax exists, I shall still conclude the same. And what I have here remarked of wax may be applied to all other things which are external to me [and which are met with outside of me]. And further, if the [notion or] perception of wax has seemed to me clearer and more distinct, not only after the sight or the touch, but also after many other causes have rendered it quite manifest to me, with how much more [evidence] and distinctness must it be said that I now know myself, since all the reasons which contribute to the knowledge of wax, or any other body whatever, are yet better proofs of the nature of my mind! And there are so many other things in the mind itself which may contribute to the elucidation of its nature, that those which depend on body such as these just mentioned, hardly merit being taken into account.

But finally here I am, having insensibly reverted to the point I desired, for, since it is now manifest to me that even bodies are not properly speaking known by the senses or by the faculty of imagination, but by the understanding only, and since they are not known from the fact that they are seen or touched, but only because they are understood, I see clearly that there is nothing which is easier for me to know than my mind. But because it is difficult to rid oneself so promptly of an opinion to which one was accustomed for so long, it will be well that I should halt a little at this point, so that by the length of my meditation I may more deeply imprint on my memory this new knowledge.

Suggested Further Readings

A vast amount has been written about the Cartesian argument for dualism. A famous critical assessment of dualism can be found in Gilbert Ryle, *The Concept of Mind* (London: Hutchinson and Company, 1949), chap. 1.

For more recent discussions of these issues, see Sydney Shoemaker, "Immortality and Dualism," in *Identity, Cause, and Mind* (New York: Cambridge University Press, 1984); Steven Yablo, "The Real Distinction between Mind and Body," *Canadian Journal of Philosophy*, Supplement 16 (1990); and Joshua Hoffman and Gary S. Rosenkrantz, *Substance among Other Categories* (Cambridge, MA: Cambridge University Press, 1994), chap. 5.

See also the suggestions at the end of the following selection.

CHAPTER 14

Body and Soul

Richard Swinburne

The world is populated by a great many people, but what is a person? The British philosopher Richard Swinburne argues that we are composite beings: One of a person's components is a material body, and the other is an immaterial soul. Our bodies are inessential to our continued existence, whereas our souls are not. In theory, we can survive with bodies other than our present bodies; indeed, we can survive without bodies—as disembodied but nonetheless thoughtful beings.

Richard Swinburne is a professor of philosophy at the University of Keele. He is the author of a number of books, including The Existence of God *(1979) and* The Evolution of the Soul *(1986).*

As stated in Chapter 1, I understand by substance dualism the view that those persons which are human beings (or men) living on Earth, have two parts linked together, body and soul. A man's body is that to which his physical properties belong. If a man weighs ten stone then his body weighs ten stone. A man's soul is that to which the (pure) mental properties of a man belong. If a man imagines a cat, then, the dualist will say, his soul imagines a cat. Talk of a man's body and its properties is of course perfectly natural ordinary-language talk; talk of a man's soul less so. The dualist would, however, claim that souls do feel and believe, even if we do not naturally talk in that way. (In ordinary talk perhaps minds, rather than souls, are, however, often given mental predicates—to be said to imagine things or feel weary, for instance.) On the dualist account the whole man has the properties he does because his constituent parts have the properties they do. I weigh ten stone because my body does; I

---

imagine a cat because my soul does. Mixed mental properties, as I defined them in Chapter 1 are those mental properties which can be analysed in terms partly of a physical component. Writing a letter is a mixed property because it involves purposing to write a letter (mental property) being followed by the hand so moving that a letter is written (physical property). The instantiation of the mental property is followed by (and, I argued in Chapter 5, causes) the instantiation of the physical property. On the dualist view the mixed property belongs to the man, because its pure mental-property component belongs to his soul, and its physical-property component belongs to his body. I write a letter because my body makes certain movements and my soul purposed that it should.

A person has a body if there is a chunk of matter through which he makes a difference to the material world, and through which he acquires true beliefs about that world. Those persons who are men have bodies because stimuli landing on their eyes or ears give them true beliefs about the world, which they would not otherwise have; and they make differences to the world by moving arms and legs, lips and fingers. Our bodies are the vehicles of our knowledge and operation. The 'linking' of body and soul consists in there being a body which is related to the soul in this way.

Some dualists, such as Descartes, seem sometimes to be saying that the soul is the person; any living body temporarily linked to the soul is no part of the person. That, however, seems just false. Given that what we are trying to do is to analyse the nature of those entities, such as men, which we normally call 'persons,' we must say that arms and legs and all other parts of the living body of a man are parts of the person. My arms and my legs are parts of me. The crucial point that Descartes[1] and others were presumably trying to make is not that (in the case of men) the living body is not part of the person, but that it is not essentially, only contingently, part of the person. The body is separable from the person and the person can continue even if the body is destroyed. Just as I continue to exist wholly and completely if you cut off my hair, so, the dualist holds, it is possible that I continue to exist if you destroy my body. The soul, by contrast, is the

---

[1]There are passages in Descartes which can be interpreted as saying that the body is no part of the person and other passages which can be interpreted as saying that the body is a part, but not an essential part, of the person. For examples and commentary, see pp. 63–6 of B. Smart, 'How can Persons be ascribed M-Predicates,' *Mind*, 1977, **86,** 49–66.

necessary core which must continue if I am to continue; it is the part of the person which is necessary for his continuing existence. The person is the soul together with whatever, if any, body is linked temporarily to it.

By saying that the person *'can'* continue if the body is destroyed I mean only that this is *logically* possible, that there is no contradiction in supposing the soul to continue to exist without its present body or indeed any body at all (although such a soul would not then, on the understanding which I have given to 'man'—see pp. 4f.—be a man or part of a man, although it would have been part of a man). Whether this normally happens, is another question; and one to which I shall come later. My concern in this chapter is to show that a man has a part, his soul, as well as his body—whether or not in the natural course of things that part continues to exist without the body.

So much for what dualism is. Now for its general defence. My initial argument in its support has two stages. I argue first that knowledge of what happens to bodies and their parts, and knowledge of the mental events which occur in connection with them will not suffice to give you knowledge of what happens to those persons who are (currently) men. Talk about persons is not analysable in terms of talk about bodies and their connected mental life. And more generally, it is logically possible that persons continue to exist when their bodies are destroyed. Secondly, I argue that the most natural way of making sense of this fact is talking of persons as consisting of two parts, body and soul—the soul being the essential part, whose continuing alone makes for the continuing of the person.

So then for the first stage of the argument. It is, I suggest, a factual matter whether a person survives an operation or not. There is a truth here that some later person is or is not the same as some pre-operation persons, but it is, I shall suggest, a truth of which we can be ignorant however much we know about human bodies and the fate of their organs.

How much of my body must remain if I am to survive an operation? Plausibly, with respect to all parts of my body other than the brain, if you remove them I survive. Cut off my arm or leg, replace my heart or liver, and I continue to exist; there is the same person before as after the operation. Remove my brain, on the other hand, and put it in the skull of another body, and replace it by a different brain, and intuitively the rest of the body that was mine is no longer. I go where my brain goes. We treat the brain as the core of the body which determines whose body it is. That is because with the brain goes the characteristic pattern of mental life which is expressed in behaviour. The brain gives rise to a man's mental states—his beliefs, including his apparent memories, and his desires, their expression in public behaviour, and his characteristic pattern of unintended response to circumstance. The brain gives rise to memory and character which we see as more intimately connected with personal identity than the digestive processes. But what if only some of my brain is removed? Do I survive or not?

The brain, as it is well known, has two very similar hemispheres—a left and a right hemisphere. The left hemisphere plays a major role in the control of limbs and of processing sensory information from the right side of the body (and from the right sides of the two eyes); and the right hemisphere plays a major role in the control of limbs of and processing of sensory information from the left side of the body (and from the left sides of the two eyes). The left hemisphere normally plays the major role in the control of speech. Although the hemispheres have different roles in adults, they interact with each other; and if parts of a hemisphere are removed, at any rate early in life, the roles of those parts are often taken over by parts of the other hemisphere.[2] Brain operations are not infrequent, which remove substantial parts of the brain. It might be possible one day to remove a whole hemisphere, without killing the person, and to transplant it into the skull of a living body from which the brain has just been removed, so that the transplant takes. There would then appear to be two separate living persons. Since both are controlled by hemispheres originating from the original person p, and since apparent memory and character and their manifestation in behaviour are dependent on factors present in both hemispheres, we would expect each publicly to affirm such apparent memories and to behave as if he had p's character. It is possible that appearances might be misleading here—that one of the apparent persons was simply a robot, with no life of conscious experience at all, but caused to behave as if it had. But, if we suppose that appearances are not misleading here, the transplant will have created two persons, both with p's apparent memories and character. But they cannot both be p. For if they were, they would both be the same person as each other, and clearly they are not—they have now distinct mental lives. The operation would therefore create at least one new person—we may have our views about which (if either) resultant person *p* is, but we could be wrong. And that is my basic point—however much we knew in such a situation about what happens to the parts of a person's body, we would not know for certain what happens to the person.

I can bring the uncertainty out strongly by adapting Bernard Williams's famous mad surgeon story.[3] Suppose that a mad surgeon captures you and announces that he is going to transplant your left cerebral hemisphere into one body, and your right one into another. He is going to torture one of the resulting persons and free the other with a gift of a million pounds. You can choose which person is to be tortured and which to be rewarded, and the surgeon promises to do as you choose. You believe his promise. But how are you to choose? You wish to choose that you are rewarded, but you do not know which resultant person will be you. You may have studied neurophysiology deeply and think that you have detected some all-important difference between the hemispheres which indicates which is the vehicle of personal identity; but, all too obviously, you could be mistaken. Whichever way you choose, the choice would, in Williams's telling word about his similar story, be a 'risk'—which shows that there is something other to the continuity of the person, than any continuity of parts of brain or body.

It is a fashionable criticism of an argument of this kind that it assumes that personal identity is indivisible. We do not make this kind of assumption with respect to inanimate things, such as cars and countries. These survive in part. If half the bits of my old car are used together with bits of another old car in the construction of a new car, my car has survived in part. And if the other bits of my old car are used in construction of another new car, then my old car has survived in part as one car and in part as another car. If we succeed in dividing humans, why should not human survival be like that? If half my brain is put into one body, and half into another body, do I not survive partly as one person and partly as another?

However, persons such as men are very different from inanimate beings such as cars. They have hopes, fears, and memories

---

[3]For the original, see B. Williams, 'The Self and the Future,' *Philosophical Review,* 1970, **79,** 161–80.

which make it very difficult to give sense to the idea of their partial survival. Consider again the victim in the mad surgeon story. If he survives to the extent to which his brain survives, his choice of who is to suffer will make no difference; however he chooses one person who is partly he will suffer, and one person who is partly he will be rewarded. In that case he has reason both for joyous expectation and for terrified anticipation. But how can such an attitude of part joyous expectation and part terrified anticipation be justified, since no future person is going to suffer a mixed fate? It is hard to give any sense to the notion of there being a half-way between one having certain future experiences which some person has, and one not having them, and so to the notion of a person being divisible.

But even if this notion of partial survival does make sense, it will in no way remove the difficulty, which remains this. Although it *may* be the case if my two brain hemispheres are transplanted into different bodies, I survive partly as the person whose body is controlled by one and partly as the person whose body is controlled by the other, it may not be like that at all. Maybe I go just where the left hemisphere goes. As we have seen, the fate of some parts of my body, such as my arms and legs, is quite irrelevant to the fate of me. And plausibly the fate of some parts of my brain is irrelevant—can I not survive completely a minor brain operation which removes a very small tumour? But then maybe it is the same with some larger parts of the brain too. We just don't know. If the mad surgeon's victim took the attitude that it didn't matter which way he chose, we would, I suggest, regard him as taking an unjustifiably dogmatic attitude. For the fact that a resultant person has qualitatively the same memory and character is certainly no guarantee that he is me—in whole or in part. For while I continue to exist quite untouched by any change of brain or character or memory, some other person *p* with my character could, through a long process of hypnosis, be given 'my' apparent memories in the sense of being led to believe that he had the same past experiences as I did. But that would not make me any less than fully me; and if I remain fully me, there is no room for *p* to be me, even in small part.

My argument has been that knowledge of what has happened to a person's body and its parts will not necessarily give you knowledge of what has happened to the person, and so, that persons are not the same as their bodies. I have illustrated my argument by considerations which, alas, are far from being mere thought-experiments. Brain transplants may well happen in a few decades time, and we need to be armed with the philosophical apparatus to cope with them. But it suffices to make my point to point out that the mere logical possibility of a person surviving with only half his brain (the mere fact that this is not a self-contradictory supposition) is enough to show that talk about persons is not analysable as talk about bodies and their parts.

My arguments so far, however, show only that some brain continuity (or other bodily continuity) is not sufficient for personal identity; which is something over and above that. They do not rule out the possibility that some bodily matter needs to continue *as well*, if personal identity is to continue. Thought-experiments of more extravagant kinds rule out this latter possibility. Consider life after death. It seems logically possible that any present person who is currently a man, having the mental properties which we know men to have and which I have described in previous chapters, could continue to be with loss of his present body. We understand what is being claimed in fairy stories or in serious religious affirmations which affirm life after death. It seems self-consistent to affirm with respect to any person who is the subject of mental properties that he continue to have them, while his body is annihilated. This shows that the very notions of sensation, purposing, etc. involve the concepts of a subject of sensation and purposing of whom it makes sense to suppose that he continue while his body does not.

This suggestion of a man acquiring a new body may be made more plausible, to someone who has difficulty in grasping it, by supposing the event to occur gradually. Suppose that one morning a make wakes up to find himself unable to control the right side of his body, including his right arm and leg. When he tries to move the right-side parts of his body, he finds that the corresponding left-side parts of his body move; and when he tries to move the left-side parts, the corresponding parts of his wife's body move. His knowledge of the world comes to depend on stimuli to his left side and to his wife's right side (e.g. light rays stimulating his left eye and his wife's right eye). The bodies fuse to some extent physiologically as with Siamese twins, while the man's wife loses control of her left side. The focus of the man's control of and knowledge of the world is shifting. One may suppose the process completed as the man's control is shifted to the wife's body, while his wife loses control of it. At that stage he becomes able to move parts of what was his wife's body as a basic action, not merely by doing some other action.

Equally coherent, I suggest, is the supposition that a person who is a man might become disembodied. A person has a body if there is one particular chunk of matter through which he has to operate on and learn about the world. But suppose that a person who has been a man now finds himself no longer able to operate on the world, nor to acquire true beliefs about it; yet still to have a full mental life, some of it subject to his voluntary control. He would be disembodied. Or suppose, alternatively, that he finds himself able to operate on and learn about the world within some small finite region, without having to use one particular chunk of matter for this purpose. He might find himself with knowledge of the position of objects in a room (perhaps by having visual sensations, perhaps not), and able to move such objects just like that, in the ways in which we know about the positions of our limbs and can move them. But the room would not be, as it were, the person's body; for we may suppose that simply by choosing to do so he can gradually shift the focus of his knowledge and control, e.g. to the next room. The person would be in no way limited to operating and learning through one particular chunk of matter. Hence he would have no body. The supposition that a person who is currently a man might become disembodied in one or other of these ways seems coherent.

Not merely is it not logically necessary that a person have a body or brain made of certain matter, if he is to be the person which he is; it is not even necessitated by laws of nature.[4] For let us assume what I shall later call into question, the most that is claimed for natural laws, that they dictate the course of evolution, the emergence of consciousness, and the behaviour and mental life of men in a totally deterministic way. In 4000m BC the Earth was a cooling globe of inanimate atoms. Natural laws then, we assume, dictated how this globe would evolve, and so which arrangements of matter would be the bodies of conscious men, and so, also, just how those men would behave and what mental life they would have. My point now is that what natural laws still in no way determine is which inanimate body is yours and which is mine. Just the same arrangement of matter and just the same laws could have given to me the body (and so the behaviour and mental life) which are now yours, and to you the body (and so the behaviour and mental life) which are now mine. It needs either God or

---

[4]I owe this argument to an article by John Knox, Jr, "Can the Self Survive the Death of its Mind?", *Religious Studies*, 1969, **5**, 85–97.

chance to allocate bodies to persons; the most that natural laws could determine is that bodies of a certain construction are the bodies of some person or other who in consequence of this construction behave in certain ways and have a certain mental life. Since the body which is presently yours could have been mine (logic and even natural laws allow), that shows that none of the matter of which my body is presently made is essential to my being the person that I am.

And so I come to the second stage of my argument. How are we to bring out within an integrated system of thought, this fact which the first stage of my argument has, I hope, shown conclusively— that continuing matter is not (logically) essential for the continuing existence of persons. For persons are substances, and for substances of all other kinds continuing matter *is* necessary for the continuing existence of the substance. If a substance S_2 at a time t_2 is to be the same substance as a substance S_1 at an earlier time t_1 it must (of logical necessity) be made of the same matter as S_1, or at least of matter obtained from S_1 by gradual replacement. If my desk today is to be the same desk as my desk last year it must be made largely of the same wood; a drawer or two may have been replaced. But the desk would not be the same desk if all the wood had been replaced. In the case of living organisms such as plants, we do allow for total replacement of matter—so long as it is gradual. The full-grown oak tree possesses few if any of the molecules which formed the sapling, but so long as molecules were replaced only gradually over a period while most other molecules continued to form part of the organized tree, the tree continues to exist. That continuing matter was necessary for the continued existence of a substance, was a central element in Aristotle's account of substances. But now we have seen that persons can survive (it is logically possible) without their bodily matter continuing to be part of them. In this situation we have a choice. Either we can say simply that persons are different—in their case continuing matter is not necessary for the continued existence of the substance. Or we can try to make sense of this fact by liberalizing Aristotle's account a little. We can say that the continuing existence of some of the stuff of which a substance is made is necessary for the continued existence of the substance. Normally the stuff of which substances are made is merely matter, but some substances (viz. persons) are made in part of immaterial stuff, soul-stuff. Given, as I suggested earlier, that persons are indivisible, it follows that soul-stuff comes in indivisible chunks, which we may call souls.

This liberalized Aristotelian assumption I will call the quasi-Aristotelian assumption: that a substance S_2 is the same substance as an earlier substance S_1 at t_1 only if S_2 is made of some of the same stuff as S_1 (or stuff obtained therefrom by gradual replacement).

Given the quasi-Aristotelian assumption, and given, that for any present person who is currently conscious, there is no logical impossibility, whatever else may be true now of that person, that that person continue to exist without his body, it follows that that person must now actually have a part other than a bodily part which can continue, and which we may call his soul—and so that his possession of it is entailed by his being a conscious being. For there is not even a logical possibility that if I now consist of nothing but matter and the matter is destroyed, that I should nevertheless continue to exist. From the mere logical possibility of my continued existence there follows the actual fact that there is now more to me than my body; and that more is the essential part of myself. A person's being conscious is thus to be analysed as an immaterial core of himself, his soul being conscious.[5]

If we are prepared to say that substances can be the same, even though none of the stuff (in a wide sense) of which they are made is the same, the conclusion does not follow. The quasi-Aristotelian assumption provides rather a partial definition of 'stuff' than a factual truth. To say that a person has an immaterial soul is not to say that if you examine him closely enough under an acute enough microscope you will find some very rarified constituent which has eluded the power of ordinary microscopes. It is just a way of expressing the point within a traditional framework of thought that persons can—it is logically possible—continue, when their bodies do not. It does, however, seem a very natural way of expressing the point—especially once we allow that persons can become disembodied. Unless we adopt the more liberal quasi-Aristotelian assumption, we shall have to say that there can be substances which are not made of anything, and which are the same substances as other substances which are made of matter.

There is therefore abundant reason for saying that a man consists of body plus soul. A man's physical properties (e.g. having such-and-such a shape and mass) clearly belong to his body and to the person in virtue of belonging to his body. If the man dies and ceases to

---

[5]See Additional Note 2.

exist (i.e. his soul ceases to exist), there need (logically) be no change in the way those properties characterize his body. A man's pure mental properties, however, belong to his soul and to the man in virtue of belonging to his soul; for it is logically possible that those properties continue to characterize the person who is that man, when his body is destroyed. Hence mixed properties belong to the person in virtue of their physical-component properties belonging to his body and their pure mental-component properties belonging to his soul.

Note that on the dualist view which I am expounding, although the identity of persons at different times is constituted by the identity of their souls (and these are not publicly observable things), it remains the case that all claims about personal identity are verifiable, in the sense that there can be evidence of observation for or against them. For although continuity of brain and of apparent memory (i.e. a man's apparent memory of who he was and what he did) do not constitute personal identity, they are evidence of it, and so evidence of sameness of soul. Why they are evidence of personal identity is an issue to which I shall come in the next chapter.

And not merely are all claims about personal identity verifiable via observations of other things, but over a short period personal identity is itself experienceable by the subject, as directly as anything can be experienced, in the continuity of his perceptions and other mental events. Human perception is perception of change. The perceptual beliefs to which our senses give rise are not just beliefs that at one time things were arranged thus, and at another time in a different way, and at a third in yet a third way. For as a result of perception we come to know not merely what happened, but in what order things happened—that first things were arranged like this, and subsequently, like that, and yet subsequently like that. Sometimes, of course, we infer from our perceptions and our general knowledge of how things happen in the world, the order in which those perceptions and so the events perceived[6] must have occurred. Knowing that, in general, babies get bigger and not smaller, I may infer that my seeing the small baby John occurred before my seeing the medium-sized baby John, which occurred before my seeing the large baby John. But not all knowledge of the order of our perceptions

---

[6]We learn through perceptions of the effects which we ourselves bring about that, in general, spatially near events are perceived at approximately the instant of their occurrence. See my *Space and Time,* Macmillan, London, second edition, 1981, p. 145.

can derive from inference. For first, we have much knowledge of the actual order of perceptions, when as far as our general knowledge of the world goes, the events perceived could as easily occur in one order as in the other—such as a ball moving on a particular occasion from left to right rather than from right to left. And secondly, in order to infer the order of our perceptions, we need that general knowledge of the order in which events of the kind perceived occur. Yet our beliefs about the latter (e.g. our knowledge that in general babies get bigger) would be without justification (and so would not amount to the knowledge which we surely rightly believe them to be) unless they were grounded in many perceptions made by ourselves or others of actual such successions.

So the perceptual beliefs to which our senses give rise include (and must include if we are to have knowledge, grounded in experience) beliefs about the order in which things happen. That is, we perceive things happening in a certain order. The most primitive things which an observer sees include not just the train being here, but also the train moving from here to there, from there to the third place. When a train moves along a railway line, the observer S on the bank has the following successive perceptions: S sees (train T at place p followed by T at place q); S sees (T at q followed by T at r); S sees (T at r followed by T at u), and so on. He acquires the belief that things were as perceived. But then that is not quite a full description of the beliefs which he acquires through perception. For if those were all his data, he would have no grounds for believing that the second event which I have described succeeded the first event (rather than being one which occurred on an entirely different occasion). Why he does have such grounds is because he also acquires, through having the succession of perceptions, the further perceptual beliefs that the first perception is succeeded by the second perception, and that the second perception is succeeded by the third perception. He acquires, through experience, knowledge of temporal succession. And, more particularly, the further perceptual beliefs which he acquires are that *his* first perception is succeeded by his second perception, and so on. The content of his further perceptual beliefs is that there has been a succession of perceptions had by a common subject, viz. himself. Using the word 'experience' for a brief moment in a wide sense, we may say that the succession of perceptions is itself a datum of experience; S experiences his experiences as overlapping in a stream of awareness. As John Foster, to whom I owe this argument, puts it, 'It is this double overlap which provides the sensible continuity of sense experience and unifies presentations [i.e. perceptions] into a stream of awareness . . . It is in the unity of a stream that we primarily discern the identity of a subject.'[7] That is, one of a subject's basic data is of the continuity of experience, which means the continuity of the mental events of a common subject, the person.

In a famous passage Hume wrote: 'When I enter most intimately into what I call *myself,* I always stumble on some particular perception or other, of heat or cold, light or shade, love or hatred, pain or pleasure. I never catch *myself* at any time without a perception.'[8] It may well be that Hume never catches himself without a 'perception' (i.e. a conscious episode) but his bare datum is not just 'perceptions,' but successions of overlapping 'perceptions' experienced by a common subject. If it were not so, we would have no grounded knowledge of succession. Hume says that he fails to find the common subject. One wonders what he supposed that the common subject would look like, and what he considered would count as its discovery. Was he looking for a common element in all his visual fields, or a background noise which never ceased? Is that the sort of thing he failed to find?[9] Yet the self which he ought to have found in all his mental events is supposed to be the subject, not the object of perception. And finding it consists in being aware of different mental events as had by the same subject.

Further, among the data of experience are not merely that certain mental events are the successive mental events of a common subject, but also that certain simultaneous mental events are states of a common subject. At a single moment of time you feel cramp in your leg, hear the noise of my voice, and see the movement of my arms. It is among the data of your experience (i.e. among basic data, not inferable from anything closer to experience) that these are all *your* mental events.

---

[7]J. Foster, 'In *Self*-Defence' in (ed.) G. F. MacDonald, *Perception and Identity,* Essays presented to A. J. Ayer, Macmillan, London, 1979, p. 176.

[8]*A Treatise of Human Nature,* 1. 4. 6.

[9]Because our awareness of ourselves is different in kind from our awareness of objects of experience, Berkeley chose to say that we have a 'notion' of the former but an 'idea' of the latter. 'To expect that by any multiplication or enlargement of our faculties we may be enabled to know a spirit as we do a triangle, seems as absurd as if we should hope to see a sound'—G. Berkeley, *Principles of Human Knowledge,* 1710, § 142.

Yet that mental events are states of the same subject is something that knowledge of brains and their states and knowledge of which mental events were occurring would be insufficient to tell you. As I noted earlier, some sensory nervous impulses (including those from the right-side limbs and right sides of the two eyes) go in the first instance to the left brain hemisphere, and some (including those from the left-side limbs and the left sides of the two eyes) go to the right brain hemisphere; and the two hemispheres control different parts of the body (the left hemisphere controlling speech, as well as the right arm and leg). However, in the normal brain the signals to one hemisphere are immediately transmitted to the other, and the 'instructions' given by one are correlated with events in the other. But if the brain operation of cerebral commissurotomy (cutting the main tract between the two hemispheres) is performed, the hemispheres act in a much more independent way, and it is a crucial issue whether by the operation we have created two persons. Experimenters seek to discover by the responses in speech, writing or other means whether one subject is co-experiencing the different visual, auditory, olfactory, etc. sensations caused through the sense organs or whether there are two subjects which have different sensations. The subject (or subjects) is aware of one or more kinds of sensation and the experimenter seeks to elicit information about his (or their) sensations from him (or them). That is not quite as easy as it sounds. If the mouth confesses to seeing a green object but not to hearing a loud noise; while the left hand denies seeing a green object, but claims instead to hear a loud noise; that is not enough in itself to show that no subject co-experienced a loud noise and saw a green object. For, first, mouth and hand may sometimes, as may any limb, give a reflex response to a question rather than a considered judgement (the reflex may be out of a subject's control without being in the control of some other subject), and the reflexes available to different limbs may relate to information of different kinds (the left hand may be able by pointing to give the answers to questions about objects presented to the left side of the visual field only without the subject being aware of the objects presented and/or the responses of the hand); and secondly, there may be kinds of belief (about his mental events) which the split-brain subject can convey only by one means rather than another. The effect of cerebral commissurotomy is not immediately evident, and various complex experiments are needed before any one hypothesis about what has happened can gain significant support.

That hypothesis about how many subjects of experience and action, i.e. persons, there are, will be best supported the better it can be filled out as a detailed claim about which beliefs, desires, and other mental events the one or more different subjects have, which explains in a simple way many observed data. For example a hypothesis that there are two persons becomes more plausible if we can in certain circumstances attribute to each not merely distinct sensations and beliefs about them, but distinct beliefs and desires of a general character, i.e. different views about what is good and bad in the world, and different inclinations to bring about long-term states of affairs, and these different beliefs and desires are continuing beliefs which explain whole patterns of limb movements—e.g. the left hand and the mouth express different complex moral claims. For then the patterns of response of the different sets of limbs would be more analogous to the conscious responses of men by which they manifest beliefs of which they are conscious, than to patterns of mere unconscious reflex. And it would be simpler to suppose that similar patterns of response (of all limbs in normal persons, and of one set of limbs in split-brain persons) have similar explanations (viz, in distinct sets of beliefs and desires) than to suppose that the unity of response in the latter case does not arise from the unity of a person with a continuing mental life.[10]

What is clear in these cases is that what the investigator is trying to discover is something other than and beyond the pattern of the subject's responses, as it is also something other than and beyond the extent of the connections between the two hemispheres.

That something is whether there are one or two subjects of experience and action, i.e. persons. Whether one person is having both sensations is something of which he will be immediately aware, but which others have to infer (fallibly) from the complex public data. In considering simultaneous experience as in considering experience over time, we see that which persons are the same as other persons are facts additional to publicly observable facts. Dualism can

---

[10]On the results and interpretation of such experiments, see Springer and Deutsch, op. cit., chs. 2 and 10, articles referred to therein (especially J. E. LeDoux, D. H. Wilson, and M. S. Gazzaniga, 'A Divided Mind: Observations on the Conscious Properties of the Separated Hemispheres,' *Annals of Neurology*, 1977, **2**, 417–21), and, most recently, D. M. and Valerie Mackay, 'Explicit Dialogue Between Left and Right Half-Systems of Split Brains,' *Nature*, 1982, **295**, 690–1.

make sense of why there is sometimes (i.e. in cases of cerebral commissurotomy) a difficult problem of discovering how many persons there are. Dualism, in claiming that a person is body plus soul, explains the problem as the problem of discovering the number of souls connected to a given brain. Since the outsider can only discover this by fallible inference from bodily behaviour and brain-states, discovering the answer can be difficult and we can always go wrong. However, co-experience is no artificial construct; it is as primitive a datum of experience for the subject as anything could be. The subject's awareness is an awareness of himself as the common subject of various sensations (and other mental events).

My conclusion—that truths about persons are other than truths about their bodies and parts thereof—is, I suggest, forced upon anyone who reflects seriously on the fact of the unity of consciousness over time and at a time. A framework of thought which makes sense of this fact is provided if we think of a person as body plus soul, such that the continuing of the soul alone guarantees the continuing of the person.

Suggested Further Readings

A natural companion to this selection is Swinburne, "Personal Identity: The Dualist Theory," in Richard Swinburne and Sydney Shoemaker, *Personal Identity* (Oxford: Blackwell, 1984).

For a very different conception of persons, see John L. Pollock, *How to Build a Person: A Prolegomenon* (Cambridge, MA: MIT Press), chap. 2.

An interesting critical examination of Swinburne's position can be found in Paul Moser and Arnold vander Nat, "Surviving Souls," *Canadian Journal of Philosophy* 23 (1993).

There are interesting things in Terence Penelhum, *Survival and Disembodied Existence* (New York: Humanities Press, 1970); Norman Malcolm, "The Conceivability of Mechanism," *Philosophical Review* (1968); Nicholas Jolley, "The Immortal Soul," in *Leibniz and Locke* (Oxford: Clarendon Press, 1986); Jerome Shaffer, "Mental Events and the Brain," in *The Nature of Mind,* ed. by David M. Rosenthal (New York: Oxford University Press, 1991); and William E. Seager, "Descartes on the Union of Mind and Body," *History of Philosophy Quarterly* 4 (1985).

CHAPTER 15

*C*onceivability and the Cartesian Argument for Dualism

James van Cleve

The concept of possibility plays a central role in many metaphysical arguments. That is certainly the case when we consider standard Cartesian arguments in favor of dualism. However, there are questions about assertions of possibility. For one thing, how do we establish that something is possible? Some theorists say that a proposition is possible if it is conceivable or imaginable. This issue is examined in the following section.

James van Cleve is a professor of philosophy at Brown University. He is the author of numerous papers on metaphysical topics.

Descartes thought he could prove that he was an incorporeal substance—a thing that thinks, but lacks extension and all traits of body. The recent critical literature has thrown a good deal of light on his reasoning, but has not given it exactly its due. I shall argue that it is more cogent than is commonly supposed, and that if it fails, it does so for reasons other than those usually given.

Descartes presents the argument I wish to discuss in the Second and Sixth Meditations and clarifies it in response to objections from Arnauld. A good reconstruction of it is as follows:

(1) It is conceivable for me that (I think & nothing is extended). (Premise)

(2) Whatever is conceivable for me is possible. (Premise)

(3) It is possible that (I think & nothing is extended). (1,2)

Source: James van Cleve: "Conceivability and the Cartesian Argument for Dualism," from *Pacific Philosophical Quarterly,* 1983, vol. 64, pp. 35–38. Copyright University of Southern California. Reprinted by the permission of Blackwell Publishers, Oxford, UK.

(4) It is necessary that (if I think, then I exist). (Premise)

(5) It is possible that (I exist & I am unextended). (3,4)

(6) If x is essentially F, then it is not possible that (x exists & x is not F). (Premise)

(7) I am not essentially extended. (5,6)

(8) All extended things are essentially extended. (Premise)

(9) I am not an extended thing. (7,8)

(Two terminological points: I shall use 'thinking' in broad Cartesian fashion to cover all states of consciousness and 'body' as a synonym for 'extended thing.')

The premises in this argument are (1), (2), (4), (6), and (8). Two of these are so obvious as to require no defense: (4) is just *cognito, ergo sum,* and (6) follows from the definition of 'essence.' A third premise, (8), though perhaps not so incontrovertible as (4) and (6), nonetheless has a good deal of intuitive appeal. That leaves just (1) and (2), the premises invoking the notion of conceivability, and it is these I wish to discuss. I shall begin with (2), which has probably drawn more criticism than any other aspect of Descartes's argument.

1.   Is Conceivability a Mark of Possibility?

Premise (2) of Descartes's argument—that whatever is conceivable is possible—was a commonly accepted maxim of 17th- and 18th-century philosophy. It received its most vigorous employment in the hands of Hume, who used it repeatedly to refute claims that this or that principle was a necessary truth by pointing out that the opposite was conceivable. Despite such impressive historical credentials, however, one may well have qualms about so audacious a principle. Why make human powers of conception the measure of possibility? Couldn't something human beings find conceivable turn out to be impossible for all that?

The answer depends in part, of course, on what meaning is assigned to 'conceivable.' Thomas Reid considered several candidates and found none of them satisfactory. 'Conceivable' cannot mean *entertainable,* for even contradictions are entertainable; indeed, we must entertain them to recognize them as contradictions. Nor can it mean *believable,* for there are plenty of impossibilities that people have believed in.

What Hume himself meant by 'conceivable' was *imaginable.* Now if by 'imagining' a state of affairs we mean forming an accurate mental picture of it, it might be thought that no impossible state of affairs is imaginable. But I do not see how to guarantee this result short of defining an accurate picture as one that shares all traits of the thing pictured, in which case next to nothing is imaginable.

Even without such stringent requirements on imaginability Hume's criterion is more limited in scope than he himself supposed. Take a state of affairs Hume said he could imagine: an event E's occurring without any cause whatsoever. Can one really form a picture of this? One can doubtless picture E's occurring without picturing a cause for it, but this is not the same as picturing E's occurring without a cause. There being no cause for E is just not the sort of state of affairs one can picture. The same goes, I think, for there being no extended objects.

Whatever we mean by 'conceivable,' we shall have to contend with the following objection. In 1742 Goldbach proposed to Euler that every even number greater than two is the sum of two primes—a conjecture that to this day has eluded both counterexample and proof. Now isn't it conceivable that Goldbach's conjecture is true? Most people to whom I have put this question say yes. But now consider the *negation* of Goldbach's conjecture: isn't *it* conceivable as well? Most people to whom I have put the question again say yes. Thus, many people profess to find Goldbach's conjecture and its negation equally conceivable. But one of them is impossible! Since either Goldbach's conjecture or its negation must be true, and since every proposition of mathematics is necessarily true if true at all, one proposition in this pair must be a necessary truth and the other an impossibility. It thus appears that at least one impossible proposition is conceivable.

If we are to avoid this objection, we must find a sense of 'conceivable' in which it is false that Goldbach's conjecture and its negation are both conceivable. Fortunately, there is such a sense. Two observations will lead us to it.

First, there is such a thing as just "seeing"—by a kind of intellectual vision—that a proposition is true. Each of us can "see" in this way that $2 + 3 = 5$, that nothing is both round and square, and much else besides. "Seeing" of this sort is what many philosophers call 'intuition' and what Descartes called 'clear and distinct perception.'

Second, there is such a thing as seeing that a proposition is *possible.* Perhaps this is a special use of the above—intuiting as true a proposition of the form 'It is possible that P.' In any case, I would claim that I can see that it is possible for there to be red things that are not round, creatures with eyes that are not creatures with ears, and much else besides.

This experience of seeing something to be possible is what I wish to propose as the relevant meaning of 'conceivable.' To distinguish conceivability in this sense from another variety to be introduced presently, I shall call it *strong* conceivability. Let us define it explicitly as follows:

> P is *strongly conceivable* for S iff S sees that P is possible.

'Sees' as it occurs here is not governed by "success grammar." That is, someone's seeing that P is possible does not *analytically* entail that P *is* possible. But it might nonetheless be good evidence for, or even a guarantee of, P's possibility; this is what we must investigate.

When conceivability is thus understood, the problem about Goldbach's conjecture no longer arises. For no one, I venture to say, really sees that the conjecture is possible; nor does anyone see that its negation is possible. When people say they find the conjecture and its negation both conceivable, I think they just mean this: they do *not* see that either one is *im*possible. This suggests a weaker sense of conceivability, which we can define as follows:

> If P is a proposition that S is considering, then P is *weakly conceivable* for S iff S does not see that P is impossible.

The Goldbach example destroys the credentials of weak conceivability as a mark of possibility, but it leaves those of strong conceivability unchallenged. Can we take strong conceivability as a guarantee of possibility? For Descartes the rule that whatever is strongly conceivable is possible would have been a corollary of his rule that whatever is perceived clearly and distinctly is true. But is clear and distinct perception a guarantee of truth? Dare we assume that intuition is infallible? Standing in the way of this assumption is the apparent fact that what one person sees to be true or possible another may later show to be false or impossible. The classic case is that of Cantor and Russell. Cantor supposedly saw that the fundamental axiom of his theory of sets—that for any predicate P there is a set whose members are just those things that satisfy P—was not only possible but true. But Russell later showed that this principle leads to contradiction. Since Russell's proof was itself based on intuition, we may say that the fundamental obstacle to assuming that all intuitions are true is that intuitions sometimes conflict.

Is there any way out of this predicament? One approach is to say that Cantor did not really see that his axiom was true—he only *thought* he did. Another approach is to distinguish two *grades* of intuition, one of which is entirely reliable even if the other is not. (Something like this, presumably, is the point of Descartes's insistence on *clear and distinct* perception.) We could then insist that Cantor's intuition was only of the dimmer and less reliable kind.

A stock objection to either maneuver is that it only relocates the problem. For how is one to know whether one is really having an intuition, or whether one's intuition is of the right kind? I do not regard this as a serious objection, however, since it presupposes that a state of intuition, clear and distinct perception, or the like can give its possessor knowledge only if he recognizes that he is in a state of that kind, and I have argued elsewhere that this presupposition is false. Nonetheless, the approach I shall adopt here concedes the fallibility of intuition.

To grant that intuition is fallible is not to grant that it is epistemically worthless. On the contrary, one may still hold that someone's intuiting P is a prima facie justifier for him of belief in P. What this means is that it is necessarily the case that anyone who intuits P is, in the absence of defeaters, justified in believing P. A defeater is a reason for thinking P false despite one's intuition of its truth; a typical example would be a proof of not–P based on premises themselves justified by intuition. If we adopt this approach, we will say that Cantor was justified in believing his axiom, but would no longer have been so had he learned of Russell's Paradox. (Of course, at no time did Cantor *know* that his axiom was true.)

Returning to Descartes's argument, my proposal is that for premise (2) we substitute the following:

> **(2′)** Whatever is strongly conceivable for me is something I am prima facie justified in believing to be possible.

The first two premises now no longer entail that the third is true, but they do entail (when the conceivability referred to in (1) is understood as *strong* conceivability) that the arguer is prima facie justified in believing it.

I realize that some people will object even to the weakened conceivability premise. But let it be recognized that those who do are not objecting to Descartes's argument in particular; they are merely indulging in a quite general skepticism. For why should intuitions of possibility be any less epistemically trustworthy than intuitions generally? And if intuition in general is not a prima facie justifier of belief, how do we even know that $2 + 3 = 5$, or that a proposition and its denial can't both be true? If $(2')$ is the *only* thing a critic can find to question in Descartes's argument, he should concede that it is no worse off than any other argument.

Suggested Further Readings

See Stephen Yablo, "Is Conceivability a Guide to Possibility?" *Philosophy & Phenomenological Research* LIII (1993); Michael Hooker, "Descartes's Denial of Mind-Body Identity," in *Descartes: Critical and Interpretative Essays,* ed. by Michael Hooker (Baltimore, Maryland: Johns Hopkins University Press, 1978); and Ian Hacking, "Possibility," *Philosophical Review* (1967), and "All Kinds of Possibility," *Philosophical Review* (1975).

CHAPTER 16

*A*n Argument for the Identity Theory

David K. Lewis

If we have immaterial souls, our psychological states are states of our souls. States of an immaterial substance are not physical states, and that means that our psychological states are not physical states. The following selection argues against this point of view. On the assumption that psychological states are causes of human behavior, there is reason to judge that such states are physical states, and that is bad news for those who postulate immaterial entitles called souls.

David K. Lewis is a professor of philosophy at Princeton University. Lewis's books include On the Plurality of Worlds *(1986) and* Counterfactuals *(1973).*

1. Introduction

The (Psychophysical) Identity Theory is the hypothesis that—not necessarily but as a matter of fact—every experience[1] is identical with

Source: David K. Lewis: "An Argument for the Identity Theory," from *The Journal of Philosophy,* January 1966, vol. LXIII, pp. 17–25. Reprinted by permission of The Journal of Philosophy, Inc. and the author.

[1]Experiences herein are to be taken in general as universals, not as abstract particulars. I am concerned, for instance, with pain, an experience that befalls many people at many times; or with pain of some definite sort, an experience which at least *might* be common to different people at different times. Both are universals, capable of repeated instantiation. The latter is a narrower universal than the former, as crimson of some definite shade is narrower than red, but still a universal. I am not concerned with the particular pain of a given person at a given time, an abstract entity which cannot itself recur but can only be similar—at best, exactly similar—to other particular pains of other people or at other times. We might identify such abstract particulars with pairs of a universal and a single concrete particular instance thereof;

some physical state.[2] Specifically, with some neurochemical state. I contend that we who accept the materialistic working hypothesis that physical phenomena have none but purely physical explanations must accept the identity theory. This is to say more than do most friends of the theory, who say only that we are free to accept it, and should for the sake of some sort of economy or elegance. I do not need to make a case for the identity theory on grounds of economy,[3] since I believe it can and should rest on a stronger foundation.

My argument is this: The definitive characteristic of any (sort of) experience as such is its causal role, its syndrome of most typical causes and effects. But we materialists believe that these causal roles which belong by analytic necessity to experiences belong in fact to certain physical states. Since those physical states possess the definitive characteristics of experience, they must be the experiences.

My argument parallels an argument which we will find uncontroversial. Consider cylindrical combination locks for bicycle chains. The definitive characteristic of their state of being unlocked is the causal role of that state, the syndrome of its most typical causes and effects: namely, that setting the combination typically causes the lock to be unlocked and that being unlocked typically causes the lock to open when gently pulled. That is all we need know in order to ascribe to the lock the state of being or of not being unlocked. But we may learn that, as a matter of fact, the lock contains a row of slotted discs; setting the combination typically causes the slots to be aligned; and alignment of the slots typically causes the lock to open when gently pulled. So alignment of slots occupies precisely the causal role that we ascribed to being unlocked by analytic necessity, as the definitive characteristic of being unlocked (for these locks). Therefore alignment of slots is identical with being unlocked (for these locks). They are one and the same state.

_____

or we might leave them as unanalyzed, elementary beings, as in Donald C. Williams, "On the Elements of Being," *Review of Metaphysics,* **7** (1953): 3–18 and 171–192. [All but the first sentence of this note was added in October 1969.]

[2]States also are to be taken in general as universals. I shall not distinguish between processes, events, phenomena, and states in a strict sense.

[3]I am therefore invulnerable to Brandt's objection that the identity theory is not clearly more economical than a certain kind of dualism. "Doubts about the Identity Theory," in *Dimensions of Mind,* Sidney Hook, ed. (New York: NYU Press, 1960), pp. 57–67.

2.   The Nature of the Identity Theory

We must understand that the identity theory asserts that certain physical states are experiences, introspectible processes or activities, not that they are the supposed intentional objects that experiences are experiences *of*. If these objects of experience really exist separate from experiences of them, or even as abstract parts thereof, they may well also be something physical. Perhaps they are also neural, or perhaps they are abstract constituents of veridically perceived surroundings, or perhaps they are something else, or nothing at all; but that is another story. So I am not claiming that an experience of seeing red, say, is itself somehow a red neural state.

Shaffer has argued that the identity theory is impossible because (abstract particular) experiences are, by analytic necessity, unlocated, whereas the (abstract particular) neural events that they supposedly are have a location in part of the subject's nervous system.[4] But I see no reason to believe that the principle that experiences are unlocated enjoys any analytic, or other, necessity. Rather it is a metaphysical prejudice which has no claim to be respected. Or if there is, after all, a way in which it is analytic that experiences are unlocated, that way is irrelevant: perhaps in our presystematic thought we regard only concreta as located in a primary sense, and abstracta as located in a merely derivative sense by their inherence in located concreta. But this possible source of analytic unlocatedness for experiences does not meet the needs of Shaffer's argument. For neural events are abstracta too. Whatever unlocatedness accrues to experiences not because they are mental but because they are abstract must accrue as much to neural events. So it does not discriminate between the two.

The identity theory says that experience-ascriptions have the same reference as certain neural-state-ascriptions: both alike refer to the neural states which are experiences. It does not say that these ascriptions have the same sense. They do not; experience-ascriptions refer to a state by specifying the causal role that belongs to it accidentally, in virtue of causal laws, whereas neural-state-ascriptions refer to a state by describing it in detail. Therefore the identity theory does not imply that whatever is true of experiences as such is

---

[4]"Could Mental States Be Brain Processes?", *The Journal of Philosophy*, 58, 26 (Dec. 21, 1961): 813–822.

likewise true of neural states as such, nor conversely. For a truth about things of any kind *as such* is about things of that kind not by themselves, but together with the sense of expressions by which they are referred to as things of that kind.[5] So it is pointless to exhibit various discrepancies between what is true of experiences as such and what is true of neural states as such. We can explain those discrepancies without denying psychophysical identity and without admitting that it is somehow identity of a defective sort.

We must not identify an experience itself with the attribute that is predicated of somebody by saying that he is having that experience.[*] The former *is* whatever state it is that occupies a certain definitive causal role; the latter is the attribute of *being in* whatever state it is that occupies that causal role. By this distinction we can answer the objection that, since experience-ascriptions and neural-state-descriptions are admittedly never synonymous and since attributes are identical just in case they are predicated by synonymous expressions, therefore experiences and neural states cannot be identical attributes. The objection does establish a nonidentity, but not between

---

[5]Here I have of course merely applied to states Frege's doctrine of sense and reference. See "On Sense and Reference," in *Translations from the Philosophical Writings of Gottlob Frege,* Peter Geach and Max Black, eds. (New York: Oxford, 1960), pp. 56–78.

[*]Here I mean to deny all identities of the form ⌈α is identical with the attribute of having α⌉ where α is an experience-name definable as naming the occupant of a specified causal role. I deny, for instance, that pain is identical with the attribute of having pain. On my theory, 'pain' is a *contingent* name—that is, a name with different denotations in different possible worlds—since in any world, 'pain' names whatever state happens in that world to occupy the causal role definitive of pain. If state X occupies that role in world V while another state Y (incompatible with X) occupies that role in world W, then 'pain' names X in V and Y in W. I take 'the attribute of having pain,' on the other hand, as a *non-contingent* name of that state or attribute Z that belongs, in any world, to whatever things have pain in that world—that is, to whatever things have in that world the state named in that world by 'pain.' (I take states to be attributes of a special kind: attributes of things at times.) Thus Z belongs in V to whatever things have X in V, and in W to whatever things have Y in W; hence Z is identical neither with X nor with Y.

Richard Montague, in "On the Nature of Certain Philosophical Entities," *Monist* 53 (1969): 172–173, objects that I seem to be denying a logical truth having as its instances all identities of the form ⌈α is identical with the attribute of having α⌉ where α is a *non-contingent* name of a state which is (either contingently or necessarily) an experience. I would agree that such identities are logically true; but those are not the identities I mean to deny, since I claim that our ordinary experience-names—'pain' and the like—are *contingent* names of states. [This note was added in October 1969.]

experiences and neural states. (It is unfair to blame the identity theory for needing the protection of so suspiciously subtle a distinction, for a parallel distinction is needed elsewhere. Blue is, for instance, the color of my socks, but blue is not the attribute predicated of things by saying they are the color of my socks, since ' . . . is blue' and ' . . . is the color of my socks' are not synonymous.)

3. The First Premise: Experiences Defined by Causal Roles

The first of my two premises for establishing the identity theory is the principle that the definitive characteristic of any experience as such is its causal role. The definitive causal role of an experience is expressible by a finite[6] set of conditions that specify its typical causes and its typical effects under various circumstances. By analytic necessity these conditions are true of the experience and jointly distinctive of it.

My first premise is an elaboration and generalization of Smart's theory that avowals of experience are, in effect, of the form 'What is going on in me is like what is going on in me when . . . ' followed by specification of typical stimuli for, or responses to, the experience.[7] I wish to add explicitly that . . . may be an elaborate logical compound of clauses if necessary; that . . . must specify typical causes or effects of the experience, not mere accompaniments; that these typical causes and effects may include other experiences; and that the formula does not apply only to first-person reports of experience.

This is not a materialist principle, nor does it ascribe materialism to whoever speaks of experiences. Rather it is an account of the parlance common to all who believe that experiences are something or other real and that experiences are efficacious outside their own

---

[6]It would do no harm to allow the set of conditions to be infinite, so long as it is recursive. But I doubt the need for this relaxation.

[7]*Philosophy and Scientific Realism* (New York: Humanities Press, 1963), ch. v. Smart's concession that his formula does not really translate avowals is unnecessary. It results from a bad example: 'I have a pain' is not translatable as 'What is going on in me is like what goes on when a pin is stuck into me,' because the concept of pain might be introduced without mention of pins. Indeed; but the objection is no good against the translation 'What is going on in me is like what goes on when (i.e. when and because) my skin is damaged.' [See J. J. C. Smart, "Sensations and Brain Processes," pp. 53–66 in this volume; and James W. Cornman, "The Identity of Mind and Body," pp. 73–79 in this volume.]

realm. It is neutral between theories—or a lack of any theory—about what sort of real and efficacious things experiences are: neural states or the like, pulsations of ectoplasm or the like, or just experiences and nothing else. It is not neutral, however, between all current theories of mind and body. Epiphenomenalist and parallelist dualism are ruled out as contradictory because they deny the efficacy of experience. Behaviorism as a thoroughgoing dispositional analysis of all mental states, including experiences,[8] is likewise ruled out as denying the reality and *a fortiori* the efficacy of experiences. For a pure disposition is a fictitious entity. The expressions that ostensibly denote dispositions are best construed as syncategorematic parts of statements of the lawlike regularities in which (as we say) the dispositions are manifest.

Yet the principle that experiences are defined by their causal roles is itself behaviorist in origin, in that it inherits the behaviorist discovery that the (ostensibly) causal connections between an experience and its typical occasions and manifestations somehow contain a component of analytic necessity. But my principle improves on the original behavioristic embodiment of that discovery in several ways:

First, it allows experiences to be something real and so to be the effects of their occasions and the causes of their manifestations, as common opinion supposes them to be.

Second, it allows us to include other experiences among the typical causes and effects by which an experience is defined. It is crucial that we should be able to do so in order that we may do justice, in defining experiences by their causal roles, to the introspective accessibility which is such an important feature of any experience. For the introspective accessibility of an experience is its propensity reliably to cause other (future or simultaneous) experiences directed intentionally upon it, wherein we are aware of it. The requisite freedom to interdefine experiences is not available in general under behaviorism; interdefinition of experiences is permissible only if it can in principle be eliminated, which is so only if it happens to be possible to arrange experiences in a hierarchy of definitional priority. We, on the other hand, may allow interdefinition with no such constraint. We may expect to get mutually interdefined families of

---

[8]Any theory of mind and body is compatible with a dispositional analysis of mental states other than experiences or with so-called "methodological behaviorism."

experiences, but they will do us no harm. There will be no reason to identify anything with one experience in such a family without regard to the others—but why should there be? Whatever occupies the definitive causal role of an experience in such a family does so by virtue of its own membership in a causal isomorph of the family of experiences, that is, in a system of states having the same pattern of causal connections with one another and the same causal connections with states outside the family, viz., stimuli and behavior. The isomorphism guarantees that if the family is identified *throughout* with its isomorph then the experiences in the family will have their definitive causal roles. So, *ipso facto,* the isomorphism requires us to accept the identity of all the experiences of the family with their counterparts in the causal isomorph of the family.[9]

Third, we are not obliged to define an experience by the causes and effects of exactly all and only its occurrences. We can be content rather merely to identify the experience as that state which is *typically* caused in thus-and-such ways and *typically* causes thus-and-such effects, saying nothing about its causes and effects in a (small) residue of exceptional cases. A definition by causes and effects in typical cases suffices to determine what the experience is, and the fact that the experience has some characteristics or other besides its definitive causal role confers a sense upon ascriptions of it in some exceptional cases for which its definitive typical causes and effects are absent (and likewise upon denials of it in some cases for which they are present). Behaviorism does not acknowledge the fact that the experience is something apart from its definitive occasions and manifestations, and so must require that the experience be defined by a strictly necessary and sufficient condition in terms of them. Otherwise the behaviorist has merely a partial explication of the experience by criteria, which can never give more than a presumption that the experience is present or absent, no matter how much we know about the subject's behavior and any lawlike regularities that may govern it. Relaxation of the requirement for a strictly necessary and sufficient condition is

---

[9]Putnam discusses an analogous case for machines: a family of ("logical" or "functional") states defined by their causal roles and mutually interdefined, and a causally isomorphic system of ("structural") states otherwise defined. He does not equate the correlated logical and structural states. "Minds and Machines," in *Dimensions of Mind,* pp. 148–179. [See also Hilary Putnam, "The Nature of Mental States," reprinted in this volume, pp. 150–161, especially section III.]

welcome. As anybody who has tried to implement behaviorism knows, it is usually easy to find conditions which are *almost* necessary and sufficient for an experience. All the work—and all the complexity which renders it incredible that the conditions found should be known implicitly by every speaker—comes in trying to cover a few exceptional cases. In fact, it is just impossible to cover some atypical cases of experiences behavioristically: the case of a perfect actor pretending to have an experience he does not really have; and the case of a total paralytic who cannot manifest any experience he does have (both cases under the stipulation that the pretense or paralysis will last for the rest of the subject's life no matter what happens, in virtue of regularities just as lawlike as those by which the behaviorist seeks to define experiences).

It is possible, and probably good analytic strategy, to reconstrue any supposed pure dispositional state rather as a state defined by its causal role. The advantages in general are those we have seen in this case: the state becomes recognized as real and efficacious; unrestricted mutual interdefinition of the state and others of its sort becomes permissible; and it becomes intelligible that the state may sometimes occur despite prevention of its definitive manifestations.[10]

I do not offer to prove my principle that the definitive characteristics of experiences as such are their causal roles. It would be verified by exhibition of many suitable analytic statements saying that various experiences typically have thus-and-such causes and effects. Many of these statements have been collected by behaviorists; I inherit these although I explain their status somewhat differently. Behaviorism is widely accepted. I am content to rest my case on the argument that my principle can accommodate what is true in behaviorism and can escape attendant difficulties.

4. The Second Premise: Explanatory Adequacy of Physics

My second premise is the plausible hypothesis that there is some unified body of scientific theories, of the sort we now accept, which together provide a true and exhaustive account of all physical

---

[10]Quine advocates this treatment of such dispositional states as are worth saving in *Word and Object* (Cambridge, Mass.: MIT Press, and New York: Wiley, 1960), pp. 222–225. "They are conceived as built-in, enduring structural traits."

phenomena (i.e. all phenomena describable in physical terms). They are unified in that they are cumulative: the theory governing any physical phenomenon is explained by theories governing phenomena out of which that phenomenon is composed and by the way it is composed out of them. The same is true of the latter phenomena, and so on down to fundamental particles or fields governed by a few simple laws, more or less as conceived of in present-day theoretical physics. I rely on Oppenheim and Putnam for a detailed exposition of the hypothesis that we may hope to find such a unified physicalistic body of scientific theory and for a presentation of evidence that the hypothesis is credible.[11]

A confidence in the explanatory adequacy of physics is a vital part, but not the whole, of any full-blooded materialism. It is the empirical foundation on which materialism builds its superstructure of ontological and cosmological doctrines, among them the identity theory. It is also a traditional and definitive working hypothesis of natural science—what scientists say nowadays to the contrary is defeatism or philosophy. I argue that whoever shares this confidence must accept the identity theory.

My second premise does not rule out the existence of nonphysical phenomena; it is not an ontological thesis in its own right. It only denies that we need ever explain physical phenomena by nonphysical ones. Physical phenomena are physically explicable, or they are utterly inexplicable insofar as they depend upon chance in a physically explicable way, or they are methodologically acceptable primitives. All manner of nonphysical phenomena may coexist with them, even to the extent of sharing the same space-time, provided only that the nonphysical phenomena are entirely inefficacious with respect to the physical phenomena. These coexistent nonphysical phenomena may be quite unrelated to physical phenomena; they may be causally independent but for some reason perfectly correlated with some physical phenomena (as experiences are, according to parallelism); they may be epiphenomena, caused by some physical phenomena but not themselves causing any (as experiences are, according to epiphenomenalism). If they are epiphenomena they may even be correlated with some physical phenomena, perfectly and by virtue of a causal law.

---

[11]"Unity of Science as a Working Hypothesis," in *Minnesota Studies in the Philosophy of Science,* II, Herbert Feigl, Michael Scriven, and Grover Maxwell, eds. (Minneapolis: Univ. of Minnesota Press, 1958), pp. 3–36.

5.   Conclusion of the Argument

But none of these permissible nonphysical phenomena can be experiences. For they must be entirely inefficacious with respect to all physical phenomena. But all the behavioral manifestations of experiences are (or involve) physical phenomena and so cannot be effects of anything that is inefficacious with respect to physical phenomena. These behavioral manifestations are among the typical effects definitive of any experience, according to the first premise. So nothing can be an experience that is inefficacious with respect to physical phenomena. So nothing can be an experience that is a nonphysical phenomenon of the sort permissible under the second premise. From the two premises it follows that experiences are some physical phenomena or other.

And there is little doubt which physical phenomena they must be. We are far from establishing positively that neural states occupy the definitive causal roles of experiences, but we have no notion of any other physical phenomena that could possibly occupy then, consistent with what we do know. So if nonphysical phenomena are ruled out by our confidence in physical explanation, only neural states are left. If it could be shown that neural states do not occupy the proper causal roles, we would be hard put to save materialism itself.

A version of epiphenomenalism might seem to evade my argument: let experiences be nonphysical epiphenomena, precisely correlated according to a causal law with some simultaneous physical states which are themselves physically (if at all) explicable. The correlation law (it is claimed) renders the experiences and their physical correlates causally equivalent. So the nonphysical experiences have their definitive physical effects after all—although they are not needed to explain those effects, so there is no violation of my second premise (since the nonphysical experiences redundantly redetermine the effects of their physical correlates). I answer thus: at best, this position yields nonphysical experiences alongside the physical experiences, duplicating them, which is not what its advocates intend. Moreover, it is false that such a physical state and its epiphenomenal correlate are causally equivalent. The position exploits a flaw in the standard regularity theory of cause. We know on other grounds that the theory must be corrected to discriminate between genuine causes and the spurious causes which are their epiphenomenal correlates. (The "power on" light does not cause the motor to go, even if it is a lawfully perfect correlate of the electric current that really causes the motor to go.) Given a satisfactory correction, the nonphysical correlate will be evicted from its spurious causal role and thereby lose its status as the experience. So this epiphenomenalism is not a counterexample.

The dualism of the common man holds that experiences are nonphysical phenomena which are the causes of a familiar syndrome of physical as well as nonphysical effects. This dualism is a worthy opponent, daring to face empirical refutation, and in due time it will be rendered incredible by the continuing advance of physicalistic explanation. I have been concerned to prevent dualism from finding a safe fall-back position in the doctrine that experiences are nonphysical and physically inefficacious. It is true that such phenomena can never be refuted by any amount of scientific theory and evidence. The trouble with them is rather that they cannot be what we call experiences. They can only be the nonphysical epiphenomena or correlates of physical states which are experiences. If they are not the experiences themselves, they cannot rescue dualism when it is hard-pressed. And if they cannot do that, nobody has any motive for believing in them. Such things may be—but they are of no consequence.

Suggested Further Readings

A good place to begin is J. J. C. Smart, "Sensations and Brain Processes," and Jerome Shaffer, "Mental Events and the Brain," in *The Nature of Mind,* ed. by David M. Rosenthal (Oxford: Oxford University Press, 1991).

For more on mental causation, see Frank Jackson and Philip Pettit, "Causation in the Philosophy of Mind," *Philosophy & Phenomenological Research* L, Supplement (Fall 1990); Jaegwon Kim, "Causality, Identity, and Supervenience in the Mind–Body Problem," *Midwest Studies in Philosophy* IV (1979); and D. M. Armstrong, *A Materialist Theory of Mind* (London: Routledge & Kegan Paul, 1968).

CHAPTER 17

"What Mary Didn't Know"

Frank Jackson

All facts are physical facts, or so say certain defenders of physicalism. That claim seems to be false, since it is possible to know all the physical facts yet lack knowledge of certain other facts. The following selection develops such a "knowledge argument" against physicalism, focusing attention on Mary, a person who spends her entire life in a room that contains no red objects. The question is: Can Mary know what it is like to see something that is red?

Frank Jackson is a professor of philosophy at Australian National University. He has written many influential papers bearing on metaphysical issues.

Mary is confined to a black-and-white room, is educated through black-and-white books and through lectures relayed on black-and-white television. In this way she learns everything there is to know about the physical nature of the world. She knows all the physical facts about us and our environment, in a wide sense of 'physical' which includes everything in *completed* physics, chemistry, and neurophysiology, and all there is to know about the causal and relational facts consequent upon all this, including of course functional roles. If physicalism is true, she knows all there is to know. For to suppose otherwise is to suppose that there is more to know than every physical fact, and that is just what physicalism denies.

Physicalism is not the noncontroversial thesis that the actual world is largely physical, but the challenging thesis that it is entirely physical. This is why physicalists must hold that complete physical knowledge is complete knowledge simpliciter. For suppose it is not complete: then our world must differ from a world. *W(P)*, for which

Source: Frank Jackson: "What Mary Didn't Know," from *The Journal of Philosophy,* May 1986, vol. LXXXIII, no. 5, pp. 291–295. Reprinted by permission of The Journal of Philosophy, Inc. and the author.

it is complete, and the difference must be in nonphysical facts: for our world and *W(P)* agree in all matters physical. Hence, physicalism would be false at our world [though contingently so, for it would be true at *W(P)*].[1]

It seems, however, that Mary does not know all there is to know. For when she is let out of the black-and-white room or given a color television, she will learn what it is like to see something red, say. This is rightly described as *learning*—she will not say "ho, hum." Hence, physicalism is false. This is the knowledge argument against physicalism in one of its manifestations.[2] This note is a reply to three objections to it mounted by Paul M. Churchland.[*]

1. Three Clarifications

The knowledge argument does not rest on the dubious claim that logically you cannot imagine what sensing red is like unless you have sensed red. Powers of imagination are not to the point. The contention about Mary is not that, despite her fantastic grasp of neurophysiology and everything else physical, she *could not imagine* what it is like to sense red; it is that, as a matter of fact, she *would not know*. But if physicalism is true, she would know; and no great powers of imagination would be called for. Imagination is a faculty that those who *lack* knowledge need to fall back on.

Secondly, the intensionality of knowledge is not to the point. The argument does not rest on assuming falsely that, if *S* knows that *a* is *F* and if *a* = *b*, then *S* knows that *b* is *F*. It is concerned with the nature of Mary's total body of knowledge before she is released: is it complete, or do some facts escape it? What is to the point is that

---

[1]The claim here is not that, if physicalism is true, only what is expressed in explicitly physical language is an item of knowledge. It is that, if physicalism is true, then if you know everything expressed or expressible in explicitly physical language, you know everything. *Pace* Terence Horgan, "Jackson on Physical Information and Qualia," *Physical Quarterly,* XXXIV, 135 (April 1984): 147–152.

[2]Namely that in my "Epiphenomenal Qualia," *ibid.,* XXXII, 127 (April 1982): 127–136. See also Thomas Nagel, "What Is It Like to Be a Bat?", *Philosophical Review,* LXXXIII, 4 (October 1974): 435–450, and Howard Robinson, *Matter and Sense* (New York: Cambridge, 1982).

[*]"Reduction, Qualia, and the Direct Introspection of Brain States," this Journal, LXXXII, 1 (January 1985): 8–28. Unless otherwise stated, future page references are to this paper.

S may know that *a* is *F* and *know* that *a* = *b*, yet arguably not know that *b* is *F,* by virtue of not being sufficiently logically alert to follow the consequences through. If Mary's lack of knowledge were at all like this, there would be no threat to physicalism in it. But it is very hard to believe that her lack of knowledge could be remedied merely by her explicitly following through enough logical consequences of her vast physical knowledge. Endowing her with great logical acumen and persistence is not in itself enough to fill in the gaps in her knowledge. On being let out, she will not say, "I could have worked all this out before by making some more purely logical inferences."

Thirdly, the knowledge Mary lacked which is of particular point for the knowledge argument against physicalism is *knowledge about the experiences of others,* not about her own. When she is let out, she has new experiences, color experiences she has never had before. It is not, therefore, an objection to physicalism that she learns *something* on being let out. Before she was let out, she could not have known facts about her experience of red, for there were no such facts to know. That physicalist and nonphysicalist alike can agree on. After she is let out, things change; and physicalism can happily admit that she learns this; after all, some physical things will change, for instance, her brain states and their functional roles. The trouble for physicalism is that, after Mary sees her first ripe tomato, she will realize how impoverished her conception of the mental life of *others* has been *all along.* She will realize that there was, all the time she was carrying out her laborious investigations into the neurophysiologies of others and into the functional roles of their internal states, something about these people she was quite unaware of. All along their experiences (or many of them, those got from tomatoes, the sky. . . .) had a feature conspicuous to them but until now hidden from her (in fact, not in logic). But she knew all the physical facts about them all along; hence, what she did not know until her release is not a physical fact about their experiences. But it is a fact about them. That is the trouble for physicalism.

2.   Churchland's Three Objections

(i) Churchland's first objection is that the knowledge argument contains a defect that "is simplicity itself" (23). The argument equivocates on the sense of 'knows about.' How so? Churchland suggests that the following is "a conveniently tightened version" of the knowledge argument:

(1) Mary knows everything there is to know about brain states and their properties.

(2) It is not the case that Mary knows everything there is to know about sensations and their properties.

Therefore, by Leibniz's law,

(3) Sensations and their properties ≠ brain states and their properties (23).

Churchland observes, plausibly enough, that the type or kind of knowledge involved in premise 1 is distinct from the kind of knowledge involved in premise 2. We might follow his lead and tag the first 'knowledge by description,' and the second 'knowledge by acquaintance'; but, whatever the tags, he is right that the displayed argument involves a highly dubious use of Leibniz's law.

My reply is that the displayed argument may be convenient, but it is not accurate. It is not the knowledge argument. Take, for instance, premise 1. The whole thrust of the knowledge argument is that Mary (before her release) does *not* know everything there is to know about brain states and their properties, because she does not know about certain qualia associated with them. What is complete, according to the argument, is her knowledge of matters physical. A convenient and accurate way of displaying the argument is:

(1′) Mary (before her release) knows everything physical there is to know about other people.

(2′) Mary (before her release) does not know everything there is to know about other people (because she *learns* something about them on her release).

Therefore,

(3′) There are truths about other people (and herself) which escape the physicalist story.

What is immediately to the point is not the kind, manner, or type of knowledge Mary has, but *what* she knows. What she knows beforehand is ex hypothesi everything physical there is to know, but is it everything there is to know? That is the crucial question.

There is, though, a relevant challenge involving questions about kinds of knowledge. It concerns the *support* for premise 2′. The case for premise 2′ is that Mary learns something on her release, she acquires knowledge, and that entails that her knowledge beforehand (*what* she knew, never mind whether by description, acquaintance, or whatever) was incomplete. The challenge, mounted by David Lewis and Laurence Nemirow, is that on her release Mary does *not* learn something or acquire knowledge in the relevant sense. What Mary acquires when she is released is a certain representational or imaginative ability; it is knowledge how rather than knowledge that. Hence, a physicalist can admit that Mary acquires something very significant of a knowledge kind—which can hardly be denied—without admitting that this shows that her earlier factual knowledge is defective. She knew all *that* there was to know about the experiences of others beforehand, but lacked an ability until after her release.[3]

Now it is certainly true that Mary will acquire abilities of various kinds after her release. She will, for instance, be able to imagine what seeing red is like, be able to remember what it is like, and be able to understand why her friends regarded her as so deprived (something which, until her release, had always mystified her). But is it plausible that that is *all* she will acquire? Suppose she received a lecture on skepticism about other minds while she was incarcerated. On her release she sees a ripe tomato in normal conditions, and so has a sensation of red. Her first reaction is to say that she now knows more about the kind of experiences others have when looking at ripe tomatoes. She then remembers the lecture and starts to worry. Does she really know more about what their experiences are like, or is she indulging in a wild generalization from one case? In the end she decides she does know, and that skepticism is mistaken (even if, like so many of us, she is not sure how to demonstrate its errors). What was she to-ing and fro-ing about—her abilities? Surely not; her representational abilities were a known constant throughout. What else then was she agonizing about than whether or not she had gained factual knowledge of others? There would be nothing to agonize about if ability was *all* she acquired on her release.

I grant that I have no *proof* that Mary acquires on her release, as well as abilities, factual knowledge about the experiences of others—

---

[3]See Laurence Nemirow, review of Thomas Nagel, *Mortal Questions, Philosophical Review*, LXXXIX, 3 (July 1980): 473–477, and David Lewis, "Postscript to 'Mad Pain and Martian Pain,'" *Philosophical Papers*, vol. 1 (New York: Oxford, 1983). Churchland mentions both Nemirow and Lewis, and it may be that he intended his objection to be essentially the one I have just given. However, he says quite explicitly (bottom of p. 23) that his objection does not need an "ability" analysis of the relevant knowledge.

and not just because I have no disproof of skepticism. My claim is that the knowledge argument is a valid argument from highly plausible, though admittedly not demonstrable, premises to the conclusion that physicalism is false. And that, after all, is about as good an objection as one could expect in this area of philosophy.

(ii) Churchland's second objection (24/5) is that there must be something wrong with the argument, for it proves too much. Suppose Mary received a special series of lectures over her black-and-white television from a full-blown dualist, explaining the "laws" governing the behavior of "ectoplasm" and telling her about qualia. This would not affect the plausibility of the claim that on her release she learns something. So if the argument works against physicalism, it works against dualism too.

My reply is that lectures about qualia over black-and-white television do not tell Mary all there is to know about qualia. They may tell her some things about qualia, for instance, that they do not appear in the physicalist's story, and that the quale we use 'yellow' for is nearly as different from the one we use 'blue' for as is white from black. But why should it be supposed that they tell her everything about qualia? On the other hand, it is plausible that lectures over black-and-white television might in principle tell Mary everything in the physicalist's story. You do not need color television to learn physics or functionalist psychology. To obtain a good argument against dualism (attribute dualism; ectoplasm is a bit of fun), the premise in the knowledge argument that Mary has the full story according to physicalism before her release, has to be replaced by a premise that she has the full story according to dualism. The former is plausible; the latter is not. Hence, there is no "parity of reasons" trouble for dualists who use the knowledge argument.

(iii) Churchland's third objection is that the knowledge argument claims "that Mary could not even *imagine* what the relevant experience would be like, despite her exhaustive neuroscientific knowledge, and hence must still be missing certain crucial information" (25), a claim he goes on to argue against.

But, as we emphasized earlier, the knowledge argument claims that Mary would not know what the relevant experience is like. What she could imagine is another matter. If her knowledge is defective, despite being all there is to know according to physicalism, then physicalism is false, whatever her powers of imagination.

Suggested Further Readings

For more on these issues, see Jackson, "Epiphenomenal Qualia," *Philosophical Quarterly* 32 (1980).

There are many interesting things in Janet Levin, "Could Love Be Like a Heatwave?" *Philosophical Studies* 49 (1986); Terence Horgan, "Jackson on Physical Information and Qualia," *Philosophical Quarterly* (1984); Derk Pereboom, "Bats, Brain Scientists, and the Limitations of Introspection," *Philosophy & Phenomenological Research* LIV (1994); Earl Conee, "The Possibility of Absent Qualia," *Philosophical Review* (1985); Thomas Nagel, "What Is It Like to Be a Bat?" *Philosophical Review* 82 (1974); Terence Horgan, "Supervenient Qualia," *Philosophical Review* 96 (1987); and William Seager, "The Elimination of Experience," *Philosophy & Phenomenological Research* 53 (1993).

See also Sydney Shoemaker, "Qualities and Qualia: What's in the Mind?" *Philosophy & Phenomenological Research* L, Supplement (Fall 1990).

CHAPTER 18

"*Mental Events*"

Donald Davidson

We may naturally judge that our minds are causally related to our bodies, that our choices and decisions bring about physical results involving movements of our bodies. If causal relations are lawlike, that suggests that there are lawlike relationships between psychological events in our minds and physical events in our bodies. But isn't this problematic? Are there really psychophysical laws? The following selection argues against this notion and poses a puzzle concerning causality and the mind. Causality involves physical laws. The problem then lies in explaining how it can be that there are no lawlike relationships between psychological events and physical events when causal relationships obtain between such events.

Donald Davidson is a professor of philosophy at the University of California at Berkeley. He is the author of Essays on Actions and Events *(1980) and* Inquiries into Truth and Interpretation *(1984).*

Mental events such as perceivings, rememberings, decisions, and actions resist capture in the nomological net of physical theory.[1] How can this fact be reconciled with the causal role of mental events in the physical world? Reconciling freedom with causal determinism is a special case of the problem if we suppose that causal determinism entails capture in, and freedom requires escape from, the nomological net. But the broader issue can remain alive even for someone who believes a correct analysis of free action reveals no conflict with determinism.

Source: Donald Davidson: "Mental Events," reprinted from *Essays on Actions and Events* by Donald Davidson (1980) by permission of Oxford University Press.

[1] I was helped and influenced by Daniel Bennett, Sue Larson, and Richard Rorty, who are not responsible for the result. My research was supported by the National Science Foundation and the Center for Advanced Study in the Behavioral Sciences.

Autonomy (freedom, self-rule) may or may not clash with determinism: *anomaly* (failure to fall under a law) is, it would see, another matter.

I start from the assumption that both the causal dependence, and the anomalousness, of mental events are undeniable facts. My aim is therefore to explain, in the face of apparent difficulties, how this can be. I am in sympathy with Kant when he says,

> it is as impossible for the subtlest philosophy as for the commonest reasoning to argue freedom away. Philosophy must therefore assume that no true contradiction will be found between freedom and natural necessity in the same human actions, for it cannot give up the idea of nature any more than that of freedom. Hence even if we should never be able to conceive how freedom is possible, at least this apparent contradiction must be convincingly eradicated. For if the thought of freedom contradicts itself or nature . . . it would have to be surrendered in competition with natural necessity.[2]

Generalize human actions to mental events, substitute anomaly for freedom, and this is a description of my problem. And of course the connection is closer, since Kant believed freedom entails anomaly.

Now let me try to formulate a little more carefully the "apparent contradiction" about mental events that I want to discuss and finally dissipate. It may be seen as stemming from three principles.

The first principle asserts that at least some mental events interact causally with physical events. (We could call this the Principle of Causal Interaction). Thus for example if someone sank the *Bismarck*, then various mental events such as perceivings, notings, calculations, judgments, decisions, intentional actions and changes of belief played a causal role in the sinking of the *Bismarck*. In particular, I would urge that the fact that someone sank the *Bismarck* entails that he moved his body in a way that was caused by mental events of certain sorts, and that this bodily movement in turn caused the *Bismarck* to sink.[3] Perception illustrates

---

[2]*Fundamental Principles of the Metaphysics of Morals*, trans. T. K. Abbott (London, 1909), pp. 75–76.

[3]These claims are defended in my "Actions, Reasons and Causes," *The Journal of Philosophy*, LX (1963), pp. 685–700 and in "Agency," a paper forthcoming in the proceedings of the November, 1968, colloquium on Agent, Action, and Reason at the University of Western Ontario, London, Canada [in *Agent, Action, and Reason*, edited by Robert Binkley, Richard Bronaugh, and Ausonio Marras (Oxford: Basil Blackwell, 1971), pp. 3–25].

how causality may run from the physical to the mental: if a man perceives that a ship is approaching, then a ship approaching must have caused him to come to believe that a ship is approaching. (Nothing depends on accepting these as examples of causal interaction.)

Though perception and action provide the most obvious cases where mental and physical events interact causally, I think reasons could be given for the view that all mental events ultimately, perhaps through causal relations with other mental events, have causal intercourse with physical events. But if there are mental events that have no physical events as causes or effects, the argument will not touch them.

The second principle is that where there is causality, there must be a law: events related as cause and effect fall under strict deterministic laws. (We may term this the Principle of the Nomological Character of Causality.) This principle, like the first, will be treated here as an assumption, though I shall say something by way of interpretation.[4]

The third principle is that there are no strict deterministic laws on the basis of which mental events can be predicted and explained (the Anomalism of the Mental).

The paradox I wish to discuss arises for someone who is inclined to accept these three assumptions or principles, and who thinks they are inconsistent with one another. The inconsistency is not, of course, formal unless more premises are added. Nevertheless, it is natural to reason that the first two principles, that of causal interaction, and that of the nomological character of causality, together imply that at least some mental events can be predicted and explained on the basis of laws, while the principle of the anomalism of the mental denies this. Many philosophers have accepted, with or without argument, the view that the three principles do lead to a contradiction. It seems to me, however, that all three principles are true, so that what must be done is to explain away the appearance of contradiction; essentially the Kantian line.

The rest of this paper falls into three parts. The first part describes a version of the identity theory of the mental and the physical that shows how the three principles may be reconciled. The second part argues that there cannot be strict psychophysical laws; this is not

---

[4]In "Causal Relations," *The Journal of Philosophy*, LXIV (1967), pp. 691–703, I elaborate on the view of causality assumed here. The stipulation that the laws be deterministic is stronger than required by the reasoning, and will be relaxed.

quite the principle of the anomalism of the mental, but on reasonable assumptions entails it. The last part tries to show that from the fact that there can be no strict psychophysical laws, and our other two principles, we can infer the truth of a version of the identity theory, that is, a theory that identifies at least some mental events with physical events. It is clear that this "proof" of the identity theory will be at best conditional, since two of its premises are unsupported, and the argument for the third may be found less than conclusive. But even someone unpersuaded of the truth of the premises may be interested to learn how they may be reconciled and that they serve to establish a version of the identity theory of the mental. Finally, if the argument is a good one, it should lay to rest the view, common to many friends and some foes of identity theories, that support for such theories can come only from the discovery of psychophysical laws.

The three principles will be shown consistent with one another by describing a view of the mental and the physical that contains no inner contradiction and that entails the three principles. According to this view, mental events are identical with physical events. Events are taken to be unrepeatable, dated individuals such as the particular eruption of a volcano, the (first) birth or death of a person, the playing of the 1968 World Series, or the historic utterance of the words, "You may fire when ready, Gridley." We can easily frame identity statements about individual events; examples (true or false) might be:

> The death of Scott = the death of the author of *Waverley*;
>
> The assassination of the Archduke Ferdinand = the event that started the First World War;
>
> The eruption of Vesuvius in A.D. 79 = the cause of the destruction of Pompeii.

The theory under discussion is silent about processes, states, and attributes if these differ from individual events.

What does it mean to say that an event is mental or physical? One natural answer is that an event is physical if it is describable in a purely physical vocabulary, mental if describable in mental terms. But if this is taken to suggest that an event is physical, say, if some physical predicate is true of it, then there is the following difficulty. Assume that the predicate 'x took place at Noosa Heads' belongs to the physical vocabulary; then so also must the predicate 'x did not take place at Noosa Heads' belong to the physical vocabulary. But the predicate 'x did or did not take place at Noosa Heads' is true of every event, whether mental or physical.[5] We might rule out predicates that are tautologically true of every event, but this will not help since every event is truly describable either by 'x took place at Noosa Heads' or by 'x did not take place at Noosa Heads.' A different approach is needed.[6]

We may call these verbs mental that express propositional attitudes like believing, intending, desiring, hoping, knowing, perceiving, noticing, remembering, and so on. Such verbs are characterized by the fact that they sometimes feature in sentences with subjects that refer to persons, and are completed by embedded sentences in which the usual rules of substitution appear to break down. This criterion is not precise, since I do not want to include these verbs when they occur in contexts that are fully extensional ('He knows Paris,' 'He perceives the moon' may be cases), nor exclude them whenever they are not followed by embedded sentences. An alternative characterization of the desired class of mental verbs might be that they are psychological verbs as used when they create apparently nonextensional contexts.

Let us call a description of the form 'the event that is M' or an open sentence of the form 'event x is M' a *mental description* or a *mental open sentence* if and only if the expression that replaces 'M' contains at least one mental verb essentially. (Essentially, so as to rule out cases where the description or open sentence is logically equivalent to one not containing mental vocabulary.) Now we may say that an event is mental if and only if it has a mental description, or (the description operator not being primitive) if there is a mental open sentence true of that event alone. Physical events are those picked out by descriptions or open sentences that contain only the physical vocabulary essentially. It is less important to characterize a physical vocabulary because relative to the mental it is, so to speak, recessive in determining whether a description is mental or physical. (There will be some comments presently on the nature of a physical vocabulary, but these comments will fall far short of providing a criterion.)

---

[5]The point depends on assuming that mental events may intelligibly be said to have a location; but it is an assumption that must be true if an identity theory is, and here I am not trying to prove the theory but to formulate it.

[6]I am indebted to Lee Bowie for emphasizing this difficulty.

On the proposed test of the mental, the distinguishing feature of the mental is not that it is private, subjective, or immaterial, but that it exhibits what Brentano called intentionality. Thus intentional actions are clearly included in the realm of the mental along with thoughts, hopes, and regrets (or the events tied to these). What may seem doubtful is whether the criterion will include events that have often been considered paradigmatic of the mental. Is it obvious, for example, that feeling a pain or seeing an afterimage will count as mental? Sentences that report such events seem free from taint of nonextensionality, and the same should be true of reports of raw feels, sense data, and other uninterpreted sensations, if there are any.

However, the criterion actually covers not only the havings of pains and afterimages, but much more besides. Take some event one would intuitively accept as physical, let's say the collision of two stars in distant space. There must be a purely physical predicate 'Px' true of this collision, and of others, but true of only this one at the time it occurred. This particular time, though, may be pinpointed as the same time that Jones notices that a pencil starts to roll across his desk. The distant stellar collision is thus *the* event x such that Px and x is simultaneous with Jones' noticing that a pencil starts to roll across his desk. The collision has now been picked out by a mental description and must be counted as a mental event.

This strategy will probably work to show every event to be mental: we have obviously failed to capture the intuitive concept of the mental. It would be instructive to try to mend this trouble, but it is not necessary for present purposes. We can afford Spinozistic extravagance with the mental since accidental inclusions can only strengthen the hypothesis that all mental events are identical with physical events. What would matter would be failure to include bona fide mental events, but of this there seems to be no danger.

I want to describe, and presently to argue for, a version of the identity theory that denies that there can be strict laws connecting the mental and the physical. The very possibility of such a theory is easily obscured by the way in which identity theories are commonly defended and attacked. Charles Taylor, for example, agrees with protagonists of identity theories that the sole "ground" for accepting such theories is the supposition that correlations or laws can be established linking events described as mental with events described as physical. He says, "It is easy to see why this is so: unless a given mental event is invariably accompanied by a given, say, brain process, there is no ground for even mooting a general identity between the two."[7] Taylor goes on (correctly, I think) to allow that there may be identity without correlating laws, but my present interest is in noticing the invitation to confusion in the statement just quoted. What can "a given mental event" mean here? Not a particular, dated, event, for it would not make sense to speak of an individual event being "invariably accompanied" by another. Taylor is evidently thinking of events of a given *kind*. But if the only identities are of kinds of events, the identity theory presupposes correlating laws.

One finds the same tendency to build laws into the statement of the identity theory in these typical remarks:

> When I say that a sensation is a brain process or that lightning is an electrical discharge, I am using 'is' in the sense of strict identity . . . there are not two things: a flash of lightning and an electrical discharge. There is one thing, a flash of lightning, which is described scientifically as an electrical discharge to the earth from a cloud of ionized water molecules.[8]

The last sentence of this quotation is perhaps to be understood as saying that for every lightning flash there exists an electrical discharge to the earth from a cloud of ionized water molecules with which it is identical. Here we have an honest ontology of individual events and can make literal sense of identity. We can also see how there could be identities without correlating laws. It is possible, however, to have an ontology of events with the conditions of individuation specified in such a way that any identity implies a correlating law. Kim, for example, suggests that Fa and Gb "describe or refer to the same event" if and only if $a = b$ and the property of being F = the

---

[7]Charles Taylor, "Mind-Body Identity, a Side Issue?" *The Philosophical Review,* LXXVI (1967), p. 202.

[8]J. J. C. Smart, "Sensations and Brain Processes," *The Philosophical Review,* LXVIII (1959), pp. 141–56. The quoted passages are on pp. 163–65 of the reprinted version in *The Philosophy of Mind,* ed. V. C. Chappell (Englewood Cliffs, N.J., 1962). For another example, see David K. Lewis, "An Argument for the Identity Theory," *The Journal of Philosophy,* LXIII (1966), pp. 17–25. Here the assumption is made explicit when Lewis takes events as universals (p. 17, footnotes 1 and 2). I do not suggest that Smart and Lewis are confused, only that their way of stating the identity theory tends to obscure the distinction between particular events and kinds of events on which the formulation of my theory depends.

property of being G. The identity of the properties in turn entails that $(x)(\text{F}x \leftrightarrow \text{G}x)$.[9] No wonder Kim says:

> If pain is identical with brain state *B*, there must be a concomitance between occurrences of pain and occurrences of brain state *B*. . . . Thus, a necessary condition of the pain–brain state *B* identity is that the two expressions 'being in pain' and 'being in brain state *B*' have the same extension. . . . There is no conceivable observation that would confirm or refute the identity but not the associated correlation.[10]

It may make the situation clearer to give a fourfold classification of theories of the relation between mental and physical events that emphasizes the independence of claims about laws and claims of identity. On the one hand there are those who assert, and those why deny, the existence of psychophysical laws; on the other hand there are those who say mental events are identical with physical and those who deny this. Theories are thus divided into four sorts: *Nomological monism*, which affirms that there are correlating laws and that the events correlated are one (materialists belong in this category); *nomological dualism*, which comprises various forms of parallelism, interactionism, and epiphenomenalism; *anomalous dualism*, which combines ontological dualism with the general failure of laws correlating the mental and the physical (Cartesianism). And finally there is *anomalous monism*, which classifies the position I wish to occupy.[11]

---

[9]Jaegwon Kim, "On the Psycho-Physical Identity Theory," *American Philosophical Quarterly*, III (1966), p. 231.

[10]Ibid., pp. 227–28. Richard Brandt and Jaegwon Kim propose roughly the same criterion in "The Logic of the Identity Theory," *The Journal of Philosophy* LIV (1967), pp. 515–537. They remark that on their conception of event identity, the identity theory "makes a stronger claim than merely that there is a pervasive phenomenal-physical correlation" (p. 518). I do not discuss the stronger claim.

[11]Anomalous monism is more or less explicitly recognized as a possible position by Herbert Feigl, "The 'Mental' and the 'Physical,' " in *Concepts, Theories and the Mind-Body Problem*, vol. II, *Minnesota Studies in the Philosophy of Science* (Minneapolis, 1958); Sydney Shoemaker, "Ziff's Other Minds," *The Journal of Philosophy*, LXII (1965), p. 589; David Randall Luce, "Mind-Body Identity and Psycho-Physical Correlation," *Philosophical Studies*, XVII (1966), pp. 1–7; Charles Taylor, op. cit. p. 207. Something like my position is tentatively accepted by Thomas Nagel, "Physicalism," *The Philosophical Review*, LXXIV (1965), pp. 339–356, and briefly endorsed by P. F. Strawson in *Freedom and the Will*, ed. D. F. Pears (London, 1963), pp. 63–67.

Anomalous monism resembles materialism in its claim that all events are physical, but rejects the thesis, usually considered essential to materialism, that mental phenomena can be given purely physical explanations. Anomalous monism shows an ontological bias only in that it allows the possibility that not all events are mental, while insisting that all events are physical. Such a bland monism, unbuttressed by correlating laws or conceptual economies, does not seem to merit the term "reductionism"; in any case it is not apt to inspire the nothing-but reflex ("Conceiving the *Art of the Fugue* was nothing but a complex neural event," and so forth.)

Although the position I describe denies there are psychophysical laws, it is consistent with the view that mental characteristics are in some sense dependent, or supervenient, on physical characteristics. Such supervenience might be taken to mean that there cannot be two events alike in all physical respects but differing in some mental respect, or that an object cannot alter in some mental respect without altering in some physical respect. Dependence or supervenience of this kind does not entail reducibility through law or definition: if it did, we could reduce moral properties to descriptive, and this there is good reason to *believe* cannot be done; and we might be able to reduce truth in a formal system to syntactical properties, and this we *know* cannot in general be done.

This last example is in useful analogy with the sort of lawless monism under consideration. Think of the physical vocabulary as the entire vocabulary of some language L with resources adequate to express a certain amount of mathematics, and its own syntax. L' is L augmented with the truth predicate 'true-in-L,' which is "mental." In L (and hence L') it is possible to pick out, with a definite description or open sentence, each sentence in the extension of the truth predicate, but if L is consistent there exists no predicate of syntax (of the "physical" vocabulary), no matter how complex, that applies to all and only the true sentences of L. There can be no "psychophysical law" in the form of a biconditional, '$(x)(x$ is true-in-L if and only if x is $\phi)$' where 'ϕ' is replaced by a "physical" predicate (a predicate of L). Similarly, we can pick out each mental event using the physical vocabulary alone, but no purely physical predicate, no matter how complex, has, as a matter of law, the same extension as a mental predicate.

It should now be evident how anomalous monism reconciles the three original principles. Causality and identity are relations between individual events no matter how described. But laws are linguistic; and so events can instantiate laws, and hence be explained or predicted in the light of laws, only as those events are described in one or another way. The principle of causal interaction deals with events in extension and is therefore blind to the mental–physical dichotomy. The principle of the anomalism of the mental concerns events described as mental, for events are mental only as described. The principle of the nomological character of causality must be read carefully: it says that when events are related as cause and effect, they have descriptions that instantiate a law. It does not say that every true singular statement of causality instantiates a law.[12]

The analogy just bruited, between the place of the mental amid the physical, and the place of the semantical in a world of syntax, should not be strained. Tarski proved that a consistent language cannot (under some natural assumptions) contain an open sentence 'Fx' true of all and only the true sentences of that language. If our analogy were pressed, then we would expect a proof that there can be no physical open sentence 'Px' true of all and only the events having some mental property. In fact, however, nothing I can say about the irreducibility of the mental deserves to be called a proof; and the kind of irreducibility is different. For if anomalous monism is correct, not only can every mental event be uniquely singled out using only physical concepts, but since the number of events that falls under each mental predicate may, for all we know, be finite, there may well exist a physical open sentence coextensive with each mental predicate, though to construct it might involve the tedium of a lengthy and uninstructive alternation. Indeed, even if finitude is not assumed, there seems no compelling reason to deny that there could be coextensive predicates, one mental and one physical.

The thesis is rather that the mental is nomologically irreducible: there may be *true* general statements relating the mental and the physical, statements that have the logical form of a law; but they are

---

[12]The point that substitutivity of identity fails in the context of explanation is made in connection with the present subject by Norman Malcolm, "Scientific Materialism and the Identity Theory," *Dialogue*, III (1964–65), pp. 123–124. See also my "Actions, Reasons and Causes," *The Journal of Philosophy*, LX (1963), pp. 696–699 and "The Individuation of Events" in *Essays in Honor of Carl G. Hempel*, ed. N. Rescher, et al. (Dordrecht, 1969).

not *lawlike* (in a strong sense to be described). If by absurdly remote chance we were to stumble on a nonstochastic true psychophysical generalization, we would have no reason to believe it more than roughly true.

Do we, by declaring that there are no (strict) psychophysical laws, poach on the empirical preserves of science—a form of *hubris* against which philosophers are often warned? Of course, to judge a statement lawlike or illegal is not to decide its truth outright: relative to the acceptance of a general statement on the basis of instances, ruling it lawlike must be a priori. But such relative apriorism does not in itself justify philosophy, for in general the grounds for deciding to trust a statement on the basis of its instances will in turn be governed by theoretical and empirical concerns not to be distinguished from those of science. If the case of supposed laws linking the mental and the physical is different, it can only be because to allow the possibility of such laws would amount to changing the subject. By changing the subject I mean here: deciding not to accept the criterion of the mental in terms of the vocabulary of the propositional attitudes. This short answer cannot prevent further ramifications of the problem, however, for there is no clear line between changing the subject and changing what one says on an old subject, which is to admit, in the present context at least, that there is no clear line between philosophy and science. Where there are no fixed boundaries only the timid never risk trespass.

It will sharpen our appreciation of the anomological character of mental–physical generalizations to consider a related matter, the failure of definitional behaviorism. Why are we willing (as I assume we are) to abandon the attempt to give explicit definitions of mental concepts in terms of behavioral ones? Not, surely, just because all actual tries are conspicuously inadequate. Rather it is because we are persuaded, as we are in the case of so many other forms of definitional reductionism (naturalism in ethics, instrumentalism and operationalism in the sciences, the causal theory of meaning, phenomenalism, and so on—the catalogue of philosophy's defeats), that there is system in the failures. Suppose we try to say, not using any mental concepts, what it is for a man to believe there is life on Mars. One line we could take is this: when a certain sound is produced in the man's presence ("Is there life on Mars?") he produces another ("Yes"). But of course this shows he believes there is life on Mars only if he understands English, his production of the sound was intentional, and was a response to the sounds as meaning something in English; and so on. For each discovered deficiency, we add a new proviso. Yet no matter how we patch and fit the nonmental conditions, we always find the need for an additional condition (provided he *notices, understands,* etc.) that is mental in character.[13]

A striking feature of attempts at definitional reduction is how little seems to hinge on the question of synonymy between definiens and definiendum. Of course, by imagining counterexamples we do discredit claims of synonymy. But the pattern of failure prompts a stronger conclusion: if we were to find an open sentence couched in behavioral terms and exactly coextensive with some mental predicate, nothing could reasonably persuade us that we had found it. We know too much about thought and behavior to trust exact and universal statements linking them. Beliefs and desires issue in behavior only as modified and mediated by further beliefs and desires, attitudes and attendings, without limit. Clearly this holism of the mental realm is a clue both to the autonomy and to the anomalous character of the mental.

These remarks apropos definitional behaviorism provide at best hints of why we should not expect nomological connections between the mental and the physical. The central case invites further consideration.

Lawlike statements are general statements that support counterfactual and subjunctive claims, and are supported by their instances. There is (in my view) no nonquestion-begging criterion of the lawlike, which is not to say there are no reasons in particular cases for a judgment. Lawlikeness is a matter of degree, which is not to deny that there may be cases beyond debate. And within limits set by the conditions of communication, there is room for much variation between individuals in the pattern of statements to which various degrees of nomologicality are assigned. In all these respects, nomologicality is much like analyticity, as one might expect since both are linked to meaning.

'All emeralds are green' is lawlike in that its instances confirm it, but 'all emeralds are grue' is not, for 'grue' means 'observed before time *t* and green, otherwise blue,' and if our observations were all made before *t* and uniformly revealed green emeralds, this would not

---

[13]The theme is developed in Roderick Chisholm, *Perceiving* (Ithaca, New York, 1957), chap. 11.

be a reason to expect other emeralds to be blue. Nelson Goodman has suggested that this shows that some predicates, 'grue' for example, are unsuited to laws (and thus a criterion of suitable predicates could lead to a criterion of the lawlike). But it seems to me the anomalous character of 'All emeralds are grue' shows only that the predicates 'is an emerald' and 'is grue' are not suited to one another: grueness is not an inductive property of emeralds. Grueness *is* however an inductive property of entities of other sorts, for instance of emerires. (Something is an emerire if it is examined before *t* and is an emerald, and otherwise is a sapphire.) Not only is 'All emerires are grue' entailed by the conjunction of the lawlike statements 'All emeralds are green' and 'All sapphires are blue,' but there is no reason, as far as I can see, to reject the deliverance of intuition, that it is itself lawlike.[14] Nomological statements bring together predicates that we know a priori are made for each other—know, that is, independently of knowing whether the evidence supports a connection between them. 'Blue,' 'red,' and 'green' are made for emeralds, sapphires, and roses; 'grue,' 'bleen,' and 'gred' are made for sapphalds, emerires, and emeroses.

The direction in which the discussion seems headed is this: mental and physical predicates are not made for one another. In point of lawlikeness, psychophysical statements are more like 'All emeralds are grue' than like 'All emeralds are green.'

Before this claim is plausible, it must be seriously modified. The fact that emeralds examined before *t* are grue not only is no reason to believe all emeralds are grue; it is not even a reason (if we know the time) to believe *any* unobserved emeralds are grue. But if an event of a certain mental sort has usually been accompanied by an event of a certain physical sort, this often is a good reason to expect other cases to follow suit roughly in proportion. The generalizations that embody such practical wisdom are assumed to be only roughly true, or they are explicitly stated in probabilistic terms, or they are insulated from counterexample by generous escape clauses. Their importance lies

---

[14]This view is accepted by Richard C. Jeffrey, "Goodman's Query," *The Journal of Philosophy,* LXII (1966), p. 286 ff., John R. Wallace, "Goodman, Logic, Induction," same journal and issue, p. 318, and John M. Vickers, "Characteristics of Projectile Predicates," *The Journal of Philosophy,* LXIV (1967), p. 285. On pp. 328–329 and 286–287 of these journal issues respectively Goodman disputes the lawlikeness of statements like "All emerires are grue." I cannot see, however, that he meets the point of my "Emeroses by Other Names," *The Journal of Philosophy,* LXIII (1966), pp. 778–780.

mainly in the support they lend singular causal claims and related explanations of particular events. The support derives from the fact that
such a generalization, however crude and vague, may provide good
reason to believe that underlying the particular case there is a regularity that could be formulated sharply and without caveat.

In our daily traffic with events and actions that must be foreseen or understood, we perforce make use of the sketchy summary
generalization, for we do not know a more accurate law, or if we do,
we lack a description of the particular events in which we are interested that would show the relevance of the law. But there is an important distinction to be made within the category of the rude rule
of thumb. On the one hand, there are generalizations whose positive
instances give us reason to believe the generalization itself could be
improved by adding further provisos and conditions stated in the
same general vocabulary as the original generalization. Such a generalization points to the form and vocabulary of the finished law: we
may say that it is a *homonomic* generalization. On the other hand
there are generalizations which when instantiated may give us reason
to believe there is a precise law at work, but one that can be stated
only by shifting to a different vocabulary. We may call such generalizations *heteronomic*.

I suppose most of our practical lore (and science) is heteronomic. This is because a law can hope to be precise, explicit, and as
exceptionless as possible only if it draws its concepts from a comprehensive closed theory. This ideal theory may or may not be deterministic, but it is if any true theory is. Within the physical sciences we
do find homonomic generalizations, generalizations such that if the
evidence supports them, we then have reason to believe they may be
sharpened indefinitely by drawing upon further physical concepts:
there is a theoretical asymptote of perfect coherence with all the evidence, perfect predictability (under the terms of the system), total
explanation (again under the terms of the system). Or perhaps the
ultimate theory is probabilistic, and the asymptote is less than perfec-
tion; but in that case there will be no better to be had.

Confidence that a statement is homonomic, correctible within
its own conceptual domain, demands that it draw its concepts from a
theory with strong constitutive elements. Here is the simplest possible illustration: if the lesson carries, it will be obvious that the simpli-
fication could be mended.

The measurement of length, weight, temperature, or time depends (among many other things, of course) on the existence in each case of a two-place relation that is transitive and asymmetric: warmer than, later than, heavier than, and so forth. Let us take the relation *longer than* as our example. The law or postulate of transitivity is this:

(L) $L(x,y)$ and $L(y,z) \rightarrow L(x,z)$

Unless this law (or some sophisticated variant) holds, we cannot easily make sense of the concept of length. There will be no way of assigning numbers to register even so much as ranking in length, let alone the more powerful demands of measurement on a ratio scale. And this remark goes not only for any three items directly involved in an intransitivity: it is easy to show (given a few more assumptions essential to measurement of length) that there is no consistent assignment of a ranking to any item unless (L) holds in full generality.

Clearly (L) alone cannot exhaust the import of 'longer than'—otherwise it would not differ from 'warmer than' or 'later than.' We must suppose there is some empirical content, however difficult to formulate in the available vocabulary, that distinguishes 'longer than' from the other two-place transitive predicates of measurement and on the basis of which we may assert that one thing is longer than another. Imagine this empirical content to be partly given by the predicate '$o(x,y)$'. So we have this "meaning postulate":

(M) $o(x,y) \rightarrow L(x,y)$

that partly interprets (L). But now (L) and (M) together yield an empirical theory of great strength, for together they entail that there do not exist three objects a, b, and c such that $o(a,b)$, $o(b,c)$, and $o(c,a)$. Yet what is to prevent this happening if '$o(x,y)$' is a predicate we can ever, with confidence, apply? Suppose we *think* we observe an intransitive triad; what do we say? We could count (L) false, but then we would have no application for the concept of length. We could say (M) gives a wrong test for length; but then it is unclear what we thought was the *content* of the idea of one thing being longer than another. Or we could say that the objects under observation are not, as the theory requires, *rigid* objects. It is a mistake to think we are forced to accept some one of these answers. Concepts such as that of length are sustained in equilibrium by a number of conceptual pressures, and theories of fundamental measurement are distorted if we force the decision, among such principles as (L) and (M); analytic or synthetic. It is better to say the whole set of axioms, laws, or postulates for the measurement of length is partly constitutive of the idea of a system of macroscopic, rigid, physical objects. I suggest that the existence of lawlike statements in physical science depends upon the existence of constitutive (or synthetic a priori) laws like those of the measurement of length within the same conceptual domain.

Just as we cannot intelligibly assign a length to any object unless a comprehensive theory holds of objects of that sort, we cannot intelligibly attribute any propositional attitude to an agent except within the framework of a viable theory of his beliefs, desires, intentions, and decisions.

There is no assigning beliefs to a person one by one on the basis of his verbal behavior, his choices, or other local signs no matter how plain and evident, for we make sense of particular beliefs only as they cohere with other beliefs, with preferences, with intentions, hopes, fears, expectations, and the rest. It is not merely, as with the measurement of length, that each case tests a theory and depends upon it, but that the content of a propositional attitude derives from its place in the pattern.

Crediting people with a large degree of consistency cannot be counted mere charity: it is unavoidable if we are to be in a position to accuse them meaningfully of error and some degree of irrationality. Global confusion, like universal mistake, is unthinkable, not because imagination boggles, but because too much confusion leaves nothing to be confused about and massive error erodes the background of true belief against which alone failure can be construed. To appreciate the limits to the kind and amount of blunder and bad thinking we can intelligibly pin on others is to see once more the inseparability of the question what concepts a person commands and the question what he does with those concepts in the way of belief, desire, and intention. To the extent that we fail to discover a coherent and plausible pattern in the attitudes and actions of others we simply forego the chance of treating them as persons.

The problem is not bypassed but given center stage by appeal to explicit speech behavior. For we could not begin to decode a man's sayings if we could not make out his attitudes towards his sentences, such as holding, wishing, or wanting them to be true. Beginning from

these attitudes, we must work out a theory of what he means, thus simultaneously giving content to his attitudes and to his words. In our
need to make him make sense, we will try for a theory that finds him
consistent, a believer of truths, and a lover of the good (all by our
own lights, it goes without saying). Life being what it is, there will be
no simple theory that fully meets these demands. Many theories will
effect a more or less acceptable compromise, and between these theories there may be no objective grounds for choice.

The heteronomic character of general statements linking the
mental and the physical traces back to this central role of translation
in the description of all propositional attitudes, and to the indeterminacy of translation.[15] There are no strict psychophysical laws because of the disparate commitments of the mental and physical
schemes. It is a feature of physical reality that physical change can be
explained by laws that connect it with other changes and conditions
physically described. It is a feature of the mental that the attribution
of mental phenomena must be responsible to the background of
reasons, beliefs, and intentions of the individual. There cannot be
tight connections between the realms if each is to retain allegiance
to its proper source of evidence. The nomological irreducibility of
the mental does not derive merely from the seamless nature of the
world of thought, preference and intention, for such interdepen-
dence is common to physical theory, and is compatible with there
being a single right way of interpreting a man's attitudes without rel-
ativization to a scheme of translation. Nor is the irreducibility due
simply to the possibility of many equally eligible schemes, for this is
compatible with an arbitrary choice of one scheme relative to which
assignments of mental traits are made. The point is rather that when
we use the concepts of belief, desire and the rest, we must stand prepared, as the evidence accumulates, to adjust our theory in the light
of considerations of overall cogency: the constitutive ideal of ration-
ality partly controls each phase in the evolution of what must be an
evolving theory. An arbitrary choice of translation scheme would
preclude such opportunistic tempering of theory; put differently, a

---

[15]The influence of W. V. Quine's doctrine of the indeterminacy of translation, as in
chap. 2 of *Word and Object* (Cambridge, Mass., 1960), is, I hope, obvious. In § 45 Quine
develops the connection between translation and the propositional attitudes, and
remarks that "Brentano's thesis of the irreducibility of intentional idioms is of a piece
with the thesis of indeterminacy of translation" (p. 221).

right arbitrary choice of a translation manual would be of a manual acceptable in the light of all possible evidence, and this is a choice we cannot make. We must conclude, I think, that the nomological slack between the mental and the physical is essential as long as we conceive of man as a rational animal.

The gist of the foregoing discussion, as well as its conclusion, will be familiar. That there is a categorial difference between the mental and the physical is a commonplace. It may seem odd that I say nothing of the supposed privacy of the mental, or the special authority an agent has with respect to his own propositional attitudes, but this appearance of novelty would fade if we were to investigate in more detail the grounds for accepting a scheme of translation. The step from the categorical difference between the mental and the physical to the impossibility of strict laws relating them is less common, but certainly not new. If there is a surprise, then, it will be to find the lawlessness of the mental serving to help establish the identity of the mental with that paradigm of the lawlike, the physical.

The reasoning is this. We are assuming, under the Principle of the Causal Dependence of the Mental, that some mental events at least are causes or effects of physical events; the argument applies only to these. A second Principle (of the Nomological Character of Causality) says that each true singular causal statement is backed by a strict law connecting events of kinds to which the events mentioned as cause and effect belong. Where there are rough, but homonomic, laws, there are laws drawing on concepts from the same conceptual domain and upon which there is no improving in point of precision and comprehensiveness. We urged in the last section that such laws occur in the physical sciences. Physical theory promises to provide a comprehensive closed system guaranteed to yield a standardized, unique description of every physical event couched in a vocabulary amenable to law.

It is not plausible that mental concepts alone can provide such a framework, simply because the mental does not, by our first principle, constitute a closed system. Too much happens to affect the mental that is not itself a systematic part of the mental. But if we combine this observation with the conclusion that no psychophysical statement is, or can be built into, a strict law, we have the Principle of the Anomalism of the Mental: there are no strict laws at all on the basis of which we can predict and explain mental phenomena.

The demonstration of identity follows easily. Suppose *m,* a mental event, caused *p,* a physical event; then under some description *m* and *p* instantiate a strict law. This law can only be physical, according to the previous paragraph. But if *m* falls under a physical law, it has a physical description; which is to say it is a physical event. An analogous argument works when a physical event causes a mental event. So every mental event that is causally related to a physical event is a physical event. In order to establish anomalous monism in full generality it would be sufficient to show that every mental event is cause or effect of some physical event; I shall not attempt this.

If one event causes another, there is a strict law which those events instantiate when properly described. But it is possible (and typical) to know of the singular causal relation without knowing the law or the relevant descriptions. Knowledge requires reasons, but these are available in the form of rough heteronomic generalizations, which are lawlike in that instances make it reasonable to expect other instances to follow suit without being lawlike in the sense of being indefinitely refinable. Applying these facts to knowledge of identities, we see that it is possible to know that a mental event is identical with some physical event without knowing which one (in the sense of being able to give it a unique physical description that brings it under a relevant law). Even if someone knew the entire physical history of the world, and every mental event were identical with a physical, it would not follow that he could predict or explain a single mental event (so described, of course).

Two features of mental events in their relation to the physical— causal dependence and nomological independence—combine, then, to dissolve what has often seemed a paradox, the efficacy of thought and purpose in the material world, and their freedom from law. When we portray events as perceivings, rememberings, decisions and actions, we necessarily locate them amid physical happenings through the relation of cause and effect; but that same mode of portrayal insulates mental events, as long as we do not change the idiom, from the strict laws that can in principle be called upon to explain and predict physical phenomena.

Mental events as a class cannot be explained by physical science; particular mental events can when we know particular identities. But the explanations of mental events in which we are typically interested relate them to other mental events and conditions. We explain a man's free actions, for example, by appeal to his desires, habits, knowledge and perceptions. Such accounts of intentional behavior operate in a conceptual framework removed from the direct reach of physical law by describing both cause and effect, reason and action, as aspects of a portrait of a human agent. The anomalism of the mental is thus a necessary condition for viewing action as autonomous. I conclude with a second passage from Kant:

> It is an indispensable problem of speculative philosophy to show that its illusion respecting the contradiction rests on this, that we think of man in a different sense and relation when we call him free, and when we regard him as subject to the laws of nature. . . . It must therefore show that not only can both of these very well co-exist, but that both must be thought *as necessarily united* in the same subject. . . .[16]

Suggested Further Readings

Davidson's position has been much in the news recently. See Louise Antony, "Anomalous Monism and the Problem of Explanatory Force," *Philosophical Review* 98 (1989); Jaegwon Kim, "Psychophysical Laws," in *Supervenience and Mind* (Cambridge: Cambridge University Press, 1993); William Stanton, "Supervenience and Psychophysical Law in Anomalous Monism," *Pacific Philosophical Quarterly* LXIV (1983); Ernest Sosa, "Mind–Body Interaction and Supervenient Causation," *Midwest Studies in Philosophy* 9 (1984); Colin McGinn, "Anomalous Monism and Kripke's Cartesian Intuitions," *Analysis* (1977); and Bruce Goldberg, "A Problem with Anomalous Monism," *Philosophical Studies* 4 (1969).

---

[16]Op. cit., p. 76.

PART V

Causality and Free Will

CHAPTER 19

*O*f the Idea of Necessary Connection

David Hume

We ask why something happened and are assured that the happening in question was caused by some previous event, but how are we to understand such talk of causation? In the following selection, David Hume (1711–1776) explores the concept of causation. Although we observe that certain events are conjoined, we do not actually observe the causal relationships between such events. Hume offers a famous definition of causation and suggests that our idea of causal necessity is itself a product of the mind's reaction to events that are in our experience constantly conjoined.

For *first;* is there any principle in all nature more mysterious than the union of soul with body; by which a supposed spiritual substance acquires such an influence over a material one, that the most refined thought is able to actuate the grossest matter? Were we empowered, by a secret wish, to remove mountains, or control the plants in their orbit; this extensive authority would not be more extraordinary, nor more beyond our comprehension. But if by consciousness we perceived any power or energy in the will, we must know this power; we must know its connexion with the effect; we must know the secret union of soul and body, and the nature of both these substances; by which the one is able to operate, in so many instances, upon the other.

Secondly, We are not able to move all the organs of the body with a like authority; though we cannot assign any reason besides experience, for so remarkable a difference between one and the other. Why has the will an influence over the tongue and fingers, not over

Source: David Hume, *An Enquiry Concerning Human Understanding*, ed. by Eric Steinberg, 1993, pp. 43–53. Indianapolis: Hackett Publishing Co., Inc. All Rights Reserved.

the heart or liver? This question would never embarrass us, were we conscious of a power in the former case, not in the latter. We should then perceive, independent of experience, why the authority of will over the organs of the body is circumscribed within such particular limits. Being in that case fully acquainted with the power or force, by which it operates, we should also know, why its influence reaches precisely to such boundaries, and no farther.

A man, suddenly struck with a palsy in the leg or arm, or who had newly lost those members, frequently endeavours, at first, to move them, and employ them in their usual offices. Here he is as much conscious of power to command such limbs, as a man in perfect health is conscious of power to actuate any member which remains in its natural state and condition. But consciousness never deceives. Consequently, neither in the one case nor in the other, are we ever conscious of any power. We learn the influence of our will from experience alone. And experience only teaches us, how one event constantly follows another; without instructing us in the secret connexion, which binds them together, and renders them inseparable.

Thirdly, We learn from anatomy, that the immediate object of power in voluntary motion is not the member itself which is moved, but certain muscles, and nerves, and animal spirits, and, perhaps, something still more minute and more unknown, through which the motion is successively propagated, ere it reach the member itself whose motion is the immediate object of volition. Can there be a more certain proof, that the power, by which this whole operation is performed, so far from being directly and fully known by an inward sentiment or consciousness, is, to the last degree, mysterious and unintelligible? Here the mind wills a certain event: Immediately another event, unknown to ourselves, and totally different from the one intended, is produced: This event produces another, equally unknown: Till at last, through a long succession, the desired event is produced. But if the original power were felt, it must be known: Were it known, its effect must also be known; since all power is relative to its effect. And *vice versa,* if the effect be not known, the power cannot be known nor felt. How indeed can we be conscious of a power to move our limbs, when we have no such power; but only that to move certain animal spirits, which, though they produce at last the motion of our limbs, yet operate in such a manner as is wholly beyond our comprehension?

We may, therefore, conclude from the whole, I hope, without any temerity, though with assurance; that our idea of power is not copied from any sentiment or consciousness of power within our-selves, when we give rise to animal motion, or apply our limbs to their proper use and office. That their motion follows the command of the will is a matter of common experience, like other natural events: But the power or energy by which this is effected, like that in other natural events, is unknown and inconceivable.

Shall we then assert, that we are conscious of a power or energy in our own minds, when, by an act or command of our will, we raise up a new idea, fix the mind to the contemplation of it, turn it on all sides, and at last dismiss it for some other idea, when we think that we have surveyed it with sufficient accuracy? I believe the same argu-ments will prove that even this command of the will gives us no real idea of force or energy.

First, It must be allowed, that, when we know a power, we know that very circumstance in the cause, by which it is enabled to pro-duce the effect: For these are supposed to be synonymous. We must, therefore, know both the cause and effect, and the relation between them. But do we pretend to be acquainted with the nature of the human soul and the nature of an idea, or the aptitude of the one to produce the other? This is a real creation; a production of some-thing out of nothing: Which implies a power so great, that it may seem, at first sight, beyond the reach of any being, less than infinite. At least it must be owned, that such a power is not felt, nor known, nor even conceivable by the mind. We only feel the event, namely, the existence of an idea, consequent to a command of the will: But the manner, in which this operation is performed; the power, by which it is produced; is entirely beyond our comprehension.

Secondly, The command of the mind over itself is limited, as well as its command over the body; and these limits are not known by rea-son, or any acquaintance with the nature of cause and effect; but only by experience and observation, as in all other natural events and in the operation of external objects. Our authority over our sentiments and passions is much weaker than that over our ideas; and even the latter authority is circumscribed within very narrow boundaries. Will any one pretend to assign the ultimate reason of these boundaries, or show why the power is deficient in one case and not in another?

Thirdly, This self-command is very different at different times. A man in health possesses more of it, than one languishing with sickness. We are more master of our thoughts in the morning than in the evening: Fasting, than after a full meal. Can we give any reason for these variations, except experience? Where then is the power, of which we pretend to be conscious? Is there not here, either in a spiritual or material substance, or both, some secret mechanism or structure of parts, upon which the effect depends, and which, being entirely unknown to us, renders the power or energy of the will equally unknown and incomprehensible?

Volition is surely an act of the mind, with which we are sufficiently acquainted. Reflect upon it. Consider it on all sides. Do you find anything in it like this creative power, by which it raises from nothing a new idea, and with a kind of FIAT, imitates the omnipotence of its Maker, if I may be allowed so to speak, who called forth into existence all the various scenes of nature? So far from being conscious of this energy in the will, it requires as certain experience, as that of which we are possessed, to convince us, that such extraordinary effects do ever result from a simple act of volition.

The generality of mankind never find any difficulty in accounting for the more common and familiar operations of nature; such as the descent of heavy bodies, the growth of plants, the generation of animals, or the nourishment of bodies by food: But suppose, that, in all these cases, they perceive the very force or energy of the cause, by which it is connected with its effect, and is for ever infallible in its operation. They acquire, by long habit, such a turn of mind, that, upon the appearance of the cause, they immediately expect with assurance its usual attendant, and hardly conceive it possible, that any other event could result from it. It is only on the discovery of extraordinary phenomena, such as earthquakes, pestilence, and prodigies of any kind, that they find themselves at a loss to assign a proper cause, and to explain the manner, in which the effect is produced by it. It is usual for men, in such difficulties, to have resource to some invisible intelligent principle, as the immediate cause of that event, which surprises them, and which they think, cannot be accounted for from the common powers of nature. But philosophers, who carry their scrutiny a little farther, immediately perceive, that, even in the most familiar events, the energy of the cause is as unintelligible as in the most unusual, and that we only learn by experience the frequent CONJUNCTION of objects, without being ever able to comprehend any thing like CONNEXION between them. Here then, many philosophers think themselves obliged by reason to have recourse, on all occasions, to the same principle, which the vulgar never appeal to but in cases, that appear miraculous and supernatural. They acknowledge mind and intelligence to be, not only the ultimate and original cause of all things, but the immediate and sole cause of every event, which appears in nature. They pretend, that those objects, which are commonly denominated *causes,* are in reality nothing but *occasions;* and that the true and direct principle of every effect is not any power or force in nature, but a volition of the Supreme Being, who wills, that such particular objects should, for ever, be conjoined with each other. Instead of saying, that one billiard-ball moves another, by a force, which it has derived from the author of nature; it is the Deity himself, they say, who, by a particular volition, moves the second ball, being determined to this operation by the impulse of the first ball; in consequence of those general laws, which he has laid down to himself in the government of the universe. But philosophers advancing still in their enquiries, discover, that, as we are totally ignorant of the power, on which depends the mutual operation of bodies, we are no less ignorant of that power, on which depends the operation of mind on body, or of body on mind; nor are we able, either from our senses or consciousness, to assign the ultimate principle in one case, more than in the other. The same ignorance, therefore, reduces them to the same conclusion. They assert, that the Deity is the immediate cause of the union between soul and body; and that they are not the organs of sense, which, being agitated by external objects, produce sensations in the mind; but that it is a particular volition of our omnipotent Maker, which excites such a sensation, in consequence of such a motion in the organ. In like manner, it is not any energy in the will, that produces local motion in our members: It is God himself, who is pleased to second our will, in itself impotent, and to command that motion, which we erroneously attribute to our own power and efficacy. Nor do philosophers stop at this conclusion. They sometimes extend the same inference to the mind itself, in its internal operations. Our mental vision or conception of ideas is nothing but a revelation made to us by our Maker. When we voluntarily turn our thoughts to any object, and raise up its image in the fancy; it is not the will which creates that idea: It is the universal Creator, who discovers it to the mind, and renders it present to us.

Thus, according to these philosophers, every thing is full of God. Not content with the principle, that nothing exists but by his will, that nothing possesses any power but by his concession: They rob nature, and all created beings, of every power, in order to render their dependence on the Deity still more sensible and immediate. They consider not, that, by this theory, they diminish, instead of magnifying, the grandeur of those attributes, which they affect so much to celebrate. It argues surely more power in the Deity to delegate a certain degree of power to inferior creatures, than to produce every thing by his own immediate volition. It argues more wisdom to contrive at first the fabric of the world with such perfect foresight, that, of itself, and by its proper operation, it may serve all the purposes of providence, than if the great Creator were obliged every moment to adjust its parts, and animate by his breath all the wheels of that stupendous machine.

But if we would have a more philosophical confutation of this theory, perhaps the two following reflections may suffice.

First, It seems to me, that this theory of the universal energy and operation of the Supreme Being, is too bold ever to carry conviction with it to a man, sufficiently apprized of the weakness of human reason, and the narrow limits, to which it is confined in all its operations. Though the chain of arguments, which conduct to it, were ever so logical, there must arise a strong suspicion, if not an absolute assurance, that it has carried us quite beyond the reach of our faculties, when it leads to conclusions so extraordinary, and so remote from common life and experience. We are got into fairy land, long ere we have reached the last steps of our theory; and *there* we have no reason to trust our common methods of argument, or to think that our usual analogies and probabilities have any authority. Our line is too short to fathom such immense abysses. And however we may flatter ourselves, that we are guided, in every step which we take, by a kind of verisimilitude and experience; we may be assured, that this fancied experience has no authority, when we thus apply it to subjects, that lie entirely out of the sphere of experience. But on this we shall have occasion to touch afterwards.

Secondly, I cannot perceive any force in the arguments, on which this theory is founded. We are ignorant, it is true, of the manner in which bodies operate on each other: Their force or energy is entirely incomprehensible: But are we not equally ignorant of the manner or force by which a mind, even the supreme mind, operates either on itself or on body? Whence, I beseech you, do we acquire any idea of it? We have no sentiment or consciousness of this power in ourselves. We have no idea of the Supreme Being but what we learn from reflection on our own faculties. Were our ignorance, therefore, a good reason for rejecting any thing, we should be led into that principle of denying all energy in the Supreme Being as much as in the grossest matter. We surely comprehend as little the operations of one as of the other. Is it more difficult to conceive, that motion may arise from impulse, than that it may arise from volition? All we know is our profound ignorance in both cases.

But to hasten to a conclusion of this argument, which is already drawn out to too great a length: We have sought in vain for an idea of power or necessary connexion, in all the sources from which we could suppose it to be derived. It appears, that, in single instances of the operation of bodies, we never can, by our utmost scrutiny, discover any thing but one event following another; without being able to comprehend any force or power, by which the cause operates, or any connexion between it and its supposed effect. The same difficulty occurs in contemplating the operations of mind on body; where we observe the motion of the latter to follow upon the volition of the former; but are not able to observe or conceive the tie, which binds together the motion and volition, or the energy by which the mind produces this effect. The authority of the will over its own faculties and ideas is not a whit more comprehensible: So that, upon the whole, there appears not, throughout all nature, any one instance of connexion, which is conceivable by us. All events seem entirely loose and separate. One event follows another; but we never can observe any tie between them. They seem *conjoined,* but never *connected.* And as we can have no idea of any thing, which never appeared to our outward sense or inward sentiment, the necessary conclusion *seems* to be, that we have no idea of connexion or power at all, and that these words are absolutely without any meaning, when employed either in philosophical reasonings, or common life.

But there still remains one method of avoiding this conclusion, and one source which we have not yet examined. When any natural object or event is presented, it is impossible for us, by any sagacity or penetration, to discover, or even conjecture, without experience, what event will result from it, or to carry our foresight beyond that object, which is immediately present to the memory and senses. Even after one instance or experiment, where we have observed a particular event to follow upon another, we are not entitled to form a general rule, or foretell what will happen in like cases; it being justly esteemed an unpardonable temerity to judge of the whole course of nature from one single experiment, however accurate or certain. But when one particular species of event has always, in all instances, been conjoined with another, we make no longer any scruple of foretelling one upon the appearance of the other, and of employing that reasoning, which can alone assure us of any matter of fact or existence. We then call the one object, *Cause;* the other, *Effect.* We suppose, that there is some connexion between them; some power in the one, by which it infallibly produces the other, and operates with the greatest certainty and strongest necessity.

It appears, then, that this idea of a necessary connexion among events arises from a number of similar instances, which occur, of the constant conjunction of these events; nor can that idea ever be suggested by any one of these instances, surveyed in all possible lights and positions. But there is nothing in a number of instances, different from every single instance, which is supposed to be exactly similar; except only, that after a repetition of similar instances, the mind is carried by *habit,* upon the appearance of one event, to expect its usual attendant, and to believe, that it will exist. This connexion, therefore, which we *feel* in the mind, this customary transition of the imagination from one object to its usual attendant, is the sentiment or impression, from which we form the idea of power or necessary connexion. Nothing farther is in the case. Contemplate the subject on all sides; you will never find any other origin of that idea. This is the sole difference between one instance, from which we can never receive the idea of connexion, and a number of similar instances, by which it is suggested. The first time a man saw the communication of motion by impulse, as by the shock of two billiard-balls, he could not pronounce that the one event was *connected:* but only that it was *conjoined* with the other. After he has observed several instances of this nature, he then pronounces them to be *connected.* What alteration has happened to give rise to this new idea of *connexion?* Nothing but that he now *feels* these events to be *connected* in his imagination, and can readily foretell the existence of one from the appearance of the other. When we say, therefore, that one object is connected with another, we mean only, that they have acquired a connexion in our thought, and give rise to this inference, by which they become proofs of each other's existence: A conclusion, which is somewhat extraordinary; but which seems founded on sufficient evidence. Nor will its evidence be weakened by any general diffidence of the understanding, or sceptical suspicion concerning every conclusion, which is new and extraordinary. No conclusions can be more agreeable to scepticism that such as make discoveries concerning the weakness and narrow limits of human reason and capacity.

And what stronger instance can be produced of the surprising ignorance and weakness of the understanding, than the present? For surely, if there be any relation among objects, which it imports to us to know perfectly, it is that of cause and effect. On this are founded all our reasonings concerning matter of fact or existence. By means of it alone we attain any assurance concerning objects, which are removed from the present testimony of our memory and senses. The only immediate utility of all sciences, is to teach us, how to control and regulate future events by their causes. Our thoughts and enquiries are, therefore, every moment, employed about this relation: Yet so imperfect are the ideas which we form concerning it, that it is impossible to give any just definition of cause, except what is drawn from something extraneous and foreign to it. Similar objects are always conjoined with similar. Of this we have experience. Suitably to this experience, therefore, we may define a cause to be *an object, followed by another, and where all the objects, similar to the first, are followed by objects similar to the second.* Or in other words, *where, if the first object had not been, the second never had existed.* The appearance of a cause always conveys the mind, by a customary transition, to the idea of the effect. Of this also we have experience. We may, therefore, suitably to this experience, form another definition of cause; and call it, *an object followed by another, and whose appearance always conveys the thought to that other.* But though both these definitions be drawn from circumstances foreign to the cause, we cannot remedy this inconvenience, or attain any more perfect definition, which may point out that circumstance in the cause, which gives it a connexion with its effect. We have no idea of this connexion; nor even any distinct notion what it is we desire to know, when we endeavour at a conception of it. We say, for instance, that the vibration of this string is the cause of this particular sound. But what do we mean by that affirmation? We either mean, *that this vibration is followed by this sound, and that all similar vibrations have been followed by similar sounds:* Or, *that this vibration is followed by this sound, and that upon the appearance of one, the mind anticipates the senses, and forms immediately an idea of the other.* We may consider the relation of cause and effect in either of these two lights; but beyond these, we have no idea of it.

To recapitulate, therefore, the reasonings of this section: Every idea is copied from some preceding impression or sentiment; and where we cannot find any impression, we may be certain that there is no idea. In all single instances of the operation of bodies or minds, there is nothing that produces any impression, nor consequently can suggest any idea, of power or necessary connexion. But when many uniform instances appear, and the same object is always followed by the same event; we then begin to entertain the notion of cause and connexion. We then *feel* a new sentiment or impression, to wit, a customary connexion in the thought or imagination between one object and its usual attendant; and this sentiment is the original of that idea which we seek for. For as this idea arises from a number of similar instances, and not from any single instance; it must arise from that circumstance, in which the number of instances differ from every individual instance. But this customary connexion or transition of the imagination is the only circumstance, in which they differ. In every other particular they are alike. The first instance which we saw of motion, communicated by the shock of two billiard-balls (to return to this obvious illustration) is exactly similar to any instance that may, at present, occur to us; except only, that we could not, at first, *infer* one event from the other; which we are enabled to do at present, after so long a course of uniform experience. I know not, whether the reader will readily apprehend this reasoning. I am afraid, that, should I multiply words about it, or throw it into a greater variety of lights, it would only become more obscure and intricate. In all abstract reasonings, there is one point of view, which, if we can happily hit, we shall go farther towards illustrating the subject, than by all the eloquence and copious expression in the world. This point of view we should endeavour to reach, and reserve the flowers of rhetoric for subjects which are more adapted to them.

Suggested Further Readings

For more information about Hume's views on causation, see Jonathan Bennett, *Locke, Berkeley, Hume* (Oxford: Clarendon Press, 1971), chaps. XI and XII; David Pears, *Hume's System* (Oxford: Oxford University Press, 1990), chaps. 5, 6, and 7; and John Carroll, "The Humean Tradition," *Philosophical Review* (1990).

In regard to causation, interesting things can be found in Brian Skyrms, *Causal Necessity* (New Haven, CT: Yale University Press, 1980); Ernest Sosa, ed., *Causation and Conditionals* (Oxford: Oxford University Press, 1975); D. H. Mellor, *The Facts of Causation* (London: Routledge, 1995); J. L. Mackie, "Counterfactuals and Causal Laws," in *Analytic Philosophy*, ed. by R. J. Butler (Oxford: Blackwell, 1962); and David H. Sanford, "The Direction of Causation and the Direction of Conditionship," *Journal of Philosophy* LXXIII (1976).

CHAPTER 20

Selective Necessity and the Free-Will Problem

Michael Slote

Incompatibilists argue that causal determinism rules out free will, whereas compatibilists deny that idea. The following selection challenges a principle that plays a central, if not indispensable, role in various arguments in favor of incompatibilism.

Michael Slote is a professor of philosophy at the University of Maryland at College Park.

A new form of argument for the incompability of free will and determinism has recently become prevalent. Carl Ginet, James Lamb, Peter van Inwagen, and David Wiggins have all mounted attacks on compatibilism which take inspiration from the fact that nothing can now be done about events in the (remote) past.[1] Unlike older discussions that seem to hinge on the assumptions of universal causation

---

Source: Michael Slote: "Selective Necessity and the Free-Will Problem," from *The Journal of Philosophy*, January 1982, vol. LXXIX, no. 1, pp. 5–24. Reprinted by permission of The Journal of Philosophy, Inc. and the author.

[1]Ginet, "Might We Have No Choice?" in Keith Lehrer, ed., *Freedom and Determinism* (New York: Random House, 1966), pp. 87–104; Lamb, "On a Proof of Incompatibilism," *Philosophical Review*, LXXXVI, 1 (January 1977): 20–35; van Inwagen, "The Incompatibility of Free Will and Determinism," *Philosophical Studies*, XXVII, 3 (March 1975): 185–199; and Wiggins, "Towards a Reasonable Libertarianism," in Ted Honderich, ed., *Essays on Freedom of Action* (London: Routledge & Kegan Paul, 1973), pp. 31–61. Incidentally, in calling these authors "incompatibilists," I do not mean to imply that they think that free will is logically incompatible with determinism. Various contingent assumptions enter into their arguments.

alone,[2] these new arguments do not make the mistake of assuming that, since all actions in a deterministic universe are *necessitated by* past events taken together with (necessary) laws of nature, all our actions are themselves necessary (inevitable, unavoidable) if determinism is true. What necessarily results from past events and laws may be necessary only *relative to* those events and laws and will be necessary or unavoidable in itself only if those past events and laws are in some sense necessary. And the above-mentioned philosophers seek to overcome the weakness of earlier treatments precisely by insisting that the past events and laws, relative to which, under determinism, our actions are necessary or unavoidable, are themselves necessary or unavoidable. This new form of argument, insofar as it recognizes and attempts to remedy a glaring deficiency of previous defenses of incompatibilism, represents a striking improvement over those earlier arguments. But it also suffers from important weaknesses which I shall detail in what follows, weaknesses that result, in particular, from insufficient attention to a kind of necessity which, despite its prevalence in ordinary thought about the world, has rarely if ever been discussed. But our first task must be to reveal and clarify the basic structure that these new arguments for incompatibilism seem to share.

For a number of reasons, I shall not present anything like a formal version of the arguments Ginet *et al.* offer us. There are differences of emphasis and assumption in their reasoning, and any detailed formal argument I gave would simply be a fourth argument (or identical with one of theirs), rather than indicate the underlying assumptions they share. I shall thus restrict myself to the informal presentation of a common argument-structure, but none of the main criticisms I shall offer can be avoided by recourse to any particular one of the more or less formal presentations offered by Ginet, Lamb, van Inwagen, or Wiggins (henceforth, GLVW, for short).

As I said above, the common argument to be discerned here focuses crucially on the past. Given determinism, there will always be some much earlier set of conditions *s* that is connected by laws of nature to any given human action *a* that takes place. But nothing can be done to alter, nothing can be *done* about those laws; and neither, it may

---

[2]Cf., e.g., Richard Taylor, *Metaphysics* (Englewood Cliffs, N.J.: Prentice-Hall, 1963), p. 46; and Roderick Chisholm, " 'He Could Have Done Otherwise,' " in Myles Brand, ed., *The Nature of Human Action* (Glenview, Ill.: Scott, Foresman, 1970), pp. 295ff.

be added, can anything be done about *s* at any time when the doing of *a* is immediately in question. Since *s* is thus necessary (e.g., unalterable) at the time when *a* is in question and since a law leading from *s* to *a* is similarly necessary (unalterable) at that time, it would seem to follow that *a* itself is necessary (unalterable, unavoidable) at that time—however ignorant of that fact the agent of *a* may be. Presumably, then, the agent in question does not act freely in performing *a,* and, since the argument has been entirely general in its assumptions, one may conclude that no human being ever acts freely in a deterministic universe.

There are, of course, differences to be found among GLVW's specific presentations of this underlying form of reasoning. Three of the authors stipulate that the set of conditions *s* exist before the birth of the agent whose freedom of action is in question. This serves to underscore the unavoidability of that set of conditions for the agent in question. But David Wiggins, on the other hand, simply places the set of conditions at some earlier time whose "contents" one can no longer do anything about (at the time of the act whose freedom is at issue). Our authors also differ in the way they conceive of those earlier conditions: van Inwagen treats them as constituting a total state of the universe at some time before the birth of the person who is to act, whereas the others treat them as a more or less delimited group of conditions or events that are lawfully connected to appropriate later actions. There is also considerable variety in the modal locutions that GLVW use to express the necessity that attaches to events or conditions that pre-exist a given individual (what we can call *pre-existent events*) or (as with Wiggins) exist before the time when a given action is in question. Lamb speaks (roughly) of our inability to refrain from an action such that, if one were to refrain from it, some true proposition describing a pre-existent event would not be the case and also, more simply, of our inability to prevent such an event; Ginet, of an individual's having no choice as to whether some pre-existent instance of a certain event-kind would occur; Wiggins, of earlier conditions which at some later time nobody can do anything about, conditions which, at that later time, are (historically) necessary and inevitable; and, finally, van Inwagen (at least by implication),[3] of a person's being unable to

---

[3]Van Inwagen explicitly says only that, if *Q* is a true proposition about states before *S*'s birth and if *S* can render the conjunction of *Q* and *R* false, *S* can render *R* false. But his whole discussion and the direction of his argument presuppose the impossibility of rendering false a true proposition about a pre-existent state of the universe; and

render false some true proposition about a pre-existent state of the universe, and, again, of things one cannot do anything about.

Of course, whatever locution is chosen to express the necessity of past or pre-existent events will also be used to characterize the necessity attaching to laws of nature in relation to what humans can or cannot do, because the argument that has recently come into prominence, unlike the earlier form of argument for incompatibilism, involves a double use of modality in its premises. Thus the old form of deterministic argument against freedom of will has roughly the form:

$$p \qquad \text{(where '}p\text{' stands for a statement that posits the existence of some earlier event or circumstance)}$$
$$\underline{N(p \supset q)} \qquad \text{(where '}p \supset q\text{' stands for some law of nature)}$$
$$\therefore Nq \qquad \text{(where '}q\text{' stands for a statement that posits some human action)}$$

And this seems clearly fallacious, whereas the more recent kind of argument has approximately the form:

$$Np$$
$$\underline{N(p \supset q)}$$
$$\therefore Nq$$

And this in no way seems fallacious and in fact corresponds to an inference that is valid in the most well-known form of alethic modal logic, the logic of logical or metaphysical necessity and possibility.[4] In that case the necessity indicated by 'N,' which is clearly not a form of logical necessity, must be exactly the same for both premises and conclusion. And this means that the proponents of the more recent defense of incompatibilism are assuming that we can no more affect laws of nature than past or pre-existent events, that the laws are every bit as unalterable as the events.

Of course, the sheer terminological force of the expression 'law of nature' would seem to rule out calling anything a law which we thought humans could alter. But there is one objection to the unalterability of laws of nature which GLVW do not consider and which may need mentioning. Could it not be held that the supposition that

---

this assumption comes explicitly to the fore both in his subsequent "Reply to Gallois," *Philosophical Studies*, XXXII, 1 (July 1977): 107–111, and in a later, as yet unpublished manuscript on freedom of will.

[4]Cf. G. E. Hughes and M. H. Cresswell, *An Introduction to Modal Logic* (London: Methuen, 1968), esp. p. 31.

humans lack the ability to alter, to affect, the laws that actually obtain involves a controversial theory about the nature of laws, namely,
that they are not just true universal generalizations with the right
sorts of predicates or systematic interrelations, but rather involve
some sort of physical necessity above and beyond these other facets?
I believe the answer here can be in the negative. In assuming that we
cannot affect laws, we need not assume that the laws themselves possess (a mysterious) physical necessity; for another explanation of our
inability to alter them would be some weakness or lack *in us*. (Consider the theological view that God can alter the laws of nature even
if humans cannot.) Our inability to alter the laws of nature may be
due to the nature of law, to our own nature(s), or to some combination of the two, and the proponents of the more recent form of argument for incompatibilism need not commit themselves to any *particular* explanation of the human inability to affect natural laws which it
seems so plausible to assume.

The arguments of GLVW also differ in the conclusions they seek
to draw from the lemma that all human actions are necessary and in
the ways they attempt to take the argument thus further. Some concentrate on free will and others on moral responsibility, but I think
all their positions can be fairly summarized in the claim that if
human actions are all necessary (and though they use different locutions, it is not clear that there are any important differences in the
kinds of necessity they talk about), then humans lack free will or the
moral responsibility that is ordinarily attributed to them. Of course,
the assumption that some kind of being able to do otherwise is necessary to freedom or moral responsibility has been called into question by Harry Frankfurt[5] and others in recent years and has always
been doubted within the idealist/rationalist tradition that thinks of
freedom as a form of rational necessity in action. But Frankfurt's arguments and examples have been attacked by one of our proponents of incompatibilism (Lamb) and by others elsewhere, and the
existence of free will would surely be highly problematic if the only
criticism one could make of recent arguments against compatibilism
was of their assumption that moral responsibility or free will entails
the ability to do otherwise.

---

[5] See his "Alternate Possibilities and Moral Responsibility," this JOURNAL, LXVI 23 (Dec.
4, 1969): 829–839.

Moreover, even if we question or eliminate the step from necessity to the absence of freedom or responsibility, the recent form of argument yields the (sub)conclusion that under determinism we can never do anything but what we in fact do, and this itself seems a sufficient challenge to deeply entrenched and cherished beliefs to make it worth while to see whether the recent arguments can be attacked at some point *before* the conclusion that all actions are necessary has been drawn. And that is precisely what I shall attempt to do in what follows. For I want to argue, in particular, that the arguments of GLVW all rest on a questionable form of inference, the very inference from the double modality of 'Np' and '$N(p \supset q)$' to 'Nq' which marks the superiority of the new kind of argument to earlier defenses of incompatibilism.

GLVW rely on this form of inference in a variety of different ways. Ginet's argument implicitly depends on the principle rule of inference: Np, $N(p \supset q) \vdash Nq$, for its validity, whereas Wiggins and Lamb explicitly formulate a modal principle that corresponds to that inference and use it as an assumption in their respective defenses of incompatibilism. And in our own terminology that modal principle— what can henceforth be called the *main modal principle*—can perhaps most readily be stated as: $(Np \cdot N(p \supset q)) \supset Nq$ (where 'N' stands for whatever form of necessity the incompatibilist argument involves).[6] On the other hand, van Inwagen makes only an indirect appeal to this latter principle or the corresponding rule of inference. Anyone who assumes the validity of arguing from 'Np' and '$N(p \supset q)$' to 'Nq' would seem to be tacitly assuming that the necessity expressed in the operator 'N' is both agglomerative (closed with respect to conjunction introduction) and closed under logical implication, so that one can, e.g., validly move from 'Np' and '$N(p \supset q)$' to '$N(p \cdot p \supset q)$' and from the latter to 'Nq'. If we do not think about these subinferences, when we move from 'Np' and '$N(p \supset q)$' to 'Nq' or assert the main

---

[6]Wiggins's and Lamb's formulations in fact differ slightly from each other and from our above statement of the main principle. What Wiggins actually states is of the form: $Pp \supset (N(p \supset q) \supset Pq)$, where '$P$' stands for the appropriate kind of possibility. But this can be altered into our principle by contraposition and trivial logical manipulations. More significantly, Wiggins uses the main principle itself as a principle of inference in a less formal version of his argument which he says he prefers to the formal version (46) and also in one of his preliminary arguments (43), Lamb's assumption 4 ("canentailment") can in similar fashion be transformed into our main principle by trivial logical means.

modal principle that corresponds to that larger inference, that is only because it is so natural to assume that any necessity operator will have the properties of agglomerativity and closure under logical implication or entailment. Van Inwagen does not in fact state anything directly corresponding to our main principle; but he does attribute agglomerativity and closure (under entailment) to the necessity he is dealing with. And, since these two properties seem inevitably to be presupposed in use of the main principle and together ensure its truth, it may not be unfair to say that van Inwagen indirectly appeals to that principle: it comes into his incompatibilist argument, so to speak, in pieces, rather than whole.[7]

GLVW's arguments make use of modal principles that correspond to valid principles of the most familiar form of alethic modal logic. Logical or metaphysical necessity is agglomerative and closed under entailment, and the principle '$(\Box\, p \cdot \Box\, (p \supset q)) \supset \Box\, q$' is valid for logical necessity under any reasonable interpretation of such necessity.[8] On the other hand, the necessity at stake in the defenses of incompatibilism we are discussing is not logical necessity or what ordinarily goes under the name of metaphysical necessity (even if it represents something weaker which may also deserve to be called metaphysical necessity). And if it turned out that the necessity involved in those arguments was not closed under entailment or was not agglomerative, or (for some reason) that the modal principle

---

[7]Van Inwagen's premise (4) corresponds to the assumption of closure under entailment; his premise (5) corresponds to the principle of agglomerativity. The latter claim may not initially be obvious, but if, as we argued in fn 3, van Inwagen is assuming the impossibility of rendering false, true propositions about the past and using it to back (5), then (5) is tantamount to the assumption that if one can't falsify a law of nature L and can't falsify a proposition about the past P_0, one can't render false the conjunction of L and P_0. And this just is an agglomerativity assumption for the necessity expressed by 'can't render false.' In "Van Inwagen on Free Will and Determinism," *Philosophical Studies,* XXXII, 1 (July 1977): 99–105, André Gallois makes practically the same point about van Inwagen's need for a principle of agglomeration and gives (what amounts to) an argument against agglomerativity which is interestingly different from anything mentioned in the present paper. But, unfortunately, van Inwagen's "Reply to Gallois" (*loc. cit.*) focuses on other aspects of Gallois's article. Note finally that van Inwagen employs our main principle itself in the forthcoming manuscript mentioned in fn 3 and that Lamb's assumption 7 ("union inefficacy") is trivially transformable into a principle of agglomeration.

[8]For some doubts, however, see Martin Davies, "Weak Necessity and Truth Theories," *Journal of Philosophical Logic,* VII, 4 (November 1978): 415–439.

'$(Np \cdot N(p \supset q)) \supset Nq$' was simply invalid for the sort of necessity involved in GLVW's arguments, then I take it that those arguments would be thoroughly undermined.

Such an eventuality may at this point seem both purely speculative and wildly implausible, since it would initially appear that anything deserving the name 'necessity' would have to be closed under entailment and agglomerative, and thus require the validity of our main modal principle. But a look in the right direction may help to persuade our second thoughts that this is not so.

It is generally agreed that 'A knows that p' and 'A knows that $(p \supset q)$' do not entail 'A knows that q' for appropriate substituends. People may fail to make inferences they are entitled to make. But the fact that such epistemic necessity is an exception to our main modal principle may well be thought to have little bearing on the necessity involved in GLVW's arguments. For these involve forms of situational inevitability and unfreedom that seem to be nomic and metaphysical matters, and Kripke's *Naming and Necessity* has surely taught us to be wary of arguing from epistemic or epistemological considerations to (corresponding) metaphysical or nomic conclusions. What, however, if other, nonepistemic modalities offer similar exceptions to our main principle?

Obligation is often said to be a form of deontic necessity. The very fact that we speak of something being "released" from an obligation by the person to whom it is owed shows that we think of someone under an obligation as being in some sense bound and not at liberty. And even when an obligation is overridden by some more important moral consideration, there is still an obligation to make amends to the person one was under an obligation to, and this too is some measure of the moral necessity that attaches to the fulfillment of obligations. But, as has sometimes been noted,[9] obligations in the most ordinary sense of the term are always obligations to particular individuals (or groups) and arise from the actions of the person who puts himself under an obligation. Most typically, a person will deliberately undertake an obligation to some other person to perform in

---

[9]A. John Simmons's "The Principle of Fair Play," *Philosophy and Public Affairs*, VIII, 4 (Summer 1979): 307–337, p. 317f., offers some reasons to think that a person's obligations cannot arise (entirely) from the actions of others.

some specific way: one promises a person to do something in his or her behalf, and, if circumstances are right, one thereby comes to be under an obligation to that person to do the thing promised. By a more or less natural extension, we also speak of a father's obligation(s) to a child even when there has been no deliberate undertaking of obligations by the father in question. It is thought here that the very act of procreation can put parents under obligations of support and the like to those whom they have procreated, but once again the putative obligations arise from certain kinds of actions and are owed to specific individuals in virtue of the actions that give rise to them.

This relativity or relationality is an important feature of obligations, both intrinsically and in connection with our present investigation of modality. If I am under an obligation to one friend to return his book and under an obligation to another friend to keep a promise to meet him at a certain time, there is no one to whom I am under an obligation to *do both* of these things. Nor will my actions with respect to each of these people somehow give rise to a corporate individual to whom the obligation to do both these things would be owed. Human undertakings can give rise to obligations to collective entities only when the undertakings concern such entities. If I promise a pair of friends to attend a party they are jointly holding, then I may properly be said to owe it to the two of them to attend, and, perhaps because of their joint efforts, that obligation is owed to the pair of them considered as a (temporary) collectivity. Certainly in other cases one can undertake obligations to universities, corporations, and governments and by that means come to have obligations to collective entities. But nothing of the sort required has occurred in the situation described above where I separately undertake to return one person's book and to meet another at a certain time. And in those circumstances there is no such thing as the obligation to do both those things. I am under an obligation to return the book, and this obligation is owed to a particular friend; under an obligation to meet another friend at a certain time, this obligation being owed to that other friend; but those are the only obligations that need exist in the situation I have described. And in that case it will be obligatory that I return the book, obligatory that I meet my friend, but not obligatory that I perform the joint act of returning-the-book-and-meeting-my-friend.

Obligation (obligatoriness) thus fails to be agglomerative, and the reason why clearly has something to do with its relationality and with the specificity of the performances required to give rise to a (relational) obligation. Obligation is a moral boundness that exists only in relation to some person or collectivity owed the obligation and in virtue of certain specific kinds of performance: most typically, undertakings. And where each of two (or more) individuals is owed an obligation in virtue of some undertaking, there may have been no undertaking to do the (joint) act required by agglomerativity and thus no person or collectivity to whom the obligation to do such a (joint) act is owed. Agglomeration will thereby fail for such cases.

It is worth noting, however, that relationality alone cannot explain why a given form of deontic or moral necessity fails the principle of agglomeration. Timothy Smiley has, for example, suggested that the moral 'ought' may express relative necessity, so that 'ought p' is true if and only if 'p' follows logically from some ideal moral code, i.e., is necessary in relation to (the fulfillment of) such a code.[10] But such relational necessity is agglomerative: if 'p' and 'q' both follow classically from a code, so does their conjunction. On the other hand, some forms of relational necessity can arise only in certain narrowly circumscribed ways; and when restrictions on the way a given kind of relational necessity can come into being unhinge it from agglomerativity (or closure or our main principle), we may say that such necessity is *selective*. Thus if obligation is nonagglomerative, that is, as we have seen, because of limitations on the way (relational) obligations can arise; it is because obligations to do specific things typically derive from *undertakings* (to individuals) *to do those very things*. So obligation is not only relational, but selective. And both these factors enter into the "logic" of the notion.

The fact that moral obligation exists only when a specific kind of performance makes some act or kind of action morally necessary in relation to some individual also have implications for the closure of obligation under logical implication or entailment. Even if doing x entails doing y, I may have promised and be under an obligation to do x, without having promised or being under an obligation to do y. Thus if I promise to meet you at three o'clock tomorrow, I may be under an obligation to you to do so; but have I promised to stay alive till tomorrow? Do I have a specific obligation to be alive at that time? If I die before tomorrow, I will, presumably, have failed to fulfill a

---

[10]See his "Relative Necessity," *Journal of Symbolic Logic*, XXVIII, 2 (June 1963): 113–134.

promise and an obligation to meet you at three o'clock; but not many people will be tempted to say that I (also) have an obligation to stay alive that I shall (also) have failed to fulfill, even though meeting someone may logically entail being alive.[11] And *no one*, I think, will want to say that I have promised or am under any obligation (to you) to exist at some moment in human history, though this too is entailed by my meeting you at three o'clock. Such examples illustrate the selectivity of obligations. Even promising to do something that entails doing or being *x* need not give rise to an obligation to do (be) *x*, if I am not *promising* to do (be) *x* and it is merely presupposed that I shall. Moreover, once we have spotted failures of agglomeration and closure under entailment in the area of obligation, it also becomes easy to find the obligatory counterexamples to our main principle. I may, for example, have an obligation to *x* to bring him a certain book and I may promise *y* to visit her if I ever bring the book to *x* (they are neighbors). But for reasons already rehearsed, it seems doubtful that I have an obligation to visit *y* outright. To whom would I owe it?

Clearly, then, the notion of obligation provides a plausible example of nonepistemic necessity failing agglomeration, closure under entailment, and our main principle.[12] But at this point the defenders

---

[11]Of course, one may be able to come under an obligation to stay alive by promising to do so. (Imagine a suicidally depressed individual and a well-meaning friend.)

[12]In "Ethical Consistency," in *Problems of the Self* (New York: Cambridge, 1973), Bernard Williams makes a tentative effort to show that (the moral) 'ought' is nonagglomerative, by adducing moral conflicts, like Agamemnon's, where two acts that cannot both be performed seem morally called for. But his argument requires him to assume that 'ought' implies 'can' and that, in the circumstances, Agamemnon really ought to kill his daughter and really ought to spare her. Many of us will wonder how both the latter 'ought's can be true—especially when, given his choice of example, we can so much more easily speak of there being two conflicting, and important, *obligations* in the circumstances (and thereby perhaps account for the need for regret, remorse and reparation, whatever Agamemnon does). Williams may be right, nonetheless, but it is harder to argue for the nonagglomerativity of 'ought' than to do so for 'obligation' just because of the relationality and selectivity that attach to obligation. We can get nonagglomeration for 'obligation' in circumstances where there is no conflict of obligations, indeed no moral conflict whatever; but such circumstances are typically ones where we feel no problem whatever about agglomerating 'ought's. And that is why, in situations where 'ought's seem to conflict, it is hard to be sure that agglomerativity really fails and that paradox can best be avoided by insisting upon that failure. [Similar remarks apply to Bas van Fraassen's "Values and the Heart's Command," this JOURNAL, LXX 1 (Jan. 11, 1973): 5–19.]

of the incompatibilist arguments we are examining will, perhaps, have one more defense. They will grant the (perhaps initially surprising) fact that something that is reasonably thought of as a form of (nonepistemic) necessity flouts principles of inference that hold for logical or metaphysical necessity; but they will then point out that the kind of necessity involved in the incompatibilist arguments of GLVW is causal or physical. Since causal necessity is generally considered to be one form of alethic necessity among others, why, it will be objected, should we take a page from the book of deontic modal logic when we have the example of the alethic modal logic of strict or logical necessity to go by? The latter clearly does obey agglomerativity and closure under entailment, and surely it is more reasonable to hold that other forms of alethic necessity will conform to these intuitively plausible rules/principles, than to be swayed by counterexamples from the totally different realm of the deontic. But what if counterexamples to these rules/principles can be found within the alethic realm itself?

If we unexpectedly run across someone whom we haven't seen in years and are very pleased to see, we can naturally express our pleasure by saying or thinking: how lucky that we both should be here at the same time, what a wonderful accident! But even if it is accidental that two people should both be at a certain place at a given time, the presence of each one separately at the place (and at the time) in question can seem like no accident at all. Each one, for example, may have been sent by his superior to the place in question, e.g., a bank, as part of a well-known routine or plan of office functioning. (There was no last-minute substitution of the person who would go to the bank, no unusual delay in getting there: everything went normally for each of the individuals concerned.) If, then, we let 'Jules' and 'Jim' stand for the individuals in the example, it would appear to be no accident (not accidental) that Jules is at the bank when he is, no accident (not accidental) that Jim is there when he is, but a benign and lovely accident (accidental) that Jim and Jules should both be there at that time. Most people who take the trouble to think about it would recognize it to be a main feature of (non)accidentality that things that in themselves appear perfectly regular and nonaccidental may "come together" to create something that is accidental, and this feature precisely is the nonagglomerativity of the nonaccidental. And yet even in the face of such examples, it is hard to deny that nonaccidentality is a causal/nomological matter concerning

how things are in the world and a form of alethic *necessity* in particular. For those who distinguish lawlike universal truths, i.e., laws of nature, from nonlawlike ones, call the latter accidental. And it is natural to equate the accidental with the contingent and to treat
noncontingency as a form of necessity.[13] So it would appear that
there is at least one form of alethic necessity that fails of agglomerativity.

Nonaccidentality also appears not to be closed under entailment.
It may be no accident that I am in a certain place right now (I was sent
there by a superior in accordance with a routine plan of business operation), yet nevertheless be an accident that I am still alive right now
(only an accidental and unintentional swerve on my part has prevented
me from just being flattened by a runaway truck).[14] Failing that, it may
at least be an accident that I ever exist at all (imagine a suitable tale of
contraceptive woes), yet that too is entailed by my being where I am at
the present moment. If closure thus fails for nonaccidentality, we can
perhaps go on to deny that it is governed by our main modal principle,
on the grounds that in the above cases where it is no accident that I am
at a certain place and yet something of an accident that I still (or ever)

---

[13]Cf. Nelson Goodman, *Fact, Fiction, and Forecast* (Indianapolis: Bobbs-Merrill, 2d ed.,
1965) p. 73.

[14]It is sometimes said that, under determinism, *nothing* is accidental, and if that were
so then we couldn't say that it was an accident that I was still alive or that the truck
missed me. Ordinarily, however, we distinguish cases of accident from cases of
nonaccident quite independently of the issue of determinism. Thus even people who
believe in (macroscopic) determinism are willing to speak of traffic accidents. And
since no one seems inclined to deny the possibility of *coincidences* under determinism,
perhaps I can best pinpoint the ordinary usage of 'accidental' I have in mind by
saying that it is a usage according to which accidentality is *entailed* by coincidentality.

Of course, ordinary claims of accidentality may be context-relative or relative to
a favored standpoint, but that very fact may actually support our present position.
When Jules (say) thinks it a lovely accident that he and Jim should simultaneously be
at the bank, he may well be making that judgment, and the judgment that it is no
accident he himself is at the bank, from his own limited point of view. But if
agglomerativity holds for (non)accidentality thus relatively affirmed, Jules should also
be willing to claim that Jim is (relative to Jules's standpoint) accidentally at the bank.
For, on the assumption that Jim is not accidentally there, agglomerativity must
commit Jules to rejecting the accidentality of the meeting or the nonaccidentality of
his own presence at the bank. The fact is, however, that someone in Jules's position
will not (automatically) assume that the other person is where he is by accident, even
when he assumes that *their meeting* is an accident. And so it would seem that
nonaccidentality, even relative to a limited standpoint, is nonagglomerative.

exist, it is also (on trivial logical grounds) no accident that if I am at that place, then I still (or at some time) exist.[15]

I believe that closure, agglomeration, and our main principle all fail for nonaccidentality because of the (relational) selectivity built into that notion. When we say that some event was no accident, at least one thing that we may be saying is that that event came about according to a plan that required it. That is, nonaccidentality of the sort at issue in the case of Jules and Jim exists only in relation to a single actual plan (relationality); but the plan must also be of a very specific kind (selectivity): it must be a plan that *requires* or *calls for* the thing that occurs nonaccidentally. Thus, if Jim is at the bank at ten o'clock on the first of the month because his superior has told him (always) to go there then, it is no accident that he is there at that time. But since the presence of both Jules and Jim at the bank at ten o'clock has not in fact been planned for, is not required by anyone's plan or intention, it is natural, on this account, to call it accidental. The particular kind of relation that nonaccidentality entails, the selectivity of the notion, may also account for nonclosure. An employer who plans for an employee to be at the bank at a certain time does not *plan for* the employee to stay alive, even if he more or less implicitly knows that being at the bank involves being alive. And similarly, even if a plan calls for someone to be somewhere at a given time, it need not call for that person to stay alive till then. The fact of aliveness may simply be presupposed by such a plan.[16]

---

[15]Ordinary thought seems to treat facts of logic as nonaccidental even though no one has planned for them. But it is natural to speak of what logic "requires" in much the same way that we speak of what certain plans require, and a common sense of necessity may thus animate all our ascriptions of nonaccidentality.

Note too that, even if nonaccidentality is closed under logical implication, our main principle will be invalid as long as agglomerativity fails. For if we grant closure and our main principle, agglomerativity immediately follows: From '$Np \cdot Nq$', closure allows us to deduce '$Np \cdot N(p \supset pq)$'; and, from the latter, our main principle allows us to deduce 'Npq'.

[16]Just as there are unintended foreseen consequences of an intention or plan, so too, I am saying, there can be unintended and unplanned-for presupposed necessary conditions of the fulfillment of a plan or intention. (These cannot be means to the fulfillment of such a plan or intention.)

For material relevant to our discussion of accidentality, see Aristotle's *Physics* II 5–6 and *Metaphysics* V 30, as well as Richard Sorabji's *Necessity, Cause and Blame* (London: Duckworth, 1980),. ch. 1, and Robert Hambourger's "The Argument from Design," in Cora Diamond and Jenny Teichman, eds., *Intention and Intentionality* (Hassocks, England: Harvester, 1979; Ithaca, N.Y.: Cornell, 1980), pp. 109–131.

So the hypothesis that nonaccidentality is a form of selective necessity that (in the relevant cases) entails being required by and coming about according to a plan helps to explain the failure of agglomeration and of closure under entailment that we seem to find in ordinary thought about nonaccidentality.

Nor is nonaccidentality merely an isolated case of selective alethic/causal modality. Having recognized the selectivity of this one notion, we can quite easily recognize selectivity in others. To act from irresistible impulse, for example, is to be necessitated in a particular way. But even if a given person steals a trinket out of irresistible impulse (kleptomania) and the same person also burns down a house from irresistible impulse (pyromania), it will not follow—it would be extraordinarily odd to say—that the person had done the two things, had stolen the trinket and burned down the house, from irresistible impulse. Indeed, if someone did, perplexingly, say the latter, we would naturally (re)interpret him to be saying, dissectively, that each of those two things was done from irresistible impulse. For it is inherent in talk about acts done from (irresistible) impulse that those acts arise from a single impulse, and most of us assume that there is no such thing as a single, unified impulse to steal-and-burn. Thus what arises from irresistible impulse is necessary in relation to a particular kind of factor, a single impulse toward the very thing that is thus made necessary. And this selectivity is sufficient to unhinge the notion from agglomerativity, and from closure as well. (Via similar arguments similar thoughts also apply to the notion of doing something compulsively.)

Given the existence of alethic/causal necessities not subject to closure, agglomeration, or our main principle, one may begin to have doubts about the incompatibilist arguments of GLVW. For these revolve around alethic/causal notions of unavoidability, unalterability, or what-have-you which may be just as selective as nonaccidentality or irresistibility of impulse, and thus just as liable to failure of closure, etc.

What would, of course, more strongly recommend this conjecture would be some more definite indication of how and why the modality of GLVW's arguments might fail modal principles that operate in the case of logical or strict metaphysical necessity, some account, for example, of the form of selectivity involved in the notion of what is unavoidable or unalterable by us. And though I am not absolutely convinced that "unavoidability" and the like are selective in the way needed to unhinge familiar modal principles/rules, and it is not my intention here to give a full analysis or formal semantics of these concepts, I would like to point out one specific way in which they may plausibly be thought to be selective.

When we say that some event before our birth is something we can now do nothing about—is now unavoidable by, inevitable for, us—I think we may be saying that that event is necessary or inevitable *in relation to* a *particular kind* of factor. We have seen that the particular kind of factor "selected" in judgments of nonaccidentality is a certain sort of effective plan-requirement and that that selected in judgments of irresistible impulse and compulsiveness is a certain sort of unitary impulse (or compulsion). What (we may ask) is the corresponding factor in claims of inevitability and the like? Perhaps we should take a clue from the fact that, with the sole exception of Wiggins, all the proponents of the new form of incompatibility argument single out past events occurring before the birth of an agent, in speaking of what that agent cannot do anything about. What such remote pastness seems intended to ensure is that the event in question be beyond the causal reach of desires, beliefs, and abilities the agent *might* have acquired during his life, i.e., that whatever brought it about should not include any possible desires, etc., of the agent. And I believe similar considerations may well be inherent in *all* talk about unavoidability. When we say of any past event that we can *now* do nothing about it, I think we are saying that our *present* desires, abilities, beliefs, characters, etc., are no part of the explanation of it. And, more generally, the particular kind of factor in relation to which unavoidability exists at any given time, the factor "selected" by such necessity, is, simply, some factor (or set of factors) that brings about the unavoidable thing *without making use of (an explanatory chain that includes) the desires, etc., the agent has around that time.*[17]

---

[17]Our present gloss leaves out some factors relevant to unavoidability: e.g., unconscious compulsions. More accurately, we could specify the selectivity of unavoidability and the like as requiring (only) that what is unavoidable not be brought about by means of *accessible* current desires, beliefs, and the like. But even this is not quite accurate (there are problems, e.g., about future desires and abilities and about certain cases mentioned by Frankfurt, *op. cit.*); and one would want, in any case, to know more about the notion of accessibility.

Note further that our rough selectivity analysis of unavoidability is (at the very least) foreshadowed in Gallois, *op. cit.,* p. 103f.

A straightforward argument against the main modal principle of incompatibilist arguments then becomes available. Given the above assumptions, we cannot now do anything about past events because they are due to factors that brought them about via a causal chain that did not include our present abilities, desires, etc. And appropriate laws of nature have the same sort of necessity because whatever it is that makes them be as they are (certain deeper laws, the basic structure of the universe or what have you) is surely something that does not involve our present abilities and desires. But even if our deliberate actions are determined, that determinism operates, nonfatalistically, by means of (causal chains involving) the approximately coeval desires, abilities, character, and beliefs of human agents. So if the necessity involved in incompatibilist arguments selects factors that bring something about (make it exist) without making use of such coeval desires, etc., then most of us *can* do something about the actions we are about to perform and the main modal principle of those arguments fails. Certain past events will be necessary in the relevant sense (necessary in relation to the right sort of factor) and certain laws leading from them to an agent's later actions will also be necessary; but it will not follow that those actions are themselves necessary at some later time when the agent is considering whether to perform them.[18] Of course, those actions will be *determined by* and presumably *predictable in terms of* factors prior to the agent's desires and abilities. But those earlier factors nonetheless bring such actions about only by means of (causal chains

---

[18]After giving his defense of incompatibilism, Wiggins characterizes its notion of historical necessity/inevitability as implying that something is inevitable at t' just in case whatever anybody or anything does at t' or thereafter (consistently with laws of nature) can make no difference to that thing (45). But in ordinary usage, the latter locution has counterfactual import and entails that the thing in question would occur even if, at t' and after, people were to deliberate, choose, or act differently from the way they actually will. So when Wiggins argues from the inevitability of laws and the inevitability of the past to the conclusion that all our actions are inevitable by the time we are considering whether to perform them, his particular sense of 'inevitable' saddles him, in effect, with an argument for *fatalism*, the absurd view that we would perform the various actions we do even if appropriate initial conditions were different. And Wiggins himself not only fails to recognize this consequence of his views but seems eager to dissociate his argument from fatalism. (Cf. his discussion of 'Theaetetus sits at t', p. 59f.) Had Wiggins recognized that under determinism (something equivalent to) our main principle leads from true premises to a form of inevitability that entails fatalism, he might have rejected the main principle. For Wiggins's understanding of inevitability is in fact somewhat similar to our own: we

involving) later desires (roughly coeval with the actions they help to bring about). And what I have been claiming is that it is precisely this further aspect of the matter which is crucial to whether a given act is avoidable. There *might* be a notion of relative necessity that merely involved being determined, but I am suggesting (roughly) that the ordinary notions of avoidability, inevitability, and the like involve the idea of being determined in a particular sort of way; and such selective necessity would account for the failure of those notions to comply with the main modal principle of recent incompatibilist arguments.

However, if appropriate selectivity undoes recent defenses of incompatibilism by undermining their main modal principle, then it must also undermine either agglomerativity or closure under logical implication (or both), since the latter principles together entail or validate the former. And this we find to be so. Let 'p' represent a proposition ascribing existence in a canonical way to some (preexistent) past event, and let '$p \supset q$' be a conditional true by virtue of the laws of nature which connects that past event with some particular about-to-be-performed action represented by 'q.' Given the selective necessity we have postulated, 'Nq' is clearly false, but 'Np' and '$N(p \supset q)$' are both true. Now, if such necessity is closed under logical implication, it is closed under logical equivalence, and '$N(p \cdot p \supset q)$' will be true only if '$N(p \cdot q)$' is. Our selectivity analysis suggests, however, that '$N(p \cdot q)$' is true only if (roughly but intuitively) some set of factors not operating through our desires and abilities makes p and q be true together. And since it is natural to assume that something cannot make a pair of things true without making each of them true,[19] we can reasonably conclude that '$N(p \cdot q)$' is true only if something independent of our desires, etc., makes q true, i.e., only if 'Nq' is true. But we are assuming that 'Nq' is false, so '$N(p \cdot q)$' is also false, and thus, by closure under logical implication (equivalence), '$N(p \cdot p \supset q)$' is false as well. So, given our other assumptions and a selectivity analysis of the modality involved, agglomeration fails if closure

have been *denying* the inevitability of some of our future acts, even under determinism, on the grounds that their "necessity" is *not* in the appropriate sense independent of initial conditions like desire and ability. And the fact that our sort of gloss on inevitability comes naturally even to an incompatibilist like Wiggins is surely some sort of reason for accepting that gloss and for rejecting modal principles that, on such a gloss, lead directly from determinism to fatalism.

[19]Cf. Frederic B. Fitch, "A Logical Analysis of Some Value Concepts," *Journal of Symbolic Logic*, XXVIII, 2 (June 1963): 135–142.

under logical implication holds. (A similar argument can be used to show that if we assume agglomeration, closure must fail.)

The selectivity that is plausibly attributed to the necessity involved in recent defenses of incompatibilism distinguishes between factors within and factors external to agents. For, on our rough gloss, what is effected without the "help" of an agent's (coeval) character, abilities, desires, etc. is (then) unavoidable, unalterable, inevitable, but what is brought about via a causal chain that includes appropriate internal factors is not.

Now both Wiggins and van Inwagen say that the distinction between internal and external factors, between character and circumstance, in no way affects the soundness of their arguments. Wiggins claims that "no subtleties about *in the agent* or the agent's *will*" can affect the validity of his general form of argument, and van Inwagen has been reluctant to allow that the validity of his argument in any way depends on the inadequacy of so-called "conditional analyses" of ability, analyses that highlight the importance of the internal/external distinction by explaining ability in terms of what an agent would succeed in doing if he made a certain effort or choice.[20] More recently, however, van Inwagen (at least) has been willing to concede that, if ability were conditionally analyzable and compatibilism were true, some of the modal principles he assumes would fail; but he also insists—correctly, I believe—that this fact alone hardly vindicates the compatibilist. For if van Inwagen's general modal premises are plausible before one makes any assumptions about how 'can' is to be analyzed or about the truth of determinism, then his arguments have definite force *against* compatibilism and *against* conditional analyses of ability.[21]

But at least part of the reason for thinking that the necessity involved in free will is agglomerative, closed under logical implication, and obedient to our main principle comes from the powerful example of "standard" alethic modal logic, the logic of logical necessity and possibility. (I think GLVW's modal principles would seem much less compelling to educated nonphilosophers than they do to those acquainted with modal logic.) Those principles clearly hold for the

---

[20]Wiggins, *op. cit.*, p. 50; van Inwagen, "The Incompatibility . . . ," p. 196f.

[21]See his "Reply to Narveson's 'Compatibilism Defended' " *Philosophical Studies*, XXXII, 1 (July 1977): 89–98, p. 95f.; and his "Compatibilism and the Burden of Proof," *Analysis*, XL, 2 (March 1980): 98–100, esp. p. 100.

most familiar forms of alethic modality, and indeed no specific example of alethic necessity flouting such principles has previously been discussed or argued for.[22] So, by unearthing plausible instances of alethic necessity that do fail those principles, the present paper may serve to weaken the feeling of inevitability and obviousness that (for most philosophers at least) initially attends the modal principles used in the recent arguments for incompatibilism. Previous suggestions that we analyze ability conditionally in order to defend compatibilism from the arguments of GLVW have seemed ad hoc in the absence of any other example of alethic necessity not subject to our main principle or agglomeration or closure; but when we supply such examples and explain how various necessities can flout those principles, the selective necessity that we have claimed may be involved in the free-will controversy is made to seem part of a plausible pattern, rather than an isolated case. None of this may absolutely demolish the recent arguments for incompatibilism, but I believe it has some force against them nonetheless, force that previous replies to GLVW, because of their ad hocness and special pleading, have failed to carry.[23]

I can also think of one positive reason for claiming that the necessity involved in those arguments fails of agglomeration, closure, and our main modal principle. Consider our common-sense intuitions, what we are normally inclined to say, about the things we cannot or can do something about. Most people, when asked, would grant that we can do nothing either about the past or about (whatever) laws of nature (exist). And yet the belief that we *can* do something about what actions we are going to perform has a tendency to resist extinction in practical life, even among those who in the study or the classroom espouse determinism. Through its reliance on agglomeration, closure, or our main model principle, the kind of argument presented by GLVW in effect seeks to undermine this "natural assignment" of truth values and to declare it and us inconsistent, as a consequence. But surely there are philosophical grounds, at least philosophical motives, for trying to avoid such a charge, and if we say that the necessity involved in recent incompatibilist arguments fails of agglomeration, etc., we can succeed in doing this. Of course, before

---

[22]One exception, however, is the article by Martin Davies mentioned in fn 8, above.

[23]I particularly have in mind Richard Foley's "Reply to van Inwagen," *Analysis*, XL, 2 (March 1980): 101–103; and his earlier "Compatibilism and Control over the Past," *Analysis*, XXXIX, 2 (March 1979): 70–74.

we had any reason to believe there were forms of alethic necessity that failed these principles, we could not perhaps have deployed such a consistency argument. For the example of the alethic modal logic of logical necessity and possibility could make it appear impossible for any form of alethic necessity to fail those principles, and in that case the claim that the necessity involved in arguments for incompatibilism was an exception to the principles would enable us to avoid one inconsistency—that of our natural assignment of truth values—at the cost of embroiling us in what seemed to be another—the denial of irrecusable modal principles. The examples of nonaccidentality, of irresistible impulse, of compulsivity, and, even, of obligation, however, make us see that nonagglomerative, etc., alethic necessity is not only possible, but in fairly plentiful supply in our conceptual scheme; and this, in turn, allows the motive of self-consistency in our common-sense judgments about things positively to recommend the idea that GLVW's arguments involve a nonagglomerative, etc., form of alethic necessity and are thus doomed to failure.

In any event, we have pointed out some clear cases of selective necessity expressible within ordinary language and have seen that, even if some modal principles/rules are common to every form of alethic necessity,[24] others have only a limited application within the alethic realm. Recently, there has been some discussion of modal logics lacking agglomerativity and our main principle,[25] but there is an obvious need for technical investigations of the logic and semantics of the selective necessities we have mentioned and various others that are undoubtedly waiting to be discovered. I believe such projects may be worth pursuing, quite independently of any relation that exists between selectivity and the specific problem of free will, for the insights they are likely to give us into modal thinking in general.

---

[24]D. P. Snyder, *Modal Logic and Its Applications* (New York: Van Nostrand Reinhold, 1971), p. 5ff., mentions some of these common principles.

[25]See, e.g., Krister Segerberg, *An Essay in Classical Modal Logic* (Uppsala: University Press, 1971), and Brian Chellas, *Modal Logic: An Introduction* (New York: Cambridge, 1980). However, what also needs to be explored (though there is no space to explore it here) is the possibility that there are indexical aspects to (some of) the necessity operators of ordinary language, that (various) apparent failures of agglomerativity and the like involve subtle shiftings of context rather than any flouting of "normal" modal principles, and that recent arguments for incompatibilism commit some sort of fallacy of equivocation.

Suggested Further Readings

An articulate critical treatment of Slote's position is presented in John Martin Fischer, *The Metaphysics of Free Will* (Oxford: Blackwell, 1994).

See also Timothy O'Conner, "On the Transfer of Necessity," *Nous* 27 (1993), and Peter van Inwagen, *An Essay on Free Will* (Oxford: Clarendon Press, 1983).

CHAPTER 21

Freedom and Foreknowledge

John Martin Fischer

For the sake of argument, assume that an omniscient (all-knowing) supernatural being exists. Can it then be true that we act freely? There are arguments opposing this idea, but there is also an "Ockhamist" defense of the compatibilist position that divine omniscience can be reconciled with free will. The Ockhamist position is explained and critically evaluated in the following selection.

John Martin Fischer is a professor of philosophy at the University of California at Riverside. He is the author of The Metaphysics of Free Will *(1994).*

A powerful argument can be made that God's omniscience is incompatible with human freedom. If God is eternal and omniscient, then it might seem that my freedom now to do other than what I am doing must be the freedom so to act that a fact about the past (God's prior belief about my present activity) would not be a fact about the past. But since the past is "fixed," it seems that if God exists, then I am now not free to do other than what I am doing.

Many philosophers have been attracted to an Ockhamist response to this argument. Both the Ockhamist and the incompatibilist can distinguish between "hard" and "soft" facts about the past; the hard facts are fixed while the soft facts need not be fixed. But the Ockhamist claims that God's prior belief about my present activity is a soft fact about the past and hence not fixed; my freedom is thus preserved. Some Ockhamists even claim that the very existence of God is also a soft fact about the past.

I shall argue that a very attractive presentation of the Ockhamist approach, one explicitly formulated by Marilyn Adams, is inadequate.

Source: John Martin Fischer: "Freedom and Foreknowledge," from *Philosophical Review*, 92 (1983). Copyright 1983 Cornell University. Reprinted by permission of the publisher and the author.

There are significant problems with Adams's attempt to characterize the hard fact/soft fact distinction. Further, I shall present a general challenge to *any* sort of Ockhamist attempt to explain this distinction.

1.   Pike's Argument

Nelson Pike claims to exhibit the incompatibility of human freedom and divine foreknowledge, relative to certain plausible assumptions about God's nature. These assumptions reflect central features of the standard Judeo-Christian conception of God. Pike explicitly adopts the assumption that if God exists, then God is essentially omniscient and God is eternal. On Pike's account, God is omniscient if and only if God believes all and only true propositions, and we might say that God is essentially omniscient if and only if God is omniscient in all possible worlds in which God exists. Pike says that God is eternal if and only if God has always existed and always will.

Following Pike's presentation in a different article, I assume that the term "God" is a descriptive expression used to mark a certain *role,* rather than a proper name. Whoever occupies the role of God is omniscient, omnipotent, eternal, etc. In contrast, the term "Yahweh" is a proper name; it refers to the person who actually occupies the role of God (if God exists). It is not necessarily true that Yahweh is omniscient, omnipotent, eternal, etc.; it is logically possible that some other person has been God.

Since "God" is being used here as a non-rigid designator, there is some ambiguity in the assumptions about God's attributes. "God is essentially omniscient" does not mean that the person who is in fact God is essentially omniscient, but rather, that necessarily, whoever is God is omniscient. In terms of possible worlds, God is essentially omniscient just in case for any possible world in which there is a person who is God, that person is omniscient. (One can assume that if God is eternal in a particular world, then it follows that there is one and the same person who is God at all times in that world. Pike need not accept this particular assumption, as it is not crucial to his argument.)

Though this is the approach to the term "God" that Pike appears to adopt, it might seem to be an unusual and unappealing position. I shall follow Pike in adopting this interpretation, but it is important to note that Pike could just as easily embrace the stronger interpretation according to which the person who is in fact God is essentially God. Nothing in Pike's proof, or in my criticism of Adams's Ockhamism, rests on adopting the weaker rather than the stronger interpretation of God's attributes.

In effect, Pike also appears to adopt what might be called the "fixed past" constraint on power attributions:

(FPC) It is never in any person's power at a time *t* so to act that the past (relative to *t*) would have been different from what it actually was.

Pike's view about the fixity of the past implies not only that one cannot causally influence the past; it implies that no person is free to do something which is such that, were he to do it, the past would have been different from what it actually was.

Pike's argument is essentially as follows. Suppose Jones did X at time t_2 and God exists. Since God exists, it follows from God's eternality that He existed at t_1 (a time prior to t_2). Let us call the person who was God at t_1, "Y." Since Jones did X at t_2, it follows from God's omniscience that He believed at t_1 that Jones would do X at t_2. Now if it was within Jones's power at t_2 to refrain from doing X, then (1) it was in Jones's power at t_2 to act in such a way that Y would have been God and would have held a false belief at t_1, or (2) it was in Jones's power at t_2 to act in such a way that Y would have been God but would not have held the belief He held at t_1, or (3) it was in Jones's power at t_2 to act in such a way that Y would not have been God at t_1.

But (1) is ruled out by God's essential omniscience, and (2) and (3) are ruled out by (FPC). Hence it was not in Jones's power at t_2 to refrain from doing X. If the argument is sound, it can easily be generalized to show that God's eternality and essential omniscience are incompatible with any human agent's being free at any time.

It should be pointed out that incompatibilism about divine foreknowledge and human freedom need not entail incompatibilism about human foreknowledge and human freedom. The problem is deeper with divine foreknowledge because of God's essential omniscience; perhaps it was in Jones's power at t_2 so to act that Smith (who actually held only correct beliefs) would have held a false belief at t_1. Pike wants to insist on an *asymmetry* between divine and human foreknowledge.

2.   Hard and Soft Facts

It is sometimes in one's power so to act that facts about the past *would not* be facts. John Turk Saunders discusses such a fact:

> Although it is true that if I had refrained from writing this paper in 1965, Caesar's assassination would have been other than it is in that it would not have preceded by 2,009 years my writing this paper, it would be absurd to argue that I therefore did not have it in my power to refrain from writing this paper in 1965.

It is obvious that the mere fact that if Saunders had refrained from writing his paper, then Caesar's assassination would not have preceded Saunders's writing his paper by 2,009 years did not render Saunders incapable of refraining; relative to 1965, "Caesar died 2,009 years prior to Saunders's writing his paper" expresses a soft fact about the past. Of course, it was not in Saunders's power so to act that Caesar would not have died on the steps of the Senate. Relative to Saunders's lifetime, the fact that Caesar died on the steps of the Senate is a hard fact about the past.

Pike agrees with the Ockhamist that there are both hard and soft facts about the past. It is not easy to provide a precise characterization of the hard fact/soft fact distinction. Pike himself provides no such account, though he claims we can recognize clear examples of each sort. The disagreement between Pike and the Ockhamist is about where to draw the line. Pike's position is that if the ordinary notions of belief and existence are applied to God, then God's belief at t_1 and God's existence at t_1 (including the fact that Y was God at t_1) are hard facts about the past relative to t_2. And if they were soft facts about the past relative to t_2, this would show that we were ascribing beliefs and existence to God in a special, nonstandard way.

Given the hard fact/soft fact distinction, the appropriate interpretation of Pike's claim about the fixity of the past should be made explicit:

> **(FPC*)** It is never in any person's power at a time t so to act that any hard fact about the past (relative to t) would have been different from what it actually was.

Marilyn Adams presents an account of the distinction which she believes supports compatibilism against Pike's attack. It will be useful to consider Adams's attempt at giving an account of the distinction:

> **(B)** "Statement p is at least in part about a time t" = df. "The happening or not happening, actuality or non-actuality of something at t is a necessary condition of the truth of p."

Thus the statement, "Caesar died 2,009 years before Saunders wrote his paper" is at least in part about 44 B.C., since Caesar's death at that time is a necessary condition of the truth of that statement. It is also at least in part about A.D. 1965 since Saunders's writing his paper in A.D. 1965 is also a necessary condition of the truth of that statement. Given (B) the notion of a "hard" fact may be explained as follows:

(C) "Statement p expresses a 'hard' fact about a time t'' = df. "p is not at least in part about any time future relative to t."

Adams uses this account to present an Ockhamist response to Pike's argument. On her account, God's belief at t_1 and the fact that Y was God at t_1 are deemed soft facts about t_1.

Adams claims that her account shows why "Caesar died 2,009 years before Saunders wrote his paper" does not express a hard fact about 44 B.C. But her account does *not* explain this unless it is interpreted to imply that *no* sentence expresses a hard fact. Adams says that "Caesar died 2,009 years before Saunders wrote his paper" is at least in part about 1965, since Saunders's writing his paper in 1965 is a necessary condition of the truth of that statement. But this seems plainly false; the statement entails that Caesar's death and Saunders's writing his paper be separated by 2,009 years, but it does not entail any two particular dates for the two events. The statement entails that the two events stand in a certain temporal *relation,* but it does not entail that they occur on any specific dates. Hence, Saunders's writing his paper in 1965 is *not* a necessary condition of Caesar's death being 2,009 years prior to Saunders's writing his paper, if we interpret "q is a necessary condition for p" as "p entails q."

One might reply that since it is true that Saunders wrote his paper in 1965, "Saunders wrote his paper in 1965" is *materially implied* by "Caesar died 2,009 years prior to Saunders's writing his paper." So if we interpret "q is a necessary condition for p" as "p materially implies q," Saunders's writing his paper in 1965 is a necessary condition of the truth of "Caesar died 2,009 years prior to Saunders's writing his paper." But it is obvious that if this sense of "necessary condition" is adopted, then *no* sentence will express a hard fact about 44 B.C. So Adams's account of Pike's intuitive distinction is inadequate as it stands. Adams gives no explication of the notion of a necessary condition by reference to which she can say that "Caesar died 2,009 years prior to Saunders's writing his paper" does not express a hard fact about 44 B.C.

Consider also the statement, "John F. Kennedy was assassinated." Given the entailment interpretation, this statement expresses a hard fact about 1961, since it does not *entail* the occurrence of anything subsequent to 1961. Of course, there are logically possible worlds in which Kennedy was assassinated in 1961. But we want to say that in 1962 (and in 1963, until November 22), it was within Oswald's power so to have acted that Kennedy would not have been assassinated. And again, it is obvious that the material implication interpretation of "necessary condition" is inadequate.

Complex statements further illustrate the inadequacy of the entailment account of "necessary condition." If Jones did not believe at t_1 that he would do X at t_2, then "Either Smith knew at t_1 that Jones would do X at t_2 or Jones believed at t_1 that Jones would do X at t_2" should *not* express a hard fact about t_1; the Ockhamist would say that Jones might have been able so to act at t_2 that this disjunctive statement would be false. Yet on Adams's account, the statement expressed a *hard* fact about t_1, since its truth does not entail that anything happens after t_1; the truth of the disjunction does not entail that anything happens (or fails to happen, etc.) after t_1.

In defense of Adams's approach, one might offer the following account of a necessary condition: q is a necessary condition for p if and only if p would not be true (or have been true) if q were not true (or had not been true). Let us call this interpretation the "counterfactual" account of a necessary condition. It *is* plausible to say that if Saunders had not written his paper in 1965, then it *would not* have been the case that Caesar died 2,009 years prior to Saunders's writing his paper. Thus, Adams could say, on the counterfactual account, that "Saunders wrote his paper in 1965" is a necessary condition of "Caesar died 2,009 years prior to Saunders's writing his paper." Also, it is perhaps reasonable to say (though I am not sure) that if Oswald had not shot Kennedy in 1963, then Kennedy would not have been assassinated. If this is so, then Adams could say that "Oswald shot Kennedy in 1963" is a necessary condition of "John F. Kennedy was assassinated." Similarly, if Jones had not done X at t_2, then it would have been false that either Smith knew at t_1 that Jones would do X at t_2 or Jones believed at t_1 that Jones would do X at t_2. Thus, Adams could say that "Jones did X at t_2" is a necessary condition of the disjunction.

But there is another sort of problem which afflicts both plausible accounts—both the counterfactual and entailment interpretations of "necessary condition." Suppose "Smith existed at t_1" is true. It is a necessary condition of the truth of this statement (on both the counterfactual and entailment accounts) that it is not the case that Smith existed for the first time at t_2. It is obvious that Smith's existing at t_1 entails that he does not exist for the first time at t_2. And if Smith had existed for the first time at t_2, then he would not have existed at t_1, so the counterfactual account fares no better than the entailment account. Thus, by (B), the statement "Smith existed at t_1" is at least in part about t_2; by (C) the statement *fails* to express a hard fact about t_1. But since Smith need not be eternal (or essentially omniscient), this is a disastrous result for Adams's account. The same sort of argument shows that Adams must say that "Jones believed at t_1 that Jones would do X at t_2" does not express a hard fact about t_1. This is because "It is not the case that Jones believed for the first time at t_2 that he would do X at t_2" is a necessary condition of "Jones believed at t_1 that he would do X at t_2."

Also, it is a necessary condition (on both interpretations) of the truth of the statement, "Piece of Salt S dissolved at t_1," that S did not dissolve at t_2. One wants to say that this statement expresses a hard fact about t_1, but Adams's account does not capture this intuition (since the statement is at least in part about t_2).

It is not easy to see how Adams could provide an account of "necessary condition" which would avoid all the problems raised above. Without such an account, she has not presented an adequate explanation of the distinction between hard and soft facts.

3.   The Incompatibilist's Constraint

Various contemporary Ockhamists have argued that on any acceptable account of the distinction between hard and soft facts, God's prior belief will be a soft fact about the past. I shall not here further discuss particular compatibilist accounts of the distinction; rather, I shall sketch a constraint on the accounts of the distinction which an incompatibilist might use to defeat *any* compatibilist characterization of the distinction. That is, I shall develop an explanation of the claim that God's prior belief is a hard fact about the past; this explanation will *not* imply that *human* foreknowledge is also a hard fact about the past. This might provide a way in which Pike could defend both his incompatibility claim and the asymmetry thesis—the thesis that God's foreknowledge undermines human freedom in a way in which human foreknowledge does not.

Consider the fact that Caesar died 2,009 years prior to Saunders's writing his paper. What lies behind our view that this fact is not a hard fact about 44 B.C.? We might say that it is a soft fact about 44 B.C. because one and the same physical process would have counted as Caesar's dying 2,009 years prior to Saunders's writing his paper, if Saunders wrote his paper in 1965, and would *not* have counted as Caesar's dying 2,009 years prior to Saunders's writing his paper, if Saunders had not written his paper in 1965. This captures the "future dependence" of soft facts; a soft fact is a fact *in virtue* of events which occur in the future.

Similarly, suppose that Smith knew at t_1 that Jones would do X at t_2. Smith's knowledge is a soft fact about t_1 because one and the same state of Smith's mind (at t_1) would count as knowledge if Jones did X at t_2, and would not count as knowledge if Jones did not do X at t_2. Exactly the same sort of future dependence explains why both facts—the fact about Caesar's death and the fact about Smith's knowledge—are soft facts.

Thus an incompatibilist might insist on the following sort of constraint on an account of the hard fact/soft fact distinction: the only way in which God's belief at t_1 about Jones at t_2 could be a soft fact about the past relative to t_2 would be if one and the same state of mind of the person who was God at t_1 would count as one belief if Jones did X at t_2, but a different belief (or not a belief at all) if Jones did not do X at t_2. But it is implausible to suppose that one and the same state of the mind of the person who was God at t_1 would count as different beliefs given different behavior by Jones at t_2.

Suppose again that Jones did X at t_2. Y (being God) believed at t_1 that Jones would do X at t_2. Let us say that Y's mind was in state s at t_1; this constituted His believing that Jones would do X at t_2. Now if Y's mind were in state s and Jones did *not* do X, Y's mind being in s would still count as a belief that Jones would do X. (In this case, Y would not be God, since he would have a false belief.) Hence, Y's mind being in s at t_1 would *not* count as one belief if Jones did X at t_2 and another belief (or not a belief at all) if Jones did not do X at t_2.

Someone might agree that the incompatibilist's constraint is appropriate but disagree with what I have said about its application. That is, one might argue that if Jones had not done X at t_2, then the state of God's mind that actually constituted His believing that Jones would do X would not have constituted that belief. This position might be supported by extending Putnam's point that meanings and beliefs ain't in the head. According to Putnam, my belief that water is wet—the state of my mind that constitutes in fact, my believing that—would have been a different belief—the belief that *XYZ* is wet—if lakes and oceans on earth had been filled with *XYZ* rather than water. On this approach, the state of God's mind at t_1 that counts as His belief that Jones will do *X* at t_2 counts as that belief partly in virtue of the fact that Jones does in fact do *X* at t_2.

But this picture of God's omniscience is highly implausible. God's omniscience would be seriously attenuated if the same state of God's mind at t_1 would constitute different beliefs about Jones, depending on Jones's behavior at t_2. The following is a more appealing picture of God's omniscience. An Ockhamist might deny the appropriateness of the constraint, claiming that while it is not true that one and the same state of God's mind at t_1 would constitute different beliefs, depending on Jones's behavior at t_2, it is true that God's mind would have been in a *different* state at t_1 (from the one it was actually in), if Jones had not done *X* at t_2. Whereas *Y*'s mind was actually in state *s* at t_1, it would not have been in *s* had Jones not done *X* at t_2.

If the Ockhamist makes this move, however, he weakens his argument to the conclusion that God's belief at t_1 is a soft fact about t_1. There is now an *asymmetry* between soft facts such as Caesar's dying 2,009 years prior to Saunders's writing his paper and Smith's knowing at t_1 that Jones will do *X* at t_2, on the one hand, and God's belief at t_1 that Jones will do *X* at t_2, on the other. But it was the assimilation of these sorts of facts that was the ground for claiming that God's belief at t_1 is a soft fact about t_1.

The incompatibilist can agree with the Ockhamist that the facts discussed above about Caesar's death and Smith's knowledge are "spurious" facts about the relevant times. They are temporal analogues of facts involving "mere Cambridge" spatial properties, such as the property of being ten miles south of a burning barn. But if the incompatibilist's constraint is rejected, then it is open to him to argue that God's prior belief is a *genuine* fact about the past.

The constraint I have proposed captures the incompatibilist's notion of the fixity of the past. If this constraint is acceptable, then Pike could defend both his incompatibility claim and the asymmetry thesis.

There is, however, one form of Ockhamism that is not defeated by the proposed constraint. Consider again, "If it was within Jones's power at t_2 to refrain from doing *X*, then (3) it was in Jones's power

at t_2 to act in such a way that Y would not have been God at t_1."
There are two ways in which it might be true that it was in Jones's
power at t_2 so to act that Y would not have been God at t_1. First,
Jones could have had it in his power at t_2 so to act that Y would not
have existed at t_1. Second, Jones could have been free at t_2 to act in
such a way that Y (though existing) would not have filled the role of
God at t_1. The Ockhamist might agree with Pike that the existence of
a particular person is a hard fact about a time, but he might insist
that the fact that the person is God is *not* a hard fact about a time.

Thus, the Ockhamist might claim (following Adams) that the fact
that Y had the property of being God at t_1 is a soft fact about t_1. This is
because the fact that Y was God at t_1 depends on the truth of Y's beliefs
about future contingent events; indeed, since God is eternal, the fact
that Y was God at t_1 depends on the fact that Y existed at t_2.

But the incompatibilist should point out that from the claim that
Y's occupying the role of God at t_1 is a soft fact about t_1 it does *not* follow that Jones could have at t_2 so acted that Y would not have been
God at t_1. There are soft facts about the past which are such that one
cannot now so act that they would not have been facts. For instance, on
Tuesday it was a soft fact about the past that on Monday it was the case
that the sun would rise on Wednesday morning. But on Tuesday, one
could not have acted in such a way that it would not have been the case
that on Monday it was true that the sun would rise on Wednesday.

Thus, even if the fact that Y was God at t_1 is a soft fact about t_1,
this does not *suffice* to establish that Jones could have so acted at t_2
that Y would not have been God at t_1. Further, it is theologically implausible to suppose that any human agent is free so to act that the
person who is actually God would not be God. This would make the
identity of God dependent on human actions in an unacceptable
way; such a God would hardly be worthy of worship. So, whereas the
fact that Y was God at t_1 might be a soft fact about t_1, an Ockhamist
who claims that one could have at t_2 so acted that Y would not have
been God at t_1 would posit an unacceptable view of God. Incompatibilism can be defended even if Pike's claim that the fact that Y was
God at t_1 is a hard fact about t_1 were false.

4.   Conclusion

Adams's formulation of Ockhamism is inadequate. I have not here
argued that *no* account of the hard fact/soft fact distinction can be

given which captures the Ockhamist intuition. Rather, I have posed a challenge to Adams's Ockhamism and have presented the incompatibilist's motivation for thinking that any Ockhamist account will be unacceptable. I have thus issued a twofold challenge to the Ockhamist: first, to formulate the hard fact/soft fact distinction in a way which yields Ockhamism, and second, to explain why the incompatibilist's constraint is inappropriate.

Suggested Further Readings

See Thomas B. Talbott, "On Divine Foreknowledge and Bringing about the Past," *Philosophy & Phenomenological Research* 46 (1986); John Martin Fischer, "Ockhamism," *Philosophical Review* 94 (1985); Marilyn McCord Adams, "Is the Existence of God a 'Hard' Fact?" *Philosophical Review* 76 (1967); Nelson Pike, "Divine Omniscience and Voluntary Actions," *Philosophical Review* 74 (1965); and Alvin Plantinga, "On Ockham's Way Out," *Faith and Philosophy* 3 (1986).